COGITO, ERGO SUM

RENÉ DESCARTES (1596–1650)
BY JAN-BAPTIST WEENIX · 1643
Centraal Museum, Utrecht

Richard Watson

Cogito, Ergo Sum

THE LIFE OF RENÉ DESCARTES

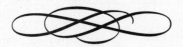

*Liberty and leisure are two things I possess so perfectly,
and that I value so highly, that no monarch on earth
is rich enough to buy them from me.*
René Descartes, 1630

I love storm, and dread it when the wind drops.
Queen Christina, 1650

DAVID R. GODINE, *Publisher*
BOSTON

First published in 2002 by
DAVID R. GODINE · *Publisher*
Post Office Box 450
Jaffrey, New Hampshire 03452
www.godine.com

LIBRARY OF CONGRESS

CATALOGING-IN-PUBLICATION DATA

Watson, Richard A., 1931–

Cogito, ergo sum: the life of René Descartes

p.   cm.

Includes bibliographical references and index.

ISBN 1-56792-184-1 (hardcover : alk. paper)

1. Descartes, René, 1596–1650.

2. Philosophers—France—Biography.

I. Title.

B1873.W38   2002

194—dc21

[B]   2001040858

FIRST EDITION 2002
Printed in Canada

CONTENTS

ILLUSTRATIONS

COGITO, ERGO SUM

INTRODUCTION

The curse of Cartesianism

René Descartes, the Father of Modern Philosophy, one of the greatest mathematical geniuses who ever lived, laid the foundations for the dominance of reason in science and human affairs. He desacralized nature and set the individual human being above church and state. Without Cartesian individualism, we would have no democracy. Without the Cartesian method of analyzing material things into their primary elements, we would never have developed the atom bomb. The seventeenth-century rise of Modern Science, the eighteenth-century Enlightenment, the nineteenth-century Industrial Revolution, your twentieth-century personal computer, and the twenty-first-century deciphering of the brain — all Cartesian. The modern world is Cartesian to the core — this world of high technology, mathematical physics, calculators and robots, molecular biology and genetic engineering — a world in which deductive reason guides and controls not only our science, technology, and practical action, but most of our moral decisions as well.

The objective is in, the subjective is out. Descartes triumphed precisely because his method of treating all natural objects — even human bodies — as machines works. He promised that with his method we could become masters and possessors of nature. And he delivered the goods.

Descartes set out on a quest for certain knowledge. He begins his search for certainty in his *Meditations on First Philosophy* (1641) by classifying all knowledge into three categories according to whether it comes from authority, from sensory experience, or from reason. Then he shows how to doubt each kind of knowledge. The underlying principle is that you should not trust any source that has ever deceived or misled you even if only once.

Descartes points out first that one can doubt any knowledge that comes from authority. This is because experts differ, and we have no sure way of deciding among them. Here is a story that illustrates the problem. At the onset of the Protestant Revolution, the Catholics said there was no way of telling whether or not Luther and Calvin were crazy (as you might suspect of anyone who thought he was in contact with God). On the other hand, Catholics can know the truth, because the pope is infallible. The devious Protestants did not challenge papal infallibility. They simply asked this question: Who is the pope? There is no way a fallible human being can tell who the pope is. Only the pope knows for sure. And there have been times when more than one cardinal claimed to be pope. So much for authority. Obviously this story also shows you how to doubt a very influential sort of authority in Western Christendom, that of revelation. Perhaps God did reveal some truths to the biblical fathers, Moses, for example. But how did they know it was God? And if it was God, did they understand? And if they understood, did they get it down right? And if they did get it down right, how do we know *we* understand? And so on.

Our sensory knowledge is doubtful, too. We could be misled, for example, about the colors and sizes of things because of bad light or poor eyes or by illusions. Or we could be drunk, deluded, dreaming, or demented. Of course, I think I am perfectly sane, but so does Napoléon Bonaparte who lives at the funny farm down the lane.

More than that, Descartes claimed that all the sensations we have are inside our minds and that we do not have direct experience of the external world at all. People think they see, touch, hear, taste, and smell material bodies directly, but they do not. Instead, the world acts on sensory organs that send messages through nerves to one's brain. Then brain states (neural firings, to be up to the minute in brain science) cause the mind to have sensory experiences of sight, touch, sound, taste, and smell. We know the world by way of these sensory representations of it. Our sensory experience is confined to a circle of mental images caused by the material world. We take these sensory images to be like the material bodies. But we can never know if the material world is like the sensory experiences we have of it, because we can never compare these mental experiences with the world itself. This is a Cartesian conundrum. To know if the world is like our sensations of it, we would have to know the world directly to compare our sensations with the material bodies. But the only way we can know the world of material bodies is by way of our sensations of it. It is naive, Descartes said, to think we see things in the external world as they really are. And more than that, the material world is nothing at all like our sensory experiences. This seems clear enough for emotions, feelings of pain, and so on. Bodies may cause you to feel hot, for example, but they don't feel hot to themselves, their atoms are just moving around fairly fast. But what about the sizes and shapes of bodies? Don't we see them as they are? Here are some exercises to convince you that you don't even see correct sizes and shapes.

Hold up your thumb and look at it. Now push on one eyeball. So what do you see? Two thumbs. But there is only one thumb there, so what you see is different from what is there. OK? Actually, I never do that one myself because it gives me the creeps to push on my eyeball. So try this one.

Hold your thumb out in front of you at arm's length. Now bring it slowly closer and closer to your eyes. What happens? It gets bigger. But your thumb doesn't get bigger just because you move it closer to your eyes. So what you see is not your thumb, but merely a visual image of your thumb. You never see your thumb, only images of it. Or rather, you see images you think are like your thumb. Remember that you can never perceive the thumb directly to check to see.

If you are still not convinced. the great British philosopher Bertrand Russell will set you straight. He points out that when you look at the sun — through smoked glass — the light that impacts your eyes left the sun eight minutes ago. Does this light cause you to see an image of the sun as it is now? No, it causes you to see an image of the sun as it was eight minutes ago. So what you see is a picture in your mind, not the sun. It is the same when you feel a pin prick your thumb. It takes time for the message to go from your thumb through your nerves to the brain, and only *then* do you take notice of the pain, a sensation that occurs after the pinprick, so it cannot be the same as the pinprick. So what you feel is a sensation in your mind, not the pin pricking your thumb. A pain is not like a pinprick in any case.

As for the third source of knowledge — reasoning — it cannot be trusted even when you are normal and wide awake. Everyone has reasoned to incorrect conclusions. Think of the errors you have made just in simple arithmetic, not to mention those in more complex matters of cognition, errors made because of lack of knowledge, inattention, fatigue, or memory failure. You have to watch all the time. The method Descartes used to revolutionize scientific research almost reduces to the admonition always to check your results to see if things are really the way you concluded. Even when you check, it is always possible that you are making a mistake when you review the steps of your reasoning. You can never be too careful.

This possibility that in reasoning you may have drawn the wrong conclusion is brought out in one of my father's favorite stories. A man stands his small son up on a high wall, steps back, and says, "Jump, my son, and I'll catch you." The trusting little lad jumps, his father steps back, and the poor child slams onto the ground. "There!" his father says. "Let that be a lesson to you. Never trust anyone."

For a universal doubt-making finale, Descartes imagined an all-powerful deceiving demon who fills your mind with the sensations and thoughts you have throughout your life — although there exists nothing but your mind, the demon, and the feelings and ideas he causes you to have. All your experience would be *as though* you had a body and there were a world full of other people and things. But in fact there would be no material world, nobody else, just the demon and deluded you. This would be worse even than being a brain in a vat fed fantasies through electrodes by a mad scientist, for you would not even have a brain. Only the demon, your mind, and your sensations and thoughts would exist.

Are you worried yet? Maybe the demon is God. The story in the Old Testament of what God did to Job suggests that God is a trickster. God took everything from Job to test his belief. Job remained faithful, so God gave everything back. But as my daughter pointed out to me in disgust after I had read the story to her when she was very small, God did not give back the same sons and daughters he had killed. Instead, he gave Job new sons and daughters. And that is not the same thing at all.

Even if only your mind and God existed, and there were no bodies in the world at all, God could give you experiences just as if there were. This is what some people think happens to disembodied souls in heaven and hell. Even if you do not have a body, your mind can be titillated or tortured.

Suppose you don't believe in God. Suppose there is no God. Then maybe the only thing in the world is your own mind causing itself to have the batch of experiences you are now having. This is called solipsism, solo for one, and in effect it makes you God. But, aha! you say. If I were God, I'd be having a lot more fun than I've had so far. Descartes himself made that objection. But he was just whistling in the dark. How do you know that you aren't just a perverse, sadomasochist soul, causing yourself the pain you crave?

A little thought thus shows that we don't really know anything much for certain at all. Would you bet your life that what you see before you is a dagger? Or a pot of flowers? Absolutely not. Moviemakers and stage magicians, scientists and pharmaceutical technicians can engineer some pretty fancy illusions. At those stakes and in these days of virtual reality, I'm betting nothing. But I will act on less than certain knowledge. I have to. Even Descartes himself said that if you had to be *completely* certain that you were doing the right thing before you did it, you would never do anything at all. Given that we know nothing for certain, practical action in this world requires that you play the probabilities. But what do you do when the odds are even? Descartes said to chose one course at random and *stick to it*. That's Cartesian rationalism for you.

It would seem that you can doubt everything. But then in the depths of your skeptical despair, it turns out that there is one thing you can know for certain.

Let me tell you a story.

One day Morris Raphael Cohen, a legendary professor at City College New York, gave a lecture on Descartes's method of doubt in which he left uncertain the question of the existence of everything. The next morning when Professor Cohen arrived at his office, he found waiting for him a young man who was obviously in great distress. Professor Cohen opened his door and ushered the student inside. "Tell me, Professor Cohen," the student blurted out at once, "I've been worrying all night. Tell me, do I exist?" Professor Cohen fixed him with a steely eye and in his eminently imitable Yiddish accent, said "Zo who vants to know?"

Providing the punch line for a thousand jokes and cartoons, in his *Discourse on Method* (1637), Descartes said, "I think, therefore I am." It is a statement nobody can doubt who thinks it. It is true for God if he thinks "I am that I am," and equally so for the dog who thinks "I bark, therefore I am" — if barking dogs think. It is true whenever you notice that *you* are doing something. Whoever self-consciously walks or talks, or just thinks about walking or talking, or only dreams about walking or talking, exists. This is a certainty of direct experience, not of reason or argument, so in his later *Meditations* (1641), Descartes dropped the "therefore" to say merely, "I think, I am." It is intuitively, self-evidently certain that while I know I am doing something — even merely thinking — I exist. I write these words: Presto! I am. My own existence is confirmed by the mere silliness of my trying to doubt it.

Descartes went on to say that there is a second thing that we can know for certain: that God exists. Descartes gave several proofs for the existence of God. One of the neatest is that God is perfect, but if God did not exist, He would not be perfect, therefore, he exists. Alas, these proofs prove nothing, for Descartes had already shown that reasoning cannot be trusted to give you certain truth. The doubtfulness of reasoning, then, leads to the insidious Cartesian Circle. You have to reason to prove the existence of God. But before you can trust your reason, you have to know that God exists and guarantees that your reason does not deceive you. The fatal circle is that you have to trust your reasoning to prove that God exists, but you have to know that God exists before you can trust your reasoning. You must have A to prove B, but also you must have B to prove A, so you go nowhere, round and round.

The same thing goes for Descartes's alternative claim that God's existence is known not by reason but by intuition. Before you can trust your intuition, you have to know that God exists and guarantees that your intuition is not deceiving you. Descartes finally says that belief in God's existence must ultimately rest on faith, which he claimed he had.

The question of the certainty of God's existence is very important to you if you are concerned about the salvation of your soul. If you are, you would probably very much like to know which of the thousands of religions is the true religion. Christians, for example, say God commands us all to have no other gods before Him. He is ready to impose some very severe penalties on those of us who disobey. If He exists, it might be nice to know. Even for those philosophers who do not believe in God, the search for certainty has been a major — and largely fruitless — intellectual pursuit for centuries.

American pragmatists from John Dewey to Richard Rorty deplore this hopeless quest for certainty, and the pragmatists are surely right. We ought to give up the wasteful, futile, disabling search for certainty. It gives philosophy a bad name among ordinary folk, who would like now and then to read a good book of philosophy for guidance and edification. But what do they find in philosophy today? Abstruse linguistic analysis and mathematical logic, which Descartes, of course, helped invent.

The amusing thing about this is that Descartes himself did not in fact take the problem of certainty seriously. He never thought we could have certain knowledge of the world about us, neither did he worry about it. As for God deceiving us, he said that the demon hypothesis is metaphysical and hyperbolical, which means just what you think. It would be very rash to doubt God's existence, and it would be really dumb to worry about not having certain truth when you have to make a living. For God's existence, we have faith. For practical affairs, we have always gotten along with probable knowledge and always will. We use ordinary reasoning for which Descartes provides a method that allows every individual to get along as well as any other. Just begin with the best knowledge you have. Break problems down into parts and solve them in order from simple to more complex (like adding a column of figures step by step). Then always review the steps of your reasoning and check your results. This is also the foundation of Cartesian egalitarianism. Using his method, your powers of reasoning are as good as anyone's. Go for it!

The modern world is Cartesian, then, not because it led professional philosophers to seek certainty (and to end up peering into their own navels) but because Descartes's method of analytic reasoning allows ordinary people to be masters and possessors of nature. Descartes made control easy, step by step.

Prior to Descartes, Scholastic philosophers believed that everything has a spirit or soul that has desires and the power to seek its satisfaction. Aristotle said that all bodies have the urge to move to the center of the earth. You can test it. Just drop something and see if the earth's center isn't exactly where it tries to go. Get out of its way if it's heavy. Acorns strive to become oak trees, and some of them succeed. This is a panpsychic view, that everything has a soul that desires to be something, somewhere. So to control a thing, you try to figure out what its desires are, and then try to manipulate it by withholding or providing satisfaction of those desires. Or by talking to it nicely.

Utter, stupid nonsense, Descartes said. Such persuasion has never been known to work with things. It does, however, work with people. As it should, Descartes agrees, because people (and only people) do in fact have spirits or souls or minds. And only people with minds have desires and can do things. Bodies have no desires, no powers. They move only because their gears interact, so to speak, when they bump into one another. All you have to know to control them is which way to push.

Nature was thoroughly desacralized by this new mechanistic science of soulless bodies that move only when bumped. Descartes derailed the supernatural. Because bodies don't have souls, they aren't self-conscious; they don't feel and they don't think. They don't *do* anything themselves because they have no selves. They just get pushed around. Even living bodies are machines made of matter, inert stuff. Human bodies not attached to souls would not be people, they would just be bones and meat, zombies, robots, androids. There is nothing special or spiritual or sacred about the body at all. So you can do anything you want with bodies.

Here is another story.

One day in 1664, Père Nicolas Malebranche picked up a copy of Descartes's posthumously published *Treatise on Man* at a book- stall in Paris on the banks of the Seine. He started reading the book right then and there, and he got so excited that he had to go home and lie down to ease the palpitations of his heart. By the way, if you have never gotten that excited from reading a book, I can't tell you how sad I feel for you. As for Père Malebranche, he became Descartes's most famous seventeenth-century disciple.

One day a few years later, Père Malebranche was strolling down the rue St. Jacques chatting with a group of his friends that included La Fontaine, the writer of those great animal fables, like the one about the fox who jumped and jumped but couldn't reach a succulent bunch of grapes. Finally the fox quit trying, and was heard to remark as he walked away that those grapes were surely sour anyway.

While Père Malebranche and his friends were walking along, a pregnant dog came fawning up to them. Père Malebranche knelt down to fondle her. Then, making sure his friends had their eyes upon him, he stood up, pulled back his cassock, and kicked the poor animal in the stomach as hard as he could. The dog ran yelping down the street, and Père Malebranche's companions exclaimed in horror. Then Père Malebranche hardened his voice, and this is the essence of what he said: Fie on ye! Restrain yourselves. That dog is nothing but a machine. Rub it there, it scratches. Whistle, it comes. Kick it, it yelps and runs away. There is a button to push and a mechanism for each of its actions. It is nothing but a machine. Save your compassion for *human* souls.

Père Malebranche is always characterized as one of the sweetest and most compassionate men of his time.

Descartes said — both famously and infamously — that all animals are machines. He said *all* animals are machines. Even the human body is a machine. Human animals would be automata — like all other animals — living robots acting unconsciously by stimulus and response, except for the fact that each human body is united with a soul. And only *human* animals have souls. This soul for Descartes is the human mind. It is the mind that is conscious, not the body. The human self, the person, is the mind, not the body. And the mind has free will, the ability to cause the human body to act in ways contrary to the way it would respond to environmental stimuli alone.

You know how it goes. For thirty years I have walked the same route, a mile from my home to my office on the Washington University campus. But I very seldom do it consciously. I know this because sometimes I start along that route to go to a bookstore about halfway there, and as often as not I find myself well past the bookstore and even in my office before I realize that I was on automatic and had walked the entire distance without thinking about or watching what I was doing at all. Let me just remark here that we human beings are conscious a lot less time than we think we are, and I mean a *lot*. Almost everything we do, we can do, and often do do, without conscious thought. But, Descartes said, what makes us human is that we *can* direct our bodies' movements, or at least some of them, if we pay attention. Descartes did not know how it works, but neither does anyone else. But it *does* work. Descartes's view that all material things, all bodies, all animals — including the human body — are machines, led to a revolutionary advance in science that is still booming. If bodies are machines, then by using Descartes's method of mechanistic models, scientists can figure out how they work and thus how to control them. Not as our minds control our bodies from within, but from the outside — by giving them a good kick in the right place.

Descartes's notion of animals as machines obviously grounds behavioristic psychology. Animals don't think, they just behave. That is, they are pushed by other bodies, so they move around. Thus you can understand them and predict their movements merely by observing their behavior. The thesis that animals are machines was also a great boon to anatomical and physiological research. Because nonhuman animals have no minds or souls, they are not conscious. They do not know themselves because they have no selves. So they don't feel things and they have no pains or pleasures. Consequently, you can cut open living animals to see how they work without worrying about hurting them. If they squirm and scream, this is merely the automatic response of a robotic machine to stimuli.

Descartes gave instructions like these: Take a live rabbit and open its chest so you can see its heart beating. Now take scissors and cut the artery leading out ... and so on. You may have done it yourself, to a frog, in biology lab, in high school. Descartes's notion that animals have no feelings made it possible for even the squeamish to practice vivisection, to which practice we are indebted for so much of our knowledge about how the living animal body works.

This view that all animal bodies are unfeeling machines is, by the way, a direct inference from the Christian interpretation of Descartes's mind-body dualism, the view that there are only two kinds of things in the world, thinking active souls or minds, yours and mine, and unthinking passive matter of which all bodies are made. When we die, our bodies rot and our souls survive. What about dogs? You ask about dogs? Did God say there would be dogs in heaven? Of course not, that would be ridiculous. Dogs have no souls. Dogs don't sin. Jesus didn't die for no stinking dogs! Only people with souls can sin and be washed in the Blood of the Lamb.

So if Descartes were alive today, would he be in favor of abortion and genetic engineering? Certainly not abortion, but genetic engineering? You'd better believe it. The body, after all, is just a machine, and if we can improve it, do it! God did not forbid improving the breed.

Here we are, then, in the modern world with the Cartesian view that all bodies — living or not — are machines that work on the basis of mechanistic interactions among their parts. The entire material world is but an elaborate mechanism that can be taken apart piece by piece to see how it works and then put back together again with the appropriate modifications to suit our purposes. Find the right buttons to push and you can get anything to do anything you please. Descartes's mechanistic physics — refined by Isaac Newton and Albert Einstein — is the juggernaut of progress in the modern world. Of course the mechanisms now include gravitational, electro-chemical, and weak and strong nuclear forces, plus neural nets and DNA.

But if matter just gets pushed around, how did it ever get organized into the intricate and complex present-day world? How did it get started moving in the first place? Descartes says God introduced a certain quantity of motion into a world full of uniform matter that then whirled about until bodies developed, all sheerly by mechanistic interactions. The amount of motion was conserved and the world evolved. It had to, because matter could, and eventually would, combine in all possible ways. Descartes's pious younger contemporary, Blaise Pascal, remarked acidly that Descartes's God was necessary merely as the finger that flicked matter to set it into motion. This was evidence enough for Pascal that under it all, Descartes was an atheist.

Nonsense. Descartes said God created the world and the natural laws determining the interactions of material bodies. You can see that by reading the first chapter of Genesis. Our job is to figure out how things work. As Pascal bitterly complained, Descartes disdained theological questions except as problems in physics. In a lifetime of trying to stay on the right side of the Catholic Church, Descartes got into serious trouble only once. He made the mistake of explaining how, according to Cartesian physics, the tiny bits of matter of which flesh and blood are made could be reorganized to have the same surface expression as bread and wine. Then they would look and taste like bread and wine. The problem with Descartes's explanation is that it turns the workings of transubstantiation into a mere matter of mechanistic physics. It actually turns blood into wine and flesh into bread. Christians like Pascal do not want mechanistic explanations of miracles.

In fact, although Descartes had the right approach in science, only a few of his own explanations of how bodies work are accepted today. His notion that light consists of little round bouncing globes that cause us to see different colors depending on their speed and spin is in the right ballpark. But his physics of colliding bodies is out in left field. He was wrong about the conservation of motion (Leibniz and Newton got it right, the conservation of energy, not motion). And his claim that all of space is filled with matter won't work, because if everything is full up, how can anything move? Descartes's explanation that things move into spaces left by other things that have moved into spaces left by still other things is incoherent, because for him, a space itself is a material thing. Even if things did move by filling the spaces left by other things, everything would have to move all at once, and everything would be over in a moment. Well, don't fuss about it. Newton replaced Descartes's plenum with material bodies moving in lots of empty space.

In anatomy and physiology, however, Descartes scored big, both with some great results concerning muscle oppositions and conditioned reflexes and with his fabulously successful analytical method. Because of Descartes, the method of procedure seems obvious to us now: Dissect, nay, vivisect by functional anatomical parts. This method is foundational in medical research today. Even the human genome is being taken apart to see how to put it back together to improve the human body. Descartes assisted in the dissection of human cadavers in Amsterdam in the 1630s, in an amphitheater just like the one Rembrandt painted in his famous *The Anatomy Lesson of Dr. Tulp* of 1632. If Descartes were alive today, he would be in charge of the CAT and PET scan machines in a major research hospital.

In his own time, however, Descartes was best known as a mathematician. Even his contemporaries knew he was one of the three or four greatest mathematical geniuses of all time. His most important invention is analytic geometry, a way of representing mathematical problems both geometrically and algebraically. He invented the Cartesian coordinates you learned about in freshman geometry in high school. Using this technique, you can solve geometric problems with algebra, and algebraic problems with geometry. This method of analysis led Newton and Leibniz to the infinitesimal calculus that all scientists and engineers have to know because it is the basis of mathematical physics and modern technology. Here is a basic problem that calculus solves. Zeno of Elea set up two paradoxes about motion based on the view that space and time are infinitely divisible. In the story of the race between Achilles and the tortoise, if you give the tortoise a head start, then Achilles will never catch up. The reason is that Achilles has to reach where the tortoise started before he can pass the tortoise. But during the time it takes Achilles to reach the tortoise's starting point, the tortoise has moved on. So Achilles has to reach the place the tortoise is now. But when he gets there, the tortoise has moved on again. And so on ad infinitum. No matter how small a distance, the tortoise always moves on during the time Achilles takes to reach where the tortoise just was, so Achilles can never pass the tortoise.

Another paradox reverses the problem. Suppose you shoot an arrow at a target. Before it reaches the target, it has to get halfway there, which takes a certain amount of time. But before it gets halfway there, it has to get one fourth the way there, which takes a certain amount of time. And before one fourth, one eighth, and so on *ad infinitum*. It isn't just that the arrow cannot reach the target. The arrow can't even get started on its way.

This is all very silly, of course, because men can beat tortoises in races, and arrows reach their targets all the time. What the paradoxes show is the impossibility of using mathematics based on infinite divisibility to represent the physics of moving bodies. Using as a basis Descartes's analytic geometry, Leibniz and Newton showed that all you have to do is introduce limits to divisibility. You divide time and movements into small increments, and then Achilles and the arrow can move right along — click-click-click — just like the second hand on a Swiss railroad clock.

In sum, the modern world is Cartesian to the core because all science and technology today is based on describing the material world mathematically as a vast machine whose various parts interact according to uniform laws of motion. Descartes set the task of figuring out how things work — how they are put together, what follows what, how to take them apart and put them back together again. And since there is nothing spiritual or sacred in nature, the entire value of the natural world resides in its utility for humankind. Finally, despite insisting on an absolute distinction between mind and body, Descartes treats even human passions mechanistically. In his last book *The Passions of the Soul* (1649), he explains how to control the passions by pitting one against the other. The desire for glory, for example, is set against the fear of death to result in courage for going into battle.

That was Descartes in the seventeenth century. Have things changed since? Not in the least. Modern science is still mechanistic in the grand sense that includes electricity, chemistry, and subatomic interactions. The name of the game at the beginning of the twenty-first century is the same as in the first half of the seventeenth — control. Our goal is to be masters and possessors of nature.

Ha! you might say. *This* is the curse of Cartesianism — Descartes's making methodic reason and objective analysis superior to subjective feeling and intuitive sensibility. He has cursed us with the belief that what is important is not the subjective sensations and emotions we have within us but rather the objective things in the outer world that cause them. Descartes is the father of machismo, of the ideal of the big tough hard stoical rational man. Grin and bear it. Emotions are subjective, trivial, useless, meaningless, and misleading. There are no emotions in the real world, so they should not be allowed to interfere with man's serious, objective work of controlling nature.

17

More than that, the success of Descartes's method of analyzing things into their separate parts to see how they work rules out, as a practical matter, considering the world and its organisms as a seamless whole. Descartes's materialist construction of nature is the antithesis of the anti-individualist Hegelian or Buddhist notion that the world itself has an oceanic soul into which our own souls merge like raindrops. Descartes's method is in opposition to the life-force ideology of deep ecologists, mystically inclined environmentalists, and defenders of the rights of nature. Cartesianism promotes the view that everything but the human mind is just inert matter, so sentiment for animals and nature is ridiculous. Only the self-conscious human soul has value. Everything else merely exists, insentient, unthinking, and without awareness of being. Descartes opposed psychism, pantheism, and spiritualism — the views that mind or spirit pervades all of existence. Descartes posed himself directly against the Aristotelian Scholasticism of his time, the view that occult forces or powers of the essences or forms of material things cause them to develop as they do. An acorn grows into an oak tree, Descartes says, not because an acorn has the power to fulfill its desire to be an oak tree. But rather an acorn turns into an oak tree merely because it is a mechanism that is pushed around in a certain way by its material environment.

Descartes did not believe in ghosts or witches or tree fairies, or in the powers of crystals, pyramids, magic numbers, and planetary conjunctions. Whatever is soft and sentimental, mythical and poetic, mystical and magical, supernatural and miraculous, superstitious and mysterious, Descartes scorned. This was one hard man, hated in his lifetime by the devout, hated by those who reason with the heart ever since. In our time, René Descartes is the most vilified innovator this side of Karl Marx.

In 1950, I started collecting quotations of great attacks on Descartes and Cartesianism. Back then, Cartesian often meant simply a pedant, compulsively orderly and methodic, someone who puts reason above the emotions, cares more about abstract than particular things, follows logic rigidly to absurd conclusions, and is not all that much fun to have around. But during the second half of the twentieth century, this picture got meaner. As we enter the twenty-first century, Cartesians are said to follow reason to inhuman conclusions. Now it is claimed that it was Cartesian of the Nazis to build efficient ovens in which to gas Gypsies and Jews. The whole notion of efficiency at the expense of humane treatment of human beings is said to be Cartesian. It is Cartesian to treat people as things, workers as interchangeable, expendable cogs in a machine. The rationalization of commerce and industry to increase production and profits by reducing the pay and number of workers (by robotization or by shipping the factory to some Third World country) is Cartesian. Of course it is Cartesian to test cosmetic chemicals by plastering them into the eyes of live rabbits (they don't feel a thing). It is Cartesian to mine coal in open pits, to clearcut forests, to think that there is a technological fix for the dangers of radioactive waste and the warming of the earth's climate. Indeed, the essence of Cartesianism is distilled in the belief that with technology, humans can solve not just any technological problem but any problem at all. (Does this depress you? Here, take this pill.)

This throws on Descartes the guilt for most of man's inhumanity to man in the modern world. His championing of technological efficiency and passionless reason is taken to be the source of selfish, narcissistic Cartesian individualism. Descartes's possessive individualism (first of all, of course, I own myself and my body, with which I can do as I please) has made consumer capitalism the dominant social and political force of our time. Cartesianism is the antithesis of community. Furthermore, Cartesian insensitivity to all of nature is blamed for universal commodification. In the labor market, even people are property, to be bought and sold.

The whole modern world is cursed by Cartesianism, and a lot of people don't like it. I soon quit collecting pejorative uses of the word Cartesian. No one needs a file. Just pick up any book promoting religion, holism, communalism, sacralization or resacralization, any tome opposed to modern science and technology, to the inhumaneness of individualism, any book promoting community, advocating deep ecology, a new environmental ethic, eco-religion, or rights for animals, any book defending hypotheses that the earth is alive or was designed especially for human beings, opposing vivisection and animal research in medicine, advocating eco-sabotage, any tract urging you to get in touch with your feelings, to emote, to follow New Age programs in opposition to reason, any attack on logic, efficiency, paternalism, meritocracy, technocracy, and elitism, any book in which the author claims that the subjective is what makes us human and the objective is what makes us beasts, the gobbledygook of gurus who ask us to dream, empathize, meditate(!), to relax and let our instincts take command, to trust intuition, the heart not the brain, cooperation instead of competition, feminine compassion over masculine reserve, tribe or group or community or state over the individual, the sentimental over the realistic, faith over reason, attacks on the Enlightenment, the French Encyclopaedists, and the French revolution, diatribes against the Age of Reason, attacks on atheism and godless humanism as the cause of all the world's problems, attacks on narcissism and individualism, attacks on sociobiology, genetic engineering, and the selfish gene, books with such titles as *The Dictatorship of Reason in the West* or *Descartes's Mistake* — any of these will provide you with crackerjack quotations denouncing Descartes and Cartesianism.

And you know what? All these accusations are true. Descartes is the architect of our modern world of individualistic, materialist science and technology. And no doubt about it, were he to arrive on the scene today, he would look around with immense satisfaction. As for the bad things technology supports, such as gas chambers, Descartes was used to ethnic and religious wars. In his time, the French expelled the Jews (1615) and slaughtered the Protestants (1628). He was in Northern Europe (1620s) when whole regions were depopulated by war, famine, crop failure, and plague. There have *always* been bad things. Descartes saw them all. Even then, he thought human life was improving because of the advance of science. And it has. Electricity, painless dentistry, indoor toilets.

This reminds me of another story. I met the great Marxist philosopher and guru Herbert Marcuse only once. His *One Dimensional Man* was the bible of a lot of student revolutionaries around the world in the 1960s. I was driving him from one place to another on the Los Angeles freeway, and I complained about the traffic.

"You like toast for breakfast?" Marcuse said dryly.

"Yes," I replied

"Then you have to put up with this," he said, gesturing with his arm at Los Angeles.

What Descartes would notice today is not toast and traffic, but medicine. His only child died of scarlatina at the age of five. It devastated him. Her death was probably an important factor in his decision to devote the rest of his life to medical research. Now we can cure scarlatina, smallpox, the plague. And, by God! Descartes might say if he were profane (which is one thing he was not, because he believed in the God of Abraham, Moses, Jesus, Mohammed, Calvin, Luther, and Unified Science — and was looked on unkindly by zealots for his ecumenical tolerance), by God! he might say in elation: Following my method, medical scientists have learned how to cure a fever. How about that!

Socrates advocated the principle my country right or wrong and accepted a death sentence he thought unjust rather than support civil disobedience, yet few people see him as the intellectual giant behind Stalinist totalitarianism. Jesus started a religion one of whose most distinguishing characteristics is the presentation of women, marriage, and human sexuality as evil, and in whose name hundreds of millions of people have been slaughtered, yet Christianity is revered as a religion of love. If we are to blame the ills of the modern world on great dead white men, Socrates and Jesus have as much to answer for as does Descartes. But neither of them gets near the bad press Descartes does. Our hero is a real bad man.

Well, you might say, someone has to take the rap for the deep malaise, the dissatisfaction with material goods, and the sense of spiritual vacuity that infect the soul of Western man. (I've never felt this myself, but who am I to piddle against the wind of pop psychologists and earnest culture critics?) Even in his own time, Descartes was accused of skepticism and atheism, and these two views of the world without certainty and without God are what anti-Cartesian critics most deplore today. Descartes complained that he was unjustly accused of skepticism because he refuted the skeptics, and of atheism because he proved the existence of God. But the accusations are fair enough because despite his sincere attempts, instead of refuting skepticism he demonstrated its irrefutable strength, and instead of proving the existence of God he showed it can't be done. That is why the life of René Descartes is important.

There are two main traditions of Descartes biography. In his *La Vie de Monsieur Des–Cartes* (1691), Adrien Baillet started the French Catholic apologetic tradition, the goal of which is to establish that Descartes's life is worthy of the Great Metaphysician. It has been continued most recently by Geneviève Rodis-Lewis in her *Descartes: His Life and Thought* (1998). Baillet was recommended by the fact that he was undertaking a seventeen-volume *Lives of the Saints*. He demurred that he knew little about Descartes, but then he threw himself into the task with the zeal of a full-fledged member of the Saint Descartes Protection Society. The founder of this society (this joke probably goes back at least to Descartes's death in Stockholm in 1650) was the French ambassador to Sweden, Hector-Pierre Chanut, who refused to allow Descartes's remains to be buried in a Lutheran cemetery. Descartes's reputation was then managed for many years by Chanut's brother-in-law, Claude Clerselier.

Clerselier edited Descartes's letters, deleting passages that conflict with church doctrine and adding passages of his own composition where they were most needed to illustrate the faith proper to a pious Catholic philosopher. This can be checked, however, only against a few letters of which there are independent copies, for none of the original manuscripts, papers, notes, and letters that Clerselier and Baillet had are extant today. They were given to Jean-Baptiste Legrand, and after he died, to his mother in 1706. Despite many searches, that is the last we ever hear of them.

The second main line of Descartes biography has most recently been continued by Stephen Gaukroger in his *Descartes: An Intellectual Biography* (1995). In this tradition, the stress is on the analysis of Descartes's works to show him as the Great Scientist who founded not only Modern Philosophy but also Modern Science.

The present work belongs to neither the religious nor the scientific apologetic tradition. Given how much paper has been lost since the seventeenth century, I cannot look at original sources for much of the story I tell, but must depend on editors and chroniclers such as Clerselier and Baillet, who are not fully trustworthy. The result is a skeptical biography, as full of doubt about tradition and authority as was Descartes himself.

Here, then, is the life of René Descartes. It is the first biography of Descartes since 1920 that is based on substantial new research, and the only one ever written for general readers. It is the story of the man, not of the monument.

PROLOGUE

On the Zeedijk

LATE IN DECEMBER 1628 or early in January 1629 René Descartes arrived in Franeker in Friesland. He was thirty-two years old, and just a few weeks before, he had been summoned to a private interview with Cardinal Bérulle, founder of the Society of Oratarians in France, rival of the Jesuits, who was deeply involved with the Catholic League and the Company of the Sacred Sacrament, a militant secret society of laymen pledged to fight for the Catholic cause by eliminating Protestantism in France. The cardinal was a strange mixture of astute politician, courtier, and mystic. He talked familiarly with God, angels, and the queen mother every day. He had convinced First Minister Richelieu — also a cardinal — to crush the last stronghold of Protestantism in France, La Rochelle, which fell under siege and starvation in late October with Cardinal Bérulle marching triumphantly among the victors.

No one knows what Cardinal Bérulle, flushed with triumph, said to Descartes — himself a Catholic — but the result was that within weeks Descartes was about as far away from militant Catholicism as you could get in Europe in the seventeenth century, standing on the steps of a Protestant university founded in 1585 and known as a haven for persecuted Protestants from all over Europe. He did not return to France for fifteen years, not until both Cardinal Bérulle and Cardinal Richelieu were dead, and then only for a visit.

In Franeker — literally God's Acre — Descartes lived in a château nearly as large as the Reformed church it faced down the wide main street. It was owned by the Sjaerdemas, a prominent Catholic family. In this château Descartes wrote the first draft of his famous *Meditations on First Philosophy* in which he bases certainty on the phrase, "I think, [therefore] I am" and which earned him the title of the Father of Modern Philosophy. But in that winter of 1629, although he had a high reputation as a mathematician and philosopher, he had as yet published nothing. He sat in his room, looking north out over the flat polder to the zeedijk, the low wall that held back the sea.

I sit now in an old fisherman's cottage under that zeedijk and look across the flat polder six miles south toward Franeker, visible only at night as points of orange light. I wonder why Descartes came here.

The Netherlands is a land of low relief but of infinite variation. When I was being shown around the grounds of Endegeest Castle near Leiden (a small but very elegant château that Descartes later rented for two years — servants, livery, and moat), Alexandre Schimmelpenninck, editor at the Kluwer publishing house, said, "See that drop-off over there? We're on higher ground here. That's what protects the castle during floods."

I strained to see.

"There, at the line of trees."

Then I saw it. Eighteen inches. In fact, my guide said, it is slightly over three feet because it slants down gently after the drop-off.

"You'll begin to see the differences after you've been here awhile," he said.

But I lived under the zeedijk for several months before I saw what someone pointed out to me, that inland was a parallel road on a lower dike, and beyond that another ridge, even lower and barely discernible. Three lines of defense are common against the sea. They are known as the waking dike, the sleeping dike, and the dreaming dike. Like Descartes, I thought, who liked to lie awake in bed of a morning, who slept late, and who found his profession as a philosopher in a dream.

Soon after we arrived in the Netherlands, my wife Pat and I went into a large cheese shop. "What shall we get?" she said.

On the shelves were perhaps a hundred large wheels of hard yellow cheese, six inches thick and nearly three feet in diameter. We had just spent seven months in Paris, eating cheese. I looked at the array and laughed. "It doesn't matter," I said. "They're all the same."

The proprietress heard me and was outraged. First, they differ as to the farms where they were made. Then they differ in being young, middle-aged, and old. Middle-aged cheese is belegen, just lying there, aging, between youth and old age, and this middle-aged cheese is also divided into young, middle-aged, and old. But more than that, in a fine shop like hers, we were not restricted to only five ages. She could give us cheese of any age, month by month, from one to twenty-four. So what did I want?

"The oldest," I said.

She grumbled quietly as she cut a piece. It was the right choice, and the most expensive. This is plain cheese. It also comes, all ages, spiced with cumin or cloves or various herbs. Very old clove-spiced cheese is most Frisian, the finest product. The whole cloves have become soft, there are many of them, and you chew them up. Descartes must have eaten such cheese — and smelled such pungent spices in the Netherlands — and perhaps he was as bemused as we were.

Descartes said nothing about Dutch cheese in his letters. He did have strong opinions about food, and he recommended that one should eat lightly — not easy in the Netherlands. And he once said that if the Netherlands did not have as much honey as God promised the Israelites, it surely had more milk. Even today it is said that the Netherlands is a country in which you can be assured that you are never more than 500 feet from a cow. Descartes was said to be a virtual vegetarian, and like any Frenchman who has a piece of ground at least a meter square, he kept a garden. Here in Friesland in winter he would eat turnips, beets, and bread, carrots and cabbage, onions and parsnips, leeks and lentils, of which you can be sure there are many varieties.

The wind is almost always blowing in Friesland. In the dead of winter it reaches gale force for days at a time and will knock you flat if you are not prepared for it. We sleep in a loft under the eaves. The wind howls around our ears and the roof tiles clack and clatter. Like being on a ship in a storm on the North Sea, Pat says, without the inconvenience of a heaving deck. When we sit by the stove reading at night, the wind rages with such fury that you imagine that you are on the Russian steppes. But if you step outside, although the wind may take your breath away, it is not cold. All winter the temperature has ranged between 33 and 45 degrees Fahrenheit. It has rarely been below freezing, with ice on the pond in mid-December for only three or four days, and then not thick enough for skating. They say 1987–1988 has been an unusually mild winter — no doubt like the one Descartes complained of in 1633–1634 when he was writing his *Meteorology*, during which he managed, he said, to study only one snowflake. Claude de Saumaise, a French exile like Descartes, characterized the Netherlands as four months of winter and eight months of cold. A neighbor said the prediction for this year is that it will warm up in July. He tells of the year you could eat outside from mid-April to mid-October. This mid-April the temperature continues the same, but the length of the day has increased from pitch-black at 4 PM in December to dusk now at 9 PM. The birds are nesting and the jonquils are in bloom.

There is not a lot of sun here. Pat marks time by referring to the day the sun shone all day. When the sun does shine on a warm day — which means no wind — everyone moves dinner tables outside to eat. On a street in Leiden where the houses are continuous and face right onto the sidewalks, one noontime we had to walk in the street because so many people were sitting at tables on the sidewalk in front of their houses eating dinner.

The weather changes a dozen times a day. Fog, overcast, light rain, heavy showers — squalls, actually, for we are in fact right out in the middle of the sea — the water held back by the zeedijk, our house a stationary boat planted on the sea bottom, nothing but the zeedijk keeping us from casting adrift in our bed. Snow flurries, sleet and hail, and sun. The sky is enormous as are the clouds, and huge rainbows reach almost to the zenith. Sun and moon through clouds, spectacular sunrises and sunsets in tulip colors, rays of sun and shadow on the sky. All that billows and blows...

But on the ground all is straight lines. The green line of the grass-covered zeedijk, the brown reeds along the long blue pond, the green and brown fields beyond extending into blue haze on the horizon. Farmhouses, small villages, steeples rise tiny out of the flat polder in the distance. All colors shade into pastels. Out every window are Dutch landscape and skyscape paintings, always the same, always different.

Why did Descartes come here? He said he preferred living in a desert, where there are few people, where there is silence and solitude so one can think. In Paris, the bustle and busyness of the city ran away with his thoughts. His friends and relatives importuned him. In Friesland he could escape. He could be alone.

"In what other land," he wrote in 1630 to his friend the poet Guez de Balzac, "can one enjoy freedom so entire?" He was living in Amsterdam then, but for him it was another desert. "In this great city," he said, "where I am now, there is no other man except me who is not engaged in commerce. And each is so concerned about his own profit that I could live here all my life without ever being seen by anyone. I walk every day among the confusion of a great people with as much liberty and repose as you enjoy in your country lanes, and I pay no more attention to the people I see than if they were the trees in your forests or the animals that dwell there." This is perhaps the first statement, not of alienation, but of the joyful anonymity one can have in a great city and nowhere else.

But most of Descartes's years in the Netherlands were spent just outside such small towns as Franeker, Egmond, Santpoort, Hardewijk, Alkmar, Amersfoort in isolated houses like our fisherman's cottage. He tended his garden, he dissected animals for his treatise on anatomy, he lay abed thinking and writing. In his leisure — but his life was his leisure — he rode, hunted, fenced, listened to music, and talked with friends. He answered letters, solved problems in mathematics, and replied to objections to his philosophy. He claimed that he did not read books. Of course he did, but on 25 December 1639 he wrote to his Parisian correspondent Mersenne that the only books he had taken with him to the United Provinces were the Bible and a copy of Saint Thomas Aquinas's *Summa Theo-logica*. He was enthusiastic about the use of the organ in the Reformed Church. But he complained that country neighbors can sometimes be more bothersome than city friends. Probably visitors just dropped in then, as now, and thought nothing of staying for four or five hours. Descartes apologized for his Dutch, although he wrote and spoke it fluently, and he must have picked up some Frisian. We know neither, but Frisian and English make up a sub-group of the Germanic family of languages. Knowing German and with Frisian the closest relative of English, we often halfway understand.

Our closest neighbors are a retired zeedijk worker and his sister, about a hundred yards down the road. They loaned us a book on dikes. The land is sinking and the sea is rising and "a day will come when nothing more can be done. Then the time will have come for the Netherlands, like children's sandcastles when the tide comes in, to disappear from the scene." The first zeedijk here was built in 1570 and was 6.6 feet high. It was raised to 9.2 feet in 1571 and was at that height when Descartes was here. In 1930, it was raised to 17.2 feet, and then after disastrous storms and floods to 30.8 feet in 1975. It cannot be raised higher because additional weight would just make it sink into the soft sea bottom on which it rests. Our house is 3.3 feet below mean sea level, the fields out there a bit lower. At night we can hear waves rolling onto the zeedijk.

We are from St. Louis, Missouri, the home of Switzer's licorice, which we have loved since childhood, so we were naturally attracted to the open bins of licorice in the stores here. Licorice is called drop. Drop ranges in color from light brown to dark black, and in hardness from very soft to crystal, but on first view drop species differ most obviously in shape. There is always a bin of small cats, one of farmers and farmhouses, another of money — fat disks with a number impressed on one side and a dollar sign on the other — and many, many more. I picked up a licorice drop and popped it into my mouth and promptly spat it out. It was licorice, but...

Licorice drops come in mild, medium, and severe strength; these in plain, or in low sweet, medium sweet, and double sweet, and in low salt, medium salt, and double salt. I had made my first test on a double salt. Drop differs also in brand name. My classification is the result of empirical tests, but I thought I might be exaggerating the number of kinds, so I asked a native Frisian. He was aghast.

"There are forty or fifty varieties *at least*," he said. And this merely in taste alone. He warned me against an inferior brand of his favorite small cats. He recommended laurel leaf licorice — not only in the shape of laurel leaves but molded around laurel leaves — that he particularly liked. Licorice also comes molded around mint leaves and flavored with sal ammoniac. He also told me that I had missed a distinction in the cheese. All varieties come either 48, 40, or 28 percent fat.

In the village of Tzummarum two miles from our house, there is an excellent bakery, Striksma's. (All Frisian surnames end in the letter *a*, meaning "of".) The bread comes with hard or soft crust in white, whole wheat, and rye; fine, medium, and coarse grained; and plain or sprinkled on top with oatmeal, poppy seeds, or sesame seeds. They bake all of these every day and all are delicious. When I remarked on this to our landlords who live in The Hague, they commiserated with us and brought samples from their neighborhood bakery that produces a dozen different kinds of white bread alone, and varieties of another dozen different kinds of dark bread.

Fifteen years is a long time to stay away from your native land when it is virtually just around the corner. In a few days Descartes could have been in Paris. But this was not his first sojourn outside France. When he was twenty-two, he had gone to the Netherlands where he spent more than a year studying mathematics and military architecture in the school run by Maurice, prince of Nassau, the most brilliant military strategist of his time. Maurice was an excellent patron saint for Descartes. The prince loved mathematics. On his deathbed in 1625, a minister asked him to state his beliefs. "I believe," Maurice said, "that $2 + 2 = 4$ and that $4 + 4 = 8$. These gentleman here," he said, pointing to some mathematicians at his side, "will inform you of the details of the rest of our beliefs."

Then for the next nine years between 1619 and 1628, Descartes traveled in Denmark, Germany, Poland, Hungary, Austria, Moravia, Bavaria, Bohemia, Venice, Italy, and France. He was in Paris off and on during the two years before his interview with Cardinal Bérulle and had talked about locating in the country. The Descartes family owned houses and farms in Poitou, Touraine, and Brittany. He had wide choice and obviously enjoyed his stays in the French country-side. He apparently said nothing about settling in the Netherlands. But soon after seeing Cardinal Bérulle, he packed up and was gone.

These flat polders and this cool, even climate are a great change from the hilly, wooded land where Descartes grew up. I feel the dif-ference because the landscape in southwestern Iowa where I was born is much like that of Descartes's birthplace in Touraine. Did he miss the lack of mystery in the hidden folds of hills, the continual change of prospect that the flat, treeless polder rules out?

Descartes left his financial affairs in the hands of his closest friend in Paris, Claude Picot, later known as the Atheist Priest. This is probably because of the notorious story of Picot's deathbed benefice. Picot was traveling in rural France — this was long after Descartes's own death — when he was taken violently ill. They could see that he was dying at the inn where he lay, so they summoned the village priest. Picot said to this priest that he would bestow a very handsome benefice on the local parish, on one condition. No mumbo jumbo. No chanting, no last rites, no Latin. He was himself a priest. His conscience was clear. Just let him die in peace. The local priest was not happy with this but agreed. Then when Picot seemed very near the end, in a coma apparently, the priest could restrain himself no longer. He began the incantation. Picot opened one eye and said, "I can still take back the money." So the priest fell silent and Picot died in peace.

Koek is gingerbread. It comes spiced mild, medium, and strong; fine, medium, or coarse textured; dry, medium, and moist; in loaves, long slices (called calves' legs), and cupcake. It also comes in the form of cake, brownies, cookies, and puff pastry. Also plain, with raisins, or with frosting. In fact, I am told that this is all wrong. Just because all these items are basically what I perceive as brown gingerbread, they do not at all belong to only one category. Mine is an outsider's empirical categorization that the Dutch do not recognize. But no outsider could ever get it right. Once I held up two packages of very dark, moist German rye bread and asked the grocery-van driver (he came by our cottage once a week) if they were the same. He was scandalized.

"*Very* different," he said, but without enough English to be precise. I bought them both. Indistinguishable.

Catholic commentators say Descartes would have been perfectly safe living and publishing in France. But the Parliament of Paris passed a decree in 1624 forbidding attacks on Aristotle on pain of death. Descartes trivialized Aristotelian logic and argued that Aristotelian physics was false. Vanini had been burned alive in 1619 for giving natural explanations of miracles — one of the advantages Descartes claimed for Cartesian physics — and more than a dozen heretics were burned alive in France during Descartes's lifetime. What is more, Descartes was making fun of astrology right at the time Cardinal Richelieu was having horoscopes cast for making decisions of state.

In 1623, there was a Rosicrucian scare in Paris — placards appeared saying the Brethren were moving, invisible among the populace. Descartes was accused of being a Rosicrucian and is said to have defended himself with mock indignation by pointing out that everyone could see that he was not invisible. He rejected the magical and mystical beliefs of the Rosicrucians, but he took their motto as his own: He who lives well hidden, lives well. Like them, he practiced medicine without charge, tried to increase human longevity, was optimistic about the usefulness of science in improving the human lot, did not marry, and changed residence often. During twenty-one years in the Netherlands, he lived in at least eighteen different places but moved more times than that. Having lived here awhile myself now, I suspect he may partly just have been looking for a change. In any event, traditional scholars are scandalized at the suggestion that Descartes might have been a Rosicrucian, or anything else than a very pious Catholic. But if it were not for the Saint Descartes Protection Society, Descartes might be known now as the Greatest Rosicrucian (just as Sir Isaac Newton might be classified as the Greatest Alchemist). We are so in need of squeaky-clean heroes that we present our great thinkers as Paradigms of Truth and Virtue rather than as the cranks they really were. Of course great men have to get only one or two things right for people to forget the hundreds of things they got wrong.

Descartes's happiest time in the Netherlands was when he lived with Helena Jans from 1634 to 1640. He prepared his greatest works for publication during those years. He and Helena had a child, Francine, who died at the age of five of scarlatina; she couldn't breathe, she turned purple, and she died. Descartes said her death was the greatest sorrow of his life and that he was not one of those philosophers who thought a man should not cry.

A number of Descartes's biographers do not even mention his daughter. Or they speak of the deplorable incident of his illegitimate child. But Francine was baptized and is listed in the register of legitimate births in the Reformed Church at Deventer. What this might mean about Descartes's religious beliefs is more horrifying to good Catholic Cartesian scholars than illegitimacy.

The Dutch are precise. Our house is rented by the week, in seven-day measures, not by the imprecise month. That means that in twelve months there are thirteen four-week rent periods. (The Dutch have been the world's most astute capitalists for four centuries. Even the French still rent by the month.) It is a weekend house but it has everything we could want. First, no telephone. A grand piano. Good beds and chairs. It is the only house we have ever been in except our own where there are good lamps for reading everywhere, and even for the piano.

Dutch houses have huge picture windows, and it is considered antisocial to pull the drapes or shades, day or night. In the seventeenth century when Descartes was here, foreigners commented on how beautiful Dutch interiors were, how elegant the furniture, how clean. The old paintings show it. You can still look in the windows to see. I run four or five miles every morning and cannot help but look into farmhouse windows as I pass by. Anyone inside looks back and waves. The window is not a barrier. I sit writing far back in a corner from the big windows facing onto the road, but everyone who walks by peers in, sees me, and waves. It is still surprising to me, but I wave back. The best views into houses are at night. We leave bare the windows facing the pond, but when we sit by the stove reading at night we pull the drapes across the windows facing the road. There really is no one out there, but it makes us feel more easy. We hope our neighbors will just think us foreign, not rude.

This openness may be a heritage of Calvinism. Nothing to hide in here! No one knocks when they come to the door; they just walk in. Neighbors, meter readers, postmen, repairmen, a schoolteacher from Franeker who heard we were here, and a newspaper reporter from Leeuwarden who learned from the schoolteacher that I was writing a book on Descartes. The schoolteacher stayed five hours. He was my informant about licorice drops. When the reporter left after two hours he said he would return to interview me.

"I thought that was what you were doing," I said.

"Oh no," he replied. "I wasn't taking notes."

Some days later he came and stayed the afternoon. The reporter warned me that after his story appeared, other reporters would come and disturb my solitude. I said I'd chance it. That was six weeks ago. The story has not yet appeared. He said when it did he would bring me a copy. Things are slow out here on the polder below the zeedijk. That is one reason why Descartes came here.

The reporter had been a philosophy assistant at Groningen University, so he knew all about Descartes. There is very little hope of finding a permanent place in the Dutch university system these days, so he became a reporter. In 1988, the government eliminated 250 teaching positions throughout the Netherlands. The university business is shrinking all over Europe, but jobs of all sorts are scarce in the Netherlands. Government propaganda promotes the view that you have performed a national service if you are willing to go on unemployment or take early retirement to allow someone else the opportunity to work. The retired dike worker down the way looks to be fifty or so. He did not want to retire. He takes long walks along the dike half a dozen times a day.

"It is very difficult," the reporter said. "The Dutch like to work."

Storm warning! All out for the zeedijk! It is in their blood. The Netherlands is the grandest sandcastle ever made on a beach. Who would not cry at being pulled away from such colossal play?

Someone sent me a clipping from Ripley's *Believe It or Not*: "René Descartes (1596–1650), the French philosopher and mathematician, learning that he would have to arise at 5 AM in a lucrative teaching position, warned that the cold morning air would be fatal to him — and died within four months."

Descartes had been invited to the court of Queen Christina of Sweden. Sweden had been a big winner at the end of the Thirty Years' War in 1648, and that made Queen Christina one of the most powerful and important monarchs in Europe. She was accumulating great scholars and writers, so why not add Descartes to her collection? Descartes had already turned down a handsome pension from a French nobleman. He said he did not want to be anyone's servant and that he did not need the money. But he was flattered at the thought of being philosopher to a queen.

Descartes must have forgotten that when Plato went to teach a monarch, his friends had to buy him back.

Descartes was fifty-three. Christina was twenty-two. She had a reputation for disconcerting the composure of dignified men. Once she taught her maids — who purportedly did not know French — to sing some dirty French songs and then had them perform in front of Thuillerie, the very old and distinguished former French ambassador to Sweden. She knew perfectly well Descartes's reputation for lying in bed in the morning, so she perversely had the great philosopher rise early enough to get dressed and ride in a carriage across town — he was staying with the current French ambassador, Hector-Pierre Chanut — to give philosophy lessons to her at 5 AM. She also asked him to write the statutes for a Swedish Academy of Arts and Sciences. Descartes had already got the message. He specified that foreigners could not be members of the Academy. He wanted out.

While delivering these statutes, at five o'clock in the morning on 1 February 1650, Descartes caught a chill. Ten days later, in a land where in winter (he said) men's thoughts freeze like the water, he died. This denouement is sometimes spoken of as Sweden's only contribution to Modern Philosophy. Descartes had expected to live to be a hundred. Christina quipped that the great mathematician miscalculated by nearly fifty years.

Queen Christina also said, "I love storm, and dread it when the wind drops."

On the rare day here when the wind does drop, the silence is deafening. Once I awoke in the middle of the night with the same sensation I had years ago waking up in port with the engines turned off after having crossed the Atlantic on an ocean liner. A few times in Paris I have woken up in the middle of the night because it is suddenly quiet. But there, after a few moments, the noise starts up again with the roar of cars and trucks. One is bombarded with noise in a city: construction, people, radio and television, the telephone, sirens, and bells — all jarring and startling, not like the wind. City noise, in itself and for what it draws your distracted attention to, is destructive of meditative thought. Descartes said it whirled you into higher and higher flights of fantasy. City thoughts seldom come to rest.

The sugar cookies here are excellent — plain, or with peanuts, almond slices, raisins, or frosting on top. Yellow cake varies from bakery to bakery according to amount of butter, sugar, and eggs. Pudding is called vla and is sold in wide-topped milk bottles. It comes in plain, vanilla, lemon, chocolate, and strawberry. A pretty combination is half-and-half strawberry and chocolate, lengthwise in the bottle. Again, our city landlords scoff at this paucity of country flavors of vla. We should see the selection in The Hague.

I had the most difficulty working out the differences in pap, which is porridge that also comes in wide-mouthed milk bottles. Whole or skimmed milk or buttermilk, made with barley, wheat, corn, or rice flour, with or without whole grains mixed in. Sweet or sour, plain or caramel flavored. Before I knew it was porridge that you were supposed to eat hot, I was testing it cold. The grocery-van driver set me straight. The next week I complained that when heated it is almost as runny as plain milk, not like porridge at all. Using a combination of English and Frisian, he led me to understand that any respectable family makes its own porridge at home, as thick as you please.

The days pass.

"In what other land," Descartes also said to Balzac, "could one sleep with such security?" Not in France where the windows are narrow and shuttered at night like fortresses. Not in Germany. I don't really understand why here. It is not as though these picture windows have not been smashed time and again by invaders over the centuries, most recently barely sixty years ago. The peace since World War II is the longest Western Europe has ever known. Perhaps it doesn't matter. There won't be a next time. Not another afterward, I mean.

A Sunday in the middle of March was still, and the sun was brilliant. Everyone was out in cars, on motorbikes and bicycles, or pushing baby strollers. Children of ten or eleven were walking across fields carrying poles ten or twelve feet long that they use to vault across the ditches. They were looking for eggs. We know there are millions of birds here. We watch them all the time, but we still dislike this spring egg-hunting sport. A man and his small son came along the other side of the pond, beating the reeds with sticks as they do to scare up nesting ducks. I rushed out to try to warn them away from the lake-coot nest I watch just by lifting my head and looking out the window.

"Nest? Where?" the man laughed, looking closer and beating with his stick. The coot sat tight and he missed her nest.

I have been watching the coots all winter and have become so involved with their lives that I would have to write a book to explain. There are thirty-five of them on the pond, black and pot-shaped, about the size of guinea hens, with big white beaks that sweep back up onto their foreheads. It has been a most frustrating obsession because they all look exactly alike — I can't even tell males from females. Pat says, "The coots know." I have no doubt that they differ from one another in many subtle ways.

There are both radio and television sets in this house, but we unplugged them when we moved in. We know the U.S. primaries must be over now, but we don't know who the candidates are. Probably it makes no difference. My brother does send us clippings from the *New York Times*. They include a running documentary on the changing prognoses of the future of AIDS, which certainly will make a difference to the future of humankind. In January we learned that "one of every 61 babies born in New York City last month carried antibodies to the virus, indicating that their mothers were infected and that many of the babies were also carriers." Where there are mothers and babies there are also fathers. When 2 or 3 percent of a population has a so-far incurable sexually transmitted disease, it won't take long for it to become 20 or 30 or 90 percent.

Descartes may have moved around so much to avoid the plague. In 1635, nearly 15,000 people died of the plague in Leiden. It was thought at the time that bad air — like that in Italy — spread the plague. Descartes was wrong about bad air, but he had the right idea when he moved away from infected areas. There is not going to be any moving away from AIDS, however. It follows us right into our beds.

Descartes truly was something of a health nut. He told his friend Guez de Balzac that besides the bad air, Italy was too hot. The Netherlands might be cold, but in a cold climate you can always get warm near a stove. In a hot climate there is no way to get cool. People like me who suffer serious heat debilitation in hot weather understand. Even air conditioning is inadequate. The body knows.

Descartes advocated government funding for cooperative research aimed at benefiting humankind. I do not believe the government needs to take as much of my income in taxes for my own good as it claims, but since it does take it, I would like to see about half of what now goes for "Defense" transferred to research on AIDS. It is not that I have ever doubted the menace of the nuclear holocaust, but AIDS is a threat that one can relate to as an individual.

We may all of us, like Descartes, overestimate the amount of time we have left. Descartes, however, frustrated with his lack of progress in finding a way to increase the length of human life, said he had come to a better solution: Don't fear death.

"I am out of my element here," Descartes said in the depth of the Swedish winter in the glacial atmosphere of a snow queen's court filled with intrigue.

"But it doesn't make any difference that he had to be up at five in the morning," a Swede remonstrated with me. "It is dark all the time in Sweden in winter, anyway, so people don't pay attention to the hour. It doesn't matter."

The wind blows, the light changes continuously, and the urgent clouds fly over the patient polder.

In Franeker, just over there on the horizon, Descartes wondered about the possibility that he might be deceived in thinking that the world exists. There might be nothing but his own mind and a demon making him think he is experiencing a world. The town is built on a low pancake-shaped mound a few yards higher than the surrounding ground. You hope you can reach the church built on the highest part of the mound if the zeedijk breaks. One day it will. There are limits to all things. Descartes invented analytic geometry, the essential foundation of the infinitesimal calculus that operates on the principle that between any two points there are an infinite number of divisions. I sit here at dusk looking at the everchanging sky. We all live between two points. Separated by infinite variations.

THE HOUSE IN LA HAYE WHERE DESCARTES WAS BORN

Photograph by Jean-Henri Roy

I   ✄   CHILDHOOD

Since my childhood,
I have been nurtured on books.

RENÉ DESCARTES was born on 31 March 1596. In 1637, when he was forty-one, he set the problem of how the human mind is related to the human body, a puzzle that has baffled Western philosophy and science ever since. The Cartesian mind-body problem is today at the head of the agenda for twenty-first-century science. Do human beings have immortal souls, or are their minds merely their brains that rot when they die? How that question is resolved will have repercussions on humankind greater than any atom bomb. Descartes is one of those rare geniuses in human history, like Socrates and Jesus Christ, whose ideas dominate human thought for millennia.

In all his writings, Descartes speaks of his childhood only six times. Writing to Princess Elisabeth of Bohemia when he was forty-nine years old (she was twenty-six), he says he inherited a dry cough and a pale complexion from his mother, afflictions that made all the physicians who examined him predict that he would die young. But the cough left him and his complexion turned ruddy in his early twenties, and he enjoyed good health thereafter. He continues to Elisabeth that his mother died a few days after his birth, but in fact she died thirteen months later on 13 May 1597, six days after giving birth to another son who died three days after she did.

Then in a letter of 6 June 1647 to Hector-Pierre Chanut who was at that time French resident in Stockholm, Descartes gives an example of imprinting on the brain. When he was a child he loved a playmate, a little cross-eyed girl. As an adult, he forgot all about her but found himself unaccountably attracted to cross-eyed women. One day he remembered his childhood friend and thus figured out the cause of his attraction, and that was the end of that.

Then he makes some comments that, while they may still be true of Descartes, are old saws (as is his remark about doctors predicting his early death). In his *Discourse on Method* of 1637, he remarks that since his childhood he had been nurtured on books and was eager to learn. But, alas, most of what he learned from books turned out to be false. Eminent authorities are often as ignorant as old wives. Descartes wheeled out another old saw in 1641 when Jacob Revius, who had converted from Catholicism to Protestantism, tried to convert him in turn. Descartes responded with the popular saying that his religion was that of his king and his nurse. A friend of his young manhood, the poet Guez de Balzac, used the same line. Finally, on 23 April 1649, Descartes wrote to the French resident in The Hague, Henri Brasset, that having been born in the gardens of Touraine, he was reluctant to travel to Sweden, a land of rocks and ice and bears.

Concerning his early years, Descartes says nothing about his father or his brother Pierre who was five years older, neither anything about his sister Jeanne who was probably six years older, nor about his step-mother whom his father married when René was four, nor his half brother Joachim II born when he was seven, nor his half sister Anne born when he was fifteen. Neither does he mention his two grandmothers (his grandfathers were long dead when he was born), nor several great-uncles, one of whom surely had a hand in raising him.

Obviously Descartes thought his childhood was negligible, or at most something whose influences — false opinions and warped impressions — were to be overcome. And in his *Meditations on First Philosophy*, published when he was forty-five, his solemn rejection of the importance of his parents is droll. He asks rhetorically if his existence could have come from them. Definitely not! For one thing, the question would immediately be raised of where his parents' existence came from, and so on ad infinitum. But supposing that they did produce his body, they cannot have produced the soul, the mind, the thinking spirit he calls himself. He concludes firmly that his existence comes solely from the first cause, God, who sustains it.

Despite how little he himself says — and his previous biographers have said little more — a great deal can be said about Descartes's childhood. The only way to begin is before the beginning, with a very involuted genealogy that provides great illumination on Descartes's life. If you like labyrinths, you will love Descartes's genealogy.

But look, the next seven pages are very dense. They are necessary for the biography because they contain all that is known about Descartes's background. You can skim them rapidly if you like. I don't want to lose you.

On 30 October 1543 in Châtellerault in Poitou in France, a marriage contract was signed between Pierre Descartes, age unknown, and Claude Ferrand, who was eleven or twelve years old. Twenty years later in December 1563, their only known child, Joachim, was born. Joachim Descartes married Jeanne Brochard on 15 January 1589, and on 31 March 1596, the fourth of their five children was born — René Descartes, who became one of the most important thinkers of all time.

René's grandfather Pierre Descartes was the son of Pierre Desquartes and Jeanne Poisson. Pierre Desquartes's brother Gilles Desquartes II was treasurer of the Cathedral of Tours. Their father was Gilles Desquartes I who had been mayor of Tours, and their mother was Marie Hubaille. That is as far back as the Descartes line has been traced, and we know of no other members than these few.

Pierre Descartes's father-in-law referred to him as "Squire," the lowest rank of the nobility, and spelled his name Desquartes, and then later in Latin as Deschartes. Pierre Descartes's great-grandchildren pretended that he was a descendant of the fifteenth-century nobleman, Giles Descartes, distinguished in military service for the kings of France. The name Descartes, however, is common as dirt — or as any crossroads where four corners need a name — and there is no evidence that Pierre Descartes descended from that Giles Descartes. Adrien Baillet (in his thousand-page two-volume life of Descartes, published in 1691, that is both immensely valuable and totally unreliable) says that Pierre Descartes traced his heredity without interruption back to the time of Charles V in the fourteenth century in order to demonstrate his nobility to the Court of Aids in Paris against the officers of Châtellerault who were trying to tax him (exemption from taxes being a major privilege of nobility). Baillet cites the Court of Aids Register of 4 September 1547, but this document is now missing from the National Archives. But even if a Pierre Descartes did so defend himself, it would have to be established that it was the Pierre Descartes who was René Descartes's grandfather. Certainly no one since has been able to find the connection.

In any event, no relations of Descartes along his father's line are known to have played any role in his life. And this is very strange. As anyone who looks into seventeenth-century family relations knows, people knew their relatives and lineages wide and deep, and they depended on the help and support of relatives extending even to third and fourth cousins. René Descartes's own godmother illustrates how far removed you could be and yet remain in the net. She was the wife of his maternal grandmother's cousin. And the Descartes children inherited money from their maternal grandfather's sister. Then there is Étienne Charlet, the rector at La Flèche where René Descartes went to school, who is said to have taken a special interest in the lad because they were relatives. Now on the only evidence we have, the closest they could have been related is somewhere down the line of a (hypothetical) brother of René Descartes's maternal great-great grandfather Jean Brochard's wife, Radegonde Charlet. That's pretty far removed.

Pierre Descartes became a medical doctor, and on 30 October 1543, he was contracted in marriage to Claude Ferrand, one of the nine children of Jean Ferrand I, who had been physician to the wife of François I, Queen Éléonore of Austria, and was in 1543 a surgeon practicing in Châtellerault. Jean Ferrand I was married to Louise Rasseteau, the daughter of Pierre Rasseteau, who was himself married to Prégente Brochard. Prégente Brochard's brother, Aymé Brochard, conservator of privileges at the University of Poitiers, was the grandfather of Jeanne Brochard, René Descartes's mother. Thus René Descartes's great-great grandmother Prégente Brochard up his paternal grandmother's line was the sister of his great-grandfather Aymé Brochard up his maternal grandmother's line. This is why René's father Joachim Descartes had to obtain special ecclesiastical dispensation to marry Jeanne Brochard, who was . . . his cousin.

On the line of René Descartes's paternal grandmother Claude Ferrand Descartes, her sister Martine Ferrand married Barthélemey de la Vau, who was mayor of Poitiers. Claude Ferrand Descartes's brother Antoine Ferrand I was lieutenant (a police post) of Châtelet in Paris as was his son Antoine Ferrand II after him. Her brother Louis Ferrand and her brothers-in-law René Rapin, Pierre Bruneau, and Antoine Desmons, were lawyers in the présidial (the civil and criminal courts) of Poitiers. Her brother Michel Ferrand I — who was one of René Descartes's two godfathers — was lieutenant general (judge) of Châtellerault from the 1580s until his death in 1606. Michel Ferrand I's son Michel Ferrand II was dean of the Parliament of Paris in 1646. Michel Ferrand II's son Pierre Ferrand was treasurer of war in Poitou.

On the line of René Descartes's mother Jeanne Brochard Descartes, her father (René Descartes's maternal grandfather) René Brochard I was lieutenant general of the présidial of Poitiers. Her father's sister, also named Jeanne Brochard, was married to Jean de Moulins, who was a counselor in the présidial of Poitiers. Jeanne Brochard de Moulins was René Descartes's godmother and she left property to the three surviving children of Joachim Descartes's first marriage: Jeanne, Pierre, and René. René Descartes's mother's brother Claude Brochard was a counselor in the présidial of Poitiers. Another of Descartes's mother's brothers, René Brochard (Descartes's godfather after whom he was named), was in Paris in 1614 as deputy of the États Généraux (meeting called by the king of the three estates — the nobility, the priesthood, and the bourgeoisie). This was the last États Généraux held in France until after the French Revolution in

1789. Thus there were strong republican interests on both sides of his mother's family — his uncle René Brochard II being a deputy in that famous last États Généraux in 1614 and his cousin Michel Ferrand II being dean of the Parliament in Paris in 1646.

René Descartes's maternal grandmother Jeanne Sain Brochard was the widow of René Brochard I. Her father Claude Sain was a merchant. His brother, Pierre Sain, was a tax controller in Châtellerault, as was Pierre Sain's son, Jean Sain, whose wife Jeanne Proust Sain was, as remarked, René Descartes's godmother. Her son René Sain was a financial officer in the French army in Italy, who died in Turin in 1623.

This brings the count to nineteen of René Descartes's (known) immediate relatives who were in government service as legal, police, or finance officers. Moreover, during his lifetime, his father, his brother Pierre and Pierre's son Joachim, his sister Jeanne's son François Rogier, and his half brother Joachim II were counselors in the Parliament of Brittany.

Now back to René Descartes's paternal grandmother, Claude Ferrand Descartes. Her paternal grandfather Jacques Ferrand was rector of the University of Poitiers in 1568. Her father (René Descartes's great-grandfather) Jean Ferrand I and her brother, Jean Ferrand II (René Descartes's great-uncle), were medical doctors. Prior to 1547, Jean Ferrand I was (as remarked above) the physician of Queen Éléonore, Francis I's second wife. Jean Ferrand I was a surgeon who specialized in the kidneys and the bladder, especially in lithotrity, the breaking up of gallstones inside the bladder into pieces capable of being voided, an extremely painful procedure. And dangerous. He also practiced lithotomy, the cutting into the bladder to remove gallstones. The anaesthetic was alcohol, taken internally. In 1570, Jean Ferrand I published *Of the Inflammation of the Kidney and Gall Stones* (in Latin) in Paris, a book consisting of descriptions of many dissections and autopsies he did on his deceased patients. In it he describes how in 1566 he dissected the body of his son-in-law Pierre Descartes (René Descartes's grandfather), who had died of large kidney stones. The Ferrand family reprinted this book in 1601 when René Descartes was five years old. Perhaps the boy even saw his grandfather Descartes's kidney stones in his great-grandfather Ferrand's collection. As a young man, he surely read his great-grandfather's book.

Jean Ferrand II was even more distinguished in medicine than his father, being named on 10 February 1563 as counselor and physician of the queen mother, Catherine de Médicis. Jean Ferrand II later became physician to Henri, duc de Montpensier of Châtellerault, to whom in 1601 his own book, *A Little Book on Fevers* (in Latin) was dedicated.

But enough, even though I have not even listed all of René Descartes's known uncles and aunts. Or his dozens of cousins. Baillet says that great men, like saints, owe nothing of their greatness to family origins, implying that this is true of René Descartes. Just the opposite is true. His family is shot through with thinkers, university officials, legal and medical men, physicians and surgeons, lawyers and judges. René Descartes learned argumentation, as it were, in the cradle. And his choice of medicine during the mature years of his life as the study most important to the benefit of humankind, even his lament that he never learned to cure a fever, comes from the family heart — or kidney, one might say. But the immediate point is that René Descartes came straight out of a powerful family tradition of law and medicine.

As for his grandfather Pierre Descartes, he was a doctor of medicine who must have been Jean Ferrand I's surgical assistant. He was well enough thought of by his employer or partner that the older man gave him his prepubescent daughter, Claude Ferrand, in marriage. As marriage settlement, Pierre Descartes promised his wife an income of thirty livres tournois a year. That is perhaps just large enough to live on, but certainly small enough to show that Pierre Descartes was not rich. In turn, her father settled on her a dowry of 600 livres tournois and a trousseau worth 100 livres tournois. In 1543, a village priest might get 100 livres tournois a year.

When the marriage took place is unknown, but the contract says it would be when Claude Ferrand reached the age of puberty, which in law was age twelve, which she reached a year or two after the contract was signed.

Marriage contract on 30 October 1542, their only known child Joachim born on 2 December 1563 in Châtellerault when Claude was thirty-two years old. Probably there were other children who did not survive. Pierre Descartes himself died in 1566, less than three years after the child Joachim was born. And Claude Ferrand Descartes's father Jean Ferrand I died in 1569 when Joachim was six years old.

I am looking for the reason why Joachim Descartes (René Descartes's father) took a law degree rather than a medical degree like his father and paternal grandfather. It would be because they were dead and his uncle Jean Ferrand II, a medical doctor, was in the service of the king of Poland and then of Catherine de Médicis, and was not there to encourage him to be a doctor. Only later, after Joachim was through with his schooling, was Jean Ferrand II physician to the duc de Châtellerault. So the child Joachim Descartes, fatherless at the age of three, grandfatherless at six, probably had his education directed by his maternal uncle Michel Ferrand I, lieutenant general of Châtellerault. Probably he was the one who sent Joachim to get his law degree at the University of Paris, where Joachim then registered as a lawyer in the Parliament. Michel Ferrand I would also have helped finance the later purchase of a counselorship in the Parliament of Brittany on 14 February 1586 for Joachim Descartes when he was twenty-two years old.

Joachim Descartes and Jeanne Brochard were married on 15 January 1589. Their first child Pierre was born on 19 October 1589 and soon died. Jeanne, who lived, was probably born in 1590. Their third child, also Pierre, was born on 19 October 1591 and survived. Then on 31 March 1596, René Descartes was born.

Descartes himself verified this date by protesting that he did not want it on his portrait drawn by Frans Schooten II in 1644 because he did not want people casting horoscopes on him.

René Descartes was born in the home of the widow Jeanne Sain Brochard, his maternal grandmother, in the small town of La Haye on the right bank of the wide Creuse River in Touraine. She had separated from her husband René Brochard I to move from Poitiers to La Haye by 1578. Descartes's father was thirty-two and his mother probably around thirty when he was born. He was baptized four days later in the Catholic Church of Saint-Georges in La Haye by a Curé Grison. The baptism is dated 3 April 1596 by inference from the dated entries that precede and follow it.

Saint-Georges was not in fact the parish Descartes's grandmother lived in. Her regular church, Notre Dame, had been turned over for use by Protestants in 1589, when La Haye and Châtellerault were declared free for Protestant worship. In the Church of Saint-Georges today, you can dip your fingers in the font at which Descartes was baptized. The Church of Notre Dame is falling into ruins. The baptismal registry page for René Descartes is under glass in the house where Descartes was born, now a museum.

On René Descartes's day of birth, his father was not in La Haye. He was serving his annual term of three months (February–March–April) in the Parliament of Brittany in Rennes. He was in Brittany also the following year when his wife died on 13 May 1597 after childbirth in La Haye.

René Descartes had two godfathers already remarked — one an uncle, his mother's brother René Brochard II, and the other a great-uncle, his paternal grandmother's brother Michel Ferrand I. He had one godmother, his aforementioned maternal grandmother Jeanne Sain Brochard's father Claude Sain's brother Pierre Sain's son Jean Sain's wife, Jean Proust Sain.

For the baptism, René Descartes's uncle René Brochard II would have to come from Poitiers sixty-two miles away and his great-uncle Michel Ferrand I and his godmother Jean Proust Sain from Châtellerault eighteen miles away. Time spent notifying them and waiting for them to arrive would explain why René Descartes was baptized four days after his birth.

There is another wonderful story to explain why René Descartes was baptized only on the fourth day after his birth. He was born in a ditch beside a field, Pré-Fallot, near the farm buildings of La Sybillière in Poitou halfway between Châtellerault and La Haye, while his mother was on her way to her mother's house in La Haye. After the delivery, René's mother was so weak that she had to rest a few days, and then they traveled on to La Haye where he was baptized.

The problem with this great story is that it is based totally on hearsay. In 1804 and 1807, the historian of Châtellerault, Abbé Lalanne, published accounts of René Descartes being born near Châtellerault but specified no exact place. Then in 1897, three hundred and one years after René's birth, during a dispute between advocates of his birth in Châtellerault in Poitou and advocates of his birth in La Haye in Touraine, Jules Duvau published the account of Jules de Milan d'Astis that Descartes was actually born in a ditch bordering Pré-Fallot. (Pré-Fallot means Torch Pasture or Lantern Meadow, a very evocative name for the future philosopher of light.) The story is supposed to have been passed down through the generations by members of a family that had owned La Sybillière since 1582. The owner in 1596 was Jacques Bonenfant I, whose son Jacques Bonenfant II was mayor of Châtellerault in 1596, and thus would have been a friend of the Descartes family and particularly of the newborn's great-uncle Michel Ferrand I.

What is more, the field Pré-Fallot is said to have been among the pieces of land belonging to Descartes's grandmother Brochard and her sister-in-law Jean Brochard de Moulins from whom René Descartes inherited Le Perron and from which he took the title sieur du Perron. As Jean-Henri Roy, the historian of the Descartes family in Châtellerault remarks, this is a very curious coincidence.

I have seen the ditch.

"This is the place," Monsieur Duhesme, the 1988 owner of the property, said.

"But you say this farm, La Sybillière, belonged to the Descartes family," I protested. "If Descartes was born here, surely they would have taken his mother to the house."

Monsieur Duhesme stubbornly kept his back to the house a hundred yards away. "That is most reasonable," he said. "But these things happen when they must."

We strolled back to the house.

"Of course they were trying to reach the house," Monsieur Duhesme relented while taking out his Descartes folder. He sighed and spread out his Xerox copies.

Pat and I had been hiking from one former Descartes property to the next — the Descartes family had owned at least fourteen farms around Châtellerault, and we were trying to get a feel for the ground. At each farm, the current owner knew the history of his farm and often had a Descartes folder.

"Perhaps they made it," Monsieur Duhesme finally said. "Perhaps Descartes was born right here, in this very kitchen." Monsieur Duhesme sat back and nodded at his wife, who was serving tea.

It is now a modern kitchen, recently remodeled, as were the rooms around the courtyard, a retreat for the families of Madame and Monsieur Duhesme and their two sons. But the stone walls and floors were the same. He sorted through the Xeroxed pages. Scholars had long noted that Descartes had taken the name du Perron, after another of the Descartes family's farms in Poitou. He was known to Isaac Beeckman in Breda in 1618 as a Poitevin, and he signed his name as a Poitevin at Leiden University in 1630.

All the Descartes farm properties were in Poitou. The town of La Haye is across the Creuse River in Touraine. So even though Descartes once spoke of being raised in the gardens of Touraine — which is true to the extent that his grandmother Brochard cared for him there in his infancy — he nevertheless is, Monsieur Duhesme concluded, a man of Poitou.

As Pat and I were leaving, Monsieur Duhesme made us promise to come to his celebration of the 400th anniversary of Descartes's birth, at La Sybillière, in 1996.

"It will be a rival celebration to the one in La Haye. Here we shall gather at the true birthplace of Descartes," he said, pointing his chin in the direction of the ditch. "Not in that museum at La Haye." He refused to call the town Descartes, to which name the city fathers had recently changed it.

We told Monsieur Duhesme that we would come to his celebration. Alas, ill health prevented him from organizing it. The celebration sponsored by the city fathers of La Haye prevailed.

In fact, none of the ancestors of the neighbors of La Sybillière passed on to their descendants any story of Descartes being born in a neighboring field. Furthermore, the grandfather and father of Jules de Milan d'Astris, who told the story in 1897, said nothing about it in 1802, 1849, and 1852, when officials in La Haye erected statues of Descartes to claim him as a native son. Fabulous as is the story of the great philosopher being born in a ditch, there is not a shred of evidence that he was (Barbier, 1898, 777-788).

Almost the first thing that happened to Descartes as soon as he was born is that he was swaddled in diapers and then in long bands of cloth to bind his arms straight down at his sides and keep his legs straight. It was thought that otherwise a child's limbs would grow crooked. Sometimes boards were added to keep the back straight, and iron hoops to hold the head, which was also wrapped, upright. Trussed up thus like cords of wood, babies were easy to handle and hang up on wall hooks.

In the seventeenth century, a baby's arms were released after one to four months, but the rest of the body was restrained for six to nine months. Babies are said to cry less and to sleep more when swaddled. But the rationale, besides the need to force their limbs to grow straight, is that otherwise they will flail about, tear off their own noses and ears, and dislocate their joints, so uncoordinated are they. For their own protection and development, then and not for the convenience of parents and nurses, babies were swaddled.

It is also possible that René Descartes had the connecting tissues under his tongue cut. A tongue attached underneath tightly and far along was thought to impede sucking. So the attachment was often snipped to loosen the tongue, with scissors, or the wet nurse might do it with her fingernails.

For Descartes certainly had a wet nurse. It was the almost universal custom among royalty, the bourgeoisie to which the Descartes family belonged, and even the relatively poor, to turn their babies over to wet nurses immediately after birth for as long as eighteen to

THE HOUSE IN CHÂTELLERAULT WHERE DESCARTES WAS
BROUGHT UP BY HIS GREAT-UNCLE, MICHEL FERRAND
Photograph by Jean-Henri Roy

twenty-four months or more until the child was weaned. A wet
nurse might become a member of the household in wealthier families, but most babies were sent to live with their wet nurses who
were very often poor, ill fed, and burdened with children of their
own — or maybe not with children of their own. The condition of
producing milk is, after all, brought on by the having of a baby,
which baby will be starved and neglected and will likely as not die if
its poorly fed mother hires out as a wet nurse. In the late sixteenth
century when René Descartes was born, infanticide was tacitly
accepted, even common. Infant mortality was anywhere from 25 to

50 percent depending on the prevalence of poverty, disease, crop failure, and other disasters. For every wet nurse, there was probably at least one dead child.

Often, the dead child was the client's, because wet nurses were certainly not always caring and dependable. If a family wanted to rid itself of an unwanted girl child — and statistics that show a large surplus of boys surviving over girls far exceeding the biological norm indicate female infanticide — the child could be sent to a wet nurse known for her inability to keep babies alive.

Even if mothers nursed their own children, but if they got pregnant again soon, a wet nurse was brought in. Descartes's mother was pregnant four months after his birth, and died thirteen months later. His survival in such a case makes it certain that he had a wet nurse. Then after two years or so he was weaned all at once. Mustard was smeared on the breasts to discourage sucking, but on the other hand, children that age were old enough to talk and to be reasoned with. Lloyd de Mause quotes from Héroard's diary about the childhood of Louis XIII that his younger sister Elisabeth was told by her nurse, "Madame, you will nurse no more. You must be weaned." To which Elisabeth replied, "Goodbye, dear breast, I shall no longer nurse."

Descartes said he was sickly. One source of evidence of how he would have been treated is in the daily journals concerning the childhood and youth of Louis XIII kept by his physician, Jean Héroard. The future king was born in 1601, so was five years younger than Descartes, virtually his contemporary. He, too, was sickly when young, and he was given purges, suppositories, and enemas almost every day of his childhood. Such methods of cleaning children out were common — it was thought that food putrefied in them — and René Descartes would have gotten his share.

Another popular theory was that childhood is a disease. Children are always ill because their humors are out of balance. According to Hippocrates and Galen, there are four humors or fluids in the body related to the four elements: atrabile-earth, blood-air, bile-fire, and phlegm-water. When these four fluids are in balance, one is healthy;

when not, not. Blood is hot and humid, whereas atrabile is cold and dry. So when a baby has a fever, it has too much blood, and should be bled. When it is choleric, it has too much atrabile, and should be warmed up and fed things that make it produce more blood. For a weak chest and a pale complexion, Descartes would have been given sweetened syrup of horehound, violet, and maidenhair. Milk was prescribed, the best being the milk of a woman, then of a donkey, third of a goat, and last of a cow.

It was thought good not to overfeed children, and healthful even to starve them a bit to toughen them up. Cold baths were also thought good for them. And children were beaten. The French were world champion spankers. Even the future king did not escape. Young Louis XIII is reported to have said on the day of his coronation when he was eight years old, "I would rather do without so much obeisance and honor if they wouldn't have me whipped."

Children were thought to be small animals, who certainly exhibited little control over their bodily functions and instinctual desires, always seeking instant satisfaction at the expense of everything else. They weren't really human until they reached the age of reason, which Pascal placed at twenty. Thus Descartes's disdain for whatever he learned in childhood fits the ideas of his time. For example, Cardinal Bérulle said that "the state of infancy is the most vile and most abject of any human state other than death." Saint François de Sales said that "during infancy we are like beasts deprived of reason, discourse, and judgment." La Bruyère said that children possess all the faults of an adult without any tempering by reason. Like beasts, they know only force. Bossuet said he would efface his childhood if he could.

The animal behavior that seemed to exercise people the most was how little children, if let loose, will crawl about on all fours like dogs and pigs. To forestall this, children were put into walking chairs well before they could stand up, thus to be held in an upright position with only two feet on the floor like human beings. Underfeeding and premature walking led to stunted growth and bowed legs.

Comenius finally said that children are innocent, although weak and susceptible to the world's bad influences. About the time of Descartes's childhood, this modern notion of children as innocent but in need of control and training began to overcome the notion that children are beasts. But note that the beast hypothesis fits better with the Christian doctrine of original sin than the notion that little children are innocent.

Potty chairs were not uncommon, but children were not particularly toilet trained until they were three or four years old. From unchanged diapers and swaddling they had perennial rashes that were treated with vinegar, wine, and rosewater. And like everyone, they had fleas and lice. But as for defecating and urinating after they were untied (literally, because once out of swaddling, leading strings were sewn to their clothes and attached to their nurses or mothers until they could get about on their own), they ran around in dresses and smocks without any bottoms. This solved the problem of wet and dirty diapers. In an era when courtiers relieved themselves in corners and on stairways of court and castle, and where farm animals had access to the lower floors of buildings where people lived, unhousebroken little children did not cause any great anxiety. Of course our hero René was not a peasant or a prince, but the future king wore no bottoms, and neither did René. If he was farmed out to a peasant nurse in the country, then he ran about with other toddlers as incontinent as chickens.

If Descartes's upbringing fit the norm, not only was he beaten fairly severely at least a few times when he was a child, his penis was admired and fondled by his mother and nurse, by older children and servants, and by his adult relatives. When Louis XIII was small he was continually complimented on the size of his penis, a circumstance that some historians speculate contributed to his apparent inability until very late to produce an heir.

It was not an age of prudery, and children often slept in the same beds in which their parents made more babies. Piles of children often slept in the same bed. Perhaps this was not the case in the Descartes household, but the children at least slept in the same bedroom with their parents. If Descartes did not have a good knowledge of sex by the time he left for school in La Flèche at the age of ten, he was sure to have been instructed by his classmates soon after he arrived. Students were separated not by age, but by level, so students of eight and eighteen could be side by side on the same bench, taking the same course of instruction. Again, in an era when boys were doing full-time men's work at ten or eleven, and girls got married at twelve or thirteen, adulthood for most people (if not for Pascal) came early.

The most we might make of what Descartes actually says concerning his childhood and his mother, and his lack of comment about his father, is that he may have thought of himself as deprived, and that after his infancy he was raised in a house in which books were common.

This raises the question of where René Descartes spent his childhood. Three years after his mother's death in 1597, his father married Anne Morin in Rennes. And by the way, add another member of the legal profession to the family. Anne Morin's father, Jean Morin, was first president of the Chambre des Comtes (the Exchequer) in Nantes. Joachim had married up a second time. Then beginning in 1601, Joachim Descartes's required time in the Parliament of Rennes doubled from three to six months a year. But he did not settle permanently in Rennes until 1610. So from the time René Descartes's mother died when he was thirteen months old until he was sent to the Royal College in La Flèche in 1606 when he was ten, he probably lived at least six months a year with one of his relatives.

Tradition has it that the three children, or at least Jeanne and René, were left in La Haye to be raised by their grandmother Brochard and a nurse. This is perhaps true for Jeanne who is recorded as a godmother in La Haye nine times between 26 December 1598 and 3 June 1609 in a range of dates that suggests that she lived there year around. Pierre is recorded as a godfather twice in La Haye — October 1598 and January 1599 — which suggests that he was not in La Haye after he was seven years old, but probably in Châtellerault being tutored under the supervision of his great-uncle

Michael Ferrand I. René Descartes is not registered in La Haye as a godfather, but in Châtellerault he is registered as a godfather in August 1599 (he was only three years old). His brother Pierre is registered in Châtellerault six times between 1600 and 1602. There is thus no documentary evidence that René was ever in La Haye except for his baptismal record.

When René's mother died in 1597, and his father began his move to Brittany, the closest, senior, local, male family head along the paternal line was his godfather Michel Ferrand I, the brother of the children's grandmother Descartes in Châtellerault. The logical choice of guardian for the two boys (never mind the girl) was obviously not their grandmother Brochard alone in La Haye, but their great-uncle Michel Ferrand I, living in their father's hometown, seconded by the boy's grandmother Descartes, both of whom probably lived in the Ferrand family home.

This reasoning pertains even more strongly to the first son, Pierre, than to the cadet (second son) René. Certainly Joachim Descartes paid more attention to his elder son and heir Pierre than he did to René.

The major argument that the boys were raised by their grandmother Brochard in La Haye is a letter from one of them to her from La Flèche with the salutation to "Dear mama." Some scholars say it is from René, but the signature is easily read as Pierre. The sender remarks that his brother's health is good.

Even if René Descartes was raised as an infant in La Haye, either at his grandmother Brochard's house or farmed out to a peasant nurse, by the time he was four or five he was probably living and being tutored in Châtellerault.

On the other hand, La Haye was not a mere backwater town. As Haya in Roman times it was on a major road. The navigable Creuse River shortly runs into the Vienne that flows into the Loire, a major thoroughfare. La Haye was the crossroads of a number of battles during the Wars of Religion although in the town itself Protestants and Catholics got along well. The Huguenot Protestants occupied both Châtellerault and La Haye in 1569. And in 1587, La Haye was overrun by the Protestant army of Henri de Navarre who converted to Catholicism and became Henri IV of France in 1589. Châtellerault and La Haye became free cities for the practice of the Protestant religion by Henri IV's ordinance of 23 March 1589, and as remarked above, the Church of Notre Dame in La Haye in the parish where Descartes was born was ceded for use by the Protestants.

I also remarked above that in 1641 in Holland when being hassled to convert to Protestantism by Jacob Revius, Descartes replied that he was of the religion of his king and his nurse. His king, the king of his youth, was Henri IV, formerly the Protestant king of Navarre, who contributed the property for the Royal College at La Flèche where Descartes went to school. Descartes saw the deposition of the actual heart of Henri IV in the chapel in La Flèche in 1610. When Henri de Navarre converted in 1595 to become Henri IV, the totally in-character story was spread that he quipped that Paris was worth a Mass. He was also the master politician who promised his people a chicken in every pot. So Descartes's king was an opportunistically converted Protestant. In 1610, Henri IV wore a green silk suit and was known as the Green Gallant. When Descartes left for Sweden in 1649, he wore a green silk suit in the highest fashion of Henri IV's days.

As for Descartes's nurse, in either La Haye or Châtellerault, it was perfectly possible in 1596 that she could have been a Protestant. Given that Descartes was born and spent his childhood in free Protestant towns and then spent the major part of his life in Protestant armies, Protestant lands, and Protestant courts, one has to consider the question of whether or not he was a Protestant, in sympathy if not in fact. It is a neat joke about his king and his nurse. I cannot imagine that Descartes was not aware of it.

Many of Descartes's best friends were Protestants, and he obviously had pronounced sympathies for Protestants. This attitude to Protestants certainly was not shared by his Catholic friends in France. But in his childhood Descartes evidently got the idea that Protestants are pretty much like anyone else. Perhaps the little cross-eyed girl was a Protestant. But the most likely possibility is

MICHEL FERRAND (1568-1610)
DESCARTES'S MATERNAL GREAT-UNCLE AND GODFATHER
Engraving photographed by Jean-Henri Roy

that Descartes learned tolerance for Protestants from his great-uncle Michel Ferrand I.

In 1597, hundreds of Protestants from all over France gathered in Châtellerault with the king's representatives to work out the provisions of what was ratified as the Edict of Nantes by Henri IV on 13 April 1589. This edict gave great freedoms and protection to the Protestants in France. Descartes's great-uncle Michel Ferrand I was counselor to the king and lieutenant general of Châtellerault in 1589 when Châtellerault and La Haye were made free cities in which Protestants could practice their religion. He held those offices during the negotiations in Châtellerault in 1589, as he did still when the Protestants from throughout France assembled there again in 1605 to protest their treatment by Catholics and to request more sureties.

The king's first minister Sully (a Protestant) presided over the Edict of Nantes proceedings, but as first officer in the king's courts in Châtellerault, Descartes's great-uncle must have played a role in all three negotiations.

Barbier, writing a local history of Poitou in 1897, makes the remark that Michel Ferrand I was a zealous Catholic who strongly opposed the Protestant cause in Châtellerault. Barbier does not say how he knows this. He may have been nervous because Michel Ferrand I was involved with the Protestants in 1589, 1597, and 1605 and it was René Descartes's great-uncle who surely raised him. Perhaps Barbier threw that comment in just to protect Descartes's reputation as a good Catholic, as does Baillet so often in his pious biography. It seems just as likely that as Lieutenant General of one of the major towns in a region where Protestants and Catholics had lived together peacefully since long before 1589, Descartes's great-uncle would have a certain tolerance for Protestants, if only as a matter of professional pragmatics. There were more Protestants in Poitou than in any other province — 900,000 by 1630.

In 1597, René Descartes was only a year old, but in 1605 he was nine, and if he was at the time living in the home of his paternal grandmother and his great-uncle in Châtellerault, he certainly would have known about and shared the excitement of so many Protestants meeting in Châtellerault. If René did not hear his great-uncle talking about matters, he would have heard gossip from his tutor, servants, cousins, and friends.

Descartes's grandmothers, uncles, and aunts owned houses in La Haye, Châtellerault, and Poitiers, fourteen farms, and other plots of ground around Châtellerault. The farms are on rolling hills spotted with forests of oak and pine, with rivers not far away. Pat and I hiked from Châtellerault to all of them along ancient roads and trails as Descartes might have done when he was young. The land is wide and fertile for wheat, and provides good grazing for sheep and cattle. When following Descartes around to the eighteen places where he lived in the Netherlands, Pat and I were struck simultaneously by the realization that Descartes almost always lived in the sand-dunes or on low rolling hills reminiscent in small of the landscape of his youth.

So suppose Descartes was raised in rural La Haye until he was sent to school. Here is what small boys did for excitement in that small town. They swam and fished in the river and they fooled around with anybody's boats who would let them. They hunted hares with sticks and the village dogs, and they moved hay and poked under granaries to flush out mice and rats for cats to catch. They killed small birds with slings and stones. In the spring they looked for birds' nests, and they ran in the fields at harvest and when hay was made. They found an old broken-down horse they could catch and ride three at a time. They watched after cows and teased milk-maids, and they scratched the family pig behind the ears while it grunted contentedly. Later they held up pans to catch the blood when that pig was strung up and its throat cut for butchering.

Most wondrous of all, in La Haye they explored the subterranean passages extending under a large portion of the town from the ruins of the old château at the river's edge. This network consisted of half a mile of passages nine feet high, with gently sloping entrances wide enough for a team of horses pulling a carriage. The excavated rock was used to construct fortifications, and the system was designed both for storage of munitions and supplies and for protection and escape routes during siege. Many of the older houses of La Haye were connected to the network; some of those passages are still accessible. One passage runs under the street right in front of the house in which Descartes was born. It is a most remarkable set of tunnels, calculated to generate excitement in all small boys and this old cave explorer.

Later, Descartes's good friend Villebressieu invented hand-clamps for climbing a rope, and a double spiral device for descending a rope on rappel, that (modified and improved) are indispensable for modern cave explorers today.

"I esteemed eloquence highly, and loved poetry," Descartes remarks in the *Discourse*. These would seem to be the words and sentiments of someone who learned to read early and got lost in the world of books. Descartes's later scorn for history and his insistence that he did not read books (which was an outright lie) was due to his expressed need to put aside all his earlier learning to make his own way in the world of ideas. But a small, pale, thin, sickly child reading books in his great-uncle's library? It rings true.

He was hidden with a book beneath the library table to escape his older brother Pierre, who hassled him. All eldest sons made life miserable for their cadet or younger brothers, who were supposed to be their servants. In later life, Descartes never betrayed the slightest affection for his older brother. Truth to tell, he hated and mistrusted him, and not without good reason. On the other hand, Pierre had most excellent reasons for disliking, neglecting, and scorning his shiftless younger brother René, who was wasting his inheritance by pretending to be a philosopher instead of increasing the family fortune.

In 1600, Joachim Descartes married Anne Morin, whose father was first president of the Exchequer in Nantes. Their son, Joachim II, was born in 1601. Note that in terms of inheritance, René, the second son of the first marriage, was shifted into third place by the birth of Joachim II, the first son of the second marriage. (His brother Pierre's first son was also named Joachim. Unmarried Descartes was out of the running in those sweepstakes.) Then René's half brother Claude was baptized in 1604 in the village of Oyré where Joachim had family property near Châtellerault. That child died, as did another, François, baptized in Chavagne near Nantes in 1609. Then in 1610, Joachim Descartes moved to the townhouse in Rennes, and a daughter Anne, who survived, was baptized there in 1611.

And now the stage is set. René Descartes was born in 1596.

In 1597, James I of England published his *Demonology*, in which he advocates burning at the stake for all witches, and he thought there were a lot of them.

In 1598, the Edict of Nantes — negotiated in Châtellerault, the Descartes family seat — was signed providing freedom and protection for Protestants in France. But even more auspicious for Descartes was the reform in mathematics that same year in which Arabic numerals in decimal display were introduced to replace the impossibly cumbersome system of Roman numerals. In historical retrospect, that simple change in notation made an explosion in mathematical innovation inevitable. It lit Descartes's fire.

In 1599, Feuillant published his summation of Scholastic philosophy that Descartes later studied.

In 1600: Giordano Bruno was burned at the stake in Rome for professing a naturalistic pantheism and for supporting the heretical Copernican thesis that the earth revolves around the sun. And Henri IV married Marie de Médicis.

In 1601: The great astronomical observer Tycho Brahe died. Hector-Pierre Chanut, the future French ambassador to Sweden who lured Descartes there in 1649, was born. And so was Louis XIII.

In 1602: The Dutch East Indies Trading Company, in which Descartes or his bankers probably invested, was incorporated.

In 1603: Henri IV recalled the Jesuits, whom he had banned in 1594 after one of their students had tried to assassinate him, and he gave them the château in La Flèche in which he was conceived.

In 1604: The Jesuits founded in La Flèche the Collège Royal that René Descartes attended. Also in 1604, Père Louis Richeome published that all-time best-seller, *The Pilgrim of Loreto*, which later may have given Descartes the idea of making the pilgrimage himself.

In 1605: The Protestants assembled in Châtellerault again to state grievances. Francis Bacon published *Advancement of Learning* and Cervantes *Don Quixote* in which he makes fun of Descartes's favorite romance, *Amadis de Gaul*.

In 1606: René Descartes was ten years old. Just after Easter, he was sent to begin his schooling at the Royal College in La Flèche. It was, for him, the year of childhood's end.

II ⚄ SCHOOLING

It is the best school in France.

IN 1606: RENÉ DESCARTES was ten years old. His older brother Pierre, who was fifteen, has been at the Royal College in La Flèche since it opened in 1604. His father, stepmother, and four-year-old half brother Joachim II come and go, six months in Rennes, six in Châtellerault. The rhythm has been set for as long as the boy can remember. But this is the year of death and change. First, his great-uncle Michel Ferrand I died. Then his grandmother Brochard died. Probably they were ill awhile before, and he had seen them sick in bed, propped up on a bolster, white caps on their heads. Wherever Descartes was living then, in Châtellerault with his great-uncle or in his grandmother's home in La Haye, the household was closing down. Just as well. It was high time for the second son of a parliamentarian to leave home for school. Tradition has it that because of his weak health, he was not put in school to suffer the hard winter. Only after Easter was René sent to La Flèche, a hundred miles from home. Henri IV gave the château in which he had been conceived to the Jesuits for a college. He also provided for teachers above and beyond the Jesuits: four professors of jurisprudence, four of engineering, and two of anatomy and medicine. It was to be the best school in the realm. A year after its opening, the school had 1,200 students.

The students had only one week of vacation a year, but more than fifty religious holidays. Pierre Descartes went home for Easter in 1606, and René went back to school with him. Also in that year, their distant relative, Père Charlet, took a post at La Flèche, and in 1607 he became rector. In a letter of 9 February 1645, Descartes addressed Père Charlet as "You who took the place of my father during all the time of my youth," and again, "you who I considered as my father." Considering Descartes's relations with his own father, this may not be saying much.

There was a standard way of sending a son off to school. His father put him in the charge of a friend who was going in that direction. At a parting of the ways, his guardian would pass him on to someone he knew who was going the right direction and so on until the young man reached his destination. It was at least as safe and sure as sending a child alone on an airplane today. There were coaches, but La Flèche was across the grain of the main post road from Châtellerault (it went to Paris).

On the other hand, the brothers could have ridden a horse from Châtellerault to La Flèche. The same horse. With arguments. Pierre always rode in front, with René holding on behind, because the cadet always followed. The cadet seconded and served the firstborn. René and Pierre never got along, perhaps because René did not take easily to kowtowing to his brother.

Or maybe the boys took a boat down the Vienne to the Creuse to the Loire down to Angers and up the Loir (a tributary of the Loire) to La Flèche. But most likely they walked in a group of students going to La Flèche. It would have been a grand adventure — whatever way they went — one hundred miles from home.

In 1606, René and Pierre stayed in someone's house in La Flèche, for the dormitories were not completed until 1609, and the few students who got to stay in the château were from families of much higher rank than that of the Descartes brothers. The college took over whole houses, the boys were gathered into groups, and young priests lived with them to keep order.

They came from all over the realm. By the end of 1604, there were five hundred sons of barons, counts, marquis, dukes, lords, and knights, and 11,500 more students of humble squires such as Joachim Descartes, and even of peasants, for tuition was free and anyone who could pass the exams was admitted. The Jesuits gave destitute students jobs in the kitchen, gave them food and even money. Jean Tarin, who arrived barefoot with only the shirt on his

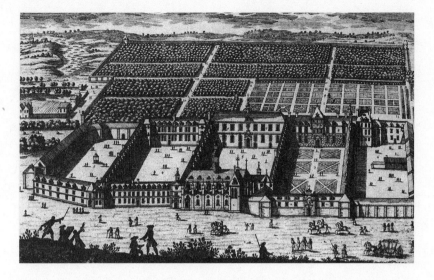

THE ROYAL COLLEGE OF LA FLÈCHE AROUND 1610
Bibliothèque Nationale de France

back and a sack of nuts and pieces of bread, went on to become rector at the University of Paris.

Jesuit educational policy was to treat all students the same, whatever their family background. In a letter of 12 September 1638 to an unknown correspondent, Descartes says they were treated "nearly" equally, and this cosmopolitan egalitarianism is one advantage he offered in recommending La Flèche as the best school to which to send the man's son.

Baillet and others have perpetrated several myths about Descartes's years at La Flèche, one being that his distant relative Père Étienne Charlet, who was rector at La Flèche from 1607 to 1615, allowed the delicate and precocious René to lie abed until eleven every morning in his own private room and to attend classes as he pleased. This is so alien to the severe Jesuit educational principles — up at five, fifteen minutes to wash and go to the toilet, etc. — as to be totally unbelievable. If anything, Père Charlet would have made sure that René was treated like the others to make a man of him. But beyond that, there were only twenty-four private rooms at

La Flèche with a base yearly cost of 240 livres, plus the costs of valets and tutors that went with them, bringing the minimum cost of a private room for one year to at least 480 livres, and this at a time when 300 livres was thought to be a decent yearly stipend for a village priest. The total cost of semiprivate rooms containing four (or more) students was at a minimum 240 livres a year. And this does not include costs of firewood, laundry, and candles. Furthermore, books and lessons in dance, music, writing, drawing, and fencing were all extra. If Joachim Descartes had been capable of and inclined to pay this kind of money for the lodging of either of his sons, it would not have been the cadet René. Most likely both Pierre and René lived in the general open dormitory, or even cheaper, in one of the rooming houses in town. Those twenty-four single rooms, and also the semiprivate rooms, were certainly occupied by the sons of higher nobility to whose fathers expense was immaterial. René Descartes may have lain abed of the mornings in later life, but he did not do so at La Flèche.

Outside school, the students played trictrac, checkers, chess, quilles, lawn bowling, barres, and tennis. They fenced and rode horseback and took excursions of up to four hours in the local countryside. By law, however, no prostitutes were allowed within eight miles of La Flèche.

The great event during the Descartes brothers' years at La Flèche was the interment of Henri IV's heart in the school chapel in 1610. Henri IV had been assassinated by a Catholic religious fanatic named Ravillac, who was incensed at Henri IV's plan to invade Germany to help Protestants against the Catholics of the Holy Roman Empire. Ravillac leaped into the king's carriage and stuck a knife into the very heart that was now being ceremoniously delivered to the college church.

So the Jesuits and the Catholic League (who never forgot that Henri IV was formerly the Protestant king of Navarre) finally got Henri IV, who wanted to go to war with holy Spain. The view that the Jesuits and the Catholic League instigated the assassination, however, is not a very popular way of stating the matter among Catholic historians. What happened is that a student from the Jesuit college at Clermont in Paris had tried to assassinate Henri IV in 1596 and failed. Then Ravillac, another Catholic student, got him.

It is classic. The Jesuits had been teaching the perfidy of Henri IV for years. This or that priest had told his students that France would be better off if Henri IV was dead: Will no one rid us of this man? As has happened more than once in such circumstances, some dedicated young man decided to do the deed in the name of God. He acted alone. The Jesuits were not to blame.

Nevertheless, in Cartesian mechanistic terms, the arm that drove the knife into Henri IV's heart was a piston connected directly to that powerful machine, the Jesuit Order. Henri IV's assassination was the result of workings of which individual men were mere parts, matter in motion. It does not matter that there was no spoken conspiracy, no commands, no commission. Mechanically, the connection is simple and direct. The Jesuits in 1597 and the Catholic League in 1610 were in heavy opposition to Henri IV. It is not at all surprising that one of their members or followers should wield a knife. It happens all the time.

Here is (abbreviated) the awesome funeral scene as described by Baillet. The town, the college, and the churches were decorated in black mourning emblazoned with Henri IV's initials, his coat of arms, skulls, tears, silver lilies, emblems, designs, and epigrams. At the head of the parade was Henri IV's heart in a carriage all its own, then on foot the king's magistrate and a squad of archers from Paris. Then 1,200 students of the college, the Recollect priests, nineteen priests from outside parishes, then those of the town of La Flèche, the Jesuits of the college, then sieur de la Varenne with his son Baron de Sainte Susanne, then the twenty-four gentlemen students boarding at the college, followed by the officers of justice and citizens carrying lighted torches. They marched around the town and then twenty Jesuits from the court in Paris, plus those from La Flèche, stood behind Père Armand, provincial from Paris, who took up the heart of Henri IV.

Preceded by a herald and two exempts and escorted by twelve

officers of the police holding pistols in their hands, plus two men supporting Père Armand's arms that were holding Henri IV's heart aloft, followed by all the laymen, they went to the Church of Saint Thomas where Père Coton pronounced the funeral oration. Then Père Armand presented the heart to the duc de Montbazon who took it to the college court where they passed through an arch twenty-seven feet high and twenty-six wide. The duc de Montbazon presented the heart to the herald on a scaffold, who held it up for everyone to see. He cried out three times, then put Henri IV's heart into an urn, which was then placed in front of the altar of the college chapel.

In the course of this description, Baillet remarks in passing that René Descartes was one of the specially chosen twenty-four gentlemen students marching in ceremonial procession behind Henri IV's heart. But out of all those sons of barons, counts, marquis, dukes, and knights, if in the name of egalitarianism they had chosen just one son of a low-ranking squire and had that lad been fortuitously a Descartes, it would have been the eldest son, Pierre, not the younger son, René. But even that is quite unbelievable. The Descartes story is not, after all, a fairy tale.

When Pat and I visited La Flèche in 1987, we were disappointed with this town. Through it now runs a major highway connecting the port of Nantes with Paris, and the noise of huge trucks is deafening day and night. The Loir River, which was navigable in Descartes's time, has been lowered by dams and diversions for irrigation. La Flèche is a very small town, surrounded by fields of corn (maize) which certainly was not the case in 1610. The school of La Flèche is concealed behind a long high wall. Today it is France's number two military school, the Prytanée Militaire.

We found an unlocked door in the wall and stepped into a graveled courtyard. No one was about, so we walked through an opening into another court to confront a man in a civilian suit who took evasive action like any harassed professor who wanted to avoid parents. We corralled him. Could we possibly, I asked him, go look inside the chapel, and at the old books I knew were on display somewhere in the school? "You'll have to ask the director," he said, "who is coming there," and he rushed off.

The director was a small, compact man, somewhat less than medium height — as Baillet said about the adult Descartes. He was in a sweat suit and had obviously just come in from a run. I asked him my questions. Standing there with his hands on his hips, breathing heavily, he brushed aside my French and answered in impeccable Oxford English, or perhaps it was Sandhurst. "To be sure," he said. "But of course you know that except for the chapel, nothing inside the buildings is like it was when Descartes was here. Everything has been gutted and rebuilt inside. We don't even know what wing he might have been in. That room they called the Observatory of Descartes and showed for so long as his private room was a complete fraud." The director gave us directions, nodded a pleasant adieu, and as he went off said, "Be sure to see the gardens. The layout has never been changed and it is a place where Descartes and his professors would have walked."

We went into the chapel, which was dirty and dusty and unused. There were urns high on the wall on either side of the altar. The one on the left was for Henri IV's heart and the one on the right for the heart of his second wife, Anne of Austria, queen mother of Louis XIII. But none of the dust in those urns was from those hearts, for during the uprisings preceding the revolution of 1789, their contents were burned and scattered to the winds.

The book display was very modest. There were none of the esoteric books Descartes said in his autobiographical sketch in the *Discourse on Method* he had been allowed to read, but there was a copy of the book of poetry — *Tears from La Flèche* — written mostly in Latin in 1611 by students in honor of the first anniversary of Henri IV's death. It was open to the poem celebrating Galileo's discovery of the moons circling Jupiter.

Finally, Pat and I went into the garden — dry, old, neglected, as these places often are in France, laid out in formal squares and rectangles. Constricting, as though people and things were smaller then than people and things are now (actually, they were much smaller). In her 1910 biography of Descartes, Elizabeth S. Haldane, whose English translation with David Ross of Descartes's works was the standard for nearly a hundred years, said this of the main building of the school: "The Château Neuf was situated on the Loire [*sic.*] 'queen of the gracious valley,' and round it was a park planted with great trees forming shady alleys through which we can imagine the meditative boy wandering alone" (p. 13).

Pat and I sat on a bench. Behind the walls the noise of the traffic was dimmed. Yes, of course Descartes once walked these lanes. But it was a long time ago. The wraith of "the meditative boy" was not evident. Even ghosts have left places like this behind.

Descartes took the standard eight-year course of study at La Flèche. During the first three years, he studied grammar and humanities, then the next two, rhetoric. All the courses were taught in Latin, and student work, oral and written, was in Latin. But Greek and French were also taught. He read the Greek poets such as Ovid and Seneca the Tragic, whom he later quotes, and he knew the *Compendium of Latin Poetry* edited by Pierre Des Brosses and published in two editions in 1603 and 1611. He read Virgil, Horace, Cicero, and Ausonius.

But the Jesuits taught far more than book learning. Young René would have had training in diction, theater, music, dance, fencing, and equitation. He could have learned mechanics, surveying, watchmaking, and optics. There was training in meteorology, hydrography, and geography. Many of these students were destined to be military engineers, so they learned military architecture and the placement of fortifications. The students were taught good manners, savoir faire, how to greet, to stand, to talk, to cast one's eyes, to take leave, how to make speeches to win friends and influence people or to insult them in a gentlemanly way. How to defer to betters while maintaining one's own dignity and how to treat inferiors without patronizing them. In short, how to be gentlemen. And in particular, how to carry on disputations, which was the main way they were tested in their courses. Everything was reduced to rules, to practice, to memory and repetition.

The goal of Jesuit pedagogy was the formation of the will. In his *Passions of the Soul* of 1649, Descartes describes the characteristics of a gentleman. It is not surprising to find him stressing justice, uprightness, goodwill to equals and subordinates, reserve with superiors, dignity, sobriety, regularity of morals, courage, and resolution. The Jesuits had a method and they trained their man.

The boys' father would have paid the extra fees for training in these essential skills for future parliamentarians. Descartes even wrote a short treatise on fencing, perhaps in 1615 when he was studying for his law exams. At least in a letter of 4 November 1630, he asks Mersenne to tell Guillaume Gibieuf and his other friends in the order of the Oratory that he was "studying something other than fencing."

And he was a believing Catholic. The Jesuits say: "Give us a boy in his formative years..."

Descartes also read Montaigne's *Essays* first published in 1580, Pierre Charron's Christianization of Montaigne's skepticism, *On Wisdom* of 1601, and *Amadis de Gaul*, a sixteenth-century romance of chivalry available in many editions. Descartes apparently dipped into *Amadis* all his life — it was continued in umpteen volumes by a sequence of authors. So in trying to follow Descartes's life, I have tried to read *Amadis de Gaul*. I cannot. It is so unbelievably bad that you can only be grateful that it inspired Cervantes to write *Don Quixote*, a wonderfully readable satire of the light reading that charmed, entertained, and perhaps even inspired Descartes.

These books would not have been part of coursework, to be sure, and they were not those most curious and rare books Descartes says he was allowed to read at La Flèche. They are supposed to have been in astrology, alchemy, and magic, although this breach of rules seems most unlikely and out of order. When Descartes later cites or remarks on Raymond Lulle (memory tricks), Agrippa (skepticism), and Giambattista della Porta (optical illusions), he does not exhibit longtime familiarity with their works. We don't know what rare and curious books he read at La Flèche.

If he did not read Galileo in school, at least he heard about him, for he must have known the poem that is on display in La Flèche today. It is one of only three poems in French in that book full of Latin verses published in 1611, all anonymously. Its title is "Sonnet on the Death of King Henry the Great, and on the Discovery of Some New Planets or Stars Circling Around Jupiter, Made Last Year by Galilei Galileo, Celebrated Mathematician of the Great Duke of Florence." Some scholars have said that because René Descartes was later interested in Galileo, he wrote this poem and it is his first published work, at the age of fifteen. This reasoning is, to say the least, very thin. One of the poems in *Tears from La Flèche* may in fact be by Descartes, but if so, it is much more likely to be one of the hundreds of good students' compositions in Latin, and not one of the three odd ones in French.

The last three years at La Flèche were devoted to logic and morals, physics and mathematics, and, in the final year, metaphysics. Logic was taught by François Fournet, with texts by Francisco Toletus and Petrus Fonseca. This is Aristotelian syllogistic logic in which you learn such things as that all men are mortal, Socrates is a man, therefore Socrates is mortal. Descartes later remarked that this method of deriving conclusions that are already apparent in the premises is useless for the advance of scientific knowledge, which should be aimed at finding out what we don't know, not at deriving truisms from what we know already.

Morals were theological, with stress on faith and service to God. But the pragmatic Stoic morality that Descartes later presented in his *Discourse on Method* was derived from his Jesuit training in the classics and their stress on willpower directed toward effective practical action. The Jesuits did not stress theology. They preached uncomplicated faith and strict obedience, like the army they were.

What really impressed young René, he said later, was mathematics, because of its certainty, which no other subject provided. His mathematics teacher was Jean François from 1612 to 1614. The algebra text was probably Clavius, published in 1609. The method of mathematical analysis Descartes later presented consists of reduction of problems to proportions. In 1655, François summed up some of his teaching in his *Treatise on Quantity*, in which he talks of proportions. It is a very general characterization not original to François, although Descartes was probably introduced to proportions by him.

Descartes's method of mathematical analysis is a way of reducing quantities and proportions to lines and curves and of solving geometric problems algebraically and algebra problems geometrically. For this, he devised what we all learned about in freshman geometry, the Cartesian coordinates (Des Cartes, the four quarters, the four quadrants).

Descartes did not invent analytic geometry as a schoolboy, and he did not embarrass his professors at La Flèche by setting them problems that they could not solve. This is another story made up in retrospect. I infer this from the fact that later in life, Descartes was suspicious of youthful prodigies in mathematics. For example, in 1639 at the age of sixteen, Blaise Pascal published a brilliant little book on conic sections. He was the darling of the Parisian mathematical world. But Descartes was a sourpuss about it. He said it was impossible for a mere schoolboy to do that work, and he pointed to the work by Gérard Desargues from which he figured Pascal had cribbed. That was before he had finished reading Pascal's book. After he read it and saw that Pascal had gone beyond Desargues, he suggested that Pascal's father Étienne, a well-known mathematician, had done the work. Conclusion: Descartes himself was not a schoolboy genius in mathematics. Blaise Pascal, in fact, was.

The crown of the Jesuit pedagogical system was the disputation. One student would defend a proposition, another would attack it, and then there would be a general discussion that included the professors. Sometimes it became a free-for-all.

We have Descartes's own testimony that he was judged in school to be as good as those who were getting their doctorates and were destined to be teachers, but he himself was never a professor. He did, however, teach mathematics to three of his valets. Gérard Gutschovven went on to occupy the chair of professor of mathematics at the University of Louvain. Another, Jean Gillot, went on in

1638 to teach fortifications, navigation, and mechanics at the School of Engineers in Leiden. Later, Gillot taught mathematics in Paris. Gillot was succeeded by a man called Limousin, to whom Descartes also taught mathematics. Limousin went on himself to teach mathematics.

In 1647, Dirck Rembrantsz, a shoemaker who lived in Nierop, brought some of his mathematical work to Descartes. He was turned away twice by Descartes's valet, but after he refused money the second time, Descartes took notice. He taught his method of mathematical analysis to Rembrantsz, who then went on to become a prominent Dutch astronomer, and published books on astronomy, logarithms, arithmetic, and geometry. Descartes also had as a student, Princess Elisabeth, who merits a chapter of her own.

Descartes's greatest contribution as a teacher are his rules and method, treated later. But a summary statement of his pedagogy would make him sound like John Dewey. When Descartes was asked to see his library in 1645, he showed the inquirer a calf he was dissecting. He said you cannot learn anatomy without doing it yourself. And given that you can think up lots of possible causes of the way things work, you have to experiment to see which theory is right. He said he could have been an artisan, a technician, and would have lived a happy life. This is sheer romanticizing on his part. He instructed Jean Ferrier on how to build a lens-grinding machine, but never built one or even ground lenses himself.

René started school in April 1606 at age ten and stayed at La Flèche at least until April 1614, when he finished the eight-year course. He later said he spent eight or nine years at La Flèche, so let's give him 1615 there, and then 1616 to study law in Poitiers, where he passed his exams and received his baccalaureate (with distinction) in canon and civil law on 9 and 10 November 1616.

On 21 May 1616, René Descartes was the godfather in Poitiers of René Chenault, the son of a tailor, with whom Baillet presumes Descartes was staying. It would be a nice touch, but the family did not name the child after their roomer. The baby's father was named René, too. It is not, however, necessarily the case — or even likely —

that Descartes was renting a room from a tailor. His uncle René Brochard II, who was his godfather and his mother's brother, and who later named René Descartes as his heir (although René received no money from it), lived in Poitiers. He had been dean of the présidial, dean of aldermen and sheriffs, and mayor of Poitiers, so probably he had a house large enough to provide a room for his godson nephew.

It was an exciting time to be in Poitiers. The Protestants were in virtual revolt, taking over the town on occasion. There is not a word in any of Descartes's writings about these matters.

But enough about school and schooling! It is time for our hero to enter life.

III ⚜ ISAAC BEECKMAN

You have awakened me.

AFTER DESCARTES RECEIVED his law degrees in November 1616, he went to Rennes to discuss with his father what he was going to do with his life. His law degrees were a step, as he himself later remarked, on the road to wealth, distinction, and power. The lowest age for entering Parliament, however, was twenty-seven, so if Descartes had ambitions along that line, he would have to wait seven years. He could, however, have gone to court as a lawyer, as had his brother Pierre before he was of age, and as did so many of his uncles and cousins. He chose not to. He stayed at home awhile. He signed as godfather in October and December of 1617 in Sucé near his father's country estate. The estate included the large and imposing château of Chavagne-en-Sucé, composed of two straight-walled wings at right angles to one another, with two dozen rooms, substantial outbuildings, and a large pond. Today the château is divided into several apartments but is still very handsome. The estate itself is composed of woods and rich, rolling farmland. Probably Descartes lounged and read novels of chivalry such as his favorite *Amadis de Gaul.* But his father certainly expected him to do something soon toward making his way in life.

The first son inherits his father's title and his position if it is hereditary or if the family owns it, as Joachim Descartes did own his counselorship in the Parliament of Brittany, and the title he married into, sieur de Chavagne. His eldest son Pierre did, then, in 1618 at the age of twenty-seven, take over his father's counselorship. Legally, two brothers could not be in the same Parliament, although this could be negotiated. And in fact, after giving his place to Pierre, Joachim Descartes promptly bought another counselorship in his own name, destined not for René, but for his son Joachim II, first son of his second marriage. A second first son! This made René Descartes a second son twice over.

Second sons traditionally were destined either for the church or for the army. René decided for the army. And a romantic army it was, one of the fabled French regiments in the service of the prince of Orange, Maurice of Nassau, commander in chief of that tiny Protestant republic, the United Provinces, that had won its freedom by fighting the Catholic Empire's Spaniards to a standstill. Mighty Maurice, who once when asked who was the world's best general, replied magnanimously that Spinola of Spain was number two. Descartes wore a dashing flagrantly bright orange scarf, like all the rest of Maurice's troops.

Descartes signed up with either the solid Saint-Simon, Baron de Courtmour, or the dashing Gaspard de Chastillon, the leaders of the two French regiments. The regiment lists for that period are lost, so we don't know which. We do know, however, that each of these regiments had a Protestant minister. One of them, Jean de Nérée, translated for the troops the Acts of the Synod of Dordrecht. This was called to resolve the conflict between very orthodox Calvinists who wanted a theocratic state and liberal Calvinists who thought that church affairs should be kept relatively separate from state, and particularly from business, affairs. The business capital of the United Provinces was Amsterdam, where the "father of the country" Oldenbarnevelt was in power. Prince Maurice, who was not religious, thought the orthodox Calvinists might make him king, so he cynically gave the order to execute Oldenbarnevelt, who was beheaded on 13 May 1619. Prince Maurice was not subsequently made king.

Two weeks after the execution, Descartes left Holland. There is no evidence that Prince Maurice's attempt to subvert the republic influenced Descartes's decision to depart. Descartes never said a word about it. In any event, Descartes did not return to the United Provinces permanently for ten years, after Prince Maurice was dead and his liberal half brother, Prince Frederick-Henry, had allowed the liberal Calvinists to hold their views openly once again.

Descartes was, at twenty-two, still thinking something like a schoolboy, for Maurice's camp at Breda was known as a training ground where mathematicians and engineers taught the fundamentals of military architecture, fortifications, and engineering. Besides these subjects, Descartes remarked that he was also studying painting and Dutch. In later years, although he apologized for his Dutch, he spoke and wrote it readily enough.

It is not as though there was no military business at home for young Frenchmen. He could have gone to war in France. On 25 November 1616, a fellow Poitevin, Cardinal Armand-Jean du Plessis de Richelieu, took over as secretary of state for war and foreign affairs for the regent, Queen Mother Marie de Médicis. Then on 25 June 1617, her son, the sixteen-year-old Louis XIII, pulled off a coup d'état with the help of his advisor the duc de Luynes. The Protestant dukes Henri de Rohan and de Bouillon were in revolt, and Louis XIII promised to reestablish Catholicism in Béarn and Navarre (where his own father Henri IV had been born and raised a Protestant). Poitiers, where Descartes took his law degrees, was in the midst of the Protestant uprisings. But rather than getting involved in the religious wars internal to France, Descartes went to the United Provinces in February 1618.

The United Provinces was a Protestant republic, but it was also Catholic France's ally against Catholic Spain and the Holy Roman Empire. Cardinal Richelieu was guiding France toward the separation of church (at least the imperial Roman church) and state, to forge an independent nation. So to fight for the United Provinces was to fight for France. But more than that, during the first half of the seventeenth century, the United Provinces was where it was at for footloose and fancy-free young Frenchmen. Not only was it the most liberal state in Europe (where a young man could escape the strictures of church and family), it was also commercially the most successful and was fast surpassing Spain in wealth (some of which came from booty as Dutch gunboats captured ships from the Spanish merchant fleet). There were then (as now) plump and blonde, cheerful and friendly, rosy-cheeked Dutch girls. There was horseplay and gambling, whoring and drinking, riding to the hounds after hares. And because a twelve-year truce had been signed with Spain in 1609, there was no danger of going into battle and getting killed.

Descartes must have had an allowance from his father. Only later did he sell the property he, his brother Pierre, and his sister Jeanne inherited from their mother, their maternal grandmother, and a maternal aunt. One of the properties was a small farm called Le Perron that Descartes sold for only 2,500 livres. It had a rather charming house that is still occupied today. Leading up to a second story porch over the main entrance is a very attractive and prominent outdoor stairway — known as a perron in French. When Pat and I were snooping around what appeared to be a place with nobody at home, I was startled on peering through a glass door by a deep-voiced "Vous! Entrez!" coming from inside. I opened the door and went into a bedroom where an enormous old woman lay in bed. She was clutching a heavy cane in one hand. I explained why we were there, and she nodded knowingly, saying, "sieur du Perron," which was what Descartes called himself in Prince Maurice's camp in Breda, and now and then for the rest of his life. The old woman said that if we would wait, her son would return and give us something to drink. We said no, we had hiked on foot out from Châtellerault and had to be moving along. Only later did it occur to us that had we offered to get the bottle, she might have been willing to have a nip herself.

This title sieur du Perron is puzzling when one sees how small the farm is. Baillet says it was one of the largest estates thereabouts with a noble heritage, but he made this up. It is hard to escape the probability, then, that Descartes was trading on the title of Cardinal Jacques Davy du Perron, who died in Paris that year, 1618. He had been born a Protestant, but when he was twenty he converted to Catholicism in the court of Henri III. It is said that he was not very sincere in his religious beliefs. And the following story is told. One day in front of the king he presented a devastating attack against atheism and gave several proofs for the existence of God. Henri III thought this performance magnificent and said so. Du Perron modestly said that was nothing and offered to return the next day and use exactly the same evidence to argue for atheism and to prove that God does not exist. Henri III was outraged and banished du Perron from the court, but not for long because his golden tongue was useful. Keep this story in mind for reference when we get ten years down the line to Descartes's encounter with an alchemist named Chandoux at Cardinal Bagni's residence in Paris in 1628.

After Henri III died, du Perron played the role of instructor in Catholicism for Henri IV, who converted as the price for becoming king of France. Du Perron was made cardinal in 1604 after negotiating in Rome to get Henri IV's reign regularized. And here is another story to remember for later on, quoted directly from Pierre Larousse's *Grand Dictionnaire Universel du XIX Siècle*: "It has been remarked as a bibliographical curiosity that Cardinal Duperron always printed his works two times. The first edition was uniquely destined for his friends, whose observations and criticism served him for correcting the edition he delivered to the public" (VI, p. 1495).

Baillet says Descartes eschewed his title and that it was imposed on him by his father, but this is most unlikely. Descartes used his title freely as a young man, and also when he was demanding that the French ambassador for the United Provinces extract him from an indictment in 1648. Certainly everyone who was anyone in France, on meeting "sieur du Perron" would think of the wily cardinal of the same name.

The young René Descartes, newly sieur du Perron, had enough money (and pride) that he did not have to sign up as a real soldier who would have to take orders or go into battle. The last was ruled out anyway since the United Provinces was in the ninth year of the above-mentioned twelve-year truce signed in 1609 with Spain. Baillet says that Descartes took only the symbolic sovereign when he signed up and kept it as a souvenir. This was the dashing thing to do in those days, so Baillet has our hero do it.

It also turns out that there was no military school in Breda during Descartes's fifteen-month residence. Prince Maurice was not even there, having gone off to consolidate his inheritance at his deceased brother's château, no doubt taking with him the distinguished engineers and mathematicians he liked to have around. But still there would have been other engineers and mathematicians in Breda with whom Descartes could have studied, as he said he did.

But he also probably chased women, drank, smoked, brawled, gambled, rode around on horses, practiced fencing, and perhaps even insulted another officer sufficiently to provide grounds for the great excitement of a duel.

Dueling was a dangerous game. Kings and generals hated it because they lost many of their best men that way. In France, Louis XIII definitively outlawed dueling in 1627 after his previous order was defied by the great swordsman François de Montmorency, comte de Bouteville, with his cousin Rosmaduc, comte de Chapelles. On 21 June 1627, in Paris, they fought against the marquis de Beauvon and the marquis de Bussy, three on three (that is, each team had a second, so three fights were going on at the same time) at noon in the Place-Royale (today known as the Place des Vosges). Rosmaduc killed his opponent.

High noon! With all the courtiers circled around watching. It must have been wildly exciting, the combatants dressed in highest fashion with their capes, boots, and feather-plumed hats, their sneers and insults, and their noble French pride. And what a way to defy the king, who after all was just another fellow nobleman. And not that much of a swordsman when it came down to it, either.

Well, you just don't execute nobility of that rank, but Louis XIII executed both Bouteville and Rosmaduc anyway — despite the pleas of the entire nobility. He did allow the families to take the bodies and bury them. Beuvron escaped and was pardoned two years later. But the executions showed that Louis XIII was serious about abolishing the time-honored custom. The king had cause, after all. He was losing too many good men. Several hundred of his best lieutenants were killed in duels every year. Bouteville was twenty-eight when he was executed. He had started dueling at the age of fifteen and had been in twenty-two duels. Billy the Kid had nothing on Bouteville, either in his cold-blooded love of the game, or in his great notoriety.

As for gambling, the preferred game in those days was cards, at which you could lose, or win, a lot of money. Rich young nobles lost their inheritances at cards. Descartes was not rich, but there is no question but that he was a gambler. In a letter to Princess Elisabeth of November 1646, commenting on the famous demon that Socrates claimed spoke into his ear on crucial occasions to tell him what to do, Descartes says that he always found when gambling that he did best when he had a happy feeling that he was going to win. He certainly did believe in the power of positive thinking, but he won because he was a mathematical genius who could figure out the odds. Descartes surely counted cards, a method as old as the game. Everything about his life (except its end) suggests that he was cautious enough that he did not lose.

As you may have noticed, I don't quite know what to do concerning traditional stories about Descartes for which either there is no evidence or for which there is conclusive evidence that they are false. The problem is that some of the false stories are so striking that if you tell them, and then refute them, most people will remember the story and forget the refutation. You know the old political campaign trick: My opponent did something *really* bad (described in detail). Next day: Oh, I'm so sorry, I got that wrong; it was someone else.

On the other hand, if I don't tell the false stories on the grounds that I am not going to perpetuate them, scholars will accuse me of not knowing them. So with all that buildup, here comes a traditional story followed (like a little yapping dog) by my immediate, vehement, and imploring refutation.

The crucial event in Descartes's life, the pivot on which his whole career turned, the moment when he saw the future and it was his, that stroke of lightning that made Descartes Descartes, was his meeting with Isaac Beeckman. And *that* much of the story is absolutely true. So here we go. Hoary tradition has it that they met in the street in Breda looking at a poster put up by a young mathematician out to make some money by challenging tyros to solve a problem he had set. This was a popular sport among young noblemen. You signed up, and if you could solve it, the problem setter would pay you a set sum. But if not, you had to pay him. But only after he had shown you that he could prove it himself. There were math sharks as well as card sharks in those days.

Descartes is supposed to have asked a man standing there to translate the problem. The man was Isaac Beeckman who complied with amusement and said mockingly to the young soldier that if he solved it, he'd like to see the results. A few hours later, Descartes came to Beeckman and showed him the proof. Beeckman then took a double take, recognized Descartes's genius, took him as his master, and so on.

What we have are Beeckman's private journal. The story is surely false, because Beeckman is strong on details in his journal, and his record of meeting Descartes for the first time on 10 November 1618 in Breda contains not a word about a poster problem. The fact is, it is an old story. Baillet himself remarks without comment that it is exactly like the story of how Descartes's great mathematical predecessor of the previous generation, François Viète, solved in three hours the problem Adrien Roman had set in challenge to all the mathematicians on earth. He sure showed them...

What Beeckman recorded in his journal is that his new friend Descartes, who, incidentally, he refers to at one point as Duperron (which is the way the cardinal usually signed it), is something of a jokester. He told Beeckman that an angle cannot exist because a line drawn through the point where the two lines of an angle meet would necessarily have to divide the point in two. But this is impossible because the point is dimensionless. So Descartes claimed to have proven that an angle cannot exist. Descartes also said that if he could get properly situated inside a large hollow spinning top, he could float free in the air.

Sure, Beeckman said. Then he asked Descartes to figure out mathematically how far a body would fall in a given period of time. Descartes gave an incorrect graphical solution to the problem of falling bodies, which Beeckman corrected.

Beeckman outlined another project for Descartes, to describe and give an exposition of the mathematical ratios of harmonic vibrations of strings. Descartes apparently worked on this problem night and day, and after just a few weeks, on 31 December 1618, he presented his *Treatise on Music* (in Latin) to Beeckman with an effusive dedication and apology:

> *Now that I see land, I hasten toward the shore. I omit many things here, much for concision, much because I have forgotten it, more from ignorance. However, unformed as it is, I release this offspring of my mind to the bears, to go to you as a souvenir of our intimacy and as the surest affirmation of my affection for you, on condition that you keep it eternally hidden in the drawers of your desk so it will not affront men's judgment. They would not avert their eyes from its imperfections, as I am sure you will do to concentrate on those pages where I have traced from life some lineaments of my mind. Above all, they would not know that it has been composed in haste for you alone among the ignorance of soldiers by an idle man submitted to a way of life entirely different from his thoughts.*

Many years later, after Descartes's death, in his effects was found a notebook that included some important juvenilia. At the top of the notebook is the date, 1 January 1619. Probably this notebook was a return gift to Descartes from Beeckman. Beeckman left for Middelburg on 4 January 1619 in pursuit of a teaching job and a wife. Descartes himself left for parts Germanic on 19 April 1619, and they did not meet again until 8 October 1628.

Isaac Beeckman was born in Middelberg on 10 December 1588. He went to the University of Leiden from 1607 to 1609. In 1612, he went to France where on 18 August 1618 he received his bachelor's degree and license in medicine from the University of Caen. He arrived in Breda on 16 October 1618 just in time to be the gadfly, the burr beneath the saddle, that by its bite and sting brought Descartes to life. Beeckman was also one of the first and best of the early practitioners of mathematical physics. Besides his development of the law of falling bodies (independently of Galileo) Beeckman's carefully written and illustrated notebooks (not published until 1939) contain the first known approach to the law of inertia.

Beeckman wrote that he thought the problem with a lot of young natural scientists was that they were too eager to publish and protect any little discovery they made. They should hold on, get their discoveries integrated, and then publish them. He never published his own. But in January 1630 he bragged to Mersenne who was visiting the United Provinces (and who handled Descartes's correspondence in Paris) that he had been Descartes's teacher. Baillet says he showed Mersenne the *Treatise on Music* as his own work. And here the story gets fishy again.

Beeckman did write in August 1629 that "Ten years ago I communicated to Descartes what I had written on the causes of the sweetness of harmony." He surely did do that when he set Descartes the task of writing the *Treatise on Music*. But it is unlikely that Beeckman told Mersenne that he wrote the *Treatise* himself, as Mersenne rushed to tell Descartes.

Nevertheless, the story is that Beeckman showed Mersenne the *Treatise on Music* claiming that it was his own work. Not only that, Adam says Beeckman showed Mersenne other work he claimed as his own that was stuffed full of propositions that were Descartes's. You wonder. Beeckman had loaned his journal to Descartes, so perhaps Descartes's journals contained propositions from Beeckman.

There is something else bothersome about this. Mersenne was a master at the game that my father called "Let's you and him fight." Mersenne (like my father) loved to get people into disputes, and by controlling the information people sent him, Mersenne could instigate and prolong arguments between almost any of them at will. He did a lot of that, purportedly to advance knowledge and science. Mersenne was fabulously successful in setting off Descartes, who had, Mersenne knew by then, a very short fuse anyway.

"I am extremely obliged to you," Descartes wrote Mersenne on 8 October 1629, "for advising me of the ingratitude of my friend." First, Descartes got back the copy of his *Treatise on Music* that he had given Beeckman in 1619. Then in September or October 1630, he wrote a really nasty letter to Beeckman:

I took back my Music from you last year not because I needed it but because someone said that you spoke of it as if I had learned it from you.... Now that I have confirmed that you prefer stupid boasting to friendship and truth, I tell you in two words that even if it were true that you have taught something to someone, it would be odious of you to say so, and if false, even more odious. But it is most odious of all when you have learned from that person yourself.... As for me, I don't care, but in the name of our friendship, I warn you that you greatly harm your own reputation by boasting that way in front of those who know me. And I warn you not to show them my letters as proof because they know I am accustomed to learn even from ants and worms.

This ought surely to be enough, but Descartes had worked himself into such a frenzy that when Beeckman wrote him to suggest that he come to see him to discuss his work, Descartes exploded on 17 October 1630 with the following incredible reply:

You claim you deserve great praise for teaching me about the hyperbola. Certainly, if I did not pity you for being sick, I wouldn't be able to keep from laughing, because you don't even know what a hyperbola is except in its grammatical sense.... I would never have suspected that your stupidity and ignorance of yourself is so great that you truly believe that I have learned more from you than I am accustomed to infer from other natural things. Don't you remember when I was occupied with studies you did not understand ... how much you importuned me and asked to hear about them at greater length? ... Now it is obvious to me from your last letter that you sin not by malice but by insanity.

So much for the man to whom Descartes had written on 23 April 1619:

If, as I hope, I stop somewhere [he was on his way to Germany], I promise you that I shall undertake to put my Mechanics or my Geometry in order, and I shall honor you as the first mover of my studies and their first author. For you, in truth, have awakened me from my idleness, and evoked in me a science I had nearly forgotten. You have brought me back again to serious occupations and have improved a mind that had been separated from them. If, therefore, I produce anything that is not contemptible, you have a right to claim it as yours. As for me, I shall not forget to send it to you, not only so you can profit from it, but also so you can correct it. (Cole's translation revised, p. 121)

The hyperbolic excessiveness of Descartes's vitriolic outburst some eleven years later is embarrassing. But Baillet rushes to Descartes's defense. That devious, plagiarizing Beeckman, that stupid ungrateful Beeckman, he got all that was coming to him.

Surely someone misunderstood, either Mersenne what Beeckman said, or Beeckman what Descartes said. Or more likely, Descartes what Beeckman was proud of. Beeckman *did* set Descartes the music problem. And anyone would be proud — as Beeckman rightfully was — to have had Descartes for a student.

I very much doubt that Beeckman told Mersenne that he himself wrote the *Treatise on Music*. Beeckman surely did tell Mersenne that he had designed the project. But we still have not reached the source of Descartes's vicious attack.

When you read the correspondence between Descartes and Beeckman from January through May 1619 the explanation is clear. Descartes fell in love with Beeckman. Descartes says in a letter of 24 January 1619, "Love me and be assured that I would forget the Muses before I would forget you, because they unite me to you by a tie of eternal affection." Descartes did all he could to please Beeckman, worried constantly about what Beeckman thought of him, and had for nine years reconciled himself to the merely mild warmth with which Beeckman responded to his affections.

The possibility that Descartes's love for Beeckman was homo-erotic makes Baillet and Adam nervous. They quote the letters in which Descartes sends Beeckman his love and asks to be loved in return and explain that these phrases seem more suggestive, more intimate, in the French translations than they are in the Latin where such pleas are just a matter of form. But this is ingenuous, because Descartes's Latin is plain and direct.

I think Descartes simply wanted Beeckman to love him like the father figure he was (and as Descartes's own father perhaps did not). Beeckman was eight years older than Descartes. He had a profession, that of mathematical physics, and he had those notebooks of worked-out problems and wonderful drawings. Descartes, who heretofore had talent but no direction, suddenly yearned to be like Beeckman. He realized almost at once that something great could be made out of the application of mathematics to mechanical prob-lems. Not that this was a new idea in the world but that something came together when Beeckman showed Descartes his work. Des-cartes now saw that the bits and pieces of mathematical analysis he was already using to solve geometrical problems could be applied to practical problems in physics.

Descartes wrote to Beeckman from Copenhagen on 29 April 1619, saying that he should send a letter, no matter the address, everyone in the port knew he was expecting a letter from Beeck-man. He went looking for it every day. And on 6 May 1619, Beeck-man did write a letter to Descartes and copied it in his journal. We don't know either whether Beeckman sent it or whether Descartes received it, but if delivery was made, that letter would have quickly cooled the young man's ardor. Beeckman wrote as a pedagogue, as maddeningly all-knowing and condescending as teachers and pro-fessors have always been, heartily making heavily humorous appeals to the young man to shape up, and ending with this parabolic tale:

There came here from your homeland a certain Frenchman, who professed in public the finest arts, fountains from which the water runs perpetually, of war and of medicine, ways to multiply the supply of daily bread — although he himself was utterly destitute. I went to see him, and, when I examined him, he turned out to be completely ignorant of everything, even those things that he was professing publicly. So he won't stand the test, and we must send him farther north, where the numb-skulls welcome illusionists and charlatans. (Cole's translation, p. 125)

If Descartes got this letter, he could not have been less than furious. But time passes and passions cool. When he returned to the United Provinces in October 1628, the first thing he did was go to Middelburg where he had left Beeckman. This is good evidence that they had not communicated for nine years because Beeckman had gone on to the Latin School in Utrecht later in 1619, and in 1627 he was named rector of the Latin School in Dordrecht, which is where Descartes found him on 8 October 1628. Beeckman's proud journal entry about this meeting shows that if there had been a breach in their mutual admiration, it had been healed:

After having traveled through Germany, France, and Italy, he affirmed that he had not been able to find anyone other than me with whom he could discuss after his own heart and from whom he could hope for assistance in his research. He found everywhere a scarcity of true philosophy, of that he calls the work of the valiant. For my part, I prefer him to all the arith-meticians and geometers I have ever seen or read.

But then Mersenne ignited Descartes's fury with his cockamamie story that Beeckman was palming off Descartes's work as his own, and this suggests that perhaps Descartes did get that incredibly awful letter from Beeckman and that despite his continuing affection for the man, he was just waiting — as any unrequited lover would — for a chance to blow his stack.

The whole affair makes me wince because I am a professor and I empathize with Beeckman. Professors are embarrassed, sometimes, by the rare student who sees in us the idol and inspiration for all his or her vague aspirations. And we all have hurt students deeply by speaking or writing as pompously and as callously as did Beeckman to Descartes, all in the name of improving and instructing the neophyte who needs shaking and shaping up. Would that just one of those each of us has bruised should take from our spark a light a tenth as bright as that of Descartes.

But here, in a moment I will be sounding like Baillet. Descartes was lazy and he deserved a good dressing down. Beeckman delivered it, and it did the young fellow a lot of good.

Of course Descartes knew this, begrudging as he was to admit that anyone had pulled up his bootstraps but himself. Also, Descartes knew Mersenne's predilection to incite arguments. Within a year of Descartes's vicious letter to Beeckman, they dined together. The older man, master teacher, had no doubt patiently calmed Descartes down.

Descartes had his revenge, then he lost interest. He had outgrown Beeckman. He was no longer infatuated. When Beeckman died on 20 May 1637, Descartes wrote to the Protestant minister Andreas Colvius, who had told him, that he was sorry to hear it. Descartes continued that he had been one of Beeckman's best friends (note the precision of the tense) and then he added this bromide: "But, Monsieur, you know better than I do that the time we live on this earth is so short in comparison to eternity that we ought not to care much if we are taken a few years sooner rather than later." A really cheery consolation, and, in fact, totally and hypocritically in opposition to Descartes's own conviction that the greatest work he could undertake for the benefit of humankind was medical research toward the prolongation of life. Maybe we ought not care about a few years one way or the other, but Descartes himself cared a lot.

IV ⚔ MAGIC KINGDOMS

I have made the most marvelous discovery.

AND NOW for the next three years — 1618–1620 — our young hero drops into a black hole — the war zone of North Central Europe. From those years we have only three dispatches. In his *Discourse on Method*, Descartes says that while he was returning from the coronation of the Emperor Ferdinand II (so he must have been in Frankfurt sometime between 20 July and 9 September 1619), he stopped in early winter to do some meditating in an oven-heated room somewhere between Frankfurt and Vienna. Let's say Ulm, which was an imperial city that had an engineering school and was a center of mathematical studies. Surely Descartes would want to see the great Rosicrucian mathematician Johannes Faulhaber who lived in Ulm. And there is some suggestion in Faulhaber's letters that Descartes was there.

From Descartes's journals, we know what he was thinking about in that oven-heated room, and most wonderfully, we know that there on the night of 10 November 1619 he had three dreams. He wrote them down. In his notes there is also a tale of derring-do while traveling. But for all those years, not one word of war.

Then there is another blank of more than two years, from the time he says he left Ulm "before the end of winter" in 1620 until he signs a contract with his brother Pierre in Rennes on 3 April 1622 (in which he promises not to sell the property he inherited without his brother's consent). He had probably returned home to Rennes to be there on 31 March 1623, his twenty-fifth birthday, on which day he came of legal age. It was an important year for his father, too, for in 1623, Joachim Descartes became dean of the grand chamber in the Brittany Parliament and thus the king's deputy.

In the *Discourse*, Descartes says that he had gone out to prove himself, so biographers have helpfully placed in him several battles. But the evidence that Descartes ever participated in a battle reduces to the fact that he was somewhere in North Central Europe while they were going on and his using as an example in his *Passions of the Soul* the case of a soldier being wounded without noticing it. There really is no evidence that Descartes was ever in battle. Nevertheless, he did set out for the war zone. And he claimed later that when he was young he had fire in his belly.

It was a good time for a war lover. The mature period of Descartes's life exactly corresponds with the Thirty Years' War, a religious war between Protestants allied with Catholic France against Catholic Spain and the Holy Roman Empire, which dates from 23 May 1618 when some Protestant nobles threw several of the Catholic king Ferdinand's representatives out a window of a castle in Prague. (It was Ferdinand's elevation to emperor of the Holy Roman Empire in Frankfurt in 1619 that took place when Descartes was there.) The Thirty Years' War began with this famous defenestration (it was the ground floor, so only their dignity was hurt), and ended on 24 October 1648 with the treaty signed in Westphalia. France entered the war (on the Protestant side against Catholic Spain) in 1635. The 1648 treaty in fact ended eighty years of conflict between Spain and the United Provinces, whose representatives, by making a separate peace and gaining final independence in 1648, left France to battle Spain alone. (France eventually won in 1659.)

Descartes thus had his choice of army in which to fight. He could join the Catholic forces of Ferdinand supporting Spain or the Protestant forces supported by France. Protestants and Catholics had been fighting in Northern Europe since at least 1582. The forces were regularized by the formation of the Protestant Union in the Palatine in 1608 and of the Catholic League in Bavaria in 1609. Henri IV of France supported the Protestant Union and was about to go to war against Spain in 1610 when he was assassinated. This delayed France's formal entry into the war for twenty-five years, but during most of that time France openly supported the United

Provinces and Sweden against Spain. With money, where it counts.

Descartes certainly knew all about this. It would be stock and trade shoptalk of the young officers at Breda. And there all sentiments would be for France. The French military mission in the United Provinces was designed precisely for the purpose of helping First Minister Cardinal Richelieu establish France's independence of the Holy Roman Empire led by Imperial Spain. Never mind that France was Catholic too. It was time to get out from under the thumb of the Holy Roman Empire, to establish a state power independent of religious control, and to ally with the United Provinces and Sweden who were also resisting the Spanish threat to their power and independence. That they were Protestant was incidental. Richelieu understood this, but Philip III of Spain did not. Thus by the end of the seventeenth century, France was the strongest state power in Europe and Spain was a backwater. Richelieu understood that in the modern world, commercial, industrial, mercantile power is more important than religion. The Holy Roman Empire spent its wealth (all that gold from the New World that made Spain the richest country in the world in the sixteenth century) trying to rid Europe of Protestants and Jews to make it entirely Catholic. But statesmen in France, Sweden, and the United Provinces, harking to what was called the reason of state, reduced religion in foreign affairs to a ploy to be used or not depending on the tactical advantage it provided. In the conduct of foreign policy, the fact that Richelieu was a cardinal was as irrelevant to his decisions in the seventeenth century as was President John F. Kennedy's Catholicism to his conduct in the twentieth.

Descartes knew that religious affiliation was becoming incidental in commerce and affairs of state. The United Provinces were a haven of intellectual and religious tolerance, they were independent, and they were booming with trade and prosperity. In Breda, Descartes was a Catholic French citizen in a French regiment in a Dutch army opposed to Spain. His king approved.

But when the biographers sign Descartes up with an army in Germany, they put him with the Catholic forces of Emperor Ferdinand II supported by Spain, probably because he said he was in

Frankfurt at the emperor's coronation. But if he did join an army, surely it would have been that of the Protestants supported by France. On the other hand, if he did not intend to fight, which is likely, it probably doesn't matter which army he joined. It has been suggested that all his membership in an army amounted to anyway was a passport, a way to travel safely, to maintain the rights and protection of an officer, and to obtain garrison housing.

Descartes must at least have seen the results of war. During the Thirty Years' War, the population of Northern Europe declined from twenty million to seven million people. Thirteen million dead. Northern Europe did not again reach the population level it had in 1600 until 1750. This loss of thirteen million people (on top of earlier losses) was not all directly due to warfare. Soldiers were killed in battle and civilians starved because crops were destroyed, but also the plague and other diseases were endemic throughout Europe.

Moreover, the mid-seventeenth century was the height of the Little Ice Age — the Mander Minimum, it is called in geological preciseness. The minimum was in sunspots. There were practically none, which decreases the heat the sun sends out. The average annual temperature of Europe fell as much as 5 degrees Fahrenheit and there were years without summer. Drop the temperature 10 degrees Fahrenheit and you're in a full-scale glacial age. It was the time when all those paintings were made of quaint Dutch citizens in bloomer trousers ice skating on the canals, a time when glaciers advanced over mountain villages in the Alps. And a time of crop failure, famine, and death.

You could get killed out there. Not just soldiers and citizens, but travelers, tourists, pilgrims, merchants, messengers, statesmen. An avalanche in the Alps, the plague, robbers — a dozen ways to die leaving a lost or anonymous corpse. When Descartes set out for the wars in 1619, he wrote to Beeckman, "Don't worry, you who love me. I'll be all right." And he describes a roundabout itinerary to avoid the heart of darkness. But we don't know which route he actually took, although he did avoid getting killed.

Not that the man was not feisty. As well as can be determined,

Descartes's feat of derring-do occurred on his way back from the wars. Baillet tells the tale from Descartes's notes. He was returning by the northern route, apparently on his way to the United Provinces. Along the Friesland coast, he hired some seaman with a boat to take him and his valet from somewhere to somewhere. The sailors, thinking the two knew only French, talked among themselves in Frisian or German or Dutch, conspiring to rob and kill the passengers and throw their bodies overboard. But Descartes did understand, and — and this is the sort of thing in which Baillet excels. Here is how he tells what happened:

> *M. Descartes, seeing what had to be done, suddenly stood upright, altered his countenance, drew his sword with a haughtiness they had not anticipated, and said to them in their own language in a tone of voice they well understood that he would instantly run them through if they dare attempt to harm him. (B I 103)*

Then Baillet goes into a panegyric about Descartes's bold, daring, and audacious cheek, to conclude that all this had "a marvelous effect on the state of mind of those wretched scoundrels."

Perhaps something like the above was in Descartes's notes, but I really doubt it. Keep the style of this story in mind when I quote Baillet's story of Descartes's encounter with Faulhaber below. The very serious problem is that although Baillet sometimes virtually reproduces entire pages from Descartes's published works, he quotes only two lines of verse from Descartes's journals for 1618–1621. All the rest is paraphrased, and the journals are lost. The fact is that Baillet may very well have repeated some of Descartes's own words, but there is no way to tell how much he improves and adds to them. I think that in many cases, Baillet just makes things up. Baillet was writing an edifying story of the life of a man who was being touted as the greatest French philosopher who ever lived. He was painting the picture of a paradigm of virtue, piety, heroism, and genius. He presented Descartes as he understood the game.

On the way to Germany in 1619, Descartes wrote to Beeckman that he had spent three days in a tavern talking to an old man about the memory techniques of Raymond Lulle, and he asked Beeckman to check Lulle's book to see if there really was a secret key. Beeckman replied dryly that it was in the book and did not amount to much. Descartes was also curious about the claims of astrologers, alchemists, magicians, and the rumors from Germany of a new Protestant brotherhood of the Rosy Cross. Members of this fraternity were supposed to have certain magical powers and to have as one of their goals the improvement of the natural sciences for the practical betterment of humankind. In particular, they were concerned with medical research to counter the ravages of aging and to increase the length of human life.

Given that these aims are also later those of Descartes, the question has been asked as to whether Descartes himself might have become a Rosicrucian when he was in Germany. Almost all scholars claim that he could not have been a Rosicrucian because in the seventeenth century, there never was a formal fraternity of the Rosy Cross. But this is logic chopping. There may have never been a formal fraternity, but there were lots of self-designated Rosicrucians, and Descartes may for awhile have fancied himself one of them. But they were Protestants. This would be a terrible blow to the Saint Descartes Protection Society. Baillet is so worried that people might think Descartes was a Rosicrucian that he translates a Latin comment from Descartes to the effect that he knows nothing certain about the Rosicrucians as he knows nothing at all about them.

Descartes must have read the Rosicrucian literature, and the parallel between Descartes's goals and rules for life with those in the Rosicrucian texts is so strong that it is most probable that Descartes was influenced by reading them. One indication of this is that in his journals, Descartes wrote the title of a book he apparently was considering writing with a dedication to the Brothers of the R. C. Cartesian scholars usually explain this away by saying that it is a joke — Descartes was making fun of Rosicrucianism.

The literature on the Rosicrucians can be pretty wild, but much of what I say here about the Rosicrucians comes from works of erudite scholarship, *The Rosicrucian Enlightenment* (1972) by Frances A. Yates and *Rose Cross Over the Baltic* (1998) by Susanna Åkerman. Yates's story in particular casts a bizarre light on Descartes's later friendship with Princess Elisabeth, daughter of the "Winter King and Queen" of Bohemia, Frederick V and Elisabeth Stuart, exiled in The Hague. So here is the tale of the magic kingdom of King Frederick V, of his relationship to Rosicrucianism, and how it was that he was king for only one winter.

The Rosicrucian excitement began with the publication in Cassel, a Protestant principality in Germany, of two manifestos: *The Fame of the Order of the Rosy Cross* in 1614 (in German) and *The Confession of the Order of the Rosy Cross* in 1615 (in Latin). They were reprinted in Frankfurt in 1615 and 1617, and Dutch translations were published in 1617 in Leiden. The author or authors are anonymous.

In *The Fame*, it is said that the members of the Order of the Rosy Cross have a large encyclopedia that contains great wisdom. Their goal is to praise God and to attain "perfect knowledge of his Son Jesus Christ and Nature" for the benefit of humankind. To accomplish this, they apply mathematics to nature and develop scientific instruments. To this end, the brethren bind themselves to six rules:

1. *Their only profession should be that of curing the sick free of charge.*

2. *They should not wear distinctive clothing, but rather wear what is customary in the country they inhabit.*

3. *Every year on a given day they should meet together, and those who cannot must send a letter giving the cause of their absence.*

4. *Each brother should look for a worthy person to succeed him after his death.*

5. *The letters C. R. should be their seal, mark, and character.*

6. *The Fraternity should remain secret one hundred years. (Yates, p. 243; translation slightly altered)*

Keep in mind the first and second rules, which are very Cartesian.

In the *Confession*, the brethren condemn both the pope and Mahomet, call on the wisdom of God and the help of angels, and propose a new language in which the nature of all things will be expressed. The truth of natural philosophy is said to be simple, easy, and naked — if we but look for it. The book closes with an implied promise of finding a medicine to cure all diseases, which would enrich the world and benefit everyone and in particular would please God.

Then in Strasbourg in 1616, the third book in the series, *The Chemical Wedding of Christian Rosencreutz* by Johann Valentin Andreae, was published (in German). As Yates says, this is "a romance about a husband and wife who dwell in a wondrous castle full of marvels and of images of lions, but is at the same time an allegory of alchemical processes interpreted symbolically as an experience of the mystic marriage of the soul" (p. 60). The rose is an alchemical symbol, the symbol of the Virgin Mary, and a part of Luther's emblem. Also, St. Andrew's cross with roses is the coat of arms of Andreae, the author. Finally, a red cross and roses are symbols of St. George of England and the Order of the Garter. The cross, of course, belongs to Jesus. In another symbolization, the rose is flesh and the creative power of nature embracing the cross that represents death and resurrection.

Yates shows that *The Chemical Wedding* is transparently modeled on Frederick V of the Palatine and his wife Elisabeth Stuart, daughter of Charles I of England (and mother of Descartes's later friend, Princess Elisabeth). Their Heidelberg castle and garden were full of water organs and mechanical statues that moved and were made to talk through speaking tubes of the sort that appear in the tale. For example, you might glimpse through the trees naked Diana bathing, but if you tried to get closer to see, you would step on a trigger that caused Poseidon to rush out at you flourishing his trident. Some say that Descartes visited and saw these marvels, but there is no evidence for this other than that he knew about them and how they worked. The message of *The Chemical Wedding* is that a glorious future lies ahead. All seekers of truth and wisdom, of religion and science, should flock to the standard of the rosy cross.

This, Yates says, is Protestant propaganda promoting Frederick V as a candidate for the elective office of king of Bohemia and potentially for that of emperor of the Holy Roman Empire. Another item in that propaganda is a commemorative coronation print showing Frederick V and Elisabeth as king and queen of Bohemia. Four lions are present, which represent Frederick V himself, the Palatine, Bohemia, and Britain — all Protestant. These are arrayed against the Catholic forces of Austria and Ferdinand II, who was elected emperor of the Holy Roman Empire on 5 September 1619, thereby ruling out Frederick V's immediate chances. The fairy tale nature of all this is enhanced by the silly notion that the Protestant Frederick V ever had a ghost of a chance of becoming emperor of the Holy Roman Catholic Empire.

Frederick V of the Palatine and Elisabeth Stuart were married in England on 14 February 1613, St. Valentine's Day. The entertainments were amazing. Fireworks displays were wonderfully satisfying in that they injured numerous people, plays were staged by Shakespeare (*The Tempest* was appropriate harbinger of later exile), and other entertainments were designed by Francis Bacon. Finally, Frederick V and his maternal uncle, Maurice, prince of Nassau, were initiated into the British Order of the Garter.

The royal couple then moved to their castle in Heidelberg, where the greatest engineer of the day, Salomon de Caus, built an amazing formal garden, touted as the eighth wonder of the world. The really touching thing about all this, as Yates says, is that Frederick V and Elisabeth actually fell in love with each other. They spent five idyllic years in the Palatine. (They also had a total of fourteen children, and might have had more had not Frederick died of the plague on 19 November 1632 in Mainz while negotiating to get back some of his lost kingdom. He was only thirty-six years old, the same age as Descartes.)

Then in 1618 came the famous defenestration in Prague that initiated the Thirty Years' War. It was a very grave thing for the Protestant officials to throw the Catholic Ferdinand II's emissaries out the castle window, particularly given that Ferdinand II had assumed the kingship of Bohemia the year before. The first real battle of the Thirty Years' War did not get underway for another year, but the immediate significance of the defenestration was that the Bohemians were in revolt against their king, Ferdinand II. They argued that the kingship of Bohemia was an elective office, and on 26 August 1619, they offered it to Frederick V of the Palatine.

Frederick V wanted it. His mother-in-law (widow of William the Silent of the United Provinces and sister of James I of England) told him not to take it, as did the Union of Protestant Princes. But Frederick V and Elisabeth (and the Bohemians and many Englishmen) thought that Elisabeth's father, King James I, would put England behind the cause. Also Prince Maurice of Nassau advised him to take it, because he thought it might enhance his chances of being chosen king of the United Provinces. So on 28 September 1619, Frederick V accepted — only twenty-three days after the in situ king of Bohemia, Ferdinand II, had been newly elected emperor of the Holy Roman Empire.

King Frederick V and Queen Elisabeth were soon in Prague, and the Bohemian tragedy (Yates is not the first to call it so) commenced to close. Frederick V and the Bohemians had misread James I. He had married his daughter Elisabeth to the Protestant prince, Frederick V of the Palatine, but his intent had been to balance his relations to the powers by marrying his son Charles to a Catholic princess of Spain. (In fact, Charles did not marry until he became king of England in 1625, after which he married a different Catholic, Louis XIII's sister Henrietta and, unlike his father, Charles supported France's opposition to the Holy Roman Empire.)

James I did not want war, and he thought such alliances would give him an excuse not to support either side. Frederick V and the Bohemians never understood this. They thought James I would come to the aid of his daughter and son-in-law and that the other Protestant princes would follow.

The Holy Roman Emperor, Ferdinand II, was furious. He sent the duke of Bavaria to capture Prague. James I turned his back and the other Protestant princes sat tight. On 8 November 1620 at the famous Battle of White Mountain, the Catholics routed the Protestants. Frederick V and Elisabeth fled, Prague was overrun and looted, many citizens were slaughtered and officials executed, and one of the most inhumane wars in history began to decimate the population of Central Europe.

At that precise moment, Yates says, the Rosicrucian movement collapsed. Tracts with titles such as *Warning Against the Rosicrucian Vermin* published in Heidelberg in 1621 began to appear. Catholic counterpropaganda began to feature the Rosicrucians as black magicians practicing witchcraft and was so successful that in 1623 there was a Rosicrucian scare in Paris, with the brotherhood being presented, as Yates says, as a "diabolical, magical, secret society." In fact, however, Rosicrucianism did not collapse but continued as a positive force in the Baltic.

Descartes could not have avoided knowing about the Rosicrucians. The man who came on as a kind of trickster to Beeckman, who talked to an old Lullean con man in a tavern, and who had newly been inspired with the desire to find the key to the natural sciences — this man would be desperate to talk to a Rosicrucian if he could find one. And he did.

It was easy, because Yates and many other scholars of the movement are just wrong to say that there were no Rosicrucians. Throughout his stay in the United Provinces, one of Descartes's best friends, Cornelius van Hogeland, was a Rosicrucian. I do not mean that he belonged to an organized fraternity with lapel buttons or anything like that. Rather, Rosicrucians just considered themselves to be such and were known as Rosicrucians. This was against the law, but a well-known saying about the Dutch was (and is) that they just make rules so they can break them. Combined with their legendary stubbornness, this makes for some pretty powerful personalities, as was evident to everyone by the way they defeated Spain and pushed back the sea.

On 8 November 1620, then, the Protestant king, Frederick V of

Bohemia, was defeated at the Battle of White Mountain by the forces of the Catholic emperor, Ferdinand II. What a great battle for Descartes to participate in, whichever army he had joined! Most biographers have him joining the emperor's army against Frederick V. But even Baillet falters here. Descartes had just spent more than a year in the Protestant Prince Maurice's army in the United Provinces. He knew perfectly well that Maurice was the uncle of King Frederick V of Bohemia. Furthermore, French policy was totally behind the Protestants in opposition to the encroachments of the Holy Roman Empire. If, then, Descartes did join the duke of Bavaria's army in support of the Catholic emperor, Ferdinand II, he was one cynical fellow. He may well have been. But even if he did sign up with the duke, it would have been in those same terms of independence he enjoyed in Breda. That is, he wouldn't have to go into battle unless he wanted to. Supposing Descartes did sign up, where would that place him on 8 November 1620, the fateful day of the Battle of White Mountain? Baillet says that Descartes merely observed the battle. But Baillet probably would have said that Descartes fought in the battle if he had not known that Descartes later became close friends with King Frederick V's daughter, Princess Elisabeth. After all, by Baillet's lights, the Catholic side was right.

But in Descartes's journals dated 10 November 1620 is only a note announcing that he has made an admirable invention, perhaps of analytic geometry. There is no mention whatsoever of the Battle of White Mountain, or, for that matter, of any other battle in all of Descartes's writings.

Descartes was in Bohemia to look for Rosicrucians. Biographers have him finding just one, the mathematician Faulhaber. Baillet tells the story by embroidering a tale he took from Lipstorp. Baillet knows for a fact only that Descartes once cited Faulhaber without comment. It is the winter of 1620, and Descartes is holed up in his oven-heated room, probably in Ulm:

There M. Descartes occupied himself with matters appropriate to an honest man, and in particular he sought out acquain-

tance of persons with a reputation for competence in philoso-
phy and mathematics. The principal one of these whom he vis-
ited was the honorable Jean Faulhaber, who received him with
great civility. Noticing in more than one conversation that M.
Descartes was not ignorant in mathematics, and that he spoke
pertinently when matters of mathematics were in question,
Faulhaber bethought himself one day to ask Descartes if he
had heard of the analysis of geometers. The deliberate tone
with which M. Descartes said that he had made Faulhaber
doubt it. He took Descartes's immediate response as that of a
presumptuous youth, and so with the intent of embarrassing
him, he asked him if he thought he could solve some problems.
M. Descartes again said yes with an air of assurance even more
resolute than before, and without hesitation promised to solve
the most difficult problems. Faulhaber, seeing in M. Descartes
only a young soldier, laughed out loud, and to mock him, he
recited some verses from a play of Plautus, to show that he took
him for a Gascon as brave as the glorious Fanfaron [a blow-
hard; some years later, Descartes said of the great mathemati-
cian Fermat, "M. Fermat is a Gascon, I am not"]. Descartes was
stung by this extremely inappropriate comparison, and sensi-
ble of the insult this German had given him, he challenged him.
Faulhaber, who excelled particularly in arithmetic and algebra
on which he had recently published a book in German, first
asked M. Descartes some ordinary questions. Seeing that
M. Descartes did not hesitate in his responses, he proposed
some that were more difficult, which M. Descartes answered as
quickly as the easier ones. Faulhaber began to change his atti-
tude, and after apologizing for the inconsiderate way he had
treated M. Descartes, asked him very civilly to accompany him
into his study, where they conferred together quietly for some
hours. Faulhaber put in M. Descartes's hands the book he had
written on algebra in German. It contained only the problems
themselves in the most abstract terms without explications. He
had done this with the design of exercising the ingenuity of the

mathematicians of Germany, to which the problems were pro-
posed to stimulate them to give such solutions as they could.
The promptitude and facility with which M. Descartes gave the
solutions to the problems that fell under his eyes as he leafed
through the book greatly astonished Faulhaber. But he was
even more surprised to hear M. Descartes recite at the same
time general rules and theorems for deriving the true solutions
to these sorts of problems, and all others of the same nature.
This was new to Faulhaber, and completely changed his atti-
tude. He frankly admitted his own ignorance of most of the
things M. Descartes had shown him, and he earnestly asked for
his friendship. (B I 68–69)

The most interesting thing about this made-up story is that when
Descartes published his *Geometry*, he, also, did not provide the solutions. But this was not uncommon. I have already remarked that
mathematics was an upper-class competitive, gambling sport in
Descartes's time. But, alas, there is no solid evidence that Descartes
ever met or talked to Faulhaber. There has, however, recently been
found mention in Faulhaber's letters of a meeting with a young
Frenchman named Polybius. This is the name Descartes used in an
entry in his journal around 1619 or so, as the author of a book on
mathematics to be dedicated to the Brothers of the Rosy Cross.
Also, there are some parallels between the compasses Faulhaber and
Descartes used to trisect angles. Either Descartes or Faulhaber may
have gotten some geometric ideas from the other. Moreover, when
Pat and I visited Ulm in search of Descartes, the very inn he stayed
in was pointed out to us. And where he took his meals. It may be.
But there are also local champions of the nearby town of Neuberg
for the view that Descartes's oven-heated room was there and not in
Ulm. There is even less evidence for Descartes's having been in Neuberg (basically, none) than for his having been in Ulm. I spent a day
each with two people who have written books on Faulhaber. The
discussions were wonderful. Kurt Hawlitschek, a mathematics pro-

fessor from Ulm, is sure that Descartes was there. He is the one who showed me where Descartes lived and took his meals. On the other hand, Ivo Schneider, a history professor in Munich, thinks it more likely that Descartes was in Neuberg. Both of them build from the same body of data. Bulletin 2001: Schneider now thinks it was Ulm.

Scholars object when one says Faulhaber was a Rosicrucian, given that the fraternity was a religio-politico propaganda device. But in the larger picture, all those who identified themselves as Rosicrucians did so in the line of advancing science and medicine. Nothing about these goals is alien to Descartes. The manifesto of the Rosy Cross has a literal content that is inspiring on its own. Francis Bacon spoke for the age in 1605 with the publication of his *Advancement of Learning*. Let's learn more about nature so we can control it for the benefit of humankind, Bacon said. In fact, the expression of that goal goes back to his thirteenth-century namesake Roger Bacon. Aristotelianism was stagnant, dying. Scholasticism did not lead to new knowledge. The great ferment of alchemists, astrologists, and magicians fed the desires of young men like Descartes to penetrate the mysteries of the natural world. Perhaps there were secrets hidden by the ancients. Descartes was influenced by the writings of both Bacon and the Rosicrucians, either directly, or because the virus of the new science was in the intellectual air he breathed. He could not help but be infected.

And there, in Germany or Bohemia, for awhile, Descartes also seems to have fancied himself a Rosicrucian, or at least he toyed with the conceit. Later on when he set his own goals and code of life, they contained substantial, solid portions that very probably are taken from the Rosicrucian tracts.

The most direct evidence for Descartes's exposure to Rosicrucian writings is the book title he wrote down in his journal, probably in 1619: *The Mathematical Thesaurus* by Polybius the Cosmopolitan Dedicated to the Learned of the World, Especially the famous B[rotherhood of the] R[osy] C[ross] in G[ermany]. As remarked above, Polybius is the name Faulhaber used to refer to a visit in Ulm from a young mathematician, who some think must have been Descartes. The name Polybius suggests the Cartesian and Rosicrucian goal of establishing the unity of the sciences. But there is no way of knowing whether this is the title of a book Descartes was contemplating writing, or one he made up as a spoof.

Descartes also labels two portions of his notebooks *Olympia* and *Parnassus*. Part of Traiano Boccalini's *Advertisements from Parnassus* (translated from Italian) was published together with *The Fame* of 1614. And in a book *Golden Themis* (Themis is the goddess of order) about the Rosy Cross published in Frankfurt in 1618, Michael Maier, one of the most prolific writers on Rosicrucian themes, speaks of Olympic Houses where the brethren might work and dwell, an idea Descartes is later said to have had for housing and training artisans in the Louvre. This is not, of course, an idea original to the Rosicrucians.

It is at this time also that Descartes takes as a motto from Ovid, "Who lives well hidden, lives well," which the Rosicrucians also professed. Concerning the rules of the Rosicrucians in *The Fame*, Descartes himself must have mused on the coincidence that the fifth, that C.R. should be taken as their device — and that in fact is more often written R.C. — fits the initials of René Descartes. He used it on all his correspondence, gloriously beribboned.

The first rule, to practice medicine free of charge, Descartes followed later in life, particularly in collaboration with his friend Cornelius van Hogeland, himself a self-professed Rosicrucian, who made up all kinds of chemical potions and dispensed them free, as a matter of experiment as much as of charity. Descartes also apparently knew Jacques de Wassenaer I who published a collection of writings concerned with Rosicrucianism in 1624–1625. Also, both Descartes and the Rosicrucians had the goal of increasing the length of human life through medical research into the causes of aging.

Then there is the second rule, to wear no distinctive clothing, but to dress like everyone else, and to follow the customs of the country they happened to inhabit. This is no more than a matter of prudent common sense. As I once told a male graduate student during the Reagan years, "You want a job, cut off your ponytail." He did, and he got a job. I was pleased and amused a few years later to see him again flaunting a ponytail — after he got tenure.

Descartes makes such a recommendation in his *Discourse* in his most controversial moral rule. While looking for truth, one has to live somehow, so Descartes's first rule is:

> *To obey the laws and customs of my country, retaining con-*
> *stantly the religion in which by God's grace I was instructed*
> *from my childhood, and to govern myself in all other things by*
> *following those opinions that are the most moderate and far-*
> *thest removed from excess, which are commonly received and*
> *followed by the most sensible of those among whom I would be*
> *living. (AT VI 22–23)*

Catholic scholars have trouble with this. What if Descartes had been born a Protestant or a Jew? They say that Descartes means this rule only for people like himself who were safely born into the true religion.

According to Descartes's autobiography, it all came to a climax for him in a room heated by a porcelain stove somewhere in Poland or Germany. There on the night of 10 November 1619, he had his three famous dreams. Baillet paraphrases Descartes's description of them at length. He undoubtedly expands on Descartes's notes as he does throughout on every small point (such as with the Faulhaber story). Yet Cartesian scholars have almost unanimously taken Baillet's lengthy report of the dreams as true to Descartes's own words — one reason being that they appear (to these scholars) too anomalous to have been made up. But everywhere we have a control, we see Baillet elaborating his stories at length and with invented detail. And there is only one check on these stories of the dreams. Leibniz made notes on the notebooks, one of which is: "Dream 1619, Nov., in which poem 7, the beginning of which is this: 'What course in life shall I pursue?' — Auson[ius]." This verse appears in Baillet's recital of the dreams. But nothing more of the dreams appears in Leibniz's notes.

I don't trust Baillet's long recital of these dreams for one minute. I think he made them up almost entirely. But they are fun, and their various interpretations are ingenious and even enlightening. So let's go with them, however tongue in cheek.

In Descartes's first dream, he was frightened by some ghosts or spirits and felt very weak on his right side so he had to lean to the left to walk down the street to where he wanted to go. He was ashamed to walk this way, but when he tried to straighten up, gusts of wind spun him around three or four times on his left foot. He dragged along fearing he might fall, then seeing a school along his way, he entered it looking for refuge and relief. He tried to get to the school church to say his prayers, but he noticed that he had passed someone he knew without greeting him, so he tried to go back to do so, but the wind prevented him, blowing him back toward the church. At the same time someone in the middle of the school yard greeted him kindly and politely and told him that if he wanted to, he should go find a Monsieur N. who had something to give him. This, Descartes thought, would be a melon from a foreign land. He was also surprised to see that the people standing about were upright and steady, while he was still bent over and off balance, even though the wind that had almost knocked him down had greatly lessened.

Descartes woke out of this dream with a pain on his left side, so he rolled over on his right and lay awake thinking of good and evil for a couple of hours. Baillet says Descartes thought an evil spirit was trying to seduce him, so he prayed for God to protect him from the evil effects of the dream and from punishment of his sins that were, he acknowledged, enough to bring thunderbolts from heaven, although his life was more or less blameless in the eyes of most men.

Then the second dream comes with a bang. It was just a loud noise that Descartes took for thunder. He woke up terrified, but at once noticed a lot of sparks scattered around the room that were so bright that he could make out near objects by their light. He had seen sparks like this before. He soon calmed down and fell asleep again.

In his third dream, Descartes was not afraid. He found an encyclopedia on his table, which pleased him because he thought it might be useful. Then another book appeared, entitled *Compendium of Poets* (in Latin), which he had read. He opened it by chance to the verse "What course in life shall I pursue?" Then he noticed a man he did not know who recommended a poem starting "Yes and No." Descartes said the verse was one of the *Idyls* of Ausonius in the anthology on the table, and that he knew the book perfectly. But when he looked for the poem he could not find it. The man asked where he got the book and Descartes said he did not know but that there had been another that had disappeared and he did not know either who brought it or took it away. Then the encyclopedia appeared again at the end of the table, although it was not as complete as it was before.

Then Descartes found Ausonius's poems, but again the one beginning "Yes and No" was not there. He told the man he knew another better one by Ausonius beginning with "What course in life shall I pursue?" The man asked him to find it but Descartes found instead several engraved portraits and remarked that this was a very fine edition but not the one he knew. Then the man and the books disappeared.

Baillet says that without waking up, Descartes decided he had been dreaming, and immediately interpreted the encyclopaedia as representing the sciences collected together, and the book of poetry to mean the unity of philosophical wisdom. Poets may be none too bright or none too good, but they have seeds of wisdom in them from which sparks can be struck. And the verse beginning "What course in life shall I pursue?" contains good advice even of moral theology.

Then Descartes woke up. He took the poets to represent revelation and enthusiasm. The "Yes and No" was from Pythagoras meaning truth and falsehood in human understanding and science. Descartes decided that the spirit of truth had wanted to open the sciences to him. And he took the visit of an Italian painter the next day to indicate that the portraits were a sign that authenticated that this revelation was from God.

Baillet says Descartes took the two frightening dreams to be warning him about his past deviation from the true path, but the third showed him how the rest of his life would go. The melon represented the charms of solitude. The wind was an evil spirit that pushed him in the direction he wanted to go, toward the church, but God prevented the demon from succeeding, even though God had led Descartes that way in the first place. The thunder dream had to do with his sins again, but also was the spirit of truth descending to possess him.

Baillet points out that this was Saint Martin's Eve, on which people customarily got drunk, but Descartes had not drunk wine for three months. He had been in a state of enthusiasm for several days and had predicted that the dreams would come to him from on high.

After this revelation, Baillet says, Descartes vowed to make a pilgrimage to Notre Dame of Loreto in Italy. He also promised himself to finish a treatise he was writing by Easter 1620. We have no evidence that he fulfilled either of these promises. Moreover, Loreto is where the house of Mary was supposed to have been miraculously transported. It is hard to imagine the scientifically inclined young man vowing to make a pilgrimage there, but who knows?

The dreams are a great embarrassment to Cartesians who stress reason and do not like the idea of Descartes's philosophy beginning in a set of mystical dreams that he takes as a revelation from God. But I don't know why anyone who knew about Descartes's discussions and work with Beeckman would think that the *dreams* revealed his life's course to him. Baillet, of course, sets the dreams in the framework of the life of a saint. Here is the great inspirational moment all truly religious people have. Pascal had such a revelation later when he was in despair. He had looked into the starry heavens, and the infinite spaces terrified him. But then Jesus visited him. Pascal wrote his revelation down on a piece of paper he kept pinned inside his shirt the rest of his life. Descartes carried his dream journal with him all his life.

But again, even supposing that the basic content of the dreams is more or less accurately presented, one wonders if Descartes really thought they came from God. Maybe he spent a couple of hours praying and thinking about his sins and good and evil, but in none of his extant writings does he report doing anything remotely like that. All he says about prayer is that we should not ask God to change His will to alter the world to suit our purposes. If you want to pray, just pray for God to do what He decided to do in the first place when He created the world.

The fact is that even Baillet reports that Descartes says he made a marvelous discovery on that day of 10 November 1619 *before* he had the dreams, and that he expected the dreams because of his enthusiasm over this discovery. The dreams did not set him on his way. They came because he was already well along his life's way. Or, as I suspect, Baillet greatly embellished the dreams for Descartes.

And that's the way it was until Cole wrote his brilliant book. Cole's interpretation in the next chapter of the dreams is the best I have seen.

Before we get to Cole's interpretation, I want to pause to consider a very odd circumstance. For the period of more than four years from January 1618 when he left the United Provinces to April 1622 when he signed a paper with his brother Pierre in Rennes, we know the name of only one person Descartes met (or may have met) out-side France — Faulhaber. As far as that goes, for the fifteen months prior to that in the United Provinces, we know the name of only one person he met — Isaac Beeckman. Of fellow soldiers in the United Provinces and Germany, of friends or companions or acquaintances he had while following the armies, we know not one. Maybe he met Faulhaber, but if he did, he himself left no record of it. There are let-ters in later life to Englishmen, but none to any German. The same goes for the time he spent later in Italy, possibly a year and a half for which we have no records. Really, I begin to suspect that those nine years Descartes says he spent rolling about the world were in large part spent in Brittany, Poitou, and Paris. We know the names of a lot of people he frequented in France during those nine years. Ah well, I said it was a black hole.

GUEZ DE BALZAC (1579?–1654) POET
DESCARTES'S FRIEND IN PARIS
Photograph by Zbigniew Janowski

V ⚔ THE REBEL

I am not prepared for a judgeship.

DESCARTES FIRST MET BEECKMAN on 10 November 1618 and from him took the inspiration to apply mathematics to problems of natural science. This was not at all a new idea, but Beeckman's orderly notebooks with drawings and calculations and descriptions blew Descartes away. What neat stuff! He wanted a notebook like that.

On 10 November 1619, Descartes remarks in his own new notebook that on that day he was full of enthusiasm and had discovered the foundations of a wonderful new science. That night he had those three dreams that every biographer since Baillet has presented as crucial in determining Descartes's life course. Then, a year later, on 11 November 1620 when he was still somewhere in Germany, Descartes added a marginal note saying that on that day he began to understand the foundations of his wonderful discovery.

Most commentators think that by November 1620 Descartes more or less had put together the method of mathematical analysis we know in part as analytic geometry. Its use would be in giving expositions of and solving problems in the four traditional mathematical sciences known as the quadrivium: geometry, arithmetic, astronomy, and music, as well as in optics, mechanics, and even physiology and medicine.

This method of mathematical analysis provided the foundation for the notion of unified science Descartes had been prodded toward by Beeckman. Instead of classifying the sciences according to their objects (nonliving bodies — physics, living bodies — biology, etc.) as Aristotle did, Descartes treated every kind of body the same way.

Everything in nature is a body in motion that can be described and measured. Thus Descartes's science is a universal mechanics in which mathematical representations can be given of how everything works and is related to everything else.

An incidental result of this work is that Descartes, who was already a whiz at solving geometrical problems, could now solve even the most difficult problems almost automatically. As I have insisted, he surely won bets and contests doing this, and I rather fancy him as a shark wherever the high rollers put their money on the line. But they had to have caught on to him, because at least by 1628, in mathematics, Descartes had a reputation of being a very big gun indeed.

Thus it is most likely that during the two years from 10 November 1618 to 11 November 1620, Descartes did the work that places him among the half dozen greatest mathematical geniuses of all time. But he did not publish his analytical method until 1637, in his *Geometry*.

Descartes left Germany before the end of winter in 1620, and there is no documentation of his whereabouts until more than two years later, 3 April 1622, when he signed an act regulating his accounts with his brother Pierre in Rennes. During this two-year period, Baillet has Descartes leaving the service of the duke of Bavaria (after the battle of White Mountain) to join the emperor's army led by the comte de Bucquoy to participate in the siege and destruction of Hradisch in Moravia, and in the destruction of other towns whose Protestant populations supported Frederick V of Bohemia — and thus were slaughtered. I mean murder, rape, and baby bashing. The evidence for Descartes's participation in this orgy of genocidal ethnic cleansing is less than zero. (And I'm not even a member of the Saint Descartes Protection Society. But note that it is anachronistic to deplore the Catholic scourge of the Protestants; Baillet thought that by sending him on this holy mission of death dealing, he would enhance Descartes's reputation for piety and religious orthodoxy.) Descartes himself lists genocide as one of the greatest of all crimes, right along with betraying cities and assassinating or executing princes and kings.

On 31 March 1621, René Descartes was twenty-five years old, the age of majority. So it is much more reasonable to place him in Rennes on his birthday than somewhere in northern Germany with fire in his belly and blood on his sword. On 31 March 1621, he came into his inheritance from his mother, a house in Poitiers and four small farms near Châtellerault in Poitou: La Bobinière, Le Grand' Maison, Le Petit Marais, and Le Perron, from which we know he took his title sieur du Perron. Coming into one's majority was a very significant event. Descartes's father would expect him to be front and center to hear what Joachim had planned for his second son.

So after he left Germany, Descartes surely took himself to his family in Rennes, where he requested his father's permission to sell the property he had inherited. His father's permission was not legally necessary, but it would have been unthinkable for Descartes to sell the property without it. And it must really have burned him that he had to agree not to sell without his older brother's permission. He did at least get permission to go look at it.

On 22 May 1622, Descartes signed contracts of sale in Poitiers and had written his father about it. Permission to sell was probably granted on the premise that Descartes would use the money to buy a living. To that end, on 21 March 1623, Descartes wrote to his brother and father from Paris about the death of René Sain, his godmother's son (or perhaps her husband or her nephew, sources differ). René Sain had died in Turin where he was commissary general in charge of obtaining food rations for the French army in the Alps. This was the sort of post in which one could make a lot of money, and Descartes's proposal that, as his godmother wanted him to, he go settle René Sain's affairs in Italy, would certainly suggest to the family that he might purchase the post. He had been with the military in Breda and Germany, so it made sense to allow him to sell his properties to become a commissary general. Thus by July 1623, Descartes had sold all five properties for a total of 24,000 to 25,000 livres, which was not paid all in a lump, but some at least in the form of interest, so much a year. Interest on property and investments constituted the income of many propertied people who, like Descartes, did not have jobs. In fact, most men of Descartes's age, education, and class did have positions or offices that brought in income. That Descartes never did is surely the sore point that galled his older brother. The cadet sold family property, burned up the income from it simply for living expenses, did not buy a lucrative post in the government, did not marry a rich woman — René Descartes was a drone, a family parasite.

Baillet says that his properties and sales gave Descartes an annual income of 6,000 or 7,000 livres, which Cohen properly remarks is far too much. More likely would be 600 or 700 livres, which would be enough for Descartes to live in modest independence. But family standards were considerably higher than that, and his father and brother certainly expected him to advance in the world. So they doubtless gave him permission to go to Italy to look into René Sain's affairs and possibly buy his post.

Descartes did not go to Italy at once, however, but apparently went first to Paris. Baillet has Descartes arriving in Paris in February 1623, during the big Rosy Cross scare. It was more of an excitement than a scare. Someone put up a poster saying that the brothers of the Rosy Cross were coming! They would move about the populace invisible! There were satirical songs and skits about the Rosicrucians, and Baillet says there were rumors that Descartes himself was a Rosicrucian because he had just arrived from Germany. Baillet continues that in a master stroke to curb these rumors, Descartes "made himself visible to everyone." A great story, but Adam does not deign to repeat it, nor would I except that it is one of those made-up stories often repeated in the Descartes literature that surely was told at the time about lots of wits about town. As Whistler said to Oscar Wilde who had remarked, "I wish I had said that," "You will, Oscar, you will."

Baillet says René Sain's affairs were just a pretext to go to Italy. But as for where Descartes went and what he did in Italy, Cohen says it bluntly: "Concerning this voyage, which at least he took, we know nothing" (C 412). Baillet trundles him around the usual tour, the route taken by Montaigne in 1581. It was the standard route. Everyone went to Venice to see the marriage of the Doge with the Adriatic on Ascension Day in May. Descartes would surely have been in Rome for the opening of the Jubilee year 1625. And Baillet thinks Descartes must have visited Galileo. (In a letter of 11 October 1638, he said he never met the man, but since he had just been stunned by news of Galileo's condemnation by the church, he might not have wanted to admit it even if he had.) Surely the student of military architecture would go to observe the great siege of Gavi. And a pious person would go on a pilgrimage to Loreto. Père Richeome's book *The Pilgrim of Loreto* published in 1604 contains instructions on how to do it. The book was a runaway best-seller. The Jesuits used it, and it is inconceivable that Descartes didn't read it at La Flèche. About Loreto, Adam has a nice line: "Finally, a Frenchman, a Catholic, an old pupil of the Jesuit Fathers, a voyager in Italy, who hadn't been to Loreto, would have been a minor scandal, and Descartes was never of a humor to scandalize anyone" (A 64). Adam forgets how Descartes put Beeckman on when he first met him. But basically, I agree. Descartes surely went to Loreto to see the show, either because of his pledge, or just because people go, the way Pat and I (although lacking a Catholic upbringing) have gone to Lourdes several times, just to see the show. The procession of the cripples is fabulous.

Descartes, however, only twice remarks on Italy in his writings. On 15 April 1631, Descartes wrote to Balzac about how bad the air is in Italy, how hot the climate, how many cutthroats and pickpockets there were — all in all a place to visit but no place to live for a man seeking health, peace, and security. He also crossed the Alps near Mont-Cenis in May during avalanche season, for he remarks about the noise like thunder they make, and later hypothesized that thunder was in fact caused by clouds tumbling from higher to lower regions of the air.

Descartes doubtless took the main Mont-Cenis pass, which is very old. It is the one Hannibal is supposed to have taken elephants over. And Charlemagne crossed here with his armies. The avalanches

Descartes wrote about were here. There are spectacular views of steep mountain slopes scarred with textbook examples of avalanche chutes. Descartes could have seen and heard avalanches on this route in 1623 and 1625 (going and coming) when the Little Ice Age climate was at its height, glaciers were advancing in the Alps, and May would have been a lot colder than it is now.

On 23 May 1998, Pat and I walked from Lanslebourg-Mont-Cenis in the Alps over the main Mont-Cenis pass on to the Petit Mont-Cenis col, another pass that leads down to the Ambion River and on into the town of Bramans on the main route between Grenoble in France and Turin in Italy. It was a hike of more than twenty miles and took us nine hours.

Pat and I walked down from the Petit Mont-Cenis col to the Ambion River and on down the trail — by this time a road — leading to Bramans. Along the way, we came to the Notre Dame Chapel of the Deliverance. Beside it pointing down a grassy trail wide enough to drive a car on was a sign saying "Brahmans Direct." A shortcut. We took it.

Soon we were going down a steep ridge through the trees, steeper and steeper. Then we came to an enormous quarry, a wall that dropped down 800 feet vertically on our right. But the trail went down the steep slope to the left. And before we knew it, we were on a ridge twenty feet wide with a 400-foot drop on the left and an 800-foot drop on the right.

Pat and I have done a lot of mountain hiking. And we've had forty years of experience of climbing while exploring caves. As we went on, the climbing as such was no problem. But the ridge was dirt and sand and crumbly rock.

"This is crazy," Pat said.

"I don't do this sort of thing anymore," I said.

"I'll go on a bit to check," I said.

Soon I was back.

"I think it's OK," I said.

Pat said nothing. The "I think" had silenced her.

We looked at the dirt slope down which we had come. With the drop-offs on either side, and no solid holds, it was nothing we fancied climbing back up.

The slope we were standing on was very steep, with nothing to stop a slide over the 400-foot drop. Pat was behind me but higher up. She started along the top, lying on the slope, her upper body leaning out over the edge of the 800-foot drop.

"Come down, come down," I said as softly as I could.

That edge up there was artificial, the result of blasting. I could see cracks in the rock, and was afraid it might crumble off. Pat with it.

"There's nothing to hold onto down there," she said.

"Come down," I said. "You can't go on from up there."

Finally, Pat slid slowly down toward me. I stretched out my arms and held one of her feet with one hand, then the other, lowering her until she reached my level. Now we had only the 400-foot drop-off to worry about, ten feet down the slope below us with nothing between except that damnable dirt and gritty sand. We inched along to a rock wall where we climbed down ten feet to a somewhat gentler slope with bushes and trees to hold onto. I'd already done this once, and had left my pack there, which I now picked up.

In it was my 500-page manuscript of this book and four big journals with all my notes from Descartes's letters and from the three main biographies of Descartes by Baillet, Adam, and Cohen. I wouldn't trust it to the baggage storage at the train station. So goes that pack, so goes this project. I put it back on and said, "I think we can get down just over there."

Pat was mute. Later she said she was sure she was going to slide down the dirt on that last slope and knock me off with both of us sliding over the edge to drop down 400 feet to the valley floor below.

We continued down the slope to the left and finally down a hundred-foot rock wall, sometimes holding onto the rock, sometimes onto bushes and trees, to the valley floor.

The valley floor was dry rock. I walked down it a hundred yards to where the quarry cut it off. We could have gone on around to the left on a sloping rock over the big drop-off, but we'd had enough of that.

I have always thought that I would die simply because I had

started doing something and then continued doing it long after I should have stopped, continued for no other reason than that I had begun. Very Cartesian. Before Descartes set out to find the truth, he set himself three maxims of behavior. The second is:

> *To be as firm and resolved in my actions as I can be, and to follow no less constantly even the most doubtful opinions once I have determined to accept them, as though they were very assured. (AT VI 24)*

At this point, both sides of the valley were rock walls. Pat and I started walking up the valley. A hundred feet straight up to our right (now away from the quarry) there seemed to be a forest. We couldn't tell because the wall was so steep. I started up one sand chute and Pat started up another. After fifty or sixty feet they were too steep, and each of us slid back down. We continued up the valley again, hoping not to come to a dry waterfall wall that would box us in. Almost at once we came to some tree roots hanging down. We climbed up them, up the steep face now of dirt and rock, hanging onto bushes and trees, a hundred feet, until we crawled out onto a gently sloping grassy meadow. We walked several hundred yards to a path that took us to a dirt road that led to the continuation of the trail along the paved road we had left an hour before. From then on we stayed on the main trail.

I had hoped that our hike would provide another story about searching for Descartes. But I had not known how terrifyingly it would illuminate his life. I believe that Descartes went to Sweden at the end of his life as grimly as we went down that ridge. After the first few steps, there was no turning back. And he was terrified. "I am not in my element here," he wrote to de Brégy on 23 December 1650. Six weeks later he was dead. He was not yet fifty-four.

"A sixty-six-year-old woman and a sixty-seven-year-old man shouldn't do things like that," I said to Pat after we'd walked for awhile back down the main trail. She gave me that look of disgust she has whenever I tell her something that is perfectly obvious.

As I walked down the road, I remembered that besides writing in his *Discourse on Method* that one should stick to a course once started, Descartes also recommended "those great roads that wind through the mountains, which by dint of being much traveling slowly become so smooth and easy that it is far better to follow them than to try to go more directly by climbing over rocks and descending to the bottom of precipices" (AT VI 14).

From 21 March 1623 to 24 June 1625, twenty-seven months, we draw mostly another blank. By 24 June 1625, Descartes had been back in France awhile, for on that day he wrote his father about the post of lieutenant general that was for sale in Châtellerault. It was the position his great-uncle, Michel Ferrand II, had held, and so the family would certainly approve of Descartes's buying it. The asking price was 50,000 livres, not at all unreasonable. Descartes reported that he had only 30,000 livres. (Interesting. The properties he had sold more than two years earlier had brought him only 24,000 to 25,000 livres. So he came back from Italy both wiser and richer.) He remarks that friends, which means the family, were willing to stake him the difference.

In July 1625, Descartes was staying in the Hotel l'Image Saint-André in Châtellerault. Obviously he had the go-ahead, because he sold more family properties: La Bréttallière, La Braguerie, La Durrandie, Courgère, the fief of Montbaudon, and La Parentière. That would certainly bring in enough money for him to purchase the lieutenant generalship. And he must have been considering doing it. But in the end, Descartes wrote that surely even his father would agree that his second son was not yet experienced enough to take over a judgeship, and, to make sure his father got the point, Descartes added that by the time he did get more training, he would be too old for the post.

This had to have driven Descartes's father up the wall. What did experience have to do with a purchased post? You paid the price, went through the charade of ceremonial tests, and took over. Then you discreetly made your fortune. That ought to be easy enough to understand.

Descartes's father was in Paris. But even before the letter could reach him, his son had set out for Paris himself. Then when Descartes arrived, his father had already departed for Rennes, and that is the last we ever hear about a legal career for Joachim Descartes's second son. But it was probably not the last of the affair. In Paris, Descartes stayed with his father's friend Vasseur d'Étoiles, receiver general of finances for the king, who traveled in the spring of 1626 with Descartes, once again to Poitiers and Châtellerault, and then to Rennes. The best guess is that this was a final attempt to get Descartes to purchase the post, and then the trip to Rennes was so d'Étoiles could explain to Descartes's father that you can lead Descartes to water, but you can't make him drink.

Descartes took the money and ran.

That money was the foundation of his independence for the rest of his life. Again, the only previously known source of his increasing it is gambling. Speaking of Descartes in Paris in 1624, Baillet says, "He was perfectly cured of the inclination for gambling that had formerly inspired him" (B I 131). Translation: The man was a card shark.

The family dynasty did build further in Brittany, despite Descartes's welshing out. Joachim gave his first counselorship to Pierre in 1618, but then promptly bought another for himself. Then on 2 December 1625, Joachim resigned from his second counselorship to give his post to his son Joachim II, aged twenty-three, but with the provision that he (Joachim I) would keep it four more years. And it goes on from there with details I won't provide here since they pertain only after the death of Descartes.

So here was Joachim Descartes in 1625 already arranging for the counselorship of the first son of his second marriage, and here was the second son of his first marriage, twenty-nine years old, without a post. Get him settled! Cole speaks for Descartes's father: "An honorable man should strive to achieve three things: the ownership of landed estates; a judicial office, or, failing that, a legal career; and an honorable marriage" (p. 95). René Descartes was the family failure.

If Descartes wanted to loaf, why didn't he marry someone rich? That would get him off their hands. Joachim had a modest fortune, property, and a title from his second marriage. One would think that his son René would be smart enough to do the same. The man was neither a priest nor a Rosicrucian — Naudé reported that Rosicrucians were pledged to celibacy — so why didn't he get married?

On that score, all we have is another story, a piece of gossip collected by an Oratorian, Père Nicolas Poisson, who was Baillet's leg man. Baillet cites him often. Poisson collected every story about Descartes he could find, most of which Baillet uses uncritically. This one concerns a Madame du Rosay, who having reached a certain age, often told how in her youth Descartes had courted her. One day while walking with her, he was attacked by a rival for her attentions. Descartes disarmed the man, but rather than running him through, he chivalrously returned the hothead's sword, saying he owed his life to the young lady for whom he had risked it. Shades of *Amadis de Gaul*. Baillet (through Poisson) goes on to remark that later in a barracks room conversation about women, Descartes "after having remarked to the company his astonishment at seeing so many dupes, assured them that he had never been affected that way, and that in his own experience (not to remark on the delicacy of his tastes), among the things in the world most difficult to find were a beautiful woman, a good book, and a perfect preacher" (B II 501). That line was not original with Descartes, if he ever said it. No, I don't trust the story at all, although I don't doubt that Madame du Rosay told her tale.

The post of lieutenant general of Châtellerault would have been perfect for Joachim Descartes's second son. It was modest but dignified. It would be appropriate to have it back in the family. It could lead to quite a respectable marriage and the building up again of properties around Châtellerault. What's more, the old Ferrand-Descartes house was there ready to occupy. His father had willed it to Pierre and René, although he surely would have given it to René alone if he had only purchased the post. René later had to pressure Pierre to give him some of the money after Pierre sold the old homeplace.

The wayward son took his way to Paris. On 16 July 1626, Descartes wrote a letter from there to his brother Pierre about financial affairs. And there he met Père Marin Mersenne, the Minim priest who later handled all of Descartes's correspondence from the United Provinces. The Minims were vegans; they ate no animal products at all, only fruit and vegetables. The founder of the Minims, Saint François de Paule in 1435, called them that to humble them more than the Franciscans, who were called Minor. Nevertheless, Mersenne had enough money to pay for an immense correspondence, books, and scientific experiments.

By this time, Descartes had established his mathematical reputation with three of the strongest mathematicians of the day, Claude Hardy, counselor at Châtelet; Claude Mydorge, treasurer of France at Amiens; and Florimond de Beaune, counselor of the presidial at Blois. Mydorge was also a lens grinder and was probably the source of Descartes's interest in optics. It is striking that all of Descartes's friends (except his valets and the lens grinder Ferrier) were rich. Well, maybe some of his professor friends had less money than he did, but even that is unclear. Mydorge is a wonderful example. By the time of his death, he had spent 100,000 écus (that would be some ten million dollars in 2000) on lenses, burning mirrors, and experiments in mathematics and physics, much to the distress of his heirs.

This period is also the time of a story Baillet tells that probably is the source of the idea that Descartes lay in bed meditating until 11 o'clock in the morning. Here it is:

In 1628, Descartes was staying in Paris with a friend of his father, Nicolas Le Vasseur d'Étoiles, receiver general of finances for the king (obviously a good man to know). Baillet says that Descartes found the social life there so consuming of his time and thoughts that he moved out without telling anyone where he was going. One morning five or six weeks later, Le Vasseur ran into Descartes's valet in the street. He bribed the man to lead him to Descartes.

It was about 10:30 when Le Vasseur quietly stooped down to peer through the keyhole into the room where Descartes was still in bed. There he lay with the windows wide open, the curtains pulled back. Papers covered the small round marble-topped table near the head of the bed. Le Vasseur watched as Descartes occasionally rose up on an elbow to write, and then dropped back down again to think.

After half an hour, the story goes, Descartes got up. Le Vasseur rapped on the door as though he had just arrived, and Descartes was hustled back into the social whirl, where, it is said, he very gallantly apologized to Madame Le Vasseur.

That is the only report we have for eighteen months. Then on 22 January 1628, Descartes was back in Brittany as godfather for his brother Pierre's son Joachim at Kerleu in Elven. And on 30 March 1628, Balzac sent him a letter addressed to Brittany. But he probably spent much of his time from 1626 to 1628 in Paris.

Besides his commerce with mathematicians, Descartes may have known a famous poet of the day, Théophile de Viau, and as already remarked, Guez de Balzac, the age's best stylist, was his friend. On 15 April 1631, after Descartes had moved there permanently himself, he wrote to Balzac trying to attract him back to the United Provinces. Théophile and Balzac had visited the United Provinces together in 1615, when Théophile was eighteen and Balzac twenty-five. Théophile later wrote that his associating with Balzac, whom he called a strange kind of male, a queer bird, was the most disgusting thing he had ever done. Théophile was the author of satiric, erotic, licentious, sacrilegious, and irreverent verse that was all the rage in the early 1620s. He was supported by Louis XIII's chief advisor, the duc de Luynes, for whom he wrote propaganda.

The Parnassus of Satiric Poets, which includes some of Théophile's poems, was published in 1622 and 1623, and again in 1625 under Théophile's name, the later edition apparently by his enemies to incriminate him. Another of Descartes's friends, Jacques Vallée Desbarreaux, had published some of Théophile's works in 1621 and more in 1623. Théophile had been banished in 1619, was burned in effigy in 1623, and then imprisoned in 1625. His was one of the great trials of the century, and in 1625 he was banished again. But he was protected in France by the duc de Montmorency until he died of tuberculosis at the age of thirty-six in 1626. The duc staged an elaborate funeral with, Adam says, no less than eighteen priests in attendance.

Descartes is connected with Théophile in several ways. Théophile's first publisher Desbarreaux visited Descartes in 1641. Also, in 1647, in a letter to Chanut, Descartes quoted some verses of Théophile. Finally, as remarked, Théophile had been to the United Provinces with Balzac (who disavowed him during his troubles, which may explain Théophile's nasty remark about him) and the correspondence between Descartes and Balzac shows that they knew each other rather well.

In 1628, Descartes wrote a letter in Latin (perhaps to their mutual friend, Jean de Silhon) in defense of Balzac's second published collection of letters. Three of the letters in the volume are addressed to Descartes, and they contain, as Adam says, "mitigated Stoical moral maxims quite similar to those our philosopher himself adopted in 1619" (A 80). In a letter of 30 March 1638, Balzac asks Descartes for the promised story of his life, and in a letter of 14 June 1637 accompanying a copy of his *Discourse on Method*, Descartes said here it is.

Besides these literary skirmishes, an event of great importance to Descartes happened on 24–25 August 1624 in Paris. Three men, Jean Bitault, Étienne de Claves (known as the doctor-chemist), and Antoine Villon (known as the soldier-philosopher) had posted notices announcing two days of disputations — a Saturday and a Sunday — in opposition to Aristotle. Adam says that "One of the most beautiful halls in Paris had been retained and nearly a thousand people were already assembled" (A 86) when an order came from the first president of Parliament to evacuate the hall. The three perpetrators were exiled by Parliament, and it was forbidden to teach against the ancient authors on pain of one's life. Only de Claves was caught and arrested. Villon and Bitault fled.

During this excitement Descartes was presumably in Italy, but he would have heard about it in detail on his return. And it behooved the son of Joachim Descartes to pay attention to government decrees — don't oppose Aristotle. In July 1626, Joachim Descartes was on a commission of magistrates in Brittany conducting the trial for treason of the comte de Chalais, who had conspired with Louis XIII's brother Gaston to overthrow the king. The comte was convicted on

18 August 1626 to be tortured, beheaded, quartered, his head put on a pike and his body parts hung in the street, his residences demolished, and his woods cut down. His mother got the quartering rescinded. As dean of Parliament, Joachim Descartes reported (in his own hand) on all this to the king and was duly rewarded with a letter of commendation in 1628 from the king who was on the battlefield at La Rochelle at the time.

It is time now to look at the results of noticing another set of coincidences. In *The Olympian Dreams and Youthful Rebellion of René Descartes* (1992), John R. Cole builds on a fact no other Cartesian scholar had seen fit to pursue. To the sequence of three 10–11 November (Saint Martin's Day) dates significant in Descartes's life — 10 November 1616 meeting with Beeckman, 10 November 1619 discovery and dreams, 11 November 1620 note on foundations) — Cole notes that on 10 November 1616, "Descartes successfully completes his professional training in the law(s) at Poitiers and receives his licentiate with honors" (p. 79). The key to Cole's interpretation of the dreams is their occurrence on the eve of the day of Saint Martin, the patron saint of lawyers.

"My hypothesis," Cole says, "is that Descartes's Olympian dreams concerned his rejection of the law in favor of a life to be spent in 'the search for truth'" (p. 129). The dreams occurred on the night of the Feast of Saint Martin. Saint Martin's Day is 11 November, and traditionally the judicial year begins on 12 November when contracts are renewed and lawyers and judges take their oaths.

Here is Cole's interpretation of the dreams. Descartes was on the road looking for the right way in life. In the first dream he is walking down a street and loses his strength on his right side so he cannot stand upright. He trends to the left, and this leads him later to worries about punishment for his sins and fears that an evil spirit is trying to seduce him. Left is sinister. But one clear meaning of right or droit in French is the law. In that first dream, Descartes rejects the right and spins to the left. "It is," Cole says, "just another step forward, hardly so much as a jump and certainly not a leap, to claim to *see* the younger son of the conseiller Joachim Descartes, himself a lawyer-nonlawyer saying no to the law on the anniversary of his licentiate" (p. 138).

In the dream, Descartes then meets Beeckman in the school yard scene — Beeckman who angered him by urging him to settle down and work on the new science. Beeckman is probably both the shadowy figure and the acquaintance in the dream, as well as the Monsieur N. who has a melon for Descartes. Cole works out in detail how Descartes might think the melon means the charms of solitude. Beeckman had chastised him seriously about wasting his time. So Descartes might be thinking of the proverbial friend who is as hard to find as a good melon. But finally, Cole concludes that the interpretation of the melon as representing charming solitude "would make sense if read as a reference to Beeckman's exhortations that Descartes settle down for the quiet satisfactions of intellectual accomplishment" (p. 145).

The dream progresses: Descartes isn't steady enough to join others around the Beeckman figure, and he wakes up. In the two hours he lay awake, he worried (Baillet says) about "punishment for his sins, which he acknowledged to have been great enough to call down upon his head thunderbolts from heaven" (B I 82). Then the minute he goes to sleep again, his father slams a big one down on him and wakes him up. Descartes is at first terrified. He is guilty of defying his father. But then he pushes his guilt aside by focusing on the sparkles in the air and decides that the noise came from the "Spirit of Truth," which, far from warning him off his chosen course of life, sanctifies it. A dream that started out as his father blasting him for giving up the legal profession (or for thinking of doing so) ends with God the Father blessing his choice of the search for truth.

The third dream then is obvious. It is wish fulfillment. Beeckman called his journals table books. Two books appear on a table in Descartes's dream, one an encyclopaedia suggesting the unity of the sciences. It turns out to be incomplete — Descartes will have to complete it. Then there is the *Corpus Poetarum* (*Compendium of Latin Poets*), which was a real book Descartes knew. Here, Cole makes an inference that rings very true in the context of his overall interpretation: "For a seventeenth-century Frenchman so recently trained in the law(s), *the* one great *Corpus* was the *Corpus juris civilis*, the body of Roman civil law codified under Justinian and edited by modern jurists" (p. 154). Descartes would have studied this book for his law degrees. The association is strengthened by the fact that in his dream, Descartes opens the corpus at random to come across the line from Ausonius, "What course in life shall I pursue?" Opening the Bible at random for advice is a very old practice, and Descartes takes the advice to consider seriously his future way of life. But there is more to the incident than that. "The standard format for examinations of legal competence in the courts," Cole says, "was to select laws for exposition 'by the fortuitous opening of books'" (p. 155). Probably this was how Descartes was examined on 9 and 10 November 1616 in Poitiers. Thus its appearance in the dream.

In his dream, Descartes also remembered the verse "Yes and No," and Baillet points out that this is a Pythagorean phrase meaning "truth and falsity in the human and the profane sciences" (B I 84). Cole points out further that the lines in Ausonius's *Eclogue 2* following "What course in life shall I pursue?" are "The courts are full of uproar; the home is vexed with cares; home troubles follow us abroad" (p. 157). Then in his *Ecologue 4* beginning "Yes and No," Ausonius comes to the conclusion that "Yes and No" is the answer to all questions. Descartes's answer to family home problems, to his father and a career in the law, is no. But his answer to his own career and private home problems is yes to the search for his own truth and a career in the natural sciences. Cole expands the decision as one "between the ways of his father, judicial office and honors, and of his friend [Beeckman], mathematical philosophy and liberty" (p. 162).

As Cole points out, however, Descartes was still not very confident about this. The miniature portraits in the dream could be chastising reminders of distinguished jurists like his father, or wish-fulfilling images of his own future portrait as an author. It is unlikely that he took them, as Baillet says, as a sign from God to authenticate the dream by prophesying the visit of an Italian painter the next day.

Biographers from Baillet to Cole love the dreams. One reason they make so much of them is that Descartes so seldom lets down his guard, even in his private letters that the desire to enter his unconscious just this once is too strong to resist. In fact, Descartes exposes himself plenty in his later conflicts with Voetius and other Dutch Protestant ministers in the United Provinces. But few Cartesian scholars have refrained from interpreting Descartes's dreams.

Both interpretations make perfect sense. If, like Baillet, you start with the notion that Descartes was a pious man who truly expected God to help him make a difficult decision about the way of life he should follow, then the religious trappings — thunderbolt, prophetic signs, pledge to take a pilgrimage — fit right in. Then if you start out as Cole does with a background study of the Descartes family relation to the law, Baillet's interpretation (or Descartes's own, if that is what it is) is only enriched by bringing in Descartes's guilt with relation to his father and his ambiguity concerning Beeckman.

Some Cartesian scholars discount the dreams, being embarrassed that the great rationalist's system began with anything so irrational. But the dreams are not irrational at all. The system does not start with them anyway, because Descartes made his great discovery before he had the dreams. Both Baillet's and Cole's interpretations show a sleeping mind working over a major life decision.

Never forget, however, that even if Descartes did say he had three dreams, the chances are virtually certain that Baillet made up most of his narration of them. If they were in the journal in that detail, why did Leibniz copy only this: "Dream 1619. Nov., in which poem 7, the beginning of which is this: 'What course in life shall I pursue?' — Auson." Cole says that Leibniz did not copy the dreams because of his disdain for dream analysis, but in fact Leibniz was interested in everything, and if the dreams were in Descartes's notebooks in the detail Baillet provides, I think Leibniz would have copied them out. For example, Leibniz did record details about a play he found in Descartes's papers. It is peculiar, as Leibniz notes:

> *Item, a comedy in French extending into the fourth act. The characters are Alixan and Parthenie who love each other. Both of them are children of princes, but each believes the other is a shepherd. But one thing astonished me as I leafed through it. This is that he reveals at the beginning what ought to be concealed until the end, that is, Parthenie having learned that she is a princess, then talks to herself in deliberating whether she ought to still love Alixan, and she concludes in his favor. Alixan is hidden nearby and hears this, and he declares to her on the spot that he has heard. She was the princess of the happy isle of Iceland, which had been taken from her by the Tyrant of Stockholm. (AT XI 661–662)*

This play (the manuscript is lost) is probably juvenalia from the days Descartes was associating with Balzac in Paris as a young man. Some commentators say he must have written it in Sweden, because of the Tyrant of Stockholm character. But we cannot even be sure that Descartes wrote it. It was in his papers, but Leibniz does not say that it was in Descartes's handwriting. Like everyone since, Leibniz just assumed that Descartes wrote it.

Cole gives as further argument for Baillet's accuracy that he "*does not* smooth out the irrationality of the dreams or the enthusiasm of the dreamer for a better fit with the rational thinker from the *Discourse*" (p. 198). But Baillet provides or copies from Descartes an interpretation that is quite rational in a religious context, just as Cole's interpretation is obvious once he sets up the family background.

Those two are not the only persuasive interpretations of the dreams. Paul Arnold points out that the three dreams can be seen to derive almost exactly from the great Rosicrucian work *The Chemi-*

cal Wedding of Christian Rosencreutz by Andreae published in German in 1616. The work created a sensation and Descartes surely read it. Rosencreutz hears a trumpet blast that brings him into the presence of an angel of truth. Then his progress is obstructed by a violent wind, which he escapes by going into a château, where he sees people he knows, and where he finds an enormous globe inside of which one can see the stars in daylight. Rosencreutz also sees a spray of sparkles as did Descartes in his dream. The spirit asks Rosencreutz "Where are you going?" There is an encyclopaedia that Rosencreutz recognizes, but which is not complete, that then disappears. Then an unknown man appears who asks Rosencreutz questions and guides him.

If one had nothing other than that as an interpretation, one would say that Descartes had been reading *The Chemical Wedding of Christian Rosencreutz.*

For another lead, we can be quite sure that both Descartes and Baillet knew perfectly well that Ignatius Loyola, the founder of the Jesuit Order, had three dreams that determined the course of his life. This coincidence is stressed in one of the wildest and most complete interpretations of Descartes's dreams. In *La Nuit de songes de René Descartes*, Sophie Jama relates every image in the dreams to the stories and myths that Descartes must have learned at home and in school. Her greatest coup is to point out that Descartes was born in the Easter cycle on the Sunday of the Passion. This gains immense significance when one realizes that in 1596, the year of Descartes's birth, the juxtaposition of the sun and the moon was exactly like that of the year 1, when Christ was born. This celestial event occurs only every 532 years, that is, it occurred in the years 1, 532, 1064, 1596, and will occur again in 2128. Jama believes that Descartes was named René not after his uncle René Brochard, but after Saint René as befits the extraordinary significance of the year of Descartes's birth. Re-né in French means second birth.

Jama also draws many parallels between the life of Descartes and those of Saint Martin and Ignatius Loyola. It was on Saint Martin's Eve that Descartes had his dreams, and Loyola founded the Jesuit

Order who were Descartes's teachers at La Flèche. Each of these lives pivot on a point of decision concerning whether to continue a secular life or to take the way of the devout. Jama draws parallels so extreme as to be ridiculous, but her whole scheme collapses when she tries to explain why Descartes chose the secular instead of the devout way — despite the fact (as she is certain) that Descartes's Jesuit teachers must have groomed him for the church because of his extraordinarily prophetic date of birth.

As for global interpretations, Alan Gabbey and Robert Hall concentrate on the melon. It is not, they argue, a symbol of Original Sin representing a woman's breasts and buttocks, or a symbol of friendship or solitude. It is more likely to be a pun on the Greek, a symbol of the unopened future toward which Descartes yearns. It is also a globe like the world itself, which contains all knowledge and is open to study. In the dream, the melon is replaced by a dictionary, which Gabbey and Hall trace to Rudolf Goclenius's *Lexicon philosophicum* of 1613 and 1615 that Descartes could have seen in school at La Flèche. The *Lexicon* comprises natural philosophy, metaphysics, mathematics, and logic, and can stand as a symbol for Descartes's desire to provide a comprehensive and unitary system of all the sciences.

But enough is enough on the dreams. I distrust them almost totally because I do not trust Baillet at all. Cole's interpretation of them is brilliant, and is surely correct, if the dreams occurred the way Baillet reports them. Even if they did not, Cole's inference that Descartes was defying his father and family by not going into the legal profession is ironclad.

What course of life *would* he pursue?

PÈRE MARIN MERSENNE (1588–1648)

DESCARTES'S POSTMAN IN PARIS

Photograph by Zbigniew Janowski

VI ✄ FLIGHT

Tell no one my address.

WHETHER OR NOT Descartes was religious has always been in question. Descartes's disciple Regius and his enemy Voetius accused him of presenting his metaphysical proofs for the existence of God merely to placate the church or to conceal his atheism. Members of the Saint Descartes Protection Society beginning with Chanut and Clerselier at the time of Descartes's death in 1650 concentrate on his piety and his metaphysics, treating his interests in natural science as secondary, subordinate, or even incidental.

Believers keep telling me that my own obliviousness to the sacred makes it impossible for me to comprehend that in the seventeenth century, everyone was religious and believed in God. But the claim that everyone in the seventeenth century was a believer is patently false. Yes, the notion of atheism is watered down by the fact that members of any one religious sect branded members of all other sects as atheists, and a pantheist such as Vanini was burned at the stake as an atheist. But true unbelievers did exist in the seventeenth century. And they were prominent. Prince Maurice of Nassau was one; Théophile de Viau was another. One of Descartes's best friends, Claude Picot, was known as the atheist priest. I have already described his death scene. Sacrilegious verse and libertine prose were popular. Descartes associated with both believers and unbelievers. He could have been either, whatever he wrote.

There is, however, little reason to think he was not a true believer, after his fashion. His fashion was both cosmopolitan and correct. He believed it proper for one to remain in the religion in which he was raised but remarked in his *Letter to Voetius* that Protestants and Catholics worship the same God (AT VIII-2 180). If there was a good reason to convert, he didn't put down the person who did it. In a letter of January 1646, he counseled Princess Elisabeth that the conversion of her brother, Édouard, to marry the Catholic Anne de Gonzague, sister of the queen of Poland, was according to a justifiable tradition. Why should she get worked up about it, he asked Elisabeth, given that her own ancestors had themselves converted from Catholicism to Protestantism?

In the United Provinces, Descartes almost always lived close to Catholic enclaves where Mass was celebrated, and apparently he made a point of attending to exhibit his Catholicism — although the only church services he ever comments on having attended were Protestant. And he was very defensive about that. In a letter of 13 November 1639 to Mersenne, he says:

> To those who say that I go to the sermons of the Calvinists, that is an unmitigated calumny. In examining my conscience to figure out what pretext it could be based on, I find nothing except that one time out of curiosity I went with M. de N. and M. Hesdin to a place in Leiden to see the assembly of a certain sect of people who call themselves Prophets, and among whom there is no minister, but each man or woman preaches whatever he imagines he is inspired with, so that in an hour we heard the sermons of five or six peasants or tradesmen. And another time, we heard the sermon of an Anabaptist minister who said things that were so absurd, and spoke such an extravagant French, that we could not keep from bursting out laughing, and I thought it was more a farce than a sermon. But for the Calvinist churches, I have never been in one of them in my life except that on the day your letter found me in The Hague on the ninth of this month, which is the day everyone thanked God and made bonfires to celebrate the defeat of the Spanish Fleet at Duins [on 21 October 1639], I went to hear a French minister of whom everyone spoke highly. But I behaved in such a way that no one who saw me would not understand that I was not there as a believer, for I entered only at the moment the sermon

began, and I remained in the doorway, and left the minute the
sermon was over, not wanting to assist in any of their cere-
monies. If I had received your letter before this, I would not
have gone at all, but it is impossible to avoid the gossip of those
who want to talk nonsense.

Descartes did give proofs for the existence of God, but he also
remarked to Mersenne that his metaphysics in which these proofs
appear is primarily the foundation of his physics. A reliable God can
be trusted to keep the laws of nature uniform. Descartes also was
firmly of the belief that the human soul is an independently existing
immaterial substance that can survive the death and deterioration
of the body, which is an argument for its immortality although God
certainly has the power to snuff it out should He desire to do so.

The question of Descartes's religious beliefs is crucial for understanding the second major turning point in Descartes's life. The first
turn that made Descartes Descartes was impelled by that meeting
with Beeckman on 10 November 1618, coming to a culmination
exactly one year later when Descartes made his great discovery.
After a restless night, he knew which course he wanted his life to
take. He would be a natural philosopher with the goal of seeking
truth in the sciences. To this end, he developed his analytic method
in mathematics, wrote on mechanics, and started his *Rules for the*
Direction of the Mind. But by no means was his decision fully
confirmed. His father and extended family still expected him to go
into the law, and I have already shown how the agony was pro-
longed. Descartes escaped awhile to Italy, but when he returned to
France he found himself embroiled in a family plot to place him as
lieutenant general in Châtellerault. That fought off in 1625, he went
to Paris, probably with periodic trips to his father's home in Rennes.
And Baillet says that sometime between 1626 and 1628, he took a
trip with Villebressieu to La Rochelle to observe the siege machin-
ery and the dike that Richelieu and Louis XIII had built to defeat the
last Protestant stronghold.

Descartes had known Villebressieu at least since 1627. Ville-bressieu was an inventor, of the rope climbing and descending equipment already mentioned, of that trick in which you make a wooden ball ascend and descend between two sticks, a portable bridge, a wheelchair for taking wounded soldiers off the battlefield, and an apparatus for causing optical illusions using mirrors and refraction. Villebressieu could make flames appear in the middle of the air and project images of toy soldiers on the wall so they seemed to grow larger, advance across the room, and then recede. Baillet gives Descartes credit for setting up those mirrors.

The dike at La Rochelle was built across the mouth of the harbor to keep the British fleet from supplying the inhabitants. It was built of stone, twenty feet wide at the base and seven feet wide at the top, with an opening in the middle to let the water through. Cannons in forts on each side and ships in the harbor protected the opening. Around La Rochelle itself were nine and a half miles of communications lines including two miles that were covered, ten feet high and seven feet wide, so cavalry could go protected through it. There were a dozen forts, eighteen redoubts — it was the greatest siege and the grandest exhibition of military engineering of the day — a wonderful show (for a grim purpose) that attracted hundreds of noble tourists. It would not be surprising if Descartes and Ville-bressieu went to see it. Descartes himself never said.

Baillet lists a large number of people Descartes met in Paris. Probably he did, but that he did is based mostly on inferences from letters he later wrote. As remarked above, he became friends with the Minim priest, Marin Mersenne, who published *Questions and Commentaries on Genesis* in 1623, *The Impiety of Deists, Atheists, and Libertines* in 1624, and *The Truth of the Sciences Against the Skeptics or Pyrrhonians* in 1625 — all of them huge volumes. In the third book, Mersenne claimed that there were 50,000 atheists in Paris, which would have been almost one out of five inhabitants. Despite his attack on atheism, Mersenne was a new mechanistic scientist who opposed Aristotelianism. And by writing thousands of letters in correspondence with hundreds of people all over Europe, he was in effect a one-man literary-philosophical-mathematical-scientific journal. He informed everyone of what everyone else was doing, circulated problems and suggestions, engaged opponents in disputes by leaking to each what the other had said, and handled Descartes's correspondence. While it is a reasonable inference that Descartes knew personally many of the people with whom Mersenne kept him in contact, it is not always certain.

Descartes's second turning-point year is 1628. On 22 January 1628, he stood as godfather to his brother Pierre's son in Brittany. On 30 March 1628, Balzac sent a copy of his just published *Discourse of a Christian Socrates* to Descartes. In this letter, Balzac thanks Descartes for some butter he had sent him. He said the butter had "hardly less perfume than Portuguese marmalade" and that he thought Descartes must "feed your cows marjoram and violets." It was at this time that Descartes wrote his letter against attacks on Balzac's *Letters*. In all likelihood, Descartes was then living on a farm known as the Petit-Marais (little marsh), a few miles southwest of Châtellerault on a high slope overlooking the Vienne River. He said he wanted to try living isolated in the country, and there he began work on his *Rules for the Direction of the Mind*. But he soon sold the Petit-Marais and was on his way.

Now events get compressed. Beeckman reports that Descartes came to see him in Dordrecht on 8 October 1628 and told him that he would send him a copy of his geometry from Paris. So Descartes had gone to the United Provinces and was on his way back to Paris. He would have had to hurry if he was to be at the meeting with Chandoux in November. Baillet has Descartes entering the defeated Protestant town of La Rochelle with Louis XIII's troops on 29 October 1628, but this makes the scheduling tight, and it is hard, anyway, to see Descartes triumphing over the starving survivors of that unfortunate place.

Someone who was at La Rochelle on the capitulation day was Cardinal Pierre de Bérulle, who had founded the Oratory in Paris in 1611 and who had been the strongest Catholic League voice badgering Richelieu and Louis XIII to crush the Protestants in France.

The defeat of La Rochelle did it, and Bérulle returned to Paris in triumph.

And now we begin to hear the strains of that Golden Oldie about Descartes's tête-à-tête with Bérulle that is as important to generations of Cartesian scholars as are the dreams. In this instance, let me give first the evidence — and glad we are to have it (although the letter is lost) — that the meeting actually took place. Then we'll look at Baillet's version of the story.

From an undated letter to Étienne de Villebressieu, Descartes says — and Baillet puts in quotation marks:

> *You have seen these two fruits of my beautiful rule or natural method. I was obliged to present them in the conversation that I had with the Papal Nuncio [Guido di Bagni], the Cardinal de Bérulle, Père Mersenne, and all that exalted and learned company that had assembled at the residence of the Nuncio to hear the presentation of his new philosophy by M. de Chandoux. It was there that I confessed to the whole troop of them what the art of reasoning well can do for those who are moderately learned and by how much my principles are better established, more true, and more natural than others that the learned have received. You were convinced of this, as they all were, making a point of entreating me to write them and to teach them to the public. (Cole's translation, p. 84)*

But it is most unlikely that if Villebressieu was there, Descartes would write him a letter telling him what he already knew. I strongly suspect that Clerselier composed this letter, as we know he did at least one other, to fill in a gap.

Baillet takes the following story from Pierre Borel's unreliable *Life of René Descartes* (1656) and embellishes it with reference to a (lost) manuscript by Clerselier that he cites throughout. This manuscript clearly represents Clerselier's own uncompleted attempt to write a life of Descartes. There was also a similar (lost) manuscript from Descartes's friend Chanut, the French ambassador to Sweden, and most likely Baillet just imported a lot of this material verbatim into his own biography of Descartes.

The Borel-Bagni-Bérulle-Chandoux story as told by Baillet goes like this. In late November 1628, in company with Mersenne, Ville-bressieu, Cardinal Bérulle, and a large number of others at the residence of Monsieur de Bagni, the pope's representative in Paris, Descartes listened to the presentation of sieur de Chandoux. Chandoux worked in chemistry and mechanics. He talked at length to refute Scholastic philosophy, and then proposed his own new system of philosophy, that is, of natural science.

When Chandoux finished, Baillet reports that everyone applauded except Descartes. Cardinal Bérulle noticed this and asked Descartes to tell the company his opinion of the talk. Descartes tried to excuse himself by saying that everyone else was more capable of judging it than he was, but he said it in a tone that made Bagni and others insist that he speak up. So not wanting to be impolite, Descartes praised Chandoux's eloquence and speaking ability. He approved the attack on Scholastic philosophy and Aristotelian science. But he was not happy that Chandoux replaced truth by probability, and he was even more unhappy that so many judicious people in the audience accepted this probabilism. Now hear Baillet's exact words.

He added that when it was a matter of people easy-going enough to be satisfied with probabilities, as was the case with the illustrious company before which he had the honor to speak, it was not difficult to pass off the false for the true, and recipro- cally make the true pass for the false in favor of the apparent. To prove this on the spot, he asked the assembly for someone to take the trouble to propose whatever truth he pleased, one among those that appear to be the most incontestable. Some- one did so, then with a dozen arguments each more probable than the other, he came in the end to prove to the company that the proposition was false. He then proposed a falsity of the sort one customarily takes to be most evidently false, and by means of another dozen probable arguments, he brought his auditors

to the pass of taking this falsehood for a plausible truth. The
assembly was surprised by the force and extent of genius that
M. Descartes exhibited in his reasoning, but was even more
astonished to be so clearly convinced of how easily their minds
could be the dupe of probability. (B I 162–163)

Then they all clamored to know if there were not some infallible
means of avoiding these sophisms, and Baillet says that Descartes
replied that he knew no better way than by following his own principles and method based on mathematics, and his general rule, and
so on.

This story illustrates Baillet's basic procedure. He fills out his
narratives with doctrinal material from Descartes's published works,
so every story is exemplary of Descartes's method and results.

This worries me. In that letter to Villebressieu, an old friend with
whom he had traveled and who had lived with him, Descartes is
supposed to have written the following: "The first fruit of this
method is to show at first whether the proposition is possible or not,
because the method examines and assures this (to make use of
these terms) with a knowledge and certitude equal to that which
can be produced by the rules of arithmetic" (B I 163). This in a letter to an old companion and friend who had probably already heard
it until he was sick of it? I don't know.

Let's get on with the story, and from here on, Baillet's attribu-
tions are to Clerselier's lost manuscript. Descartes went on to say
that Chandoux's philosophy was really little different from that of
the Schools, and he gives some details to show this. Descartes concludes that he thinks it possible to establish some clear and certain
principles with which one can explain all the effects in nature. At
this point, Baillet says, some people who had been convinced by
Chandoux to abandon Aristotelianism for his philosophy now
trooped to Descartes's side. And now Baillet probably tips in another passage from Clerselier's manuscript:

Cardinal Bérulle above all the others greatly appreciated all he had heard, and asked M. Descartes to talk to him again another time privately on the same subject. M. Descartes, sensible to the honor he had received from such an obliging proposition, visited the Cardinal a few days later and talked to him about his first thoughts on philosophy on the basis of which he had perceived the futility of the means commonly employed in treating it. He led the Cardinal to understand the results his thoughts could have if they were well conducted, and the utility the public could receive if his manner of philosophizing were applied to Medicine and Mechanics, from which the one would produce the reestablishment and conservation of health, and the other the diminution and the alleviation of man's work. (B I 165)

Anyone who knows Descartes's *Discourse* of 1637 will recognize that Clerselier just lifted this material from there. (And also from the letter to Newcastle of October 1645 in which Descartes says that "The conservation of health has always been the principle end of my studies.") Clerselier is setting the story up so Cardinal Bérulle can say: My son, you must give everything else up and go somewhere alone to write for the glory of God. Here is how Clerselier has him say it:

The Cardinal had no difficulty comprehending the importance of this plan, and he judged it very proper that Descartes undertake it, so he employed the authority he had over Descartes's mind to lead him to undertake this great work. He made it even an obligation of conscience for Descartes, who had received from God a power and penetration of mind for illuminating nature such as He had not given to others. (B I 165)

Clerselier (reported by Baillet) continues that the cardinal made a tremendous impression on Descartes. Then Baillet does cite the

Discourse from which the inspiration for this recital comes, and Lip-storp's *Comments on Descartes* (1653) to the effect that Descartes's friends had already been after him to publish. Then Baillet concludes:

> *Descartes now deliberated only on the means to execute his plan most commodiously, and having remarked two principle obstacles that could keep him from succeeding, namely the heat of the climate and the crowd of high society [in Paris], he resolved to retire* forever *[emphasis mine] to a congenial place to procure perfect solitude in a moderately cold land where no one would know him. (B I 166)*

I can't fill in like that (the passage is cobbled from letters Descartes later wrote to justify his choice of exile in the United Provinces), or rather I could, but doing so is to capitulate entirely to casting (or making up) an unknown early life out of the greatly honed comments the mature Descartes makes about it in his later life. Besides, Descartes never said Paris was too hot. That was Italy. About Paris, he says the air — meaning ambience — does not suit him. And look how it continues. Most incredibly, Baillet says:

> *M. Descartes had always had great veneration for [Cardinal Bérulle's] merit, and deference to his advice. He considered [Bérulle] after God as the principle author of his plans, and he had the satisfaction after [Bérulle's] death to find some of his disciples, i.e., priests of the Oratory, in whose hands he put the direction of his conscience all the time he lived in Holland. (B I 194)*

Frédérix says this is "pure fantasy" (p. 97), but alas, Frédérix explains that this is because there were no Oratorians in the United Provinces. Frédérix, who insists on Descartes's piety, goes on to say that "on the other hand, it is perfectly believable that it was Bérulle who, exhorting a Descartes already quasi-decided to go on the retreat to Holland, succeeded in determining him to go" (p. 98).

Frédérix is one of those biographers who severely dresses Baillet down for wild additions, but calls him "the honest Baillet" (p. 59) who could make no errors whenever his stories fit Frédérix's own edificatory purposes.

This long story about Bérulle is what Clerselier, Baillet, and Lipstorp think *should* have happened. Descartes did go away from France more or less forever — and wrote all his published works in the United Provinces — and this is difficult to explain for anyone who wants to write a panegyric about *France's* greatest philosopher. So there must have been a strong impetus coming from very high up. If not from God, then from Cardinal Bérulle, who was known to talk to God every day. Supposing Descartes's lost letter to Villebressieu is authentic, Descartes did say something or other about his method at the Chandoux talk, and always a name dropper as long as the names were not of people he might be accused of taking ideas from, he remarks that Bagni and Bérulle were there. He does not say he had a private conversation with Bérulle. He merely includes Bérulle in the company he spoke to. He says they encouraged him to write up his ideas, but people had already been doing that for years. So (Clerselier and Baillet probably thought), why not spin it out to a private talk with Bérulle? Clerselier was a devout — he was said to go to Mass more than any man in Paris — and he fervently supported Bérulle's totalitarian aspirations for the Catholic League. What a good idea to have Cardinal Bérulle set Descartes on his life's way! Then Descartes would have an acceptable reason for going to the United Provinces. Beeckman? A nobody. The significant, important man in Descartes's life had to be a somebody. The members of the Saint Descartes Protection Society began to refer to Cardinal Bérulle as Descartes's director of conscience. That genocidal maniac (and I speak precisely) as Descartes's director of conscience? Not bloody likely. Descartes did not want to eliminate Protestants and Protestantism. Some of his best friends were Protestants. He got along with them very well.

Cardinal Bérulle is an ultimate exemplar of excess in religious enthusiasm. I have remarked that he was a fanatic in opposition to the Protestants, taking himself to be expressing God's will in urging

Richelieu and Louis XIII to impose the horrors of death by starvation on the lost souls of La Rochelle. Descartes sought the truth, but Bérulle *knew* the truth, and he was mad to kill everyone who refused to bow down to it. Let me read back from Descartes's later works myself for a moment. Descartes said soldiery is charlatanry. Soldiers are looters and murderers. He said killing off a whole people is one of the greatest of crimes. And before he met Bérulle, he had seen, or at least knew all about, sieges. He knew what happened to the starving women, children, and old men in a besieged town (all the young men had been killed fighting). Maybe he went to see the dike at La Rochelle. But I don't think Descartes would have liked anything at all about Cardinal Bérulle. He drops his name. I'd put the accent on the verb.

But back to the story again. There is something familiar about it. Remember Cardinal du Perron, whose reputation René Descartes certainly knew when he decided to take the title of sieur du Perron. That story of how Cardinal du Perron attacked atheism and gave half a dozen proofs for the existence of God before the king. And when he was applauded he said that if the king wanted, he could give as many arguments equally good for the other side. It is the same story. I assume that in the backs of their minds, Baillet and Clerselier knew the Cardinal du Perron anecdote.

Could it have happened *exactly* as Baillet, cribbing from Clerselier's manuscript, says it did? No. In the prologue to this book I describe what Descartes's reaction was bound to be after a private interview with Bérulle. Nobody was going to recruit Descartes into his private civilian army to wipe out Protestants. Descartes left immediately for Friesland.

In the context of Descartes's giving up the law, Cole quotes another passage from Descartes, published in the *Discourse* in 1637 to be sure, but reflective of his obvious lifelong desire for freedom and independence. It is a major statement against the taking of oaths:

> *Particularly I included among excesses all promises by which we surrender any of our liberty. . . . I thought that I would have committed a great offense against common sense, if, because I*

had once approved of something, I considered myself ever after-
ward obligated to consider it good. (Cole's translation, p. 88)

This is not a man likely to take on a director of his conscience, or, if he did, not a madman like Bérulle.

It is always satisfying to see a villain come to a bad end. Thus Baillet records with evident good humor that Chandoux later tried to pass false gold and was executed for forgery. Baillet is more sober about the death of Bérulle, less than a year after the supposed conversation with Descartes. Baillet says that Bérulle had a seizure at the altar while saying Mass and died soon after. This is the standard good death for a priest, told about hundreds of them. Other reports are that Bérulle took ill while eating and was probably poisoned. He was the confessor and advisor of the queen mother, Marie de Médicis, who was in perennial conspiracy against her son, King Louis XIII. Cardinal Bérulle fanned the fires of her rebellious support for the king's enemies, the Spaniards and the Holy Roman Empire. She was a champion of the Ultra-Montanists, the Catholic League, in opposition to the principles of the reason of state to which Richelieu appealed in his move to make the king and the nation of France independent of the pope, the Holy Roman Empire, the nobles of the Catholic League, Spain, and the Catholic Church.

Bérulle was a troublemaker. To be sure, in 1625, he had arranged the marriage of Louis XIII's sister Henrietta to King Charles I of England, and Richelieu did want England as an ally. But then Bérulle managed to get himself and most of Henrietta's retinue kicked out of England for Catholic conspiring and proselytizing. Richelieu believed that Protestants could be good citizens if their religion was reduced from a political faction and party to a mere practice. That is the saving rationale behind the modern separation of church and state. Bérulle frothed like the proverbial Turk out either to convert or cut throat. (In fact, one of Bérulle's wilder schemes was to rid Europe of the Turks, that is, Muslims.)

On 15 September 1629, Bérulle argued vigorously in the court in opposition to Richelieu's Italian campaign against the Catholic League and Rome. On 2 October, he dropped dead.

It may have been one of Richelieu's well-known removals that satisfied even some church officials, for Bérulle was a loose cannon even in the church. In any event, the rumors of Bérulle's poisoning were widespread and also apparently never thoroughly looked into.

If Descartes did meet with Bérulle, and if the cardinal tried to recruit him, it would probably have been for the Catholic League's lay army in opposition to the Protestants, not for the development of a new natural philosophy (not a subject of uppermost concern in the mystical Bérulle's mind — it was the pope's nuncio Bagni who liked physics, not Bérulle). Knowing how powerful Cardinal Bérulle was in the court, Descartes may have seen flight as the only way out.

If Descartes was religious, he was cosmopolitan and pragmatic about it. He never concealed his Catholicism and at times flaunted it. But he could not stand most priests (there were several notable exceptions) and he thought most Protestant preachers stupid. Religious feeling and strife were in the forefront in France. In the United Provinces, at least for awhile, Descartes could ignore religious matters and people like Bérulle.

Descartes certainly did seem to feel threatened. More than once he asked Mersenne to tell no one his address. In point of fact, Descartes kept instructing Mersenne to lie to people about his whereabouts. To put off an unwanted visit by the lens-grinder Ferrier, Descartes asks Mersenne on 2 December 1630 to tell Ferrier that he is going to England. Over the years, Descartes makes up a dozen cock-and-bull stories for Mersenne to tell people to put them off the track. He does not want people to know he is working on dioptrics, or the rainbow. In the summer of 1632, he says to tell them he is not writing anything, he is spending his time learning to fence.

Descartes piously, yes, religiously, broadcasts that his goal in life is the search for truth, but in practical affairs, he is quite willing to spread falsehood wherever it will do the most good. Cartesian scholars tell me that it is too harsh to call this lying. It is just good sense. Queen Christina said that not to be able to dissimulate is not to be able to live. The good life Descartes maintained by remaining well hidden required a lot of dissimulation.

Let me get behind Cole's bandwagon again. By 1625, it had long been arranged that Descartes's half brother Joachim II would take his father's second counselorship in the Parliament of Brittany in July 1629 so that Joachim I could retire. He had retired once before in 1618 when Descartes's brother Pierre took over his first counselorship. This time he was retiring for good. But he was not yet content.

Joachim II told this barbed story long after Descartes had died. His father said: "Of all my children, I am dissatisfied with only one. How could I have brought into the world a son so ridiculous as to bind himself in calfskin!" Descartes's father knew you could not make any money writing books. This is in opposition to the sweet family story told by Descartes's niece Catherine — that when René was a little boy, his father referred to him as "my little philosopher" because he was so bright and inquisitive. It is doubtful that either story is true.

Joachim Descartes had two of his three sons firmly established in the courts. On 21 April 1613, his daughter Jeanne (René's sister) married Pierre Rogier, Seigneur de Crévis. His daughter Anne (René's half sister) married Louis d'Avaugour de Kergrois in July 1628. That was all his children except for that good-for-nothing René, living a life of leisure on family money in Paris. He had no post and he had no wife. Descartes was thirty-two years old in 1628. It was time to get that account settled.

Descartes took off. The last recorded time he had seen his father was on 22 January 1628 at the christening of his brother Pierre's son in Brittany. Maybe he saw his father again later in the year. Maybe Joachim made a trip to Paris to knock some sense into the prevaricating wastrel. The known facts are these. Descartes did go to the United Provinces in December 1628 or January 1629, and he did not return to France again until 1644. His father died in 1640. Descartes did not see his father for the last twelve years of the old man's life.

Descartes said he needed to get away to think. He had in hand a draft of his *Rules for the Direction of the Mind*, he had projected works on geometry and mechanics, and he wanted to work on a metaphysics that was published in part in his *Discourse on Method* in 1637 and fully in his *Meditations on First Philosophy* in 1641. The hullabaloo and social obligations with friends and relatives in Paris took all his time. And they *would* hassle him to get married and to buy a post. There were too many family connections in Rennes, Châtellerault, and Poitou. Even so, as the French have said ever since, *surely* he could have found a haven in France.

Some say Descartes was worried because he intended to attack Scholastic philosophy and Aristotelianism. There was that court order of 1624 not to attack Aristotle on pain of death. But Gassendi had published a massive attack on Aristotle in 1623, *Paradoxical Exercises in Opposition to Aristotle*. And Mersenne's *Truth of the Sciences Against Skeptics or Pyrhonnians* published in 1625 was universally mechanistic and anti-Aristotelian. Nobody touched a hair of their heads. Ah, but Gassendi and Mersenne were priests, protected by their orders. Descartes was a layman. Still, the greatly extended Ferrand-Brochard-Descartes family consisted of many respectable bureaucratic servants of the king. Descartes might have had no trouble. The pantheist Lucillio Vanini, however, was burned in Toulouse in 1619, and the deist Jean Fontanier was burned in Paris in 1621. For being atheists.

There is, however, another context, larger and more universal than those of Descartes's personal ambitions, family pressure, and School philosophy — that of politics. French Catholic scholars never present Descartes's move to the United Provinces in this larger context, but over time and in the light of history, consider how it looks.

In 1628 with the defeat of La Rochelle, the last resistance of the Protestants in France was crushed. The agreement of the Edict of Nantes that Protestants could have fortified cities was reversed. There was no longer a Protestant party in France, no more Protestant armies, no more internal religious wars. Thousands of Protestants moved to the United Provinces. In the very liberal court of Prince Frederick-Henry in The Hague were, according to Cohen, these exiles from France: "the prince de Bouillon, Frédéric de la Tour and his younger brother Turenne, the Maréchal de Chastillon, the marquis d'Hauterive, Alphonse de Pollot [later Descartes's friend] and the faithful Squire Deschamps, without mentioning lords of lesser importance" (C 425).

In France, the Protestant leaders Bouillon and Rohan were condemned. Richelieu was subduing not just the Protestants but also the entire noble class. The absolute state was being formed in opposition to the old Catholic hierarchy. On the side of the pope, Spain, and the Inquisition were Cardinal Bérulle, the Catholic League, and the noble class trying to maintain the power of the Old Regime. There was a place in all this turmoil for René Descartes, whether as a bureaucrat like his father and brothers, as a soldier for the king, or even as a natural scientist working as a military engineer in ordinance as Galileo did in Italy.

But Descartes ran out on it all. His was not just a flight from family and social responsibility. His move to the United Provinces — forever — was a revolutionary political act. He abandoned France almost at the precise moment that France began to be the first modern state. Descartes could have been in on the beginning of the reign of the Sun King, Louis XIV. He could have been a highly positioned courtier. For whatever reason, he chose not to.

I don't know that Descartes himself saw it that way, and certainly most French Cartesian scholars do not, but it is plain as can be that Descartes's move to the United Provinces at the end of 1628 was an act of solidarity with republican French Protestantism against royalist Catholic totalitarian oppression, and of liberal Christianity against the Spanish Inquisition. He was not opposed to the Catholic religion; he was opposed to the Catholic state; he was afraid of the oppressive nature and acts of the Catholicism that was the state religion of France.

Baillet and Adam point often to Descartes's clarity and use of reason to show that he was a true Frenchman. Well, Descartes was at least a modern Frenchman, to the core. He chose liberty, even though it meant leaving France. He took the money the family had destined for his buying into France and he ran. Don't tell *anyone* my address.

VII   ⚔   DESCARTES'S DOG

I go almost every day to the slaughterhouse.

Now we come to a true sea change. In his 1619 notebooks, Descartes wrote the following: "Like actors who, to play their parts, put on masks to hide their blushing faces, at this moment when I enter upon the scene in a world where until now I have been a spectator, I walk on masked." You remember that Descartes also took the motto: Who lives well hidden, lives well. And we have seen that large portions of Descartes's life during the ten years between 1619 and 1629 if not well hidden, at least are now largely unknown. But when he moved to the United Provinces, Descartes took off the mask. He still has his secrets, and he often tells Mersenne not to reveal his address. But he wrote several letters every week — some of them very long — so we know mostly where he was and what he was doing from early 1629 until his death in 1650. And if our knowledge of his personal contacts before 1629 is often a matter of inference, now we are introduced to a cast of hundreds. (Letters from Descartes to Mersenne for the first nine months of 1631, however, are missing. The explanation for this is that after Descartes's death, Chanut shipped his letters to Paris. The boat sank in the Seine and all Descartes's papers were underwater for three days. During the process of their drying — servants pinned the papers up on clotheslines — most of the letters for that period were apparently lost.)

Let's pick Descartes up in Dordrecht on 1 February 1629, on which day Beeckman wrote in his journal about Descartes's new proof of a mathematical problem. "Our Gallic Philosopher" is also mentioned in a letter Henry Reneri wrote from Amsterdam on 28 March 1629. Then Descartes went to Franeker. He registered at the university on 26 April 1629 as "René Des Cartes, French philosopher." The one professor there that we know he had something to do with is Adrien Metius, author of *Practical Arithmetic and Geometry*. His brother Jacques Metius is one of several claimants to the invention of the telescope in 1608 (although telescopes were known before that).

Also in Franeker, Descartes met Anna Maria van Schurman, the brilliant female phenomenon, aged twenty-two, her brother Jean Godschalk who was none too bright, and her widowed mother who was very enterprising in promoting her daughter.

That spring, Descartes was, so he says in his autobiography, working on a little book on metaphysics. But he seems to have been desperate for company by 18 June 1629, when he wrote to the lens grinder and maker of optical and scientific instruments and machines, Jean Ferrier, in Paris. Descartes said he had been learning a lot of new things about lenses, and he invited Ferrier to come to Franeker to live and work with him. Descartes had designed a machine to cut hyperbolic lenses. He thought his machine could cut one in fifteen minutes. Everyone else worked with spherical lenses, but Descartes figured out that a hyperbolic lens would focus more sharply. Descartes's letter of 18 June 1629 is much quoted to show how well Descartes treated subordinates.

"If I had only thought of it when I was in Paris," Descartes says to Ferrier, "I would have tried to bring you along with me." So Ferrier should come now. They needed to work on the machine together, Descartes the theoretician, Ferrier the craftsman, because a thousand little problems that could be solved with a word or two face to face could never be resolved by letters. "In nothing," Descartes says, "will you be worse off than I am. We will live as brothers." He said he would pay all expenses and send Ferrier back to Paris whenever he wanted to go. Then he gave detailed instructions on how to get to Dordrecht, but he sent no money on what Ferrier must have seen as a most peculiar excuse, that if he did, people would know his address. (I have tried to figure out what that means. Descartes could have sent Ferrier a letter of credit that could be redeemed in Paris, but maybe it would have to be signed by someone in Franeker, which would give him away. He apparently had not yet arranged for anyone to handle his finances in Paris, or he could have told Ferrier to go to him.)

Ferrier should bring his own tools, and a camp bed for Descartes "because the beds here are very uncomfortable and have no mattresses." But Ferrier was to come even if he could bring nothing. When he reached Dordrecht, Beeckman would give him money and instructions on how to find Descartes. Twice in the letter, Descartes says that if Ferrier wants to do something that surpasses anything anyone else has done, he should start right out. And by the way, he should not tell Mydorge about this. Descartes and Mydorge had worked together with Ferrier in 1627–1628 on an attempt to grind a hyperbolic lens, which failed. Descartes did not want Mydorge to scoop him now.

I particularly like the part about Descartes offering to live together with Ferrier as brothers. You know who would be the cadet.

In another long letter of 8 October 1629, Descartes wrote from Amsterdam to Ferrier describing the lens-grinding machine. He asks Ferrier to write back with a detailed description of it, so Descartes could see if Ferrier understood. On 26 October 1629, Ferrier replied in great and elegant detail, suggesting both improvements and problems. Descartes responded on 13 November 1629 with an even longer letter full of diagrams. He concludes that if Ferrier resolves to spend a lot of time on this machine, "I dare hope that we will see, by your means, whether there are animals on the moon."

But Ferrier had no intention of going to the United Provinces. He was employed by Louis XIII's brother Gaston to make some instruments, and he had applied for one of the apartments in the Louvre that were reserved for skilled craftsmen. Several people tried to help him get it, although it is unknown if he ever did. Mydorge then told Ferrier to his face that he was an inferior craftsman. The evidence is that he was a good craftsman if kept at work continually under the thumb of someone like Descartes, but on his own he had difficulty finishing anything.

Ferrier vacillated, did not write for six or seven months after the initial exchange but then, according to Mersenne, finally decided that he did want to go work with Descartes after all. But by then Descartes was totally turned off. The pompous, self-righteous tone of his letter setting Ferrier straight is a feature of Descartes's personality that Baillet always softens by putting the other guy in the wrong. It feeds the nastiness of Descartes's letters breaking with Beeckman, it poisons his relations with his disciple Henry Regius, and it gets him in more trouble than was necessary with Gisbert Voetius and other Protestant ministers who later oppose Cartesianism.

In a letter of 2 December 1630, Descartes replied to a letter from Ferrier that we don't have, in which Ferrier complains about wasting time working on Descartes's invention. Descartes says that he had warned Ferrier it would be difficult and continues, "I told you expressly, so that if you lost time as you have, you would not attribute the fault to me or complain to me." He then reminds Ferrier that he had invited him to come work with him, all expenses paid. He now adds — the man knows how to twist a knife — that he had intended for Ferrier to get all the profits if the machine worked.

Descartes did try to help Ferrier get other commissions, however, both to keep Ferrier from thinking that Descartes might come back to Paris and to keep him from changing his mind and coming to the United Provinces, which Descartes did not now want. Descartes goes on about how Ferrier deceives himself, etc., and so on. That is a big change from what Descartes wrote to Mersenne in a letter dated 18 March 1630, in which he says that in preparation for Ferrier's coming to make lenses with him, he had hired a boy who could cook the French way and that he was prepared to lease rooms for them to live together for three years.

Ferrier tried to get back into Descartes's good graces by conveying to him an invitation from M. de Marcheville to accompany him to Constantinople. Descartes says to Mersenne on 4 November 1630 that he is being mocked, that he does not know de Marcheville, and furthermore if it should chance to be true, he should be told to invite Gassendi. Descartes then relents and says to tell de Marcheuille that four or five years ago he would have thought it one of the best things that could have happened to him, but not now. Mersenne can tell people now that Descartes does not have to travel to seek his fortune.

Descartes's affair with Ferrier is a kind of repeat of Descartes's encounter with Beeckman. There Descartes courted the older man, saw himself rebuffed when Beeckman went off to get married, and eventually lashed out viciously at the friend he had once loved. Now Descartes was the mentor who courted the younger man by asking Ferrier to come live with him like a brother. And Ferrier said no. So much for him, the ingrate.

What can be said is that Descartes always did, eventually, calm down. He made up with Beeckman within a year after the break, and he again praised Ferrier's craftsmanship. After disowning his disciple Regius, he later said Regius had actually done good work. And concerning his archenemy Voetius, he said he would accept even his friendship if it were seriously offered, although considering how they truly despised each other, that offer may have been made sarcastically in the knowledge that there wasn't a whisper of a chance that Voetius would ever offer to make up. As for Ferrier, by 1638 Descartes was talking of grinding hyperbolic lenses again and said to Ferrier, "If anyone in the world can succeed, it's you!"

Long after, in 1669, the British Royal Society commissioned Robert Hooke to make Descartes's machine for grinding non-spherical lenses. Hooke said beforehand that it wouldn't work, and it didn't. Whether or not he gave it a fair test is hard to say. And he did not have Descartes with him to solve all the little problems that would come up in its construction. Actually, Huygens told Descartes on 5 December 1635 that some lens grinders in Amsterdam who had seen the design of the machine said that if it worked, they would eat glass. Descartes obviously had doubts himself, because in letters of

25 January and 1 March 1638 to Mersenne, he says he does not want to take up an offer from Richelieu to have the machine made for fear that if it failed it would reflect on his philosophy.

By October 1629, Descartes had moved from Franeker to Amsterdam, which was his primary place of residence until 1635. He lived first on Kalverstraat, then on Dam, and finally on Westerkirkstraat. He spent time in Leiden where he registered in the university as a mathematician on 27 June 1630, and there he probably sat in on the mathematics course of Jacob Golius. He also met there the astronomer Martin Hortensius and a philosopher Henry Reneri, who became a close personal friend and supporter, Descartes's first university professor disciple. What was big at the University of Leiden was the teaching of Oriental languages — Arabic, Persian, Turkish — for Calvinist missionaries going to the Levant. They got medical degrees to give them entry, and then they preached Christianity. Descartes also spent many months in 1632 and 1633 in Deventer where Reneri had been appointed to the École Illustre. When Reneri was on his deathbed in March 1639, Descartes rushed to be with him and lamented that he was too late.

During his time in the United Provinces, most of Descartes's relations with Frenchmen were necessarily epistolary, but he seems to have known personally everybody who was anybody in the United Provinces. First and foremost is a man he had met in 1630, who became his best friend in the United Provinces, Constantijn Huygens, the first secretary and advisor to three successive stadhouders (commanders in chief) of the United Provinces, the Nassau princes of Orange, Maurice, Frederick-Henry, and Henry III (as his father had been to their predecessors). Huygens was the same age as Descartes, but he lived until 1687, dying at the age of ninety-one (he had once asked Descartes how to live to be a hundred). Huygens became Descartes's greatest promoter and protector in the United Provinces. He was elegant, handsome, brilliant, witty, good-humored, rich, and powerful. Tall, with a striking, narrow face and pointed beard, he wrote poetry, he knew painting, mathematics, and music. He was a friend and patron of Rembrandt. In 1645, Corneille dedicated his play *The Liar* to him. Huygens read, understood, and defended Descartes's philosophy. With friends like Huygens, Descartes did not need to worry excessively about enemies. At the same time, Descartes met Huygens's brother-in-law, David Le Leu de Wilhelm, who soon became his investment banker.

Descartes was very content with himself during these years. In a letter to Mersenne of 15 April 1630, he said about his future:

> *I fear reputation more than I desire it, figuring that it would always diminish in some way the liberty and leisure of those who acquire it. This liberty and leisure are two things I possess so perfectly, and that I value so highly, that no monarch in the world is rich enough to buy them from me.*

Keep this passage in mind for consideration later when Queen Christina enters the scene.

He had seen Paris. He lived in that capital city for at least three years but did not like it. In a letter to Mersenne of 4 November 1630, Descartes says, "Nothing is more contrary to my purpose than the atmosphere of Paris because of an infinity of divertissements that are inevitable there. While I can live my own way, I will always dwell in the country in some land where I can be importuned by my visits from my neighbors no more than I am here in a corner of North Holland." To Chanut in May 1648 Descartes writes that in Paris, the atmosphere, the ambiance repels him. "That air makes me have chimerical rather than philosophical thoughts," he says. "I see so many people in Paris who are deceived in their opinions and calculations that I think it must be a universal sickness. The innocence of the desert where I live is much more pleasing to me than Paris."

In a letter to his old friend, the poet Guez de Balzac on 15 April 1631, Descartes says that in the two years he has been away from Paris, he has not been tempted once to return. And in this letter he raves about his life in the country:

I sleep here ten hours every night with not a care to awaken me. After my sleeping mind has promenaded for a long time in the groves, gardens, and enchanted palaces where I enjoy all the pleasures imagined in fables, I mix insensibly my daydreams with those of the night. And when I perceive that I am awake, my contentment only becomes more complete, and my senses participate in those dreams, because I am not so severe as to refuse anything that a philosopher could permit to them without offending his conscience.

Descartes did live most of the rest of his life in the country. Less than a month later, however, he was living in Amsterdam, the world's most cosmopolitan city with more than 125,000 inhabitants, a quarter of them foreigners like Descartes, and he wrote on 5 May 1631 again to Balzac, giving voice to the first and still the greatest expression of the liberation afforded to the individual by living anonymously in a great city. I have already quoted part of it, but here is the full passage:

In this great city [Amsterdam] where I am now, there is no other man except me who is not engaged in commerce. And each is so concerned about his own profit that I could live here all my life without ever being seen by anyone. I walk every day among the confusion of a great people with as much liberty and repose as you enjoy in your country lanes, and I pay no more attention to the people I see than I would the trees in your forests or the animals that dwell there. Even the noise of their activities interrupts my reveries no more than would that of a babbling brook. And when I sometimes reflect on their activities, it gives me the same pleasure that you would have in seeing the peasants who cultivate your fields, because I see that all their work serves to embellish the place where I live so that I will lack in nothing. As you take pleasure in seeing the growth of your fruits and vines, and in enjoying such abundance, think how I feel the same when I see coming into the port the ships

that bring here abundantly all the products of the Indies and
everything that is rare in Europe.

Then comes Descartes's ultimate statement concerning the city,
politics, order, the state, and civilization.

What other place could one choose in the entire world where
all the commodities of life and all the curiosities that one could
wish are so easy to find as here? What other land where one
can enjoy a liberty so entire, where one can sleep with less
inquietude, where there are always armies afoot expressly to
guard you, where poisonings, treason, calumnies are less
known, and where the innocence of former times remains?

In the anonymity of the city, the individual is free to think and do as
he will, with no one monitoring or controlling him. But even more,
Descartes enjoyed the disengagement of the expatriate. In the
United Provinces, the culture, the politics, the religion, the language
— none of these were his. He had no stake in them at all, so he could
tune out totally, enjoy the scenery, and think his own thoughts. In a
letter of June 1648, when Descartes was fifty-two years old, he told
Princess Elisabeth that he had one foot in one land, the other in
another, and that this condition made him very happy because it
made him free.

Descartes certainly toadies up to the great literary stylist Guez
de Balzac. Or perhaps he is trying to top him. None of Descartes's
other letters are so lyrical. Balzac set him straight. He answered
Descartes's flowery letter in ordinary French. Balzac also courted
Descartes, however, by including three letters to Descartes in his
collected edition. But there is another letter of Balzac's, to Hydaspe
on 1 January 1624, that suggests something else. Balzac is commenting on boring talkers and says, "But they really make me die of
boredom when they come freshly from Holland where they have
begun to study mathematics."

If Ferrier bombed out, Descartes did get a work companion, the engineer Étienne de Villebressieu. In May 1631, they traveled to Denmark together to look at hydraulic works, but Descartes got sick and returned before Villebressieu did. He told Villebressieu he would be in their lodgings in the Old Prince. In 1631, they lived together in Amsterdam, and perhaps in Paris in 1627–1628, but did not see much of each other after 1634.

There are many theories about why Descartes left Paris. I like Leibniz's wisecrack that "Descartes left Paris so he wouldn't run into Roberval anymore" (Frédérix, p. 100). Roberval was always contesting Descartes's mathematical proofs. Paris was not a large place. Perhaps Descartes was like my father-in-law, who, in a small town of 1,200 people in Iowa, said one day to another resident, "I wish you'd quit stopping and talking to me in the street. People will begin to get the idea that we're friends." There were a lot of people Descartes apparently did not want to run into on the street.

All very well, but the mystery remains as to why Descartes was a virtual fanatic about concealing his address in the United Provinces. My guess is that he was hiding from Bérulle and the fanatic Catholics. Or perhaps from his father and older brother. He had sold the farm, taken the money, and run. But they were not going to put out a warrant for his arrest even if he stayed in France. They could visit him in France, however, or sick onto him old friends such as Vasseur d'Étoiles to bark at his heels. They were not likely to follow him to the United Provinces, even if they knew his address. And letters could not harm him.

Whatever it was that drove Descartes into hiding, he soon got over it. Within three or four years, he was one of the most visible and well-connected philosophers in the United Provinces. Later when he made three visits to France, and when he went to Sweden, his friends in Amsterdam and The Hague constituted a virtual Chamber of Commerce Boosters' Club in their attempts to keep him in the United Provinces.

Scholars wonder why Descartes moved around so much in the United Provinces. But his moves are perfectly reasonable. He went to be near friends, scholars, publishers, universities — and some moves obviously were made to avoid outbreaks of the plague in Leiden and elsewhere. The plague in Leiden from 23 June through 31 December 1635 killed 14,582 people — 1,500 in one week. There is also the fact that by these moves, Descartes got to know — besides mathematicians, scientists, and professors — many important people in local and provincial governments.

Descartes had a plan. He was a man of immense self-regard and of immeasurable ambition. By 1628, he was already talking of replacing Aristotelian philosophy and science with his own. To do this, he would have to convince the Catholic Church hierarchy to abandon the Scholastic philosophy and textbooks that had been used for centuries, to replace them with Cartesian philosophy and a textbook he intended to write. Even given that there was a lot of sentiment for a new observational and experimental natural science promoted by such philosophers as Bacon and Gassendi in opposition to Aristotle, Descartes's ambition was still breathtaking. It could be viewed, and doubtless was viewed by many, as the ravings of a lunatic. This lay philosopher said he was going to convince the Jesuits to use his textbook rather than expositions of Saint Thomas Aquinas and Aristotle. The man was mad.

Remember, we are talking about someone who has a reputation as a geometer but has never published anything, let alone anything in philosophy or science. He has an idea about unifying the sciences with a method based on mathematics and has written a draft of some rules for the direction of the mind. And he has done some theoretical work on optics. That this man would set out for the United Provinces to undertake from there a campaign to replace the teaching of Aristotle with his own philosophy is wild.

But Descartes had to start his revolution somewhere. Compared to the old established French universities, Dutch universities were brand new. Leiden was founded in 1575, Franeker in 1585, Groningen in 1615, and Utrecht in 1636. Descartes remarked that the University of Utrecht was not yet corrupted. And in fact, by the mid-1630s, there were Cartesians teaching in three of those universities. If Descartes did not move to the United Provinces because he thought it would be easier to crack the Dutch universities than the French ones, he realized this soon after arrival. The more important people he knew, the more likely was his philosophy to be accepted.

If Descartes worked on metaphysics during his first nine months in the United Provinces, a period for which we have only his letter of 18 June 1629 to Ferrier, he thereafter concentrated on dioptrics, which has to do with the reflection and refraction of light. Then the report of the four false suns observed in Rome on 10 March 1629 led him to an explanation of this phenomenon and to work on his *Meteorology* published in 1637.

Dioptrics and mathematics aside, Descartes had a passion in the early 1630s for anatomy. He dissected animals with Fortunatus Vopsicus Plempius (who moved to the University of Louvain in 1633) and he lived on Kalverstraat — cow street — a street of butchers. "There was one winter in Amsterdam," he said, "when I went almost every day to the house of a butcher to see him kill the animals and to have carried to my lodgings the parts that I wanted to anatomize more at my leisure." Anatomy was a hot topic at the time. You can see that in Rembrandt's *The Anatomy Lesson of Dr. Tulp*, showing a human cadaver being dissected in an amphitheater, painted in Amsterdam in 1632.

In 1632, Descartes gave Golius some of the manuscript of his *Dioptrics* to check over. And he remarked that he had spent five or six weeks solving the ancient mathematical problem of Pappus.

Descartes then worked full blast on what he meant to be his major work, *The World, or a Treatise on Light*. As he told Mersenne, his metaphysics contained the solid foundation that assured the certainty of his physics. Once God's existence is proved and the world is shown to consist only of matter in motion following natural laws guaranteed by God, then all God needed to do to get the world going was give it a push. Descartes said that then the stars and planets, and the earth and all the things in it, would form by bodies joining and parting as they swirled around one another. To avoid objections that this is not the way it is told in Genesis, he called his story a fable. But a very useful fable, because once we know how matter moves in accordance with eternal laws of nature, we can control these movements for the good of humankind.

Descartes moved from celestial bodies to atmospheric phenomena such as rainbows to explanations of living bodies. The culmination of the fable was to be the description of how a human body could be formed mechanistically. Then all that body would need to be a man would be its union with a human soul. Of course Descartes assumes that every human being constitutes such a union. But other animals are machines, automatons that move only by stimulus and response and have no thoughts or feelings, no sense of pleasure or of pain. No souls.

You have to take these convictions seriously, even though Descartes himself had a dog named Monsieur Grat (Mister Scratch) that sounds charming. But Descartes's attachment to Monsieur Grat could not have been great, for he sent the dog to Paris to Claude Picot in February 1648, along with a bitch of the same species, to give the breed a start in France. One wonders what kind of dog it was. The standard Dutch country dog today stands eighteen inches high, has short black fur with some white spots, and is a dog for bringing in the cows. Exactly the same sort of dog is shown in paintings made by Rembrandt in Descartes's day. Monsieur Grat and mate must have been cow dogs. Now even if Descartes was attached to Monsieur Grat, he is also the man who practiced vivisection on rabbits and dogs. Here, from Descartes's *The Description of the Human Body*:

> *If you cut off the end of the heart of a living dog, and through the incision put your finger into one of the concavities, you will clearly feel that every time the heart shortens, it presses your finger, and it stops pressing it every time it lengthens. (AT XI 241–242)*

Maybe the best thing that ever happened to Monsieur Grat is that Descartes sent him off to France.

Man's best friend. Descartes speaks of dogs two other times.

Once in his *Passions of the Soul* to point out that if hunting dogs can be trained not to fear gunshots and to freeze and point rather than chase after birds, then so can human beings. Then on 18 November 1630 in the first known statement of the phenomenon of the conditioned reflex, he says to Mersenne that after you whip a dog six or eight times to the sound of a violin, the sound of the violin alone will make the dog whimper and tremble with fear. Descartes did hunt birds with his friend van Zurk. One can presume that he also experimented with the violin trick.

By the middle of 1633, Descartes had virtually completed his book on natural philosophy, *The World*. He promised Mersenne on 22 July 1633 that he would send it by the end of the year. But then a bombshell dropped. The very next day he learned that Galileo's *Dialogue on the Two Chief World Systems* published in 1632 had been condemned in the court of Pope Urban XIII in Rome for containing the thesis that the earth moves around the sun. On 22 June 1633, Galileo abjured his claims and was condemned to house arrest for the remainder of his life. Just as soon as Descartes heard the news in November 1633, he wrote to Mersenne in panic and despair:

> *This has so astonished me that I am quasi-resolved to burn all my papers, or at least to show them to no one. Because I can't imagine that Galileo who is Italian and very well received by the pope, or so I hear, could have been taken before a criminal court for anything other than that he had without doubt wanted to establish the movement of the earth, which I know was awhile back censored by some Cardinals. But I thought it was accepted even in Rome if one didn't teach it publicly. And I confess that if it is false, so are all the foundations of my philosophy, because it obviously follows from them.*

Descartes knows Mersenne will try to get him to publish anyway, so he goes on to say: "I would not for anything in the world publish a discourse that contained a single word disapproved of by the church."

Nevertheless, still protesting, but with hopes, he wrote to Mersenne in February 1634:

The knowledge that I have of your virtue makes me hope that you would only have a better opinion of me to see that I have determined to suppress entirely the treatise I have written and lose nearly all my work of four years in order to render complete obedience to the church in that it has forbidden the opinion that the earth moves. However, because I have not yet seen that the pope or the Council have ratified this prohibition set only by the Congregation of Cardinals established to censor books, I would like to know what is thought of it now in France and if the Cardinals' authority has been sufficient to make it an article of faith.

Still hoping six years later, in December 1640, Descartes wrote to Mersenne:

If you write to Cardinal Bagni's doctor [Gabriel Naudé], I would appreciate it if you would tell him that nothing keeps me from publishing my philosophy except the prohibition against the movement of the earth, which I do not know how to separate from my philosophy, because all my physics depends on it. But also that perhaps I will soon be constrained to publish it because of the calumnies of several people who, because they do not understand my principles, want to persuade everyone that I have opinions greatly removed from the truth. And would you please ask him to sound out the Cardinal on this subject, because being very much his servant, I would be very unhappy to displease him, and being very zealous for the Catholic religion, I revere generally all its heads. I do not add that I do not want to put myself in hazard of the censure, because believing very firmly in the infallibility of the church, and also having no doubts of my proofs, I have no fear that one truth contradicts another.

Cardinal Bagni never expressed an opinion.

As for publishing that the earth moves around the sun, Descartes was perfectly safe from the Inquisition in the United Provinces, and would have been, for that matter, even if he had been living in France. Both Mersenne and Gassendi, among others, published their belief in the heliocentric system after Galileo's condemnation. In 1634, Mersenne even published Galileo's *Mechanics* and also a résumé of his *Dialogue*. And despite Descartes's pleas and vows of obeisance to the church, he kept looking for a way around the prohibition. He never did, however, publish *The World*. Instead, he mined it for his *Dioptrics* and *Meteorology*, published in 1637, his *Principles* of 1644, and for his *Treatise on Man* not published until after his death.

Given that he was planning for his *The World* to replace Aristotelian natural science textbooks in the Catholic schools, Descartes's panic and concern not to cross the church is perfectly understandable. A condemned book was certainly not going to get adopted as a textbook in the Jesuit colleges.

Immediately, however, Descartes seems to have given up. "I never fancied myself as a maker of books, anyway," he writes to Mersenne in November 1633. The man was at loose ends.

At the end of March 1634 Descartes was thirty-eight years old. There is nothing in the records to indicate that he had any romantic relations with women at all up to that time other than the story told by Madame Rosay about his disarming a rival for her affections. Then on 15 October 1634, he recorded on the flyleaf of a book that on that Sunday, in a house still standing on Westerkerkstraat in Amsterdam, his daughter Francine was conceived with Helena Jans. Baillet remarks in apology that it is hard for someone as interested in anatomy as Descartes was to avoid such temptations. Yes! I picture Helena as the prettiest, rosiest-cheeked, blondest, and bounciest Dutch maiden that ever milked a cow.

VIII · FRANCINE DESCARTES

I am not one of those philosophers
who think a man should not cry.

IN THE BAPTISMAL REGISTER of the Reformed Church in
Deventer for 7 August 1635, the following is recorded:

Vader Rener Jochems	*Father René son of Joachim*
Moeder Helena Jans	*Mother Helena daughter of Jans*
Kint Fransintge	*Child Francine*

Yes, I went to see it, although I was a bit embarrassed. It took the
young man in charge half an hour to find it. Other scholars had
already combed the Deventer Archives, and he complained that it
had been authenticated, transcribed, and printed, so why did I want
to see the original? I don't know. It's the sort of thing biographers do.
There is also a baptismal record of a Helena Jansen for 17 April 1614.
If this is Descartes's Helena, then she was twenty-one years old when
Francine was born. Descartes was thirty-nine.

The marriage records for part of the period during which Descartes and Helena might have gotten married are missing. But it is
most unlikely that they did. Descartes would have had to convert to
Calvinism for that, and had he done so, the preachers would have
hooted the news to high heaven. They didn't, so Descartes and
Helena were not married.

Helena Jans was the mother of René Descartes's child. Before I
make some guesses about her, let me tell you about what Descartes
looked like and what kind of man he was in his prime.

According to Baillet, who talked to people who had known Descartes personally, "our philosopher" was a thin man, slight of build, with a large head.

I have, in fact, held the purported skull of Descartes in my hands in the basement of the Musée de l'Homme in Paris. It was sent from Sweden to Paris in 1821, after having presumably been in private hands from not long after Descartes's death in 1650. You can be assured that the story of how Descartes's purported skull got from a Stockholm grave to a museum basement in Paris is not ironclad. But that's too long after his death for me to go into here.

It is a very small skull, with no brow ridges and none of the rugosities usually associated with males. What is more, the sutures are not fully closed. "It looks like the skull of an adolescent girl," Pat said. Pat is a member of the National Academy of Sciences, but she is an archeologist, not a physical anthropologist, so she took the problem to one of her colleagues who is. Erik Trinkaus is also a member of the National Academy of Sciences, but more important, he is one of the world's foremost authorities on Neanderthals. And Descartes's purported skull is housed in the Musée de l'Homme in the same cabinet with the Neanderthal skulls. So Erik looked at the skull one day and reports that there is an 80 percent chance that the skull is male but only a 20 percent chance that it is of someone over forty years old. Descartes was nearly fifty-four when he died.

The skull is at the low end of the size scale for humans. But Baillet said Descartes had a large head? Well, he also said Descartes was below average height. One impressive thing is that although the teeth are missing, the sockets show that they were in excellent condition. And Descartes himself said that he had good teeth. There is an easy way to find out if the skull is really Descartes's. Descendants of the Descartes family live in France today, and we could compare their DNA with DNA from the skull. This would be definitive. I've suggested that the test be made, and maybe it will be someday.

The average height of a Frenchman during the first half of the seventeenth century was either five foot five or five foot three (sources differ). If that seems awfully short to you, go look at seventeenth-century suits of armor in a museum and be astonished. They

WESTERMARKT 6 IN AMSTERDAM
WHERE FRANCINE DESCARTES WAS CONCEIVED
Photograph by Raymond Lécuyer and Paul-Émile Cadhilac

look as though they were made for children. At noticeably less than average, Descartes was perhaps five foot one or two. He might have been significantly less than that, for Baillet stresses that despite his smallness, Descartes's body was well proportioned. In other words, despite his big head, he was not a dwarf.

When Descartes was young, he carried a sword and wore a feathered hat as gentlemen did, but in his forties he changed them for a beaver hat and a cloak. He had a soft voice and good eyesight. He always wore silk hose and pulled wool ones over them whenever he went out. It was wet and cold in Holland.

When he went out, it was among the Dutch. Dutchmen were big even in the seventeenth century. All that milk and honey, and butter, eggs, and beer. So were the Swedes, those Nordic supermen. Descartes's small size might have contributed somewhat both to his Dutch friends' concern to keep and protect him, and to his Dutch enemies' seeing him as a smart aleck. Descartes was always sure of himself, and he does seem seldom to have refrained from speaking his critical mind. On the other hand, being as small as a boy must also have been to his advantage when gambling with big macho soldiers.

Baillet says that Descartes's hair was black, going gray in his early forties. His forehead and lower lip protruded slightly. His eyes were black, and he had a large nose whose length, Baillet specifies, was proportionate to its size. A small growth on the fold of his right cheek scabbed off now and then but always grew back. He had a thin mustache down past the ends of his mouth, and a small pointed beard in the space below his lower lip and above his chin. This is in the style of Louis XIII, and it is indicative of the extent of French culture that Descartes's rich and powerful Dutch friend Constantijn Huygens wore his mustache and beard in the same way. So did Descartes's friend the poet Guez de Balzac.

Baillet's description of Descartes sounds very much like the Frans Hals portrait of Descartes, which would seem also to be the source of his further comments that Descartes preferred black cloth and that his hair always hung down over his forehead. (And nobody has black eyes except in paintings.) The very serious problem that now arises is that this familiar, virtually iconic portrait is neither by Frans Hals nor is it of Descartes. There are as many as a dozen copies of this portrait. The one that was exhibited for so many years in the Louvre in Paris has been taken down because of its double inauthenticity. I have tried to find out when this painting was first claimed to be a portrait of Descartes by Frans Hals but have had no luck.

There are only two portraits that we know certainly to be of Descartes — a drawing by Frans Schooten II and a painting by Jan-Baptist Weenix. Schooten drew his portrait to include with the 1644 Latin translation of Descartes's *Geometry*. It shows a thinner man than does the fake Hals portrait. Descartes's friends did not like it, but all Descartes said about it was that the beard and clothes were not right. He also asked that it not be printed, which it was not, until the second edition of 1659 after his death. The so-called Frans Hals portrait could conceivably be someone's heroic conception of how an older Descartes would have looked based on the Schooten drawing. At least the clothes and the beard are the same.

The portrait by Weenix was painted sometime after 1647. A drawing by Jan Lievens was made about the same time that is surely of Descartes, although this is not absolutely authenticated. The Weenix portrait shows that Descartes looked nothing at all like the man of approximately the same age in the so-called Frans Hals portrait. The "Hals Descartes" has firm facial features and a heroic mien. In the Weenix and Lievens portraits, Descartes has bags under his eyes, his face is puffy, and his mouth and chin are weak. The man in the fake Hals is big and tall, but Weenix and Lievens show that Descartes was a small chubby man with short arms and a double chin. And in the Weenix portrait, Descartes looks like a peasant. Constantijn Huygens was a friend and patron of Lievens and probably commissioned Descartes's portrait. Lievens painted a magnificent portrait of Huygens.

In August 1649, just before Descartes left for Sweden, his friend Bloemaert commissioned a portrait of him. My guess is that Cartesian scholars say Bloemaert commissioned a portrait by Frans Hals simply because Hals is the most famous painter of the day. I think that Bloemaert would have fancied the Weenix portrait in which Descartes is holding an open book across two pages of which in large letters is written "The World Is a Fable." This refers to Descartes's description of how the world could have evolved merely from matter in motion, which story, because it goes against the creation story in the Bible, he labeled a fable.

Of purportedly authentic portraits of Descartes, there is finally the one painted after his death by David Beck in Stockholm on commission from Queen Christina. In this painting, Descartes's face is slacker and fuller than the bogus Hals portrait from which it looks copied.

The fanciful eighteenth-century portrait engraved by C. Hellemans of Descartes with his foot on the works of Aristotle has the torso lengthened out of proportion but otherwise definitely shows a man of diminutive stature, a virtual midget stomping Aristotle. Another piece of evidence that Descartes was known to be a noticeably small man is the book *New Memoirs for the History of Cartesianism* published by Pierre-Daniel Huet in 1692. This is a satire in which Huet claims that Descartes is not dead, that he went to Lapland where he was accepted immediately as a Lap because of his diminutive stature and became a god among them.

One might infer that Descartes was small from his work on the art of fencing of which Baillet had the manuscript. Baillet says that Descartes describes moves to make when one is far out, so as to get in close to one's opponent, and then how infallibly to overcome one's opponent when one is in close. It would behoove a small, short-armed man always to be in close, to avoid being outreached at a distance. But of course if the distance is far enough, you are out of danger. You don't have to fight. This removal at a distance is a constant motif in Descartes's life. He would live in a desert.

We even know what Descartes looked like in the middle of the night. In his *Meditations* published in 1641, Descartes raises a number of reasons for casting doubt on what we think we know. "How many times," Descartes says, "have I dreamed in the night that I was right here, dressed, next to the fire, although I was totally nude in bed." Generations of undergraduates have hooted at that passage: Descartes sleeps in the nude!

Not only did Descartes sleep in the nude, Frédéric Pagès argues most persuasively that he also smoked pot. Smoking was very big in the United Provinces, and nobody who visited could have avoided trying it. Particularly not a young soldier as Descartes was when he was in Breda in 1618. And most of the tobacco at that time was laced with marijuana. So of course Descartes smoked pot. Possibly he was even under the influence when he had his dreams. In later life, however, Descartes was a health nut who spoke out against tobacco as a stupefying drug. And there is no evidence that he was ever a habitual smoker.

Descartes had a wry sense of humor. You remember that he named his dog Mister Scratch. I like the line in his letter of 23 April 1649 to Brasset, complaining that he really did not want to go to Sweden:

> *I avow that a man who was born in the gardens of Touraine and who now lives in a land where, if there is not as much honey as God promised the Israelites, it is credible that there is more milk, cannot so easily resolve to leave it to go live in a land of bears among rocks and ice.*

And Descartes put Clerselier on royally when he told him that there is nothing better than an omelet of eggs that have been brooded eight or ten days. Clerselier solemnly repeats Descartes's admonition that the result is detestable if the eggs have been brooded either less or more than eight or ten days. Do you know what is inside eggs that have been brooded eight or ten days? Yech.

But here is probably Descartes's best story, one he told in a letter of 1 November 1644 letter to Chanut when he was being harassed by the Calvinist preacher Voetius from Utrecht:

> *If only I had been as wise as they say savages think monkeys are, that is, savages imagine that monkeys could talk if they wanted to, but they don't so no one will put them to work. Since I have not had the same prudence to abstain from writing, I don't have at all as much leisure and repose as I would have, had I had the wit to keep quiet.*

Another good one is in a letter to Huygens of 27 August 1640 in which Descartes repeats the old story that the New World Indians refused to become Christians for fear that they would have to go to heaven with the Spaniards.

Again to Huygens on 12 March 1640, Descartes says that Pierre Petit is so untrustworthy that "if he told me that the Chinese commonly have two eyes like us, I would believe that China is a land with only one-eyed Cyclops." This is in the course of commenting on some stories Petit had told Mersenne, including one about a girl in Cologne who had the stigmata of Christ. Descartes doubts it, and says Mersenne is so gullible that he will believe anything. This, by the way, is one of the very few mentions of Christ in Descartes's writings, although he quotes him against Voetius several times.

We have seen that Descartes laughed at some extravagant Protestant preaching. And in a letter to Mersenne in March 1637 he says, "I wasn't able to keep from laughing in reading the place where you said that someone would have to kill me so people could see my writings." On 27 May 1638, he wrote to Mersenne that Roberval's letter haranguing him truly made him laugh, because Roberval had no good response to Descartes's comments. In the same letter, Descartes says that Jean de Beaugrand's book, *Geostatics*, on the immobility of the earth, is laughable and that he pays no more attention to the insults he gets from people like Beaugrand than he would to a parrot. On 27 July 1638, he wrote Mersenne that he would no more think of replying to Petit than he would chase after a little dog that yapped at him in the street. He uses the same line to say that he would not reply to Beaugrand.

Descartes's first book, the *Discourse on Method*, starts with a joke. Montaigne used it and Charron repeated it:

Good sense is distributed better than anything else in the world, because everyone thinks he is so well provided with it that even those who are most difficult to satisfy in all other things customarily do not desire more of it than they already have.

Descartes goes on to say that "the power to judge well and to distinguish the true from the false, which is properly what we call good sense or reason, is naturally the same in all men." Differences between men arise from application. Some people use their reason better than others. What Descartes offers is a method everyone can use to apply reason to avoid error and to attain certainty.

The twist Descartes puts on this old joke is that he believes it is true. He thinks we *are* all born with equal reasoning power. So it is not a joke at all, and you begin to realize that even when Descartes smiles because he recognizes the humorous potential in something he is saying, he is deadly serious. That joke about how many feminists it takes to unscrew a light bulb must have once run: How many Cartesians does it take to blow out a candle? One, *and that's not funny.*

To Princess Elisabeth on 6 October 1645, Descartes says that "great joys are ordinarily bleak and serious; mediocre and transient joys are what cause laughter." Our philosopher was not a jolly fellow. For example, in the *Passions of the Soul*, he says that a man mourning for his wife often would be sorry to see her resurrected. I don't think Descartes repeated that tired old saw because he thought it might bring a smile, but because he thought it a piece of sober natural history. And it reminds me painfully of Descartes's letter of purported consolation to Huygens, whose wife had died on 10 May 1637. Ten days later, Descartes wrote to Huygens:

> *Having no doubt whatsoever that you govern yourself entirely according to reason, I am persuaded that it is very easy for you to console yourself and to regain your accustomed tranquility of mind now that there is no more remedy at all, than formerly when you had occasion to fear and to hope. Because it is certain that when hope is removed, desire ceases, or at least weakens and releases its hold, and that when one has little or no desire to see again what one has lost, no strong regrets are felt.*

Huygens, who loved his wife passionately (and Descartes knew it), wrote in the margin of Descartes's letter: "By passion torn, although my hopes are dead," which is from Petrarch. Descartes ends his letter with a petty personal complaint about Mersenne not yet having sent him the privilege for publishing his *Discourse*. Then he was very annoyed when he did get it, because against his express instructions, Mersenne had included Descartes's name in the privilege, and even a panegyric about how great Descartes and the book were. But even worse was the fact that the privilege extended over further books, making Descartes look as though he was in the business of selling books, an image Descartes detested.

Descartes's talent clearly lies in sarcasm. His "Letter to Dinet" of 1642 and his 1643 *Letter to Voetius* are packed with mean jibes. I have already noted that he indulged himself by pointing out to Beeckman — for fancying himself Descartes's teacher — that his friends knew that he, Descartes, learned things even from ants and worms. Descartes says acidly that he would rather believe that Beeckman is purposefully trying to give people the false impression that he taught Descartes some important things, than what on the face of it appears to be the case, which is that Beeckman is stupid. Beeckman was a friend. Voetius never was. And when I try to think of a good sarcastic remark Descartes makes with Voetius the butt, I come to the realization that against his Orthodox Calvinist theologian enemy, Descartes is not so much sarcastic as just plain nasty. For example, he pointed out several times in his letters to Utrecht officials that he was really doing them a favor by giving them cause to get rid of that fraud Voetius. The Utrecht officials ignored Descartes's suggestion.

If not always so funny, Descartes was always devilishly clever. In the *Letter to Voetius*, his responses to attacks on his person and philosophy often depend on taking words in their most literal, narrow sense. He was, after all, a student of the Jesuits. They could weave argument adequate to annul the marriages of kings. Here is how Descartes handles being accused of having illegitimate sons. First, he comes on so strong as to have us cheering. "It has not been so long since I was young [he was forty-seven when he wrote this]; I am a man, and I have never made a vow of chastity, and I have never pretended to be more wise than the others." Remembering that he stood up and acknowledged himself the father of Francine in the Orthodox Church in Deventer at her baptism on 7 August 1635, we are proud of him. He was not married to Francine's mother. Or at least no record of it has been found. And no one ever seriously accused him of marrying a Calvinist in an Orthodox church (they said that only to slander him). For a child to be legitimate, however, marriage of the parents was not necessary, only the acknowledgement of the father. Surely this was one of Descartes's finest hours. It provides solid ammunition against insinuations that Descartes — who was writing on the development of the fetus — was simply indulging in an anatomical experiment. I doubt that he intended to vivisect Helena, or to dissect Francine (although his great-grandfather did dissect his grandfather). The ironic thing about such insinuations is that they come both from Descartes's enemies and from such denizens of the Saint Descartes Protection Society as Clerselier, who (in Baillet's report) says that Descartes did it only once. "Our philosopher" in bed with a woman? Clerselier was horrified. When Clerselier himself was sixteen, he married a twenty-year-old woman who bore him thirteen children. But a philosopher fornicating? Never! Even in 1910, Adam's image of a great philosopher is still that of an unmarried, celibate man above the temptations of the flesh. The model for this is a Catholic priest. Here is Baillet's transcription of Clerselier's solemn report:

> The mistake which he [Descartes] had made one time in his life against the honor of his celibacy ... is less a proof of his inclination for women than of his weakness: and God raised him above it promptly so the memory of his fall could be a subject of continual humiliation for him and that his repentance would be a salutary remedy for the elevation of his spirit. By this glorious reestablishment he would reenter a perfectly Christian philosophy and ... the innocence of his life. (B II 502)

If Descartes did tell Clerselier this, which I very much doubt, it is further evidence that Descartes really did have a sense of humor, at least when talking to Clerselier, the most pious man in Paris.

But alas, after Descartes's terrific string of pronouncements about being a man like other men, he says, "But I don't." Don't what? Voetius accused him of having illegitimate sons. So he had no sons, but he had one daughter, and she was legitimate, and she had been dead for a year, so generously sticking to the letter of the accusation, Descartes could stand on his dignity and say that he had no illegitimate sons, and not even a living legitimate daughter. Obviously Voetius knew no specific details about Helena and Francine. Descartes had hidden them well.

What this biographer wants is for Descartes, Helena, and Francine to have had a jolly time. Descartes should bounce both of them on his knees. I think of that famous portrait by Pourbus the Younger of Henri IV on his hands and knees covered with his children — legitimate and illegitimate — tumbling around him playing horse. Of course when it comes to women, Descartes was no Henri IV, but he did have Helena. And he did record the date of Francine's conception on the flyleaf of a book.

"How did he know that was the day of conception?" Pat asked.

"Well," I replied, "if he did it only once..."

Descartes was stunned by Galileo's condemnation in 1633. It knocked him completely off his foundations. Being in a state of near total emotional collapse, he was, one Sunday afternoon in a breezy room (I develop the one-shot hypothesis), seduced by this saucy Dutch maid. I'll bet. Actually, I think Descartes was enough of a scientist that he would have repeated the experiment several times, if only to see if the experience was the same the second and a third time.

Descartes soon got over the shock of Galileo's condemnation. During the next three years, Descartes cannibalized *The World*. He extracted his work on lenses into an essay he entitled *Dioptrics*. The work on atmospheric phenomena was shaped into his *Meteorology*. What he had done on rules for the direction of the mind was incorporated into his *Discourse on Method*, as was a condensation of his work on metaphysics. Furthermore, he satisfied Balzac's request for the story of his intellectual development by including an autobiography, highly crafted to support and exemplify the life of reason in the search for truth. Then, Descartes says, toward the end of all this writing and rewriting, he hastily put together his *Geometry*, which also already existed in various bits and pieces.

This great burst of composition resulted in the publication in 1637 of Descartes's *Discourse on Method* illustrated with the three essays demonstrating the results of his method in *Geometry*, *Dioptrics*, and *Meteorology*. What is more, somewhere in the course of going over his manuscripts, he decided to bring his philosophy into the world in French, in some part, he said, so women could read it. His daughter was named Francine. His philosophy spoke French.

This was not entirely innovative on Descartes's part. Montaigne wrote his *Essays* in French. And two works that had direct influence on Descartes were also written in French: Pierre Charron's *On Wisdom* in 1601, a Christianization of Montaigne's skepticism and relativism, and Jean de Silhon's *Two Truths, the One of God and His Providence, the Other of the Immortality of the Soul* in 1626. Silhon was a good friend of Descartes's in Paris, and there are views in his book reflected in Descartes's *Meditations* of 1641. Nobody at the time made much of this, including Descartes and Silhon.

If one wanted the serious attention of the scholars and professors in the schools, one wrote in Latin. Descartes may have thought that if the Catholics condemned Galileo, he might as well give up trying to get his philosophy adopted in the Catholic schools. How else explain the insulting explanation he gave to the erudite for writing in French?

If I write in French, which is the language of my country, rather than Latin, which is that of my teachers, it is because I expect that those who use only their pure natural reason will judge better of my opinions than those who believe only in ancient books.

He sent copies to three of his nieces and to the wives of some of his friends. Perhaps even Helena read it. We know she could read and write because she and Descartes exchanged letters. We don't know in what language.

Descartes was a conscientious man. He arranged to have Helena and Francine live with or near him. Here is the one letter we have in which he speaks of Helena and Francine. It was written on 30 August 1637, probably to Reneri:

> *Everything is going better here than we might have wished. I spoke yesterday to my hostess to find out if she wanted to have my niece [Francine] here, and how much it would cost. Without pausing to think about it, she said that the child could come whenever I wanted, and that we would easily agree on the price because it was indifferent to her whether she had one child more or less to take care of. As for the servant, my hostess is waiting for you to furnish one, and since it has been some time since she has wanted one, and so as not to annoy her too much, please send here, or better, to Mr. Godfroy, a letter saying you are looking for one, that you wanted to talk to two or three to be able to inform yourself better about them, but you have not yet decided, and that there is no need for us to go to the trouble, as you will certainly decide on one or the other. In effect, it is necessary that Helena come here as soon as she possibly can, and it would be best if she can come before Saint-Victor [the traditional day on which servants' contracts were signed] by getting someone else to take her present place. Because I am afraid our hostess will get annoyed if she has to wait too long before getting a servant, so let me know that you have told Helena all this. . . . The letter I have written to Helena is not urgent, and I would prefer that rather than giving it to your servant to take to her, you hold onto it until Helena comes to find you, which I believe she will do at the end of this week to give you the letters she has written to me.*

"The *letters* she has written to me."

Note that Descartes is again at his old trick of making up a story for someone else to tell, like the lie that he was going to England that Mersenne was to tell to Ferrier. But he does have it all planned out. And you should not think sarcastically of how decent it was of him to get Helena placed in a proper servant's job. Descartes was being realistic. They were not married. Both of them wanted to keep up appearances. She was a big strong Dutch girl. She liked to work. She wanted to work. And he wanted her and Francine to be with him.

On the other hand, although Descartes was not rich enough to support a mistress in the grand style of the nobility, he had enough money that Helena need not have worked as a servant. But at least for awhile he arranged for Helena to work in a household where he had his lodgings. From 1637 to 1640, he lived in country houses near Santpoort and Amersfort, where he kept gardens, and Helena and Francine could have lived openly with him in those places. No one was going to object.

The only things we know for sure about Helena is that she was a servant, she was the mother of Francine, she could read, and she wrote letters to Descartes, probably in Dutch. It is also virtually certain that she nursed Francine, for Dutch mothers nursed their children, unlike the French who sent theirs out to wet nurses. Many of Descartes's friends had to know about their liaison, but there is no mention of it in any of their letters. It could not have been general knowledge, because Descartes's enemies Saumaise and Voetius report having heard only rumors that Descartes had a child.

My guess is that there were letters from Helena in the trunk Descartes left in Amsterdam when he went to Sweden. He told his friends that if he died, they could burn the letters in that trunk, and probably they did, except for the letters from Huygens, which were returned to him. Later, when Clerselier asked for help on Descartes's biography from Jean de Raey, who was present when the trunk was opened, de Raey refused. De Raey would not cooperate because he said that "M. Descartes lived a simple life" and "the French will spoil it" (B I xxx).

The saddest thing is that there is nothing at all about Helena in any of Descartes's extant papers after the death of Francine. Perhaps Helena died of the fever along with Francine. Whatever happened to Helena, Descartes lived the rest of his life alone, that is, without a woman companion. Descartes never lived entirely alone because he always employed a manservant or valet.

Descartes wanted at first to publish only a few copies of his essays on *Geometry*, *Dioptrics*, and *Meteorology* anonymously, so he could sit behind a screen (as Anna Maria van Schurman had to do to attend classes at the University of Utrecht) to hear what people said about them. But everyone knew the author anyway. So in 1637 he went ahead with the full printing.

The three essays were a great success, and they were soon translated into Latin. Descartes's reputation was assured in geometry (the solution to the Pappus problem and the exposition of his analytic method), dioptrics (the law of refraction), and meteorology (the explanation of the false suns and the rainbow). Then the *Discourse on Method* that introduced them was very influential, particularly among a few young professors — mostly in the United Provinces — who saw it as providing a methodological basis for progressing in the natural sciences. But Descartes was not entirely satisfied, because the metaphysical foundations for certainty he had provided with his proofs for the existence of God were widely criticized, and — worse in his eyes — ignored as irrelevant by his best disciple in the United Provinces, Henry Regius at the University of Utrecht.

On the basis of the success of the *Discourse* and the *Essays*, Descartes started preparing for publication his *Meditations on First Philosophy* to provide a solid metaphysical foundation for his physics, so he told Mersenne. And again — like his namesake cardinal (no relation) du Perron before him — he wanted an initial publication of a few copies to send around for comments that he could use for revision before publishing a version for the public. He enclosed some objections from a Jesuit priest from Louvain, Johannes Caterus, that had been obtained for him by his friends in Harlem, the Catholic priests Bannius and Bloemaert.

Mersenne ran away with this plan. He collected two batches of objections himself, and some from Thomas Hobbes, the English materialist who had published *On the State*; Antoine Arnauld, a Jansenist (anti-Jesuit) theologian of Port-Royal; and Pierre Gassendi, an Epicurean atomist. Mersenne bundled all these objections together and published them with Descartes's replies in the *Meditations* in one volume. In 1642, a second edition appeared with a seventh set of objections by Pierre Bourdin, a Jesuit priest, and a "Letter to Dinet" from Descartes in which he complains about Bourdin's objections and also about Voetius, the Orthodox Calvinist minister in Utrecht who was attacking Descartes and Cartesianism. Descartes obsequiously implores Dinet, who was at that time Provincial for the Jesuits in France and also Louis XIV's confessor, to make it clear that Bourdin does not speak for all the Jesuits. His comments to Dinet about Voetius might appear to be gratuitous unless Descartes was — and he was — overbearingly and with great excess and lack of finesse pointing out to Dinet that he, Descartes, was a loyal Catholic being harassed by a mad dog Calvinist in a foreign land.

God knows what Dinet made of the letter. He replied with some vague remarks probably drafted by his personal secretary. But Dinet did apparently call off Bourdin, who made up with Descartes. And here we get another measure of the depth of Descartes's sense of humor. In 1644 when Descartes published his *Principles of Philosophy*, he sent twenty or thirty copies to Bourdin for *Bourdin* to distribute. Mind you, still in print was Descartes's *Meditations* with *Objections* and Descartes's *Replies*, in which he makes it clear that he thinks Bourdin is an idiot and a fool. And this is the man who now runs errands for Descartes, distributing books of the philosophy he had criticized and rejected just six years before. Yes, Descartes was willing to make friends with his worst critics and enemies — as long as they capitulated and sank to their proper level where he could wipe his feet on them.

Descartes was a proud, excitable, egotistic little man. He was acid in his wit. Dogmatic about his own views, he accused everyone who disagreed with him of misunderstanding or of being stupid. He was suspicious, quick to take offense and to anger, slow to cool. He insisted that he was unaffected by personal attacks, but he never forgot an insult, slight, or an injury. Despite his egalitarianism about human reason, he thought the true nobility (not the third estate purchased nobility of judges like his father and brother) was of finer stuff than ordinary men. But above all, he was romantic. He was flattered to be the preceptor of a princess. Against his better judgment he hoped he could teach his philosophy to a queen.

Descartes was in Leiden seeing his publisher when on 1 September 1640, he was called urgently home to Santpoort. He left immediately, without even sending the letters he had ready to go to Paris. Francine was terribly ill with scarlatina. Her body was flushed and she had a high fever. She died on 7 September 1640. (Only the year before in a letter of 20 February 1639 to Mersenne, Descartes had lamented that for all his work in medicine, he had never learned to cure a fever.)

Descartes stayed in Santpoort another week, and then returned to Leiden. Certainly he had Francine in mind when in a letter of January 1641 to Pollot he says that he is not one of those philosophers who think men should not cry and that he had recently lost two people very close to him. The other might have been Helena. There is not another word of her.

Look, a lot of people knew about Helena and Francine. Henry Reneri certainly knew — he was the liaison between Descartes and Helena. Constantijn Huygens certainly knew. Descartes's hunting companion and banker Antoine Studler van Zurk knew. Saumaise and Voetius had heard rumors. After Descartes's death, Louis de la Voyette, Frans Schooten II, Jean de Raey, and Cornelis Hogelande looked through the trunk Descartes left in Amsterdam. They knew. Descartes apparently never threw away any papers. The correspondence with Helena would have been there. Many of these people knew what happened to Helena. They destroyed the letters, to be sure as Descartes said they could.

It is amazing how mean some of the French biographers are to Helena. Léon Petit speaks of her as a "humble creature" and he quotes Barrès as saying about Francine's death: "Descartes could not console himself about the death of his small daughter. He saw her constantly with her sweet smile, her air of a small animal that needs protection [but we know what Descartes thinks of animals — mere senseless machines], and he suffered because her mother was so common that he could not share his grief with her [she would have been devastated, the Dutch absolutely love children]" (p. 266). Petit actually goes along with this (his book was published in 1969), and he quotes Rousseau (who sent his own children to an orphanage) about how terrible it is for a thinking man to have a common, uncultured wife with whom he cannot share his thoughts. The case of Karl Marx sitting at the kitchen table surrounded by children while he wrote his masterworks would probably just clinch the case for Petit.

In a letter of 23 August 1638 to Mersenne, Descartes tells about amusing a child. A fable: They are in the garden, she is three years old, sitting on his knees. He claps his hands, and the echo comes from the corner of the garden where the weeds have grown up as high as a man. The echo comes back — like the cry of a bird! The little girl runs to the corner of the garden, but there is no bird there. She runs back to her father. He solemnly claps his hands again. The echo comes back. The little girl is amazed, she shrieks with laughter, she claps, but not loud enough. Her father claps his hands again. The bird-call echo comes back. The little girl looks up into her father's face in admiration. Again. And again. He claps his hands and the echo comes back.

PIERRE GASSENDI (1592–1655)
ONE OF THE OBJECTORS
TO DESCARTES'S *MEDITATIONS*
Bibliothèque Nationale de France

IX ✒ THE GEOMETERS

*I have gone as far in mathematics
as the human mind can go.*

Tiny Tim's father Bob Cratchit sat on a high stool in
Ebenezer Scrooge's office every long day, adding and subtracting accounts, even on one famous Christmas Eve. And woe
betide the accountant who ever made a mistake. The awesome
thing about this scene is that it was set more than two centuries
after young Blaise Pascal had invented an adding and subtracting
machine. So slow did computer technology move in the seventeenth, eighteenth, and nineteenth centuries. In Descartes's days, if
you were a peasant or a nobody who was good at mathematics, you
could make a living adding and subtracting. But it was a terrible,
tedious job. When on 27 May 1635, Descartes recommended his
young friend and former valet Jean Gillot to M. de Sainte-Croix in
Paris, he said that Gillot knew arithmetic and geometry perfectly,
and in particular he could teach Descartes's method. He had been
treated by Descartes more as a protégé, a friend and comrade, than
as a valet. Descartes said he would speak for him as for a brother.
Gillot was therefore accustomed to talking to people of rank as an
equal. He could be employed as a man of letters or a secretary. But
Descartes cautioned that if Gillot were employed as an accountant
to do long calculations, he would surely revolt out of indignation
and boredom.

How far a nobody could go with mathematical talent is shown by
Descartes's bête noire Gilles Personne (personne means nobody in
French) de Roberval. And you know that Roberval was destined to
be a great mathematician, because if Descartes was said to be born
in a ditch, Roberval really was born in a field as his peasant mother

was trying to reach the house. Roberval was the third-ranked geo-metrician of his day — I speak precisely — and no one (except Roberval) denied that Descartes was number one. (Pierre de Fermat was number two.) In 1632, Roberval was awarded the Ramus Chair of Mathematics at the Collège de France. Award is correct, for it was a contest and he had to defend the chair against all challengers, which he did until his death in 1675.

The big question is when Descartes became number one. There is an outside limiting date. In his journal on 8 October 1628, Beeck-man remarks that Descartes had visited him that day and had reported that he had gone as far in mathematics as the human mind could go. Everyone who mattered knew that Descartes was the greatest by then. He did not publish his method of analysis until 1637 in his *Geometry*, but in a letter to Mersenne of 15 April 1630, he was already complaining about people sending him problems to solve. And by 1638, he was begging Mersenne not to send him any more mathematical problems. It was just a lot of pedestrian work on useless problems that anybody who knew his method could solve. Descartes was interested in a more fruitful form of mathematics than in problems that merely exercise the mind.

What Descartes found to be useful was something Beeckman introduced him to in Breda on 10 November 1618 — a form of math-ematical physics consisting of the construction of geometric mod-els of natural phenomena, such as water pressure. As I have already remarked, Beeckman asked Descartes to work out the law of falling bodies and to do a study of the harmonics of vibrating strings, which Descartes provided in his *Treatise on Music* on 31 December 1618.

Applied mathematics was not unfamiliar to Descartes. He was in Breda to study the military architecture of fortifications, sieges, and encampments at Prince Maurice's informal military school. But Descartes credited Beeckman with awakening him to the possibil-ity of applying mathematics — specifically geometry — to all phys-ical phenomena including those of anatomy and physiology.

Then came the night of dreams, 10 November 1619. In his journal, Descartes wrote that he had discovered "the foundations of a marvelous science." Exactly one year later, on 10 November 1620, he wrote that he had commenced to conceive of "the foundations of an admirable invention." The marvelous science is the notion of a unified science such that all natural phenomena can be studied and understood with one method. This method is a generalization of the analytic procedure he used in solving mathematical problems. It is outlined in Descartes's *Discourse on Method* in four steps:

1. *To never take anything to be true that I do not know evidently to be such...*

2. *To divide each difficulty that I examine into as many parts as is possible and that is required to best resolve it.*

3. *To conduct my thoughts in order by commencing with the most simple objects and easiest to know, to ascend little by little as by degrees to knowledge of the most complicated; and to assume an order even between those that do not precede one another naturally.*

4. *To make enumerations so complete, and reviews so general, that I am assured to have omitted nothing. (AT VI 18–19)*

The admirable invention is his more specific method of analytic geometry — that is, of representing quantities by lines and lines by algebraic symbols. With this method geometric problems can be represented and solved algebraically, and algebraic problems can be represented and solved geometrically. All of this put together allowed Descartes to see physics and physiology as merely the mathematics of moving bodies.

Descartes made these discoveries when he was twenty-three and twenty-four years old. He was in the prime of life for a mathematician. And like many other mathematical geniuses, except for some number rules in arithmetic that he sent to Paris on 17 May 1639, by the age of twenty-four he had taken his great discovery as far as he could. (As remarked above, Leibniz and Newton took it on to the infinitesimal calculus in the next generation.) For all serious intents and purposes, Descartes's life as a creative mathematician was over. Indeed, having gone, he said, as far as the human mind can go, it surely never occurred to him to seek something further. But he impressed people with his ability to solve mathematical problems for the next twenty years.

He was most concerned to apply his mathematical method to solving problems in optics and mechanics. He explained the phenomenon of refraction (the ratio between the sines of the angles of incidence and refraction for any two given media is a constant) known as Snell's Law, and he worked out the mathematics of the five simple machines: lever, screw, inclined plane, wedge, and windlass. He gave the correct mathematical description of the formation of the rainbow by refraction in raindrops. But he never worked out a dynamic mathematical physics as did Newton. Like Beeckman, Descartes pointed the right direction by urging the application of mathematics to physics, but he himself turned to nonmathematical studies in anatomy and physiology, although he treated them as a kind of mechanics. In a letter to Mersenne of 3 June 1638, he said that if he had to extract a square root, he would have to look up how to do it, or — just to make sure nobody got the wrong idea — he would have to invent a way of doing it. And that story about the problem posted on the wall — told equally about Viète and Descartes — is one of those should-be-true fabrications that illuminate not the factual truth but rather the essential nature of a man.

Mathematicians are divided on the general question of discovery versus invention in mathematics. If mathematics is invented, then it is a construct of the human mind, and every innovation is newly placed in the world. If it is discovered, then it was there before we were, in an eternal realm of Platonic ideas, say, or in the mind of God. Descartes believed he discovered the mathematical relations and proofs. God created them, and they are eternally true because He made them so. Mathematics is, Descartes said, the most certain and most useful of God's works. But even atheists such as Prince

Maurice loved mathematics, both for its own sake, and also for its application to military engineering. Maurice also followed it as a fan, and gathered top mathematicians around him. Geometry done with a straight edge and a compass was the queen of the mathematical sciences in the first half of the seventeenth century, and it was pursued as a pastime, a passion, and an obsessive game by numerous members of the noble class. Most of Descartes's geometer friends, then, were both rich and noble. (Roberval was none of these, neither friend nor rich nor noble. He had to make a living teaching mathematics. Descartes was putting down poor people like Roberval and classing himself with his noble mathematical friends such as Claude Mydorge when he remarked in the *Discourse* that fortunately he does not have to work to make a living.)

There were other mathematical games followed then as now by every class, rich or poor — card games. Descartes makes several references to his gambling. There is that letter in November 1646 in which he tells Princess Elisabeth that he won more readily when he took a positive attitude to the play. And like Pascal after him, he understood the odds. I suspect that some of Descartes's rich friends in the United Provinces helped support him simply by playing cards with him.

When Descartes finally published his *Geometry* in 1637, after he had exhausted all interest he had formerly had in the solving of problems himself, he gave his text a form derived from some basic elements of the competitive, game-playing background of the world of seventeenth-century mathematics. First, he posed the Pappus problem (a locus problem concerning points on a plane), which geometricians had been trying unsuccessfully to solve since the end of the third century A.D. Here is Shea's statement of the problem:

The problem is as follows. There are given n *straight lines. From the point* c, *lines are drawn making given angles with the given lines. If* n = 3, *the ratio of the product of two of the lines from* c *to the square of the third is given. If* n *is even and greater than two, the ratio of the product of* n/2 *of the lines from* c *to the product of the other* $n/2$ *lines is given. If* n *is odd and greater than three, the ratio of the product of* $(n + 1)/2$ *of the lines to the product of the other* $(n - 1)/2$ *lines together with a given line is given. It is required to find the locus of* c. *(p. 60)*

Try that with a compass and a ruler. It took Descartes five or six weeks even using his analytic geometry. Descartes gave a sketch of his solution, including, as he said, most of the essential steps but skipping the easy parts. These easy parts included gaps that had to be filled with several pages of calculations. Descartes said he did this both to give the really good mathematicians the thrill of making discoveries themselves and to keep poor geometers (he had Roberval in mind) from rushing through the proof and then claiming that they had already known it. If it were a poster problem with a bet — I'll give you 100 livres if you can solve it, and you give me 100 livres if you can't — challengers would have had to demonstrate that they actually could solve it by filling in the gaps. But it was not just the solution to the Pappus problem that Descartes left incomplete. He left gaps in the exposition of his method, also. The result is that very few mathematicians then — or now, for that matter — could read Descartes's *Geometry* and understand it straight off. In 1639, Descartes advised Desargues on how to write a popular book in mathematics. Everything has to be explained so clearly and distinctly that readers have no more trouble with it than they would in understanding the description of an enchanted palace in a novel. Descartes's own book is not of that sort.

Descartes's method was not entirely new. There was an ancient method of mathematical analysis attributed to Apollonius of Perga that Descartes refined. And then there was the greatest mathematician of the previous generation, François Viète, who invented the modern system of representing squares, cubes, etc., with number superscripts — that is, as a^2, b^3, etc. Descartes built on the old analysis and refined the use of superscripts, but he denied that he had ever read Viète. Then he said he did not want to see the book when someone offered it to him. Finally when a copy was thrust into his hands, he said he put it down after reading only a few pages because he could see he had nothing to learn from it. But of course he had already learned from it. You do not have to read a book to learn from it, and Viète's analysis was commonplace among mathematicians. But give Descartes his conceit, even if he had no need to be so jealous of his genius. As he himself insisted, it is not the pieces and parts themselves that matter; what matters are the relations in which they stand to one another and how you put them together. Descartes worked out the idea of representing quantities and ratios by lines and of mapping a geometric figure on what have come to be called Cartesian coordinates, so that, for example, a triangle can be expressed both geometrically and algebraically. With this, Descartes took a major step in the development of modern mathematics. And he knew it. The man had a maddening sense of his supreme superiority in mathematics. He drove Roberval (geometer number three) up the wall. But Fermat (number two) respectfully asked Descartes what he, Fermat, should think of his own abilities. Like Prince Maurice who answered the question of who was the best general of his time by saying Spinola was second best, Descartes told Fermat on 11 October 1638 that he had never known anyone who knew more geometry — anyone else. Even more biting was Descartes's earlier comment to Fermat on 27 July 1638, that Fermat wrote like a poet. In the *Discourse*, Descartes remarks that poets produce brilliant effects, like sparks struck from flint, but without system and without comprehending how they do it. Descartes often pointed out that contrary to Fermat and many others, he himself worked systematically, and he knew how and why he got his results.

The fact is, Descartes destroyed the game of posing and solving individual geometric problems. Descartes had no interest in individual problems. In his *Geometry*, he describes a method for working out general solutions to specific types of problems. It was very nice that Roberval and Fermat have great ingenuity in solving any individual problem set before them and general methods for solving certain classes of problems. But Descartes conceived of his own method as completely general, and with it he eliminated the competition. After Descartes's *Geometry*, anyone who took the trouble to learn his method could solve problems even as difficult as the one proposed by Pappus.

There were soon several guides to Descartes's *Geometry*, a particularly good one by his young friend Frans Schooten II and his older friend Florimond de Beaune. Descartes recommended these cribs, in which all that he had left out was filled in with elementary detail. Descartes said that he himself did not write for schoolchildren. He also said to Mersenne in December 1637, "My geometry is to ordinary geometry as Cicero's *Rhetoric* to a child's A, B, Cs."

But Descartes was not as blasé as he pretended. He was so concerned that everyone get it right that in 1640 he put off his plans to visit his seventy-six-year-old father (whom he had not seen for twelve years) to supervise the response to an attack on his *Geometry*. After that skirmish was over, he wrote a letter to his father on 28 October 1640 explaining why he had not been able to get away that fall but would come later. His father had died just sixteen days before Descartes wrote the letter.

The occasion for Descartes's delay was a challenge posed by Johan Stampioen II, twenty-nine years old, who in 1638 published a placard with a mathematics problem that he claimed only he could solve. This was ridiculous, of course, but what really incensed Descartes was Stampioen's announcement (with Stampioen's picture on it!) of his *New Method of Algebra* containing rules of method in opposition to those in Descartes's *Geometry*. Descartes certainly was not going to put up with that.

Stampioen's book was published in 1639. Immediately, Jacques de Wassenaer II, one of Descartes's protégés, published a proof of Stampioen's problem using Descartes's method and gave criticisms of Stampioen's new method. Stampioen then challenged Wassenaer to a contest including solving equations of the third degree, with each of them putting down a deposit of 600 gulden, the loser's 600 to go to the poor people of Leiden. (A fair annual salary for a university professor at that time was 600 gulden.) Four mathematicians were chosen as judges: Jacob Golius and Frans Schooten I, friends of Descartes at the University of Leiden; and two of Stampioen's friends, Andreas van Berlikum of Rotterdam and Bernard Schotanus of Utrecht. The judges were in place by January 1640, solutions submitted in February 1640, and Wassenaer declared victor in April 1640. Throughout, Descartes coached Wassenaer. He was indignant during the entire affair and wrote to Huygens on 17 November 1639 that the public had to be protected from such impostors as Stampioen: "Baseless slanders and insults posted in public by someone trying to earn credit by way of effrontery and lies cannot honestly be tolerated in a land so well ruled as this one." On 26 November 1639, Descartes further wrote Huygens that "the affair is so stupid that if Stampioen wins, I would be no less astonished than I would be if he announced that he is God the Father." Huygens organized the contest but asked that his name be left out of it.

Descartes consulted Huygens throughout this affair because it turned out that Stampioen was the mathematics tutor of Prince Frederick-Henry's son as well as of Princess Elisabeth of Bohemia. Huygens (as Frederick-Henry's secretary) told Descartes not to worry about it. Later on, in fact, Huygens himself employed Stampioen to tutor his own two sons, one of whom, Christiaan (the cadet) went on to be known as the great Huygens who invented the pendulum clock and was one of the most distinguished scientists of the second half of the seventeenth century. Moreover, Descartes was very impressed by Elisabeth's mathematical abilities, she who had been instructed by Stampioen.

After the victory, Descartes was still so worried about Stampioen, who was using something like Descartes's own method, that he immediately sent copies of the problems and solutions to Mersenne for general distribution, saying that he wanted to forestall the possibility that Stampioen might switch the proofs and send out Wassenaer's — that is, Descartes's — as his own.

Even then the affair was not over. The money had been deposited with Rector Dedel of the University of Leiden, and instead of giving Stampioen's forfeited 600 gulden to the poor, he gave the money to the Pestehuis, a hospital. Descartes was outraged. By what right could

Dedal divert these funds? "A deposit is a sacred thing," Descartes insisted, a rather amusing high horse to mount by the man who advised in the *Discourse* that one should not take oaths committing oneself to actions and opinions one might want to change in the future.

Descartes demanded that the money be given to the poor. But on 17 October 1640, he received notice that the money had been given officially to the hospital. This did make sense. The pest of the Pestehuis hospital was the plague, and the nearly 15,000 deaths in Leiden of 1635 were still freshly in mind.

There were numerous outbreaks of the plague throughout Europe in Descartes's time. Descartes never mentions the plague directly in any of his writings, but he practiced the standard method of precaution — live in the country. It was thought then that the plague was spread by bad air. This is what Descartes is alluding to when he says the air is bad in Italy, and although the context makes it seem that he meant the social ambiance, he could also have been referring to the threat of plague when he said he disliked the air of Paris, where the plague raged from 1621 to 1623. He had one thing right. The plague spread in cities where large numbers of people lived together.

This is the man who groaned every time he received problems and criticisms from Mersenne. But when Pierre de Fermat sent some of his own mathematical writings and also some criticisms of Descartes's *Dioptrics*, Descartes knew he had to respond. As usual, he sent a long letter to Mersenne, expecting him to pass it on to Fermat. But Mersenne, always eager to engage as many combatants as possible (like that great three-on-three duel fought in the Palais Royal) instead gave the letter to two of Fermat's mathematical friends, Roberval and Étienne Pascal. They prepared a response to Descartes that Mersenne at once leaked to two of Descartes's mathematical friends, Claude Mydorge and Claude Hardy, who responded on Descartes's behalf. Now if ever there were two mathematicians in the history of humankind who did not need champions to defend them, Descartes and Fermat were the ones. As excellent as the four mousquetaires were in mathematics, they only muddled the issues. So after a series of feints and misunderstandings, it was with real relief and sincerity that Descartes wrote to Fermat on 27 July 1638 accepting his offer of friendship with joy, although I have already commented that Descartes had a tendency to expect his friends to take all his writings as gospel. Fermat did not think Descartes was God the Father of Mathematics. But Fermat solved the disciple problem simply by begging off any requests to criticize Descartes's works. Mersenne asked him to contribute a set of objections to the *Meditations*, but he refused. Thereby he avoided any further disputes with Descartes.

Roberval was another matter. Roberval adored disputes and he despised Descartes. Descartes in turn could not stand Roberval. Each was a superior geometer and each had an enormous ego, but beyond that, Baillet tells exactly how they fell out with one another. It is one of Baillet's best stories, and it is possibly even true.

In 1637, 3,000 copies of Descartes's *Discourse on Method* and accompanying essays — *Dioptrics*, *Meteors*, and *Geometry* — were printed, a very large number for the time. Descartes received 200 copies to distribute. Besides these, he had a dozen separate copies of the *Geometry* printed on fine paper and elegantly bound. Most of these copies were given to Mersenne for distribution. And Mersenne chose not to give one of the special twelve copies of the *Geometry* to Roberval, who deserved one both by his rank as a top mathematician and also because of his occupying the Ramus Chair of Mathematics at the Collège de France. Even worse, Mersenne did not even give Roberval one of the 200 regular copies. Roberval, naturally, was furious. Prior to this insult, he and Descartes had had practically no relations. Descartes said he had spoken to the man only once, on the occasion of his assuming the mathematics chair. So there was no special reason why Descartes should have told Mersenne either to be sure to give Roberval a copy or not to give him a copy. The only conclusion is that Mersenne engineered what Baillet refers to as Roberval's "immortal animosity" to Descartes as another step toward his goal of furthering the advancement of science by initiating disputes among brilliant men. Roberval was a big man who was enormously visible. There is no way Mersenne could have failed to give him a copy of Descartes's *Geometry* unknowingly.

Thereafter, Roberval took every occasion to criticize Descartes. He attacked his *Geometry*, argued that Descartes had not really solved the Pappus problem, claimed that he had taken his ideas from Viète and others, and showered him with further problems to solve.

At first, Descartes tried to mollify Roberval, but soon he was begging Mersenne not to send him anything more from that man. "I'm tired of Roberval," he said. "Please don't involve me in any more brou-ha-ha with Roberval." He even tried praise. Roberval solved the problem of finding the area of the curve (called la roulette) traced out by a point on a wheel rolling without slipping on a plane in one rotation. Mersenne had invented this problem after observing cartwheels rolling along the ground. Descartes said (correctly) that Roberval's proof was brilliant. But then the question arose of constructing tangents to the curve described by the moving point. Roberval worked it out as an individual problem by applying his general method of composition of movements. But Descartes contributed a general rule for constructing tangents not just to this curve, but to any curve at all, one-upping Roberval severely.

Roberval was persistent, loudmouthed, and belligerent. Descartes was absolutely confident and firm, but he kept saying that he would let his mathematics speak for itself. Of course he could not restrain his own talent for insult and sarcasm. (In September 1641, for example, he told Mersenne not to send any more letters from another of his critics, Jean de Beaugrand, "because we already have enough toilet paper here.")

Roberval, Descartes said to Mersenne in a letter of 17 July 1638, seemed to him as vain as a woman who attaches a ribbon in her hair to appear more pretty. In a letter to Mersenne of 2 November 1646, he said Roberval reminded him of a dwarf with a head twice as large as his body, who has so little sense that he thinks this is an advantage. Or even more, Roberval reminded him of the braggadocio captain of an Italian farce, "who after having been made a fool of and had his ears boxed and his face slapped with a slipper, continues bragging and remains always victorious and invincible." Descartes goes on to say that he would rather be slapped with a slipper himself than be forced to read any more of Roberval. In a letter to Elisabeth of 29 June 1648, he says he is surprised that anyone pays Roberval to teach them, but meanest of all, to Mersenne on 19 June 1638, he says "I am astonished that this man can pass among others as a rational animal."

Of course Roberval knew about these letters. Mersenne would be sure to see to that. So soon after Mersenne died on 1 September 1648, Roberval came into his room and gathered up all of Descartes's letters and took them away. Mersenne very likely meant for him to have them. Then after Descartes died, when Clerselier was collecting his edition of letters, Roberval refused to turn over any of Descartes's letters to Mersenne. There were seventy-five of them. Oh, the terrible man! Baillet says. But Roberval comes out as a biographer's hero. For when he died in 1675, those letters were willed to the Académie Royal des Sciences in Paris, where Baillet consulted them when writing his biography of 1691. But he could not take them away, and thank God for that, for every scrap of paper Baillet had has now disappeared. We have 560 of Descartes's letters, of which 187 are in Descartes's hand, and seventy-five of these were saved by Roberval. Roberval was not as bad as Descartes painted him. He was just a justifiably frustrated great mathematician. In any other era he might have been number one.

ELISABETH DE BOHÈME (1618–1679) PRINCESS PALATINE

BY GUILLAUME VAN HONTHORST

Nationalmuseum, Stockholm

X ⚜ PRINCESS ELISABETH

No one has understood me better.

I N EARLY OCTOBER 1642, Descartes's friend Alphonse de Pollot
in the court at The Hague wrote to him about Princess Elisabeth
of Bohemia, age twenty-three. In 1635 when she was seventeen,
King Wladislas IV of Poland had asked for her hand. But he was
Catholic and she was devoutly Calvinist, so she refused. Now she was
living in The Hague with her mother, four brothers, and three sisters, supported by the charity of her mother's cousins, the successive princes of Nassau. Her father Frederick V, the Winter King, had
died in 1632 of the plague on a visit to the Palatine lands he had lost
to Emperor Ferdinand II of the Holy Roman Empire at the Battle of
White Mountain on 8 November 1620. Elisabeth had read Descartes's *Discourse*, the *Essays*, and the *Meditations*, and she wanted
to meet the philosopher. On 6 October 1642, Descartes replied to
Pollet that he would be pleased to talk with the princess. He went to
see her then, and he saw her again in The Hague in late April 1643.
He was just the age her father would have been had he lived.

Elisabeth spoke English, German, French, Dutch, and Italian, and
she knew Latin. She was very good in mathematics, and her criticisms
of Descartes's metaphysics are as astute as any he received. What is
more, while he fobbed off and insulted numerous other critics, he
answered her.

Descartes argued that there are only two substances in the world,
minds and bodies. Each can exist alone independently of the other
(and thus the mind or soul can be immortal). The essence of mind
is unextended, active thinking. The essence of body is unthinking,
passive extension. Thus the two substances are direct opposites of
one another. Now, Descartes went on, a human being is a union of a

mind and a body such that external bodies act on one's sense organs to cause one's mind to have mental sensory images. And the mind can cause one's body to move, walk, and talk.

Here is the problem Elisabeth proposed. If the natures of the mind and body are so totally opposite one another, how can they interact? How can an *inactive extended* body *act* on an *unextended* mind. And conversely, how can an unextended mind act on an extended body? Bodies move by bumping and being bumped. But minds can neither bump nor be bumped. So, Elisabeth asked, how can the human mind and body interact?

Descartes could not solve the problem and was constrained to explain to Elisabeth that we know it is possible because we experience it, and God can make it so. She was not enlightened by this answer.

Elisabeth posed this classic mind-body problem in a letter to Descartes of 16 May 1643, in which she also regretted that they had not been able to meet when he had recently been in The Hague. The forty-seven-year-old philosopher's reply of 21 May 1643 to the young princess needs to be quoted:

The favor with which your Highness honors me in sending me your commands by writing is greater than I had ever dared hope, and it is in some sense better than what I had wished for passionately, which was to receive them from you in person, if I had been permitted the honor of making reverence to you when I was last in The Hague, and to offer you my very humble service. Because had that happened, I would have had too many marvels to admire at the same time, and seeing superhuman discourse coming from a body resembling those painters give to angels, I would have been ravished in the same way that it seems to me those who come from earth must be when first entering heaven. This would render me less capable to respond to your Highness, who without doubt has already remarked this fault in me when I have had the honor to speak to you in the

*past. So your mercy relieves me of that fault, and because you
sent me your thoughts on paper where I can reread and consider them several times, I am in fact less dazzled although
without admiring them any the less, for I see now that they
appear ingenious not only at first, but also the more judicious
and solid the more I examine them.*

Despite this masterly display of a model courtier's rhetorical obeisance to a princess, Descartes could not have been overly concerned
with getting to know Elisabeth. He had been living at Endegeest
outside Leiden only seven miles from The Hague, but at the end of
April 1643 — right when he met Elisabeth — he moved to Egmond
aan den Hoef, some thirty-five miles from The Hague. From Endegeest, Descartes could go visit Elisabeth and return home in one
day, but from Egmond it was a three-day outing, two on the road. All
the evidence is that Descartes and Elisabeth actually talked face-to-
face very few times. There are also long gaps in the correspondence.

Elisabeth's sister twelve-year-old sister, Sophie, provides a portrait of Elisabeth:

*My sister, who is called Madame Elisabeth ... has black hair, a
bright complexion, brilliant brown eyes, large black eyebrows,
a noble forehead, a beautiful vermilion mouth, fine teeth, and a
thin, aquiline nose that turns red easily. She loves to study, but
all her philosophy cannot keep her from chagrin when the cir-
culation of her blood causes her nose to turn red. Then she
hides herself from all the world.... She knows all the languages
and all the sciences, and has a regular commerce with Monsieur Descartes, but this thinker renders her a bit distracted,
which often makes us laugh. (A 403)*

Sophie went on to marry Ernest-August of Hanover, and in 1714,
her son George-Louis, became George I, king of Great Britain. Sophie
grew up to be a most witty woman, well worth her own biography.

I'll permit myself one story. In her maturity, in Rome in 1644, Sophie wrote in her journal:

> *I went to see the [church] of Mary of the Victory, formerly called Jupiter of the Victory, where the Emperor Ferdinand had sent his scepter and his crown to a small portrait of the virgin that he believed was responsible for his winning the battle of Prague against the king, my father. The monk who showed me this beautiful present said to me that a great princess like me also should give something. I replied to be sure, if the virgin had been on the other side. (A 556)*

Eventually, family fortunes did look up, for Elisabeth's namesake (Sophie's descendant) sits on the throne in Buckingham Palace today.

Elisabeth lamented to Descartes on 20 June 1643 that the life she has to lead "does not give me enough free time to acquire a habit of meditation according to your rules." Descartes replied on 28 June 1643 with his famous (and false) claim that he has never spent "more than a few hours a day in thoughts that occupy the imagination and a few hours a year on those that occupy the intellect alone." He goes on to say that he has given "all the rest of my time to the relaxation of my senses and the repose of my mind," which is just what the princess-on-call cannot arrange to do, neither could Descartes himself do.

Elisabeth was in fact very harassed by court life, so much so that she was in a state of slight depression. Descartes recommended that Elisabeth think joyful thoughts and then she would be happy. In a letter of 1 September 1645, he even claimed that he never had bad dreams because he had long accustomed himself "to drive away sad thoughts." In January 1646, to counsel Elisabeth on her depression, he wrote to her that one ought not allow "the troubles that come to us from outside, no matter how great they are, to enter into our minds any farther than the sadness caused by actors when they represent very distressing actions in front of us." Descartes used theater metaphors throughout his life, to the extent that one suspects that he truly did believe that all the world is a stage. Perhaps this is a measure of his general removal from most of the cares of ordinary life. Elisabeth, in a milieu of real seduction, real murders, and real beheadings, thought that Descartes's advice to view one's life as theater was not merely impossible but absurd.

In one wonderful exchange, Descartes pontificates pompously (very like a father) and Elisabeth replies irritatedly setting him straight (very like a daughter). On 6 October 1645, Descartes writes:

> *If your Highness would but consider the reasons why she has had more leisure to cultivate her reason than most others her age, and if she would also consider how much more she has profited than others, I am assured that she will be content. And I do not see why in comparing herself to them, she should not be greatly satisfied, rather than complaining.*

Elisabeth's father, the Winter King, was the joke of Europe when he lost Bavaria in 1620, and he had the bad luck to die of the plague in 1632. Furthermore, Elisabeth's family was so extravagant that there often was no money to pay the butcher and the baker. But here Descartes tells her how much better off she is than lots of other women. On 20 October 1645, Elisabeth replied indignantly:

> *I am astonished that you want me to compare myself to those my age, particularly in things that are unknown to me, with the notion that this would be more to my advantage than focusing on problems I cannot ignore. So what if I have had more advantages in cultivating my reason than others who have not had such advantages? Knowing what others have done won't help me know whether I have profited more in cultivating my reason. And I have no doubt at all that if I had the time to relax my body requires, I would be more advanced than I am.*

Descartes knew nothing at all about the burdens Elisabeth had to bear. Her mother was frivolous, her brothers and sisters importunate, and beyond that were the demands of court civility. Elisabeth was not at liberty to think of "forest greenery, the colors of flowers, or the flight of a bird" every time her unmarried sister got pregnant, her brother committed a murder, or her uncle got his head chopped off. In his letter of 9 February 1649, Descartes points out that getting his head cut off was less painful for her uncle, Charles I of England, than if he had died of a fever, and besides it gave him the opportunity to put on a great show of bravado. Charles I in fact was terrified and had to be dragged to the chopping block and held down.

Descartes truly begins to sound like Voltaire's Candide, who proclaimed this the best of all possible worlds no matter what happened to him. On 2 March 1646, Descartes says "There are always more good things than evil in this life." In his letter of 6 October 1645, he declaims a set piece that begins: "I have sometimes asked myself the following question: Is it better to be cheerful and content by imagining that one's goods are greater and more valuable than they are, not knowing or caring to know what one lacks, or is it better to consider and know the real value of one's condition, and thus be sad?" He concludes, of course, that it is better to be wise and sad than dumb and happy. But then he goes on to say that "since almost everything in the world can be looked at from some point of view that makes it seem good ... we should look at things from the point of view that makes them seem most to our advantage, provided" he pedantically appends, "it involves no self-deception." In *Candide*, Voltaire parodies Leibniz, but his target could just as well have been Descartes.

Elisabeth was Descartes's match. My favorite letter is the one of 1 August 1644 in which she thanks Descartes for dedicating his *Principles* to her. She does not linger on the phrases of adoration that Petit thinks constitute a public declaration of love by Descartes. She thanks him for publicly witnessing his friendship and approbation and for making her a party to his glory. Then as she often does, so often it has to be conscious and even a bit sardonic, she feeds him back his own words by saying that if she understands him better than others, it is because unlike the Schoolmen, she is not corrupted by Aristotelianism. Finally, in that quite short letter, she makes two astute critical objections to highly technical details in the *Principles* he has just dedicated to her, citing page numbers and outlining her arguments.

There is also an unembarrassed exchange — which is very Dutch — about Elisabeth's obstructions in the spleen that cause a thickness in the blood, which ultimately comes down to constipation. (A painting by Jan Asselyn, painted between 1647 and 1652, shows front and center a dog defecating, and just off center left a man pissing against the wall. There are many such scenes in Dutch paintings of the time. This must mean something, but the most I can get from art historians is that the Dutch were amused by scatology.)

Sewage was dumped into gutters in all the towns to flow into the canals which, in summer, made the towns stink to high heaven. People were less squeamish about such things then than now, but even so, it is rather startling to read the exchange between Elisabeth and Descartes, like that of a patient discussing her female problems with a physician. Descartes prescribed like a physician, saying that the waters of the Spa would clear up her obstructions. Throughout, Descartes's main advice is that diet and exercise are better than medicines. Then in July 1647 Descartes made his ultimate Stoic, mind-over-matter pronouncement: "I know nothing more adequate for the conservation of health than a strong persuasion and firm belief that one's bodily constitution is so good that when one is healthy it is not easy to get sick," but he qualifies the advice by going on to say "unless one engages in notable excesses or the air or other external causes harm one."

Descartes also discussed political matters with Elisabeth, and some of his advice is very astute. The fate of the Palatine inheritance was decided on 24 October 1648 by the Treaty of Münster. The eldest son and heir, Elisabeth's brother Charles-Louis, was given the Lower Palatine, while Emperor Ferdinand II kept the Upper Palatine. Descartes advised Elisabeth to tell Charles-Louis, who wanted the whole Palatine, to take what was offered to him and to thank Sweden, France, and the Empire very nicely for giving him anything at all. Beggars can't be choosers. Anyway, each was just doing it to keep the other from getting it, so don't give them time to think it over.

In his *Descartes and Princess Elisabeth*, Léon Petit is impatient with anyone who doubts that Elisabeth was the love of Descartes's life. And what a thrill if there had been a love affair between Descartes and Elisabeth! As far as the morals of the Bohemian court went, there was no serious deterrent. In 1646, a French courtier, Jacques de l'Espinay, having been kicked out of France because he seduced the mistress of the king's brother, now seduced Elisabeth's sister Louise (after first, the gossip goes, having had his way with her mother — Louise herself was said to be no prize, but royal conquest was his game). This sport was not, however, approved by the youngest member of the family, nineteen-year-old Prince Philippe, who behooved himself to avenge the family honor by having l'Espinay assassinated by a dozen hired English thugs in the open market square in broad daylight. Prince Philippe then escaped town on a horse (and was later killed in battle at the siege of Rethel in 1655).

Elisabeth's mother believed that her daughter had urged Philippe to arrange this assassination, so she exiled Princess Elisabeth by sending her to live in Germany with her Aunt Catherine, the electrice of Brandenburg. Elisabeth left The Hague on 15 August 1646, never to return to the United Provinces. Descartes visited her in The Hague during the summer before she left for Berlin but never saw her again.

Petit bases his case for a love affair on the fever, veneration, and tenderness of Elisabeth's compliments to Descartes and on Descartes's saying that happiness for him consists in knowing Elisabeth, seeing her again, and enjoying her friendship. On 31 January 1648, Descartes says that "Nothing could keep me from preferring the happiness of living where Your Highness does, if the occasion should present itself either in my own country or someplace else, wherever it may be." And on 22 February 1649, he says, "There is no place in the world so rude or incommodious in which I would not count myself happy to spend the rest of my days, if Your Highness were there." This is all very well, but Descartes had read *Amadis de Gaul*. He knew the conventions of chivalry. Instead of moving three days away from his lady love as soon as he met her — and Petit thinks he was smitten with a "thunderbolt" on that first occasion as witnessed by the panegyric in his first letter to her — Descartes should have moved to The Hague to be at Elisabeth's beck and call. When she was banished, he should have packed up and followed her to Berlin. At the very least, he should never have let months at a time go by without writing to her.

Yet, on his visits to France in 1644, 1647, and 1648, Descartes wrote Elisabeth only two letters. After he returned from Paris in November 1644 he did not write to her until 18 May 1645, and then only because Pollot said she had been ill. He was ready to come to The Hague to check on her health, he says, when, to his great relief, he learned that she has recovered, so he stayed home and wrote her a nice letter instead. Finally, Descartes's last letter to Elisabeth from Sweden is dated 14 October 1649, and it is another four months before he dies. That October letter is full of praise for Queen Christina. Elisabeth did not reply until 14 December 1649, and that is the end of the affair.

There is no question but that Elisabeth and Descartes liked one another personally. He was even conceivably serious when he talked of possibly coming to live near Elisabeth in the Palatine. But I would guess that given his experiences later that year in the Swedish court, had he lived, he would have had enough of royalty, and in the spring of 1650 would have hurried back to Egmond never to leave home again.

The most incredible thing about Descartes's relationship with Elisabeth, however, is that he dedicated his *Principles* to her. Here is the book he intends to replace the Aristotelian textbooks in the Jesuit schools, a goal he has had in mind at least for twenty years, *and he dedicates it to a Protestant princess.* Even if she married a king (which is unlikely as she had no property), she had already shown that it would have to be a Protestant king. She had neither power nor property nor was she likely to get any. It is all the more puzzling because if he were going to dedicate a book to Elisabeth, it should have been *The Passions of the Soul,* which she asked him to write, and much of which he worked out in letters to her. In any event, Descartes's dedication of the *Principles* to Elisabeth is terribly tactless. Somehow, despite his desire to have his physics and philosophy taught in Catholic schools, Descartes went out of his way to insult the Catholic teaching establishment.

I don't like the hypothesis that the church's censure of Galileo made Descartes think the game was all over anyway. He certainly had not given up. He went to France in 1644, in part to establish his presence again, to let people see him and hear him talk, to attach flesh and blood to his books and his philosophy, so they could be less easily dismissed.

Given that, one wonders again what he was he doing dedicating the detailed exposition of his philosophy to a Protestant. I am totally baffled by this. Of course it had done him no noticeable good to dedicate the *Meditations* to the doctors of the Sorbonne (who were not Jesuits, either, as far as that goes). But at least the doctors of the Sorbonne were Catholic teachers, like the Jesuits, and they did approve the *Meditations* at least to the extent that they said nothing and so did not condemn it. Descartes's dedication to Elisabeth is a real slap in Catholic faces. And he dedicated the book not just to a Protestant, but to a woman, besides.

Five years later, Descartes dedicated his *Passions of the Soul* to another Protestant woman, Queen Christina of Sweden. Could he have seriously been considering converting and throwing the lot of his philosophy in with the Lutherans? Nobody can believe that, even if, like Humpty-Dumpty, they work hard at it for twenty minutes a day. If Descartes fell off the wall of Catholic orthodoxy, no Protestant king's horses and men would or could ever put him back together again. I don't know what game he was playing. He was terribly timid and dared not cross the church by publishing that the earth moves around the sun, but on several other occasions he was drawn to making grand gestures even though the heavens might fall (on him).

On his way back to Holland from France in 1644, Descartes was delayed for fifteen days by high winds in Calais. There on 10 November 1644, he wrote in the guest book of his host, Cornelis de Glarges,

ENGRAVING AFTER A PORTRAIT DRAWING OF DESCARTES
BY FRANS SCHOOTEN II, 1644

Rijksmuseum, Amsterdam

this epigram from Seneca: Unfortunate is the man who is well known to everyone else but who dies unknown to himself. Descartes liked this line so much that he repeated it in a letter of 1 November 1646 to Chanut.

During the time that Descartes was responding heatedly to the attacks of the Orthodox Pastor Voetius, he was counseling Elisabeth on how to control the passions. In June 1645, he wrote her that he was more interested in learning how her health was than "to know what happens to my advantage or disadvantage at Groningen and Utrecht" where he was being threatened with arrest for libeling Voetius. Descartes was a great thinker, to be sure, but his words and actions were, like those of all normal human beings, often at odds.

During the seven last years of Descartes's life, he seldom enjoyed the quiet that he told Elisabeth (and everyone) was his sole reason for moving to the United Provinces. But his fortunes did advance. The *Principles* was published in Latin in 1644, as were the *Discourse*, *Dioptrics*, and *Meteors*. Descartes supervised the French translations of the *Principles*, the *Meditations*, and the *Objections* and *Replies*, all published in 1647. In his correspondence, he explained to the Jesuit Mesland how Cartesian philosophy can be used to explain transubstantiation. He insisted to the Marquis of Newcastle, William Cavendish, that animals are machines that have no souls, no feelings, thoughts, or consciousness, which is proved by the fact that they cannot talk while even the most idiotic human being can use language. He opposed Henry More's views that God is extended and failed to answer More's question of how the mind possibly could move the body without breaching the deterministic laws of physics. In his correspondence with Elisabeth, he began to analyze the passions. He had suggested the topic, and the astute Elisabeth soon caught the lead and asked him to write *The Passions of the Soul*, which he published in 1649.

In 1644, Descartes was in Paris six months, from June to November. Then again in 1647, four months from June to September, and in 1648, four months from May to August. He was looking for a place to go, for he was worried that the Calvinist theologians were going to harry him out of the United Provinces. There is a very sad letter to Picot of 1 January 1648 in which he says he is afraid he is enjoying (in Egmond) the last tranquil period of his life. He was right.

The search for peace and quiet is the persistent theme in all Descartes's personal writings. One could say that he protests too much, for he simply did not have the temperament for sitting still, letting life go by, and always seeking out the good side of events. Even so, from about 1634 until he left for Sweden in September 1649, except for the visits to Paris, Descartes lived mostly in the country outside Santpoort, Leiden, Egmond aan den Hoef, and Egmond-Binnen. But his publications involved him in continual polemics. There was no way this man was going to be left alone to tend his garden.

Nevertheless the sort of life Descartes actually led, more than anything else, was the life of a writer. For long periods of time he sat in his room and wrote. And his philosophical works are as tightly written as anything you will ever read. More than 350 years after the appearance of his *Meditations*, hundreds of articles and many books are published every year in which the details of Cartesianism are worked out in new and intricate ways. To provide a text with that depth, a philosopher must think how every part integrates with every other part. Descartes did not leave any manuscript drafts. But it is clear that he worked like a mathematician by going over his ideas time and again in his head. Contrary to what he told Elisabeth, he did not think of metaphysics only a few hours a year; he thought for days, weeks, months, and years about metaphysics. Then slowly, painstakingly, he wrote his thoughts down in clean copies.

Elisabeth obviously admired Descartes and was truly grateful for the attention he paid her. But she was by no means supine. It is patently clear that she knows he cannot answer the question of how mind and body interact, a crucial weakness at the heart of his metaphysics. And besides her setting him straight on the inapplicability to practical life of his maxims about how to be tranquil by thinking good thoughts and always seeing the bright side of life, her letters are full of irony at Descartes's expense. Or sarcasm. In her last letter to him of 14 December 1649, she says his trip to Sweden will surely be a success and that "You will find even more marvels in the queen of Sweden than she already has a reputation for." There had been plans for Elisabeth to visit Sweden, but Christina had no interest whatsoever in having a thirty-year-old beauty, a princess and a cousin, visit her court.

One of Elisabeth's sharpest remarks to Descartes follows a report of an affliction she and her aunt suffered after walking under some oak trees in Berlin. They were thereafter covered with a red rash that itched insupportably. The peasants said it was from a venomous pollen. Elisabeth concludes her recital of 23 August 1648 to Descartes by saying: "I tell you this story because I presume that you will find in it something to confirm one of your doctrines." Let's see you think that itch away with sweet thoughts. And while you're at it, just exactly what is the good side of that experience, since you say there is a good side to everything? At least the tree didn't fall down and smash us dead? Descartes very patiently replied in October 1648 that if they had washed with eau-de-vie immediately, the itch would have been cured.

Elisabeth had already alluded sarcastically to the theme of thinking good thoughts in her letter of 29 November 1646, in which she says everyone treats her so well and the air is so good for her complexion (in Berlin, before the oak trees) that "I find myself in a state with enough power to practice your lessons with regard to gaiety." Descartes had written her just that month that gay thoughts seemed to make things go better for him.

Princess Elisabeth never married, and in later life became the Abbess of Herford, a Lutheran monastery in Westphalia, where, ironically, she had considerable property and power. There she sheltered misfits from various Protestant sects. Among them was Anna Maria van Schurman, who had become obsessed with the mystic Jean de Labadie. Descartes had warned Anna Maria long before that she was wasting her intellect on theology. Van Schurman died in 1678, having renounced all intellectual endeavors. Elisabeth died in 1680.

No, it was not a love affair. But it was a fair exchange, a meeting of minds between two exceptional human beings. Elisabeth challenged Descartes and she inspired him to write one of first works in physiological psychology, *The Passions of the Soul*. Elisabeth sought to know Descartes because he was one of the greatest thinkers of the age. And we know Elisabeth because she knew him.

CANDIDE ET GENEROSE

HENRY REGIUS (1598–1679)
DESCARTES'S FIRST DISCIPLE IN UTRECHT
Bibliothèque Nationale de France

XI ⚔ THE PREACHERS

I am not an atheist.

THE WAY TO GET IN TROUBLE in the United Provinces was to argue about religion, or to publish — as Descartes did — some metaphysical views that conflict with Orthodox Calvinism. Descartes certainly knew how heated the supposedly phlegmatic Dutch temperament could get over religion. When he was in Breda in 1618, Dutch theologians were battling over the issue of predestination. The Orthodox Calvinists adhered to the views of Franciscus Gomarus who held that God's choice of people (the elect) to go to heaven is completely arbitrary from the human point of view. Faith, good works, nothing we do can assure us a place. Only God's grace can get us to heaven. On the other side, the Remonstrant Calvinists believed with Jacob Arminius that God predetermined the elect on the basis of his foreknowledge of how people will freely behave and that our faith and good works do count in God's choice. Thus there is a real possibility that everyone can be saved. Overall, the Remonstrants thought God's ways had to appear reasonable to human beings, while the Orthodox argued that God's ways are beyond human comprehension.

The two factions split also on political grounds. Both groups believed that the state should combine with religion to maintain order, but the conservative, theocratic Orthodox thought that rulers should be subordinate to the church, whereas the liberal, republican Remonstrants thought the church should be subordinate to the state.

In 1619, the conflict came to a head at the National Synod of Dordrecht where representatives of all seven of the United Provinces voted to establish the Orthodox view. As remarked before, they were supported by Prince Maurice, who was stadhouder (commander in chief) of the United Provinces. The Union was a loose republic, with each province politically independent except for a representative body called the States General that concerned itself only with foreign affairs and national defense. The stadhouder was important because the United Provinces were engaged in the long war of independence against Spain that lasted from 1560 to victory in 1648.

Prince Maurice was an atheist who opportunistically supported the Orthodox because they were most likely to crown him king or at least treat him as such. The Orthodox, in turn, opportunistically supported Prince Maurice because they thought him most likely to crush the Remonstrants who were backed by rich and liberal businessmen in Amsterdam. We already know that Prince Maurice took the decision of the Synod of Dordrecht as an opportunity to behead the most powerful leader in the United Provinces, Johan van Oldenbarnevelt, the magistrate of Amsterdam (which commanded half the wealth of the United Provinces).

Prince Maurice died in 1625. His liberal half brother Prince Frederick-Henry became stadhouder, and the Remonstrants began to rise as a power again. The religious debates were reengaged. But none of this seemed to be of any concern to Descartes from his return to the United Provinces in late 1628 until 1638 when his disciple Henry Regius, whose father had been the Utrecht representative on the Remonstrant side at the Synod of Dordrecht in 1618–1619, got in trouble with the Orthodox minister Gisbertus Voetius, who had been at the Synod on the Orthodox side.

When Voetius looked at Descartes's philosophy, he saw the Cartesian stress on the power of human reason as dangerously supporting the Remonstrant liberal view. Descartes says anyone with faith can get to heaven, as though grace is given to anyone who yearns for it. And Descartes's optimistic view of man's goodness is transparently in opposition to the doctrine of the Fall of Man and the Orthodox Calvinist view of arbitrary predestination.

Descartes was thinking of Catholic, Jesuit theology, and not of the Calvinists. With his eye on the lofty goal of giving Cartesian explanations of Catholic dogma (the existence of God, immortality, transubstantiation), Descartes stumbled into the Calvinist hornet's nest at his feet that he had up to that time mostly ignored or disdained.

The introduction of Descartes's philosophy into Dutch universities had begun with no problems at all. Descartes met Henry Reneri in 1629 and spent a year in Deventer with him in 1631, where Reneri was teaching. Helena Jans may have been a servant in the Reneri household, and Francine was baptized in Deventer.

When Reneri was called to be professor of philosophy at the University of Utrecht in 1634, Descartes moved there to live close to his friend for another year, during which time he worked on his *Meteorology*. The winter of 1634–1635 was very cold, offering fine conditions for studying snow and crowns around stars caused by light refracted by ice crystals in the air.

Reneri quietly taught Descartes's method of investigation and scientific explanation at Utrecht. In his inaugural lecture in 1634, he stressed observation and experiment. And in 1638, he lectured on Descartes's *Discourse on Method* and the scientific essays. Reneri never said a word about Cartesian metaphysics, and he never once got in trouble for teaching Cartesianism.

Reneri died in 1639. At his funeral, his friend Antonius Aemilius gave an oration that included a panegyric on Descartes. Aemilius said Descartes was the unique Archimedes of his century, the unique Atlas of the universe, the confidant of nature, powerful Hercules, Ulysses, Daedalus, etc. This was apparently approved of by town officials but not by the theological faculty.

In 1638, Reneri had introduced Descartes to Henry Regius. Descartes was delighted with Regius, inviting him and his wife and child out to the country for ripe cherries and pears. Reneri was a good friend, but this man Regius was a true disciple, Descartes's first. Descartes told Mersenne with pride that this young professor he had never even met (not true) had written to thank him for helping him get his appointment at Utrecht where Descartes knew no one (an outright lie). But Regius really did say that he had advanced because he had learned so much from the *Discourse* and the *Essays*. And for awhile — before kicking him out of the nest — Descartes clucked over Regius like a mother hen with one chick. But almost from the beginning, Descartes found Regius difficult to control.

Regius wanted to publish a book on physics, to which Descartes objected because Regius did not follow Descartes's views exactly. Moreover, Descartes intended to publish his own physics someday. Regius did, however, publish his physics in 1646. Regius said the union of the human soul with the human body is accidental, and not, as Descartes and Catholic Church doctrine claimed, substantial. So Descartes felt that he really had to disassociate himself from Regius. The way to get back at opponents in those days was to publish a broadside. Disputants then went to the printer as naturally as we today go to the Xerox machine or Web site. So as the year 1648 began, Descartes disowned his disciple Regius by printing *Notes on a Certain Program*.

Regius had been appointed professor of theoretical medicine and botany, but he really wanted to teach natural philosophy. He was from a rich family of brewers in Utrecht, so he had the town fathers behind him. Voetius, who had been brought in from outside as professor of theology, and who had just been elected to a one-year term as rector, was taken with Regius, so allowed him to lecture on natural philosophy as a background to medicine. In November and December of 1641, Regius thus organized a series of dissertations on physics. They went all right until Regius argued that man's soul and body are not united by God as one being but are only accidentally connected. This was bad enough, but what convinced Voetius that Regius was an enemy of Orthodox religion was Regius's open support of the view that the earth moves around the sun.

Everyone took sides, and on 8 December 1641, a formal disputation at the university erupted into a magnificent mélée of foot stomping, hooting, whistling, overturned benches, shoving, and fistfights. It was wonderful, and the students loved it.

The point of the argument is this: If your soul and body are united as one being, then the resurrection of your body is necessary if *you* are to live in Paradise. But if the union is accidental, then only your soul need dwell in Paradise, and the resurrection of the body is not necessary.

Voetius immediately organized some disputations to attack Regius's views. Descartes was none too happy about it but advised Regius to reply, otherwise people would think he had been defeated by Voetius. Descartes also gave Regius the bad advice to argue that Voetius's Aristotelian views lead to the notion that the soul is material, and this is atheism. This was too much. In March 1641, Regius was forbidden to discuss physics, and the teaching of the new philosophy was banned. Even so, Regius continued to profess Cartesian science — as he adapted it — at Utrecht until his death in 1679. And like Reneri before him, he ignored Cartesian metaphysics.

Descartes was quite outraged that Utrecht had forbidden the teaching of Cartesianism, so in his "Letter to Dinet" published with the second edition of his *Meditations* in Amsterdam, he launched a violent personal attack on Voetius that is completely gratuitous in the context of the *Meditations*.

Descartes said that Voetius was quarrelsome. But Descartes himself was behaving like a mad dog. And imprudently, besides. Descartes was a foreigner, a Catholic, a layman, and here he was publishing in Amsterdam an attack on a distinguished Orthodox Dutch Calvinist minister of the gospel who was also a professor and rector of the University of Utrecht. Moreover, Descartes surely anticipated that Voetius's Remonstrant archenemy Jean Batelier would immediately translate Descartes's attack from Latin into Dutch and publish it for everyone to read. Descartes was looking for a fight even if he protested that Voetius had hit him first. (One of Descartes's old saws is that he who strikes first always has the advantage.)

In his "Letter to Dinet," Descartes declares that Voetius is a stupid pedant who uses sarcasm to appeal to the common people, and to turn them against their betters. Voetius doesn't argue, he just insults his opponents. He is an enemy of the truth (that is, of Descartes's own views). Voetius is a hypocrite who really just wants to maintain his power in the university by attacking a popular professor (Regius) who was getting more students than Voetius was.

Voetius was rightfully furious. He immediately engaged Martin Schoock to attack Descartes in a long book entitled *The Admirable Method*, published in 1634. Their strongest charge is that Descartes is actually an atheist who rejects the traditional proofs for the existence of God to substitute one so weak that anyone reading his works will be led into atheism. This is what Mersenne and others said Vanini had done. And Vanini was burned at the stake in Toulouse in 1619. Descartes is compared to Vanini numerous times in the book.

In his *Letter to Voetius* of 1644, Descartes replied that this comparison to Vanini is the vilest of criminal slanders. This is in some part because of the accusation that Descartes is deviously trying to make people into atheists. But he was also outraged because Vanini had been burned at the stake as much for homosexual acts as for his heretical theology.

Schoock later said it was Voetius's idea to compare Descartes with Vanini as an atheist so everyone would make the Sodom and Gomorrah connection as well. Descartes's total outrage shows that Voetius hit his mark. Over and over again, Descartes complains that Voetius's attack is cruel, slanderous, libelous, impudent, insolent, evil, false, and prosecutable. Descartes calls both on Voetius's university superiors and on the Utrecht town government to punish the slanderer. Descartes even tells them that he is doing them a favor by exposing the perfidious villain. In a letter of 6 July 1643 to the Utrecht city council, he says it is not just that he is defending his honor. Descartes is also trying to procure the common good by defending the town and university from Voetius.

The biggest mistake Voetius made during this whole affair was to write to Mersenne to solicit help against Descartes, whose disciples, Voetius said, were taking him to be a god. Mersenne had written a large book against atheists and would surely want to help Voetius expose this one. Mersenne asked for more information, then sent Voetius's letters to Descartes. Descartes dictated a reply to Voetius that Mersenne copied and sent unsealed to Descartes (as requested).

Naturally, the letter sets Voetius straight about the superior value of Cartesian science and philosophy. Descartes read it, sealed it, and sent it on to Voetius. In the trunk of papers that Descartes left with Hogeland when he went to Sweden in 1649, the only letters he specified that should be kept and not burned were those from Voetius to Mersenne — to keep the record straight.

Voetius has had a very bad press among Cartesian scholars who usually characterize him as a dogmatic, fanatical, quarrelsome, none-too-bright but very stubborn doctrinaire Calvinist. He truly did seem, as Descartes said, to seek out arguments, particularly with the more Remonstrant of the more liberal wing of Dutch Calvinism. Even so, when you compare the rhetoric of Descartes's nearly 200-page *Letter to Voetius* to that of Voetius (and of Schoock in his *The Admirable Method* to which Descartes was responding), they differ mostly by the wealth of Schoock's and Voetius's citations as compared to Descartes's disdain for all ancient authors, except for the Gospel writers Matthew and John. For example, Descartes cites the words of Jesus Christ from Matthew 7, "Judge not, that ye be not judged." But when it comes to diatribe, whining complaint, and calling names, Descartes and Voetius are a match.

It could have remained merely a local, personal matter. The Dutch scholar Theo Verbeek remarks that Descartes simply did not understand. University and town officials in Utrecht really did not want to touch the quarrel, so their way of handling matters was to forbid the printing or discussion — for or against — of anything about Descartes and Cartesianism. In succeeding years, they quietly appointed Cartesian professors and turned their backs on breaches of the rules. But Descartes seemed unaware that if these officials were not exactly his friends, although he was really incensed because a number of them were (for example, the burgomaster Gisbert van der Hoolck, who was embarrassed by Descartes's demands), these officials definitely were not his enemies.

Utrecht is a delightful town, with a circling canal inside it on which you can take boat tours. When Pat and I went there, we stayed in the Hotel Maliebann, because Descartes had lived in a small house next to the Maliebann when he was in Utrecht. The Maliebann is a grass playing field, some fifty yards wide and five hundred yards long. It was built — outside town back then — for university students, who played paille-maille on it. Paille-maille is something like glorified croquet, with large mallets used to drive wooden balls through hoops set up on the Maliebann. Descartes is said to have owned a mallet.

As for Descartes's relations with public officials, in a letter to Rivet of April 1640, Saumaise remarks on a large dinner that Descartes gave for the magistrates and professors of Leiden, to which Saumaise and his wife had been invited — but did not go. This is an aspect of Descartes's social life of which there is not the slightest hint in his correspondence. Saumaise goes on to complain that Descartes makes extravagant compliments to him in person, but then is sarcastic about him behind his back. Saumaise wouldn't trust Descartes at all. In this letter Saumaise repeats a rumor about Descartes's illegitimate child he had heard from Descartes's valet, who complained about going to the country so often to see the child. That valet would have been Gillot (of whom Descartes said he would speak for as a brother when he recommended him for a position). Descartes's view of Saumaise — in December 1640 to Mersenne — is that Saumaise "is a bit too easy to offend." Saumaise wrote two volumes defending usury, which he sent to Descartes, who agreed that one should be permitted to earn interest on investments, something the Orthodox Calvinists strongly opposed but all city fathers approved.

The powers-that-be in Utrecht were simply fostering Dutch tolerance, which is to go along with the people they have to live with (Voetius, a few Cartesian professors) without really doing much harm to possibly mistreated outsiders (Descartes). But Descartes would not leave it at that. He made the quarrel international by publishing his vicious attack on Voetius in his "Letter to Dinet."

As remarked, Voetius retaliated by getting Schoock to write *The Admirable Method*, published in 1643. In 1644, Descartes blasted back with the *Letter to Voetius*. Voetius sued Descartes for libel. The local government in Utrecht was now forced to examine both the

GISBERTUS VOETIUS (1586–1676)
RECTOR AT THE UNIVERSITY OF UTRECHT IN 1641
Centraal Museum, Utrecht

"Letter to Dinet" and the *Letter to Voetius*, and they concluded correctly that Descartes had libeled Voetius. Never mind that Voetius had first libeled Descartes, Voetius was the one who was suing. The case was sent to the police court.

There again it could have stopped, for the Dutch republic was a

229

wonderfully loose union. The provinces were united only for foreign affairs and national defense. A legal process undertaken in Utrecht theoretically could not touch Descartes who was a resident of Holland. There was in fact an extradition agreement between the two provinces to prosecute in one what was decreed in the other, but almost certainly no one would enforce it. Nevertheless, Descartes panicked. He asked the French ambassador, the marquis Gaspard Coignet de la Thuillerie, for help. The ambassador spoke to the prince of Orange, who asked the officials in Utrecht to cancel the lawsuit. They did not cancel it, but neither did they pursue it.

Descartes would not let well enough alone. He announced that the honor of France had been insulted. He was a French nobleman. (At this point Descartes calls himself sieur du Perron.) He did not just want the heat turned off him, he wanted it turned on Voetius. Voetius should retract, and if he would not, the officials should punish him. Again Descartes appealed to the French ambassador, this time to ask that Voetius's lieutenant Schoock be prosecuted for libeling Descartes. If they sue you, then sue them back.

Schoock, who was a professor at Groningen (and the author of a wonderful book entitled *The Chicken and the Egg*), was duly arrested and spent two days in jail. He threw the blame for *The Admirable Method* onto Voetius, supporting his case with letters from Voetius that compromised the preacher. Schoock was exonerated. Descartes then bundled up all the details of the affair and in June 1645 he sent his "Apologetic Letter to the Magistrates of Utrecht" asking for apologies. They ignored it. And that was the end of the quarrel of Utrecht.

Descartes really should have kept out of the fight his wayward disciple Regius had gotten into with Voetius. Descartes even agreed with Voetius that Regius's notions about body and soul were heretical, and he split with Regius over this matter. On 6 June 1643, Huygens had told him to ignore Voetius. "Theologians are like pigs," Huygens said. "When you pull one by the tail, they all squeal." (This sounds like a joke, but it is really a warning. Pigs are very excitable, and if you get a batch of them squealing, they may attack you, kill you, eat you, and crunch your bones.) But Descartes could not stay out of it. And as Verbeek solemnly remarks, "Tact was not among Descartes's virtues" (D&D 20). Verbeek concludes that "If Cartesianism in the end conquered the universities of the United Provinces, one could say that in some sense it was *in spite of* Descartes, who constituted the major obstacle to the spread of his own philosophy" (Q 66).

It is hard to sympathize with Descartes in these disputes. Not that Baillet had any trouble. He describes Regius as an ingrate and Voetius as an ignoramus. Neither accusation is true. Descartes gives proofs for the existence of God, but Regius said that if you have faith, you do not need proofs. Descartes also gave a proof that the soul could be immortal. Here again, Regius asks: Who needs a proof? God's promise of immortality is enough. Let's get on with the physics!

Here is a crucial point for determining whether Descartes was a "zealous Catholic" as Saumaise, his countryman in the United Provinces and the greatest philologist of the day, described him (Saumaise himself had converted to Calvinism), or whether he was a secret atheist as Voetius had him, or a secret (but not very well hidden) materialist as the Cartesian scholar Hiram Caton argues. In a letter of 26 November 1630 to Mersenne, Descartes says, "I get angry when I see people so audacious and impudent as to attack God" — that is, atheists. Of course he was writing to a priest who had written a huge tract attacking atheism. And I wonder that maybe Clerselier added that sentence. But after reading Descartes's long diatribe in response to being called an atheist himself, I think he really did believe that atheism is the worst crime. He said, for example, that no state should tolerate atheism. And it was a crime punishable by death both in the United Provinces and France. People got burned at the stake for being atheists. At the very least, Descartes was responding to that threat but not just to the personal danger. His ambition to replace Aristotelianism with Cartesianism was also in jeopardy. No university was going to adopt the philosophy of an atheist.

Descartes was stunned by the accusation that he was an atheist and that his philosophy led to atheism. Several times he complained that people accused him of being a skeptic because he had refuted skepticism, and of being an atheist because he proved the existence of God. He argued that these people totally misunderstood him. Or they were misrepresenting him to attack him. Descartes's friend Fortunatus Plempius once said that the problem with Descartes was that he would never admit that he was wrong. And Roberval remarked on Descartes's lack of response to a criticism that it was the only occasion he knew of in which Descartes had sense enough to shut up. (Descartes was in fact trying to force Roberval to write down his objections to Descartes's view that there is no vacuum, but instead all of space is filled with subtle matter. Roberval never wrote it down. After Descartes's death, Clerselier forged a letter from Descartes containing an answer to Roberval's criticisms. Clerselier apologized that everyone knew the letter was a fake.)

There was also a crisis in Leiden. Adriaan Heereboord, the professor of logic, set a number of disputations from 1641 through 1646 that were Cartesian in their defense of reason in philosophy and theology. Heereboord also defended the Cartesian method of investigating natural science mechanically. No one complained about his disquisitions on the new philosophy. Then on 18 September 1646, the theologian Jacob Trigland attacked a principle being defended by one of Golius's students, that "doubt is the beginning of undoubtable philosophy," a sentiment deriving directly from Descartes's *Meditations*. For Descartes, once you have learned that everything can be doubted, you suddenly realize the certainty of "I think, therefore I am," and from this you can proceed directly to proof of the existence of God — you had to come from somewhere, and you sure didn't cause yourself. But Trigland argued that this doubt would lead students to skepticism and atheism. The university senate agreed, and decreed that only Aristotelian philosophy could henceforth be taught at Leiden. Nevertheless, Heereboord later gave an oration in which he argued that even Aristotle and Thomas use the method of doubt to exclude falsehoods, and he praised Descartes's method of doubt as a way to reach truth by freeing the mind of prejudices.

This basic attack on Aristotelianism greatly annoyed Jacob Revius who was regent of the theological school. In Deventer, Revius had been a friend of Reneri, and he had tried to convert Descartes. Besides commenting that he believed in the religion of his king and his nurse, Descartes may have set the convert Revius straight about Catholicism being the true, mother religion. But he could also just have put Revius off with platitudes, because he did believe that "we all worship the same God" (AT VIII-2 180). A gentle evasion, however, would have required tact, which Descartes did seem capable of exhibiting — although only with transparent ingenuousness — when addressing important Jesuits.

But Descartes's views about his religion go deeper than his joke about his king and his nurse. His first maxim for getting on in life is:

Obey the laws and customs of your land, retaining constantly the religion in which by God's grace you were instructed in your childhood, and govern yourself in all other things by following the opinions that are most moderate and farthest removed from excess, which are commonly received and followed by the most sensible of those among whom you live. (AT VI 22-23)

On the basis of this maxim, many commentators say Descartes was conservative in politics and religion, which he was.

In February and March 1644 Revius attacked Descartes's method of doubt on the grounds that it would lead inevitably to doubt of God's existence. Trigland added that Descartes's hypothesis that God might be a deceiver is blasphemous.

On 4 May 1647, Descartes wrote to the curators of Leiden University asking them to settle the affair with Revius and Trigland. He covertly hinted that otherwise he would make a public scandal of it. He wanted an apology and a retraction of his being called a blasphemer and a Pelagian, that is, someone who denies original sin.

Descartes did in fact deny the doctrine of original sin in his stress on the natural goodness of man. And in a letter to Huygens of 10 October 1642, Descartes also seems to deny hell. It is one of those letters for which we have documentary evidence of Clerselier's alterations. Descartes says "I am of those who love life the most," which Clerslier changes to "I esteem life sufficiently." And when Descartes says unqualifiedly that our souls are "born for felicities very much greater than those we enjoy in this world" Clerselier adds "provided that we regulate ourselves properly and do not render ourselves unworthy, and that we don't expose ourselves to the chastisements that are prepared for sinners." Descartes, however, says without qualification, "I can conceive of nothing other for those who die than that they pass on to a life sweeter and more tranquil than ours, and that we will go find them someday." Also, to Huygens on 10 October 1642, Descartes says he would rather go to heaven with the Dutch than with his French relatives.

The Leiden curators (as had those in Utrecht) decided that no professor should discuss Descartes "for or against," and that Heereboord should stick to Aristotelian philosophy. They sent a copy of their decision to Descartes, who replied testily that the issue was not about what should or should not be discussed but about the fact that he needed an apology and a retraction. Then, as was his habit (this being the third time), he appealed to the French ambassador, who spoke to the stadhouder, the prince of Orange.

But before anything could come of this, on 23 December 1647, Johannes de Raey, who had been Regius's student at Utrecht, attacked the theologian Adam Stuart, who was giving a disputation against the new philosophy. The session ended in another wonderful uproar. What great fun these disputations must have been! The Dutch are as stubborn as God, and they love arguments, particularly loud ones.

Meanwhile, in 1647, Revius had published *A Theological Consideration of Descartes's Method* in which (Verbeek summarizes) he concludes that "it may be true that Descartes tries to free himself of all prejudices, yet there is one to which he remains singularly attached — the conviction that he is absolutely right on everything ... what Descartes means by certain words is never what other people mean by them, so his invariable reaction is that he is misunderstood" (D&D 49). Besides this astute analysis, Revius scored a number of substantial points. Heereboord leaped to Descartes's defense by scheduling a disputation to oppose Revius.

Now the stadhouder told the curators to get the matter settled quietly. Three times by way of the French ambassador, Descartes received the support of the prince of Orange, who as commander in chief was in traditional terms, if not king, at least the supreme nobleman in the United Provinces. Descartes's ability to command such high level support is impressive.

The fact is that Descartes did not arrive in Franeker or Amsterdam or Leiden as just some Frenchman of the minor nobility who had enough money to live well in a rented country house. He was already Descartes, the world's greatest geometer. This gave him access to everyone who was an amateur or professional mathematician, or who followed the progress of the game. He was like Garry Kasparov in a world where everyone plays a little chess. This is undoubtedly at least part of the explanation of how Descartes happened to know people in the municipal governments of Utrecht, Groningen, and Leiden.

Descartes also knew Henri Brasset, secretary to the successive French ambassadors for many years. Descartes even gave a copy of *The Passions of the Soul* to Brasset's daughter, who was in her early twenties. Since 1638, Descartes had been a friend of Alphonse Pollot, who was a gentleman-in-waiting to the prince of Orange. And since 1630, his best friend in the United Provinces had been Constantijn Huygens, who was secretary to three successive princes of Orange. Descartes knew how to pick his friends.

But Descartes was also close to his peasant neighbors. He even got deeply involved in a murder. He tells a good story in a letter to Huygens of January 1646, in which he pleads the case for a pardon:

> *Monsieur, I know that many things occupy you that are of more importance than to take the time to read the compliments of a man who frequents here only peasants, so I dare not write to you except when I have occasion to ask you for something. I*

write to you now to give you the opportunity to exercise your charity for a poor peasant in my neighborhood who has had the misfortune to have killed someone. His relatives intend to seek the clemency of the Prince to try to obtain his grace, and they asked also that I write to you to ask you to second their request with a favorable word in case the occasion should arise. For me, I seek nothing but security and repose, and I am content to be in a land where crimes are chastised with rigor, because the impunity of criminals give them too much license. But because all the movements of our passions are not always in our power, it happens sometimes that the best men commit very great errors, and for this the giving of grace is more useful than the law. This is because it is better that one good man be saved than that a thousand bad ones be punished. Also, the most glorious and august act a prince can undertake is that of giving pardon. The peasant for whom I plead has a reputation here of not being quarrelsome, and he has never done anything to displease anyone before this misfortune. The most one could say to his disadvantage is that his mother was married to the one who is now dead. But if one adds that she had been outrageously beaten by her husband during several years living with him until finally she separated from him and no longer considered him as her husband but as her persecutor and enemy. Now to take vengeance on her for this separation, he threatened to kill one of her children (the one in question here). So one can see that there is much here to excuse the murderer. And as you know that I am accustomed to philosophize on all that presents itself to me, I will tell you that I have looked into the cause that could carry this poor man to do such a thing so far removed from his usual humor. And I have discovered that at the time the misfortunate happened, he was extremely afflicted because he had a sick child whose death he awaited at any moment. While he was with the child, someone came to call him to help his brother-in-law who was being attacked by their common enemy. So I do not find it strange that he was not master of himself in such an encounter. Because, when one has a great affliction, and when sadness leads one to despair, it is certain that one can easily be carried away by anger by something that would not incite it at another time. Such that ordinarily the best men who, seeing on one side the death of a child and on the other the peril to a brother, will be most violently moved. That is why crimes committed without any premeditated violence are, it seems to me, the most excusable. Thus, the murderer in this case was pardoned by all the principal relatives of the dead man on the same day that they assembled to bury him. And what is more, the local judge here absolved him, but too precipitously, which has obliged the higher court to overrule the pardon. The peasant is afraid to go before the higher court, which will follow the rigor of the law without regard to individuals. But he pleads for a pardon from the Prince on the basis of the innocence of his past life. I well know that it is sometimes very useful to make examples to put fear in criminals, but it seems to me that this case is not appropriate for that. Because, other than the fact that the criminal has fled and that all one could do is keep him from returning home and thus punish his wife and children more than him, there are many other peasants in these Provinces who have committed murders less excusable and whose lives are less innocent, who nevertheless still remain here without having any pardon from the Prince (and the dead man was of their number). This makes me think that if one made an example of my neighbor, those who are more accustomed than him to draw a knife will say that only the innocent and idiots fall into the hands of the courts, and will be confirmed in their criminality. Finally, if you do something to help this poor man reunite with his children, I can say that you will have done a good act, and that this will be a new obligation that I will have to you.

We don't know what happened to the peasant, neither do we know what happened to the local judge, for whom Descartes wrote a letter to Huygens almost a year later, on 27 December 1647:

> *I formerly asked you to have grace for a poor peasant of this quarter who had killed his step-father. Now this same affair gives me occasion to ask similar assistance for the officer of this quarter, who is not accused of having killed anyone, but only of having wished with his own authority to give the pardon that we desire to obtain from the Prince.... A reason most serious and most pressing which could convince the Prince to pardon him, and the higher court not to imprison him, is that he has a very large number of children who are in need of him, such that in punishing him one would punish also several innocent children.*

We don't know what happened next, because this is the last letter we have in the correspondence between Descartes and Huygens. So let us pause here for a moment to mourn the loss of another important batch of papers concerning Descartes's life.

Huygens's letters to Descartes were returned to Huygens after Descartes's death, and he bound them with copies of Descartes's letters into books. But the last letter in those books is the one quoted just above of 27 December 1647. Theirs was a heavy correspondence, and it certainly must have continued through Descartes's stay in Sweden until his death. But the volumes containing their correspondence from January 1648 through February 1650 are missing. Not only that, Huygens kept detailed daybooks all his life, and the daybook for the period 18 January 1650 through 30 April 1650, which would contain Huygens's comments on Descartes's death, is missing. Someone must have stolen those volumes. The bound volumes of the correspondence we do have were in the library of Harry Wilmot Buxton in England who is said to have gotten them from Charles Babbage, the inventor of the modern calculating machine. Maybe the missing volumes one day will be found.

There is no question that Descartes had a distaste for court life. Despite all his court friends and his dependence on them, Descartes never himself lived in The Hague, which housed the courts of the

CONSTANTIJN HUYGENS (1596–1687)

BY JAN LIEVENS

Rijksmuseum, Amsterdam

prince of Orange, the States General (senate), and the deposed king and queen of Bohemia. In a letter of 8 April 1644 to Pollot, he apologizes for the following behavior. He had been leaving Princess Elisabeth's lodgings in The Hague when he saw Pollot and a number of Frenchmen on their way to see Elisabeth's mother, the queen. He knew they had seen him, but he pretended he had not seen them, and he rushed off, he explained to Pollot, for fear they would keep him up past his bedtime.

Descartes was well known in the court. In 1644, Brasset called him in at the request of Prince Frederick-Henry's mother to help settle a boundary dispute concerning fishing rights in a lake. Stones had been dropped to the lake bottom to set the boundaries, and her highness was arguing that they had moved downslope. Of course they moved downslope, Descartes ruled. This dispute had been going on since 1552.

Descartes was never shy about asking favors from the court. In 1647, he successfully asked Huygens to open a game reserve for his friend Antonie Studler van Zurk, who bought the seigneurie of Bergen in northern Holland near where Descartes lived. Another service Descartes performed for van Zurk was to obtain plans of various French gardens for him. In turn, van Zurk acted as Descartes's banker.

These court contacts, and the fact that on three occasions Descartes got the stadhouder to intervene on his side at three provincial capitals — Utrecht, Groningen, and Leiden — makes one wonder whether the usual interpretation is right that Descartes was in a panic because the Utrecht municipality was suing him. Henrik Bruno, Huygens's literary secretary and tutor to his children, was a friend of Descartes. In a letter of 15 December 1647, Bruno reports that Descartes "laughed heartily about a horrible pamphlet that was recently written against him by a Leiden theologian [Revius], but he hardly thought it worth a reply." And he did not, in fact, reply directly to Revius. He kept insisting, as in a letter to Huygens of 20 September 1643, that the whole affair barely bothered him at all, and he goes on to say that "I can assure you that I have not lost any weight at all, unlike Voetius, who they say has lost thirteen pounds, but not of fat, because he has never had any." In Huygens's reply of 5 October 1643, he says it would be quite easy for Regius to save himself. All he has to do is to apologize and get on with his work. Descartes should forget it and get back to work himself.

Considering that the Utrecht citation of 13 September 1643 was immediately shelved by the order of the stadhouder, and that the stadhouder forced action on Descartes's demand that Groningen try Schoock for libel against him which was settled in Descartes's favor on 10 April 1644, one can imagine that Descartes may very well have gotten over his initial fright enough to laugh at Revius's attack in 1647. And when he did decide to demand that Leiden get Revius off his back, he was confident enough about the stadhouder's support to threaten the Leiden officials with a public scandal if they did not apologize. The prince of Orange had the rector of Leiden University, Frederick Spanheim, in to talk with him about the matter on 12 January 1648. Spanheim then contained the immediate dispute between Heereboord and Revius.

Then Johannes de Raey, a twenty-six-year-old student of Regius, was forbidden to teach Cartesianism on 14 June 1648. And Stuart and Revius complained about being forbidden to discuss and refute Descartes's dangerous opinions. Rector Spanheim's method of keeping these Aristotelian theologians from fighting with the Cartesian philosophers then was simply to forbid the teaching of metaphysics of any kind. Cartesian science, however, continued to be taught. Even an Orthodox theologian, Abraham Heidanus, appointed at Leiden in 1648, whom Descartes had known at least since 1639, was tolerant. If Descartes was not hysterical, then he certainly was a meddler. But none of this hindered Cartesianism from taking over in Dutch universities soon after Descartes's death in 1650.

Descartes was obviously well known and well respected where it mattered — among higher municipal and state officials, and even by curators of the universities of Utrecht, Groningen, and Leiden. Numerous people must have visited him besides those of whom we have a record. One of the reports gives a most interesting perspective on the man and philosopher in that it amounts to a virtual interview, as though he were going to be written up as new thinkers are for *Le Monde* or the *New York Times Magazine*.

A theology student, Frans Burman, age twenty-three (Descartes knew his father), visited Descartes on 16 April 1648 and took extensive notes on their conversation. For the previous five years, Burman had been a student of theology at Leiden, so he knew all about the disputes. After his discussion with Descartes, he reported it to Johannes Clauberg, who wrote it up in Latin. The original is lost, and all we have is a copy in an unknown hand found in the university library in Gottingen in 1895, which Cartesian scholars take to be authentic on the basis of its contents — that is, there is no external evidence that *Conversations With Burman* actually is a report of the conversation. But never mind, Descartes himself noted that he had a visit from Burman. The personal picture this text gives of Descartes is of a genial, forthright, pleasant, and eminently reasonable man, concerned both to instruct the younger man and to explicate his position in answer to various critics. Both of them seem to have had a thoroughly good time. I disapprove, however, of taking an assumed copy of Clauberg's expansion of Burman's notes as gospel Descartes, as many Cartesian scholars do, even though it does show Descartes at his best.

The Utrecht quarrel, like his quarrel with Beeckman, shows Descartes at his personal worst. It also suggests how much attention he actually paid to local politics and affairs. He was worldly enough to know the right people, and he helped his neighbors, but he gained his leisure, as all expatriates do, by general lack of involvement in most social and political concerns crucial to the natives' lives. (One of his few political remarks is in a letter to Mersenne of 4 January 1643 in which he says that if Cardinal Richelieu "gave you three of his millions to do the experiments necessary to discover the nature of different bodies, I don't doubt that the knowledge gained would be very much more useful to the public than all the victories that can be earned in making war.")

Descartes thought he was setting the idiots straight. Among his critics, Descartes was decent to Mersenne (who asked leading questions), to Arnauld (who was a sympathetic Catholic theologian), and to Elisabeth (who was a princess). The rest were beyond help. They misunderstood Descartes, who might admit to being unclear here and there (probably by intent to weed out ignoramuses), but who was never wrong. In 1641, when Descartes was raging about Gassendi's objections, Gassendi said, "What can you do? It is his temperament." When Descartes said that Voetius was inciting the lower classes against their betters, that he was corrupting the youth he was being paid to teach, and that his behavior constituted sedition against the state so that the municipality should remove him and even prosecute him, he truly believed he was doing Utrecht a service by saying outright what the officials were constrained from saying by protocol. Descartes expected them to be grateful to him for getting it all out in the open so they could get rid of Voetius. They ignored his instructions.

He does seem to have been frightened when the Utrecht officials set the police on him, but as soon as the stadhouder intervened, he just got bolder. The stadhouder, for reasons of his own having to do with balancing the powers of church and state, wanted to keep down the power of the preachers.

Descartes stood on his honor: He denied that he was an atheist. He went to Paris in 1648 and then to Sweden in 1649, where he died in early 1650. There is no indication that had he lived, he would have let the quarrel with the preachers drop until he got the justice he demanded — that is, humble admission that they were wrong and he was right.

XII ⚔ THE FRONDE

It is like inviting a guest to dinner when your kitchen is in
an uproar and the cooking pot turned over.

JOACHIM DESCARTES's seventy-fifth birthday was on 2 December 1638. His second son, René, had not seen him for ten years. Perhaps his father's seventy-fifth birthday set him to thinking — if slowly — for on 30 July 1640, he told Huygens that in five or six weeks he was going to go to France for family matters. But he kept putting it off, and on 30 September 1640, he told Huygens he would not be going to France that year, after all.

From 1636 through 1640, Descartes lived in Egmond-Binnen, Santpoort, and Amersfort with Helena and Francine. He wrote his *Discourse* and the *Essays*, published in 1637, and worked on his *Meditations*, published in 1641. He had two friends in Haarlem nearby, Jean Albert Bannius and Augustin Aelstein Bloemaert, Catholic priests who were interested in mathematics and music. Bannius was a good musician who played for them on his new spinet.

Descartes's father died on 17 October 1640, just forty days after Francine. Not knowing this, on 28 October 1640, Descartes wrote a letter to his brother and father, saying that he intended to come soon to Brittany to visit them. Baillet says he told them that he lived in Holland to avoid persecution for his ideas by Aristotelians. What else he said we don't know as the letter is lost.

Only then was Descartes informed of his father's death. The fact is that Descartes communicated with his brother Pierre and his half sister Anne through Mersenne. They simply did not know his address in Holland. As for family matters, the only ones that concerned Descartes had to do with money. He lived off the interest paid on the property he had sold. Thus when his father died, Descartes arranged for Claude du Boüexic in Rennes, who became a member of the Parliament in Brittany in 1645, to handle his inheritance, the collection of interest, and contracts. Baillet had the contracts that Descartes carried with him to Sweden, but they are lost now, as is Descartes's letter of 3 December 1640 to his brother Pierre about these matters. In cash alone, Descartes's father left 126,840 livres. He willed his son René Descartes an unknown amount of money, the land and farms of Courgère near Oiré and of Beauvis, and with his brother Pierre the Descartes house in Châtellerault. Pierre immediately took over these properties and made an initial payment of 4,000 livres with an annual interest of 500 livres a year to Descartes. There is no indication of how many years any of this interest was contracted to be paid. Descartes used this money to rent the château of Endegeest on the outskirts of Leiden where he lived from March 1641 to May 1643, when he moved to Egmond aan den Hoef. (The château of Endegeest is now an insane asylum. They tell the story there of a former inmate who used to greet visitors at the gate, inform them he was the director, and show them around. Always at some point he would take off the wool stocking cap he wore summer and winter, wipe his bald head, and say, "You have no idea what it costs to keep up a place like this.")

His father dead, 4,000 livres in hand sent by his brother, Descartes rented this expensive château and again put off his trip to France. He worked on the *Replies* to the *Objections* to his *Meditations*, which was published by Michel Soly in Paris in 1641. Then for the second edition published by Ludovicum Elzevirium in Amsterdam in 1642, he worked on the "Reply to the Seventh Objection" by Bourdin and wrote his "Letter to Dinet" attacking Voetius. In 1643, Shoock and Voetius published their attacks on Descartes, to which he prepared replies already noted. He also got his *Principles of Philosophy* ready for its publication by Ludovicum Elzevirium in Amsterdam in July 1644.

In the midst of all this, Descartes had three house guests at Endegeest. His old friend Père Picot, Jacques Vallée Desbarreaux who was a counselor in the Parliament of Paris, and the younger de

Touchelaye brother, a priest, came to stay for six months in 1642. When asked what his profession was Desbarreaux said, "Seeking good wine by land and by sea." On their voyage to see Descartes, Picot is said to have avoided taking Desbarreaux through the wine country of Languedoc because he might think that in finding good wine he had found the truth. Desbarreaux and Picot did in fact praise the cuisine at Endegeest.

Out of this visit, Descartes wrote an unfinished dialogue, *The Search for Truth*. In the dialogue, Descartes is Eudoxus with his level-headed method of reasoning by the natural light of reason, Picot is the erudite and scholarly Epistemon, and Desbarreaux is the bluff, commonsensical Polyander who is to be won from his admiration of ancient learning by the practical procedures of Descartes. The dialogue is awful. Also, a number of Cartesian scholars vehemently deny that Descartes ever entertained the notorious libertine Desbarreaux. It is bad enough that nobody can deny that the libertine Picot was Descartes's close friend. At least Picot was a priest.

All of this activity obviously kept Descartes very busy, but finally in May 1644 he set out for France. He arrived in Paris in early June 1644 and stayed with Picot on rue des Écouffes. Picot had been handling Descartes's financial affairs since 1626, collecting the interest from the properties Descartes had sold in Poitou in 1625. It might seem odd that Descartes picked a Catholic priest to handle his financial affairs. Claude Picot, however, was from a family involved in financial matters. His father, his two brothers, and his two brothers-in-law were receivers, auditors, or masters of accounts for the king. So it was not as though Picot had nowhere to turn if he needed help with Descartes's financial affairs.

In Paris, Descartes renewed his friendships face-to-face with Mydorge and Mersenne. Baillet says that Descartes and Picot also went to Blois to see Florimond de Beaune, who had written the best introduction to the *Geometry*. Then to Tours to see the brothers de Touchelaye. This is all reported in a letter written by Picot (not now extant). After that, Descartes went to Nantes and Rennes for the dealings with his brothers.

Descartes left Paris for Brittany on 10 July 1644. He went directly to Rennes where his brother Pierre lived. To complete the trip, Descartes spent from 29 July to 25 August at Crévis at the home of his brother-in-law, although his sister Jeanne had died in 1640, not long after his father. Then he returned to Chavagne-en-Sucé near Nantes to stay with his half brother Joachim II, where on 9 September 1644 he signed as godfather for his nephew named René.

Descartes went to rectify the arrangements his brother Pierre had made about the properties Descartes inherited from his father in 1640. And he certainly demanded more of the 126,840 livres cash his father had left than the 4,000 livres Pierre had sent him. About the final arrangements, Descartes wrote to Picot on 18 August 1644 that they were not as good as one might hope but better than if he had sued. In this case, Descartes took his own advice to Prince Charles (that he should take the offer of the Lower Palatine without quibbling). When you have little power with which to force your case, just take what is given to you and smile.

Pierre and Joachim II were distinguished counselors in the Parliament of Brittany. Descartes had never earned a cent, was forty-eight years old, and had lived all his life on family money. Those capital payments, the interest, that money could have been used to buy a lucrative post in government, and the status gained could have set Descartes up for marriage into a rich and powerful noble family. This was what his father did on his second marriage and was what his two brothers had done. So what we have here is a virtual ne'er-do-well, author of some notoriously controversial books, appearing after fifteen years of absence and four years after his father's death to claim some of the inheritance. The brothers certainly knew that Descartes was a famous mathematician and philosopher, but what had that to do with the price of beans, or wealth, or property, or position?

The good brothers could not deny him his rights. But they were trained lawyers. They could see to it that he bled off no more of the family wealth than they absolutely had to give him.

Of the 126,840 livres inheritance, 37,625 was designated for the children of the second marriage. Pierre, René, and Jeanne's widower could, then, claim at most 88,775. The eldest son certainly got more than the cadet and the daughter's heir. So four years after his father's death, Descartes shows up holding out his hand. Perhaps they gave him 20,000 livres. I doubt that it could have been more than that, and it might have been less. Whatever it was, Descartes accepted it, thanked his brothers, and took his leave.

From Brittany, Descartes apparently went straight to Châtellerault in Poitou to deal with the properties he had inherited from his father. Baillet had in front of him a now lost copy of a procuration paper signed before a notary in Angers on 19 September 1644, in which Descartes authorized his representative in Rennes, Claude du Boüexic, to deal with the properties he had inherited from his father that his brother had taken over and to transfer all the annual interest payments from his brother Pierre to himself. This is the source of his later letter to Picot of 7 December 1648 in which he states in no uncertain terms that his brother Pierre was not his representative in business matters:

> *Concerning my brother's complaint, it seems to me very unjust. I said nothing in Poitou except that I have not charged him to act on my behalf in my affairs, and that if he attempts to do something in my name or as though it comes from me, I will disavow it. When he wails that this is prejudicial to him, he shows himself to be desirous of being my procurer in spite of what I say, as he did with the shares of the succession of my father, to rob me under this pretext, with the assurance that I would rather lose it than sue him. Thus his complaint is like that of a wolf who complains that the sheep do him wrong by fleeing in fear that he will eat them. But the affair does not merit your speaking of it to M. Père Ferrand [the Descartes brothers' cousin on their Grandmother Descartes's side], unless he asks you directly about it.*

Descartes was back in Paris in late September 1644.

While Descartes was in Brittany with his relatives, copies of his

Principles arrived in Paris. Mersenne and Picot, not to forget the humiliated Bourdin, set out at once to distribute copies of the book. Descartes had high hopes that it would be acceptable to the Jesuits. In a letter of June 1645 to Huygens, Descartes points out that Père Dinet, who had been at La Flèche when Descartes was a student there, had thereafter been confessor of Louis XIII, then confessor of Louis XIV. Furthermore, his relative, Père Charlet, who had been rector at La Flèche when Descartes was there, was now assistant to the general of the Jesuits in Rome. Dinet and Charlet were very important. So again one wonders why, given that Descartes was soliciting Jesuit support, he dedicated the *Principles* to Princess Elisabeth. Why didn't he dedicate that textbook to his old and powerful Jesuit mentors, Dinet and Charlet? Neither of these two was a dogmatic Aristotelian schoolman. They were sophisticated operators in the real world who understood that the new mechanistic science of Mersenne, Galileo, and Descartes — not to mention that of Copernicus, Harvey, and Gassendi — was superseding the old animistic science of the schools. Not only were they intelligent, they carried great weight in the schools, the church, and the court. Given Descartes's professed ambitions for his philosophy, there simply was no more tactful and fully appropriate dedication of the *Principles* than to Dinet and Charlet. Yet Descartes sends to them — with his obsequious protestations of personal admiration, professional indebtedness, and religious fealty — he even calls Charlet his "second father" — this book that is in fact dedicated to the Protestant princess, Elisabeth of Bohemia, a Calvinist exiled in Holland because her father defied — and was crushed by — Emperor Ferdinand II of the Holy Roman Empire.

The more I spell it out, the less I understand Descartes's behavior in the matter of this dedication. Maybe he was love besotted after all. But, no. He was just one peculiar nut, as hard to crack as any in the history of human thought.

Descartes does not on first examination appear to be a man who undercuts his own ambitions. And in the long run his Cartesian philosophy did successfully supersede Aristotelianism. But consider again his "Letter to Dinet" published in the second edition of the *Meditations* in 1642. In it, not only does Descartes attack by implication the Protestants of the United Provinces with his accusations against Voetius, but also he casts aspersions on the intellectual astuteness of the Jesuits in France by going on about the stupidity of Père Bourdin. He wanted his physics and philosophy to be taught in colleges and universities both in the United Provinces and in France, so you would think he would flatter them. Instead, he attacks both the Calvinists and the Jesuits.

Descartes could not decide whether or not the Jesuits were on his side. It is unlikely that he truly believed that there was any real chance of winning their support. In a letter to Picot of 9 February 1637, Descartes said he had received letters from Charlet, Dinet, Bourdin, and two other Jesuits, "which makes me believe that the Society wants to be on my side." But by 31 July 1640, he was saying to Huygens that he thought he was going to "enter into a war with the Jesuits" because Bourdin had held disputations against his philosophy at the Clermont College. Then on 11 November 1640 to Mersenne he said he thought the Jesuits might ask him to write a textbook for them.

Descartes was never a professor. What he wanted was to provide a new philosophy of nature — physics and physiology — for professors to teach. Thus his *Principles* of 1644 are set up as lessons for disputation and discussion, to replace Scholastic textbooks being used in Jesuit schools. In 1640, he asked Mersenne which contemporary Jesuit textbook he might use as a foil for his own. He decided upon the *Summa philosophia quadripartita* of Eustache de Saint-Paul, partly because Eustache was still alive and Descartes believed he could get his permission to abridge his course. Descartes's scheme was then to print his own refutations of Scholastic positions alongside the abridgements of Eustache that illustrated those positions. Then, to Descartes's annoyance, Eustache died before Descartes could ask permission to use his text. After that, Descartes lost interest in his plan of printing a proposition-by-proposition refutation of some Scholastic text in philosophy. He said that after all, the mere presentation of his own new philosophy was in itself sufficient refutation of the old philosophy. And what a novel idea that was! If only philosophers would state their own positions clearly and distinctly and be done with it. But the bulk of philosophical writing to this day continues to be an immense clutter of "he said, she said, but I say" taking in of each other's washing.

By 26 April 1642, Descartes was saying again to Huygens that to get any peace from either the Protestant ministers in the United Provinces or the Jesuits in France, "It is necessary that I make a little war."

Descartes sent copies of the *Principles* to his old mathematics teacher at La Flèche, Jean François, and to various other Jesuit priests including Vatier, Fournier, and Mesland. And also to the Oratorian Fathers Condren and Gibieuf, who were developing the society as a teaching order rival to the Jesuits. Maybe Descartes had his hopes there, although the Oratorians were insignificant compared to the Jesuits.

Picot had started translating the *Principles* from Latin into French, and the young duc de Luynes had already translated the *Meditations* into French. Some of Descartes's time in Paris was thus occupied in correcting these translations. And now the plot thickens. The duc de Luynes was the twenty-two-year-old son of Honoré d'Albert, the first duc de Luynes and of Marie de Rohan, duchesse de Chevreuse. Louis XIII was raised by d'Albert, who began as keeper of falcons but then was elevated to the level of duc de Luynes, king's advisor, and peer of the realm (a position equivalent to being the king's brother). Luynes won the lad by turning small birds loose in the halls of the Louvre so the young prince could set his hawks after them. In 1617, when Louis XIII was sixteen, he staged a coup d'état with the duc de Luyne's aid (some say the duke incited it) against his mother Marie de Médicis, who was regent, and her first minister Concino Concini who was murdered as a crucial step in the coup. Also in 1617, the older duc de Luynes married the beautiful sixteen-year-old Marie de Rohan. The Rohans were of the highest nobility, an old Huguenot family. Marie's father Hercule de Rohan was a friend of Henri IV, had been present at the birth of Louis XIII, and was in the carriage with Henri IV when he was assassinated in 1610. Marie's father and uncles were peers of the realm. There had been political conversions along the way with Henri IV, which made Marie a Catholic, but her uncles Henri de Rohan and Soubaise de Rohan were leaders of the Protestant revolt that Louis XIII and Cardinal Richelieu finally crushed at La Rochelle in 1628. Marie's two Protestant Rohan uncles were the godfathers of Charles I of England, who was Princess Elisabeth's beheaded uncle. This is a small world, which is just the point I am making.

The old duc de Luynes died of scarlet fever caught on the battlefield in 1621. Four months later his widow married the duc de Chevreuse. He was forty-four and Marie was twenty-two. The duc de Chevreuse was a suave and worldly ladies' man. He was in very high favor in the court of Louis XIII and was distinguished in battle against the Protestants in 1621 and 1622. When he was younger, he loyally gave his mistress Henriette d'Estragues to Henri IV, whose favorite she became, bearing him several children.

Marie returned to the court. There she cut a swath as wide as it was long-lived among the men of the court, where she became known as the notorious, the seductive, the absolutely irresistible Madame Chevreuse. She had honey-colored hair, and men raved about the beauty of her breasts, which were often exposed in the court dress of the day. She was Queen Anne's best friend, and she was a plotter, a conspirator, a political adventuress of the highest intelligence. She had no scruples, nerves of steel, and a total absence of fear. She flaunted the motto of the Rohans, which roughly translated reads: "Up yours to the king, and who needs a dukedom? I am a Rohan."

The first time Chevreuse got into trouble was when Queen Anne of Austria was first pregnant. Anne, Mademoiselle Verneuil, and Chevreuse (they were all about twenty-two years old) were engaged in a wild game of running and sliding on the waxed floors of Louvre (Wheee!) when Anne fell down and had a miscarriage. Of course her main purpose in life was to provide an heir. Chevreuse was promptly banished from the court by Louis XIII. She was soon back. Another story is that the miscarriage was brought about on purpose for fear that the child's father was actually duc Henri de Montmorency, who was cross-eyed.

In fact, Louis XIII had, it seemed, something of an aversion to performing his marital duties, and it was nearly fourteen years later before Anne of Austria conceived again and produced the child that was to become the future Sun King, Louis XIV, the glory of France. The joy this caused in the court evidently inspired Louis XIII, and Anne soon produced a brother for Prince Louis, Gaston, who became known as Monsieur, and who spent his adult life conspiring against the court.

After Louis XIII died in 1643, the Queen Mother Anne became regent for the young Louis XIV, age five. Cardinal Mazarin was her first minister. Chevreuse and Mademoiselle Verneuil are said to have tried to seduce Cardinal Mazarin. When they failed, they spread the rumor that he was impotent. Nevertheless, Chevreuse was still Queen Anne's dearest friend.

Madame Chevreuse caused almost as much trouble for the courts of Louis XIII and Louis XIV as her Protestant Rohan uncles. Chevreuse was one of the greatest female courtesans in French history. She was practically immune to censure. Not only was the Rohan family nearly as powerful as the king but her husband was the duke of an independent principality, that of Lorraine. Technically, she was outside the law of the realm. On top of that, she was (would history lie?) one of the most desirable women of all time.

There is a painting of the duchesse de Chevreuse by Moreelse which was owned by Charles I of England. Yes, she cut a swath across the channel, too. When she was in England she was greatly pregnant with the young duc de Luyne's sister, but that did not stop her conquests among the men of the court. What really scandalized the English, however, was that two weeks after the little girl was born, Chevreuse swam across the Thames.

In the portrait, her eyes are dark and the left side of her mouth turns up in a slight smile. The right side of her mouth is straight in the three-quarter view. Her look is one of disingenuous inquiry. Her right arm is crooked around the narrow shaft of a trident. The nipple of her left breast peeps over the low curving neck of her blouse. She holds a heavy loop of her honey-colored hair in her left hand, and her index finger points up at an unopened red rose nestled in an extravagant spray of pheasant feathers on the large turban that sits at a cocky slant on her head. Bewitched! Beware!

Now Chevreuse's young son born in 1620 during her previous marriage to the duc de Luynes had taken it upon himself to join the Cartesian retinue and to translate the *Meditations*. The young duc de Luynes was totally unlike his father and mother. He was scholarly and pious, and he later gave money to the Jansenists at Port-Royal. (In front of the main building of Port-Royal is an immense oak as old as the times we are revisiting. One can sit on a bench in its shade and look far down a long slope into the deep, thick Forest of Chevreuse.) The young duke's mother said of her son's piety: "Entirely out of character."

During Descartes's visit to Paris in 1644, all the cards for the rest of his life were laid on the table. In Paris, Descartes met Claude Clerselier, who was making a French translation of the *Objections and Replies* to the *Meditations*, and Clerselier's brother-in-law, Hector-Pierre Chanut, who engineered Descartes's visit to Sweden in 1649. Clerselier was known as the man who took communion more often than anyone else in Paris. Chanut was a rising career diplomat. Clerselier was thirty and Chanut was forty-three when the forty-eight-year-old Descartes met them. Descartes took to them both instantly, perhaps because Clerselier was translating the *Objections and Replies*, and Chanut had helped Mersenne in a (failed) attempt to repeat Torricelli's experiments on the pressure of air. Chanut may also have been among those who pressed First Minister Cardinal Mazarin to give Descartes a pension. But Chanut was neither a mathematician nor a philosopher nor a scientist. So later when Descartes asked him to tell him what he thought of the *Principles*, Chanut parried with the claim that he was not really interested in natural philosophy, but rather in moral philosophy, a field in which at the time Chanut would not have known that Descartes had done any work.

Baillet says of Clerselier that "Descartes put the acquisition of such a friend among the best fortunes of his life. He revealed to him the most intimate secrets of his heart" (B II 242). Baillet gives no reference for this allegation, although I suppose Clerselier reported this sentiment himself in his lost manuscript. The "intimate secrets" Baillet cites from Clerselier's lost manuscript are those quoted above about Descartes's fall from grace with Helena.

It is hard for an older man to have a good critical eye when it comes to younger men who admire his work. If Chanut (more Descartes's own age) lured him into the white hell of Swedish death, both Chanut and Clerselier worked hard after his death to further his immortality by gathering together his letters and manuscripts for publication and by setting up the canonical biography written by Baillet. The Saint Descartes Protection Society began to form during that 1644 visit. Maybe Descartes had some such idea in mind. The influence of Clerselier and Chanut, in any event, has been incredibly tenacious.

By 15 November 1644, Descartes was back in Holland. While he had been in France, his musician friend Bannius died. But Descartes had to have been cheered by the joy with which his friends Regius, van Zurk, Huygens, and van Hogelande greeted him. "The shining light of our land" has returned, Hogelande said. They had all feared, when Descartes left for France, that he would never return to Holland.

When Descartes arrived in the United Provinces, he went almost immediately to Egmond-binnen, just two miles south of his former residence in Egmond aan den Hoef, and Egmond-binnen was his permanent residence until he left for Sweden in September 1649.

Local lore is that Descartes actually lived in an isolated house up against the dunes halfway between the two Egmonds, a house now gone. This would place him only half a mile from the sea, and a mile from Egmond aan Zee, which was a port then, although the wide beach in front of the dunes is as straight as a ruler. Egmond aan Zee is now an attractive resort town, and one can hike for miles on trails through the dunes in either direction, as Pat and I did for several days without the slightest hazard of falling off a cliff. In Descartes's day, he and his friend van Zurk would have ridden to the hounds for hares in the dunes, and even for deer.

Today a farmhouse is nestled in some trees on the inner side of the dunes, with lush flat farmland all around. It is a location and an ambiance of enormous charm, a setting so ideal, that once seeing it, one could never again wonder why Descartes chose such a place to live.

From November 1644 to June 1647 Descartes stayed close to Egmond. He finished revising the French translations of the *Principles* and the *Meditations*, and he wrote to Pollot about his troubles with the preachers. He corresponded with Princess Elisabeth about life and the passions, with Lord Newcastle about animal machines, and with Chanut about Queen Christina. And with dire consequences, he wrote letters to a young priest, Denis Mesland, in which he gave this explanation of transubstantiation.

When we eat bread and drink wine, they are absorbed in the flesh and blood of our bodies. And our bodies are united to our souls. So in the ceremony of the Eucharist, Christ's soul unites with the bread and wine in the priest's hands, thus to become a part of Christ's body. Then when we eat and drink that bread and wine, we are really partaking of Christ's body and blood.

This was too much for Mesland's Jesuit superiors (who of course monitored the correspondence), so in 1645 they sent Mesland to Martinique to convert the natives. He died in the New World. Descartes surely understood why Mesland was sent away, but he does not indicate that he feels any responsibility. Descartes is touched by Mesland's fate, however, for he begins his last letter of 1645 to Mesland by saying, "I have read with a great deal of emotion your goodbye forever." Descartes then goes on somewhat irritably to say that "it seems to me that the talents God has given you could be more usefully employed here converting our own atheists" than in converting savages in the New World. Mesland undoubtedly thought so, too, but he dutifully went to the oblivion to which his superiors had consigned him. Clerselier was afraid to publish these letters after

Descartes's death, but they were not lost because other people made copies of them.

It was also during this period that Samuel Sorbière told the story of a friend of his who visited Descartes and asked to see his library. "Come with me," Descartes said, and took the man out to a shed where a dead calf was hanging ready for dissection. This story is always repeated approvingly to show how Descartes was committed to examining nature firsthand and not to reading and repeating things read in old books. But Sorbière was a disciple of Gassendi who was opposed to Descartes. He published Gassendi's attacks on Descartes's philosophy in Holland. He also said that Descartes was cross, surly, peevish, fickle, inconsistent, flighty, spiteful, malevolent, injurious, and prejudicial. So Sorbière could have made the library story up — wisdom in the calfskins on real scholars' shelves, stinking guts in Descartes's.

On his second trip to Paris, Descartes arrived in late June 1647. The French translation of the *Meditations* had appeared in February, and now with Picot, Descartes arranged for the French translation of the *Principles* to appear in July. Then Descartes and Picot went to Brittany where on 27 July 1647, Descartes and his brother Pierre signed notarized papers. The sense of what Baillet says seems to be that Picot presented Pierre with transference papers for three contracts with buyers of Descartes's Poitou property, showing that 11,400 livres in interest was owed to Descartes. Baillet's marginal reference says "See the papers in the inventory," which we cannot do because they are lost. But this transaction seems to be a further rectification of the arrangements Pierre had made on their father's death to receive himself the receipts from the sale of René's property. The fact that Descartes did not have to sue to recover this money shows that his brother did not deny his claims. But obviously Pierre was not going to pay any money out until René showed up to demand it, which he had done in 1644, and now again in 1647. If the annual interest payments had to pass through Pierre, and he was not sending them on, Descartes may have been hurting for funds, although he had refused money offered him by the comte d'Avaux for experiments. Of course, maybe he just did not want to do the experiments. He certainly did not want to be beholden to the comte.

In Paris again in 1647, Descartes stayed again with Picot, where he was whirled up into a continual round of social affairs. An eighteen-year-old priest, Père César d'Estrées arranged a reconciliation dinner with Hobbes and Gassendi, both of whom had attacked Descartes severely in their objections to his *Meditations*. (In a letter of 4 March 1641, Descartes told Mersenne that he thought Hobbes was just trying to gain a reputation at his expense.) Hobbes, Clerselier, Mersenne, and Roberval were at the dinner, but Gassendi stayed home, sick in bed. After the dinner, they all descended on Gassendi, to embrace him and wish him well, and the reconciliation with Descartes was made, not that either of them thought the other was right.

Then on 23 September 1647, Descartes visited the twenty-one-year-old Blaise Pascal, who also happened to be sick in bed. For protection, Pascal had called in his mathematics teacher Roberval (that old enemy of Descartes's), who demonstrated the calculating machine Pascal designed and had made, a machine that is exhibited today in the window of a bank in Paris as the very first ancestor of contemporary computers. It was truly an invention, one of the first calculators ever made for arithmetic, although the principles behind it had been developed by the craftsmen who built knitting machines.

Descartes arrived with a retinue of René de Montigny, sieur de Beauregard (who had arranged the meeting) and his young son François, Germaine Habert who was the author of a biography of Cardinal Bérulle, Charles Vion de Dalibray who was a Bacchic and erotic poet, and the mathematician Le Pailleur.

Descartes talked with Pascal for several hours. Later, he claimed that he had suggested to Pascal the Puy-de-Dôme experiment that Pascal became famous for setting up. This was to see whether the column of mercury in a tube closed at one end with the open end set in a bowl of mercury was lower at the top of a mountain than at the bottom. This result demonstrates that the weight of the air in the atmosphere — which decreases as you go higher — presses down on the mercury in the bowl to hold up the column in the tube. On this basis the barometer was invented. The more air pressure there is on the mercury in the bowl, the higher the column of mercury rises in the tube.

Descartes and Pascal disagreed about whether or not a vacuum is left in the top of the tube. In the experiment, you fill the tube completely with mercury, put your thumb over the open end, invert it and stick the end down into a bowl of mercury, and remove your thumb. The mercury in the tube drops to a level at which the column of mercury in the tube weighs the same as the outside column of air in the atmosphere. At sea level, the air will hold up a column of about twenty-seven inches of mercury. The higher you go above sea level, the lower the column of mercury, because there is less air to hold it up. (By the way, do not try this experiment, because mercury is poisonous and you can absorb it through your bare skin.) Pascal said the space left in the top of the tube is obviously a vacuum. Descartes said it is not, it is filled with subtle matter that seeps in through the pores in the glass.

Pascal's sister Jacqueline recorded the meeting between Descartes and Pascal. In the course of the discussion, Descartes and Roberval got into an argument in which Descartes accused Roberval of bad faith. Jacqueline's description of the end of the discussion is exquisite:

> *Descartes, noticing by his watch that it was midday, got up because he had an engagement to dine in Saint-Germain. Monsieur de Roberval got up also so quickly that Monsieur Descartes took him away with him in a grand coach, where the two of them were all alone, insulting each other, but somewhat louder than here. (AT V 72)*

The next day, Descartes returned alone to see Pascal again, but unfortunately Jacqueline was not there to record what they said.

One reason Descartes had returned was to give Pascal medical advice concerning his ailment. "Stay in bed," Descartes said.

Now we come to a very confused affair. Baillet reports that Descartes received patent letters from King Louis XIV dated 6 September 1647, "sealed with the great seal and verified by the Chamber carrying the gift of a pension of *three thousand livres* of interest." That is Baillet's stress. Descartes's friends had gotten this from Cardinal Mazarin, and the inscription says it is for Descartes's "great merits, and for the usefulness of his philosophy, and for research in his extensive studies on mankind, and also to help in covering expenses for his fine experiments, etc." (B II 327). Baillet's marginal reference is to the missing inventory of papers Descartes had in Sweden. Baillet says the pension was paid for two years, September 1647 to September 1649. For this information, Baillet cites a letter to Picot of 13 November 1648 and letters Descartes wrote to Marshal Charles de la Porte de la Meilleraye, who was in charge of paying it. We do not have those letters.

But then Baillet continues that only seven months later, in March 1648, Descartes received a second certificate with the royal seal embossed on beautiful parchment offering him a pension from the king, with many elegies. Baillet himself remarks that it is hard to believe that Cardinal Mazarin would give "two pensions as close together as seven months to a philosopher, that is to say, to a man of so little importance, so little a courtier, so little known as was M. Descartes, and under the same pretexts. On the other hand," Baillet continues, "we see the two letters with quite different dates." And in fact, Baillet says in a marginal note that "It was common at that time to give two or three pensions at different times to the same person for the same reasons" (B II 339).

Baillet continues that 3,000 livres was paid in September 1647 but that before anything could be paid for the next year, all pensions were suspended, which contradicts what he says earlier about the pension being paid for two years. But in Descartes's letter to Chanut of 31 March 1649 (his fifty-third — and last — birthday), Descartes says in disgust that he had gone to Paris in 1648 "to buy the most expensive piece of parchment I have ever had in my hands," that he had received nothing, and that he even had to reimburse a relative for the costs of having sent it to him in Holland.

Adam speculates that in fact Descartes left Paris in late September 1647 without knowing about the pension, and that he received notice of it only in January 1648 (A 459). So there was only one pension. This certainly fits with the fact that Descartes's first mention of any pension is in his letter to Elisabeth of 31 January 1648, in which he says he will have to return to France to get it. That the sum was 3,000 livres is mentioned in a letter to Mersenne of 16 January 1648 from a friend of Pascal's, Jacques Le Tenneur, who lived in Tours. In February 1648 Descartes was making plans to return to Paris. He received the official certificate confirming the pension in March.

Baillet also mentions a parchment from Holland written in Dutch giving Descartes a pension of 800 livres, but he does not know the date (B II 460–461). Then neither Baillet nor anyone else I have read says another word about the Holland pension. Given the efforts the Dutch made to lure the philologist Claude de Saumaise to the United Provinces and keep him there, it would not be surprising that they would give Descartes a pension. But Descartes never says anything about it, and it is the sort of thing he would have mentioned if it had happened.

Descartes was awarded at least one pension. Perhaps Chanut had something to do with it, but at the time the pension was being negotiated, Chanut was already the French resident in Stockholm, and there is nothing in his correspondence with Mazarin about a pension for Descartes. Adam says Descartes mentions de Martigny, and implies that it was really due to "the great distributor of pensions at that time. . . , Jean de Silhon, secretary to Cardinal Mazarin" (p. 463). Silhon had conceived of and had organized the Académie Royal des Sciences, founded by Richelieu in 1634. Descartes knew Silhon in Paris from 1626 to 1628, and they wrote to one another after Descartes moved to the United Provinces. Remember that in 1626, Silhon published a book on God and the immortality of the soul, *The Two Truths*, which contains some points that Descartes covers in his *Meditations* of 1641, and Silhon's ideas may have influenced Descartes. Descartes was, Silhon might muse, a fellow philosopher, even a disciple.

In 1637, Descartes published in his *Discourse* the argument that if you self-consciously think you exist, you cannot doubt it. "I think, therefore I am." Descartes repeated the argument in his *Meditations* of 1641. In *The Two Truths* of 1626, Silhon says that "it is impossible that a man who has the ability, as many do, to look within himself and make the judgment *that he exists*, could deceive himself in this judgment, and *not exist*" (A 465). Silhon says that from the knowledge that one exists, one can go on to demonstrate that God exists, which is just what Descartes does in the *Meditations*. I have never understood why scholars have made so little of this. Suffice it to say that while Descartes never cited Silhon's *The Two Truths*, Silhon really liked Descartes's work. And Descartes said he approved of Silhon's.

So Descartes was to be one of those pensioners on whom Queen Anne of Austria and First Minister Mazarin were wasting state money, although Cardinal Mazarin also spent great amounts of state money marrying his nephews and nieces into noble families. Silhon offered their mutual friend Guez de Balzac a pension in 1644 of 6,000 livres a year — be it noticed, the poet was worth twice the philosopher. Balzac refused, as did Claude de Saumaise, the great philologist Silhon tried to lure back from Holland. Silhon certainly had to approve giving Descartes a pension, and it is possible that it was his own idea.

In September 1647 Picot accompanied Descartes home to Egmond and stayed with him until January 1648. On 20 November 1647, Descartes sent Queen Christina copies of his letters to Princess Elisabeth and the manuscript of what he had written so far on the passions. Sending copies of letters without asking permission of the first recipient was a commonplace. Just like e-mail on the Internet today. If you punch that button, you are broadcasting to the world. In fact, commenting on some lost letters to Mersenne on 15 May 1634, Descartes said, "Don't write anything you don't want everyone to know."

In a 31 January 1648 letter to Picot, Descartes said that the rest of the winter would probably be the most tranquil time he could hope for during the rest of his life. Then on 4 April 1648, he wrote to Picot again saying he would not stay with him when he came to Paris this time. Instead, he asked Picot to find him an apartment near the court. Descartes wanted to be close enough that he would not need to keep a carriage. Picot found Descartes an apartment that had a nice room for dining, one for receiving guests, a study, and a room for his manservant.

No Cartesian scholar that I know of has faced up to the implications of this letter. No one likes the idea of Descartes giving up his tranquil life (the life of a philosopher, we say naively or ingenuously in our inveterate romanticizing and mythifying of the intellectual life) to enter court life. But here is Descartes methodically preparing to do just that. Remember all that advice he gave Elisabeth about her brother's taking what the great powers were offering to him. And later he offers to be her advocate in Sweden. Who did he think he was? Or rather, what did he think he was going to become, a diplomat?

In his *Discourse* of 1637, Descartes said that he would "be an observer and not an actor in the comedies of life." Ten years later he was pulling on his fancy lace courtier's gloves.

Now we pick up again the plot left thickening some pages back. Descartes arrived in Paris around 10 May 1648. He occupied his courtier's lodgings near the court, put on his green silk suit, and accompanied by his manservant strolled over to the court . . . to find that a veritable war was going on between Parliament and the regent Queen Anne of Austria (Louis XIV was only ten years old). During the five years since Louis XIII had died on 14 May 1643, Queen Anne had been running things with the counsel of Cardinal Mazarin, her first minister (and lover).

Queen Anne and Mazarin had decimated the state treasury. By the end of 1643, the projected receipts through 1645 had been used up with luxurious living and by giving gifts to this and that nobleman. And pensions. By May 1648 the situation was desperate.

Mazarin revived an old ordinance forbidding building for a certain distance outside the city walls of Paris and put a tax on the thousands of buildings that had been built in that space. On 17 February 1648, payment of interest by the government was suspended (mark well that this would have included Descartes's pension or pensions). The wages of thousands of government employees (except members of Parliament) were cut drastically or suspended. Then on 13 May 1648, Parliament refused to approve a new round of taxes. One of Mazarin's schemes for raising money threatened the hereditary nature of the nobility that counselors like Descartes's father had bought. This maneuver brought on the unanimous opposition of the entire administrative body of the government. Meanwhile, a conspiracy against Queen Anne and Mazarin was forming among the nobility, and the bourgeoisie of Paris had been storing up weapons since the beginning of the year in fear of civil war.

Descartes might as well have turned around right then and returned to Holland. Nobody was going to pay anybody a pension, and nobody in the seething court had any time for philosophy. Nevertheless, Descartes's friends prevailed on him to stay for awhile. The situation could change for the better. Descartes stayed, but he evacuated his lodgings near the court to move back in with Picot.

Now in 1648, Descartes's closest linkage in the court was to the infamous Madame Chevreuse, that devastatingly sexy woman who created havoc among men wherever she went. She was, as we know, the mother of the translator of Descartes's *Meditations*, but there is more. Descartes could not help but have remembered that back in 1626, after Louis XIII died on 14 May, Madame Chevreuse was involved in a complicated plot to assassinate the first minister, Cardinal Richelieu. Conspirators included Louis XIII's brother Gaston, their bastard half brothers César and Alexandre, the duc de Vendôme, and the twenty-eight-year-old Henri de Talleyrand-Périgord, the comte de Chalais, who was besotted with Madame Chevreuse. Their goal was to eliminate Cardinal Richelieu so the regent, Queen Anne of Austria (Louis XIV was only five years old) could take over full power.

It was a totally incompetent plot (as were most of those Gaston was involved in) about which Richelieu knew everything (he had spies everywhere). The none-too-bright comte de Chalais was the trigger man, and he blew it. Richelieu was untouched. You know that the main problem in punishing anyone when such plots are exposed is that so many of the conspirators are of such high nobility that generally speaking you cannot execute them. So various of them were banished from the court, including Madame Chevreuse. The relatively lowly comte de Chalais took the rap.

Chalais fled to Brittany where he was soon captured. The dean of the Parliament in which he was tried was Joachim Descartes, René's father. Dean Descartes had his instructions. He delivered. Chalais was decapitated. Louis XIII sent Descartes's father a letter of commendation from the battlefield at La Rochelle.

Descartes certainly remembered all of this. The woman who conspired against the king and had vamped the comte de Chalais, which led to his condemnation to death in Descartes's own father's court was the mother of the young duc de Luynes who had translated Descartes's *Meditations*. And now this woman, Madame Chevreuse, was a leader in a conspiracy against Mazarin.

On 20 August 1648, le grand Condé, cousin of Louis XIV, won a major battle against the Spanish army at Lens. He then moved his army toward Paris, ostensibly in support of Anne of Austria and Mazarin, although he did not enter Paris. Then on 26 August 1648, Mazarin arrested the president and two of the most popular counselors of Parliament. The next day, 27 August 1648, was the famous Day of the Barricades, when the people put up 1,260 barricades in the streets of Paris. (Who counted them? Reputable historians repeat these figures, but where do they get them?) The people had risen against the court, and there were rumors that le grand Condé was going to take Paris and the throne.

Civil war seemed about to break out. On the morning of 27 August, Descartes fled Paris.

Descartes's old friend Mersenne was on his deathbed, but Descartes did not tarry. Mersenne died on 1 September, four days after

Descartes fled. Some biographers say how cowardly and bad it was of Descartes to abandon his old friend. And it certainly was. I won't defend him. But I have built up a case to explain his panic as no one ever has before.

Descartes was compromised whichever way he turned. The court and Mazarin had given him the pension that had drawn him to Paris. His father had years ago condemned a lover of a main conspirator against the court who just happened to be the mother of the lad who had just translated Descartes's *Meditations* into French. And here Descartes was, preparing to be a courtier. On the other side, he had at least one close relative in the Paris Parliament, his cousin, Michel Ferrand II. Descartes's nephew François Rogier probably was also in Paris and probably was a lawyer in Parliament at the time. Descartes's brother Pierre and half brother Joachim II in Brittany would be on the side of Parliament against the queen and Mazarin. But Descartes's noble friends in Paris — certainly Silhon and Chanut — had their fortunes tied up on the side of the court with the queen and Mazarin. Talk about getting in over his head. This bird flew the coop.

The affair of 1648 is referred to in French history as the Fronde. A fronde is a sling for throwing stones. In Paris, gangs of boys and young men fought street battles with frondes. It was viewed pretty much as a game, although you could lose an eye or even get killed. After all, David killed Goliath with one of those things. The revolt of Parliament against the court was viewed in this playful light. And on 28 August 1648, the very next day after Descartes fled Paris, the president of Parliament was freed (one of the two arrested counselors escaped and the other died in prison). The barriers were dismantled, and Parliament had won for the moment. Eventually, le grand Condé threw all his weight behind Mazarin and Queen Anne, who came out on top in 1652.

Later after Descartes had returned to Holland, he wrote to Chanut two letters rife with indignation:

26 February 1649: Please excuse me for not answering the letters you sent to me in Paris that I have not answered for more than five months after my return to Holland, but concerning what happened in France, I supposed that Monsieur Clerselier had written to you, as he often writes to me with your news. And I have thought it just as well to write nothing since my return, in order not to seem to reproach those who called me to France. But I must say that I consider them to be like friends who invited me to dinner at their home, and then when I arrived there, I found that their kitchen was in an uproar and the cooking pot turned over, and that is why I have returned without saying a word, in order not to increase their embarrassment. But this encounter has taught me never to undertake a voyage on promises again, even though they are written on parchment. And though nothing attaches me to this place other than that I don't know any other that is better, I nevertheless see myself in great danger of passing the rest of my life here, because I fear that the storms of France will not soon be over, and I will become day by day more lazy, such that it will be difficult for me to resolve again to suffer the discomforts of a voyage.

31 March 1649 [Descartes's fifty-second birthday]: It seems that fortune is jealous that I have never desired anything of it, and that I have tried to conduct my life so that fortune would never disoblige me if it had had occasion to do so. I have proved this in the three voyages I have taken to France since I retired to this land, but particularly in the last, which was commanded on the part of the king. To convince me to do it, I was sent letters on parchment, finely sealed, that contain the most grand elegies, which I don't merit, and the gift of a handsome pension. Moreover, in the details of the letters from those who sent me the king's letter, they promise me a great deal more than that if I would come to France. Ah, but when I arrived there, the unex-

pected troubles made it so that instead of finding what they had promised me, I found that I had to pay one of my relatives for the postage of the letters they had sent me, and that I seemed to have gone to Paris merely to buy a parchment, the most expensive and useless that I have ever held in my hands. This, however, bothered me very little. I would have attributed it to the tribulations encountered in public affairs, and would have let it go, if I had been assured that my voyage could be of some use to those who had invited me. But what really disgusted me is that none of them exhibited any desire to know anything other than the way I looked, such that I came to believe that they wanted to have me in France only like an elephant or a panther, because of rarity, and not at all to be useful for anything.

Descartes's close relative who had to be reimbursed for the postage on the sheepskin was probably his second cousin Michel Ferrand II, who had been dean of the Parliament of Paris in 1646. He was the son of Michel Ferrand I, who I think raised Descartes when he was a boy in Châtellerault.

So Descartes's flight from Paris on the Day of the Barricades was not the bravest act of the old soldier philosopher's life, but it is understandable given his obvious political naïveté. Oh, could he have seen (as the romance school of biographers proceed) that his acceptance of the invitation to join the Swedish court of Queen Christina would turn out even worse. But foresight is not at issue here. What the serious biographer of the man has to assess (in contrast to what the serious hagiographers of the philosopher have faithfully ignored) is what it means about the man and his life that he himself says all the right philosophical things (in the romantic interpretation) about this 1648 summer adventure in Paris. That great letter to Chanut about being a zoo exhibit, and the one about being invited to dinner when the kitchen is in disorder contains the line, "This encounter has taught me never to undertake a voyage on promises again."

Yet all Queen Christina offers are promises. They do not even come from her, but from Chanut. Every romance needs a villain, Chanut is my candidate for this one. Here is the story cold. Descartes was determined to be a courtier. He was going to move away from quaint Dutch country dwellings, give up solitude (it was getting boring) and escape the Protestant theologians (who were squealing like pigs).

Descartes was going to change his life.

I had an early hypothesis about why Descartes accepted Queen Christina's invitation to her court in Stockholm. Descartes was, I speculated, like a professor in the sticks, teaching at Podunk U., waiting for the fabled call from Harvard. And lo, one day it actually comes. But alas, it is too late. He is too old, he is past his prime, he is an extinct volcano. Recognition is as much a burden as a joy to him now, but he has to go anyway, and attempt to sparkle among younger men in their prime, even if it kills him.

That does not play too badly. But compared to the French court, Stockholm, was the minor leagues — not Harvard; Ohio State maybe — despite Sweden's power and wealth and Christina's success in attracting a few stars. Descartes had been preparing to take his rightful place in the retinue of Cardinal Mazarin and Louis XIV, not out there on the Arctic ring.

So if Descartes hesitated about going to Sweden, it was because he still regretted the unfortunate outcome of that call to the French court. Oh, had it been otherwise! But it seemed to him that it was obviously all over in Paris. In fact, it was not. If only he had held on a few years, by 1655, say, he would have been able to return, and if he had actually managed to live to be a hundred as he thought possible, he could have been a sunbeam in the Sun King's court. He was too impatient. He set his jaw and set out on that boat for Stockholm in early September 1649. He arrived in Stockholm in early October, and the last act begins.

QUEEN CHRISTINA OF SWEDEN (1626–1689)

BY SEBASTIEN BOURDON, C. 1648

Statens Konstmuseum, Stokholm

XIII ✄ QUEEN CHRISTINA

Where men's thoughts freeze like the water.

T HE GEARS CREAK and crank as the wheels turn, the stage is
rotated, and the scenery changed for the last act, that final year
of Descartes's life. There, some ice! A lot of snow! Bears! And
cold, cold, crackling cold, bone-splitting, gut-wrenching cold. The
Queen of Scythes, the White Queen, the Queen of the Snows, the
daughter of the Lion of the North.

LET HER NORTHERN LIGHT BLAZE FORTH!

She stands bareheaded in the blast, indifferent to the chill. She
could walk barefoot in the snow. Her father, Gustavus Adolphus,
was killed on 16 November 1632 at the head of his troops at the battle of Lutzen. The Swedes did not pause. No, those damned Swedes
were not to be stopped by the mere death of a king. His First Minister Axel Oxenstiern took over and the battle was won. The Swedes
tipped the balance. Protestant Sweden and Catholic France, allied
for reasons of state, finally defeated Prussia and the Holy Roman
Empire to end the Thirty Years' War in 1648. It was the most awful
war ever known. Northern Europe was devastated and depopulated
and did not recover for another fifty years.

Christina was six years old when her father died. He had raised
her as a boy, and now Chancellor Oxenstiern continued her father's
plan to groom this girl to be a king.

Why had Gustavus Adolphus not sired another child, a son, a
prince? Alas, the queen had become simple. Marie-Éléonore of Brandenburg was the sister of Princess Elisabeth's father, Frederick V.
She had never been too bright. Now she was somehow crazy, a com-
pulsive talker who told everyone everything she knew about any-

thing. On an occasion when she was told to keep a secret, her niece, Princess Elisabeth, said of her sadly, "She who never had any." You don't take a chance on a son destined to be a king with a woman like that. She was banished from court. At least her daughter Christina was alert and very intelligent. Better to stick with the princess. Christina seldom saw her mother.

Christina was a very bright child, no romanticizing here. She was one sharp little girl. At age eleven, she wrote in her journal that Oxenstiern had made up the notion of God in an attempt to frighten her into behaving. As a teenager, she rode a horse all day without tiring, astride like a man. She could hit a running rabbit in the head with one bullet. But she also took books on the hunt to read when it got boring. A wise child, that.

Christina was slight, short, her face and body out of symmetry. Her voice would suddenly drop to very masculine, and then slowly recover its feminine tones. In paintings her eyes are not quite right, not crossed, too close together, one larger than the other. Strange. The French were scandalized that even though she was a queen, she took only fifteen minutes to dress. And just clasped her hair back. And wore flat-soled shoes like a man's slippers. She told Descartes she had never felt the sentiment of love, and she abdicated her crown soon after Descartes died, in part because she abhorred the thought of marriage and submitting to the duties of a brood queen.

The old French Ambassador Thuillerie sent her gifts of perfume. The French resident in Stockholm, Descartes's friend Hector-Pierre Chanut, knew better than that. What made her eyes light up were books. He sent her fine books bound in leather and embossed with the arms of Sweden and France. He had Gabriel Naudé, Cardinal Mazarin's librarian send her a book catalog. On 25 January 1648 (she was twenty-one), Chanut reported to Mazarin: "The queen has seen and has taken great pleasure in examining the catalog of books printed in France during the last five years. She has promised herself an agreeable divertissement of several hours to pick those she would like to buy" (A 527).

Christina liked to be read to. And to have things explained to her.

She had her librarian Johannes Freinshemsius and Chanut read Descartes's *Meditations* and *Principles* so they could explain his philosophy to her. Chanut took a trip with her in September and October 1648, during which he read Tacitus, Virgil, Seneca, and Epictetus out loud during the long carriage rides. She was visiting copper mines in Cupreberg and silver mines in Salzberg, and she went down the shafts. Chanut complained with morbid humor about how he might die in service as others do in battle because he had to keep his head uncovered in the cold when he was with her.

But surely the man wore a wig. Descartes always wore a wig made of human hair the color of his own. When Descartes was forty-two, he asked that strands of gray be added, like those appearing on his own head. He said it was healthy to wear a wig, as it certainly was in the ever changing weather of Holland, that land Saumaise described as having four months of winter and eight months of cold. In Sweden, it was the other way around. They may have had some oven-heated rooms in Sweden, but most rooms in most houses and public buildings were unheated and they were freezing. You may think those wigs are funny, and in a way, they are, but they keep your head warm — particularly in situations where you have to doff your hat.

Christina was crowned in 1644 when she was eighteen. She was soon overruling Oxenstiern in council meetings. When Sweden came out on top in the Thirty Years' War, the Swedes even managed to get part of the Palatine back for Princess Elisabeth's brother Charles. Not as much as he wanted (you remember), but at least the family had a kingdom again.

Besides indulging her love of books, old manuscripts, and old knowledge, Christina invited poets, grammarians, rhetoricians, and philosophers to her court. She loved the theater even more, and in 1646 sent Count Magnus Gabriel de la Gardie to Paris where he hired the theater architect Antonio Brunati to return with him to Sweden to construct a ballet theater in the latest Italian style. In January 1647 Brunati began work on a ballet ballroom 110 by 260 feet, with considerable technical equipment including mechanisms for staggered scenery seven ranks deep of mountains, gardens, seas, and perhaps even great rollers that turned to imitate waves in the sea. It was state-of-the-art, and in Sweden, too. Queen Christina adored it.

Descartes's mind wandered her and there as he meditated during the silence of misty autumn mornings while winter crept closer to Holland in 1648. When it came, everyone said it was the worst in forty years.

Descartes was fifty-two. He could now look back to his early adolescence, when he first noticed himself as a person, when he began to have his own desires and to set his own goals in life. Not so long ago, he had felt great. On 9 July 1639, he told Mersenne he had not been sick for thirty years (another noble lie). He told Huygens on 6 June 1639 that his teeth were good, and that he felt stronger and better than he ever had. He just might live to be a hundred, or at least another thirty years. But by 15 June 1646, he had been so discouraged about finding medical ways to prolong life that he told Chanut he had found a better way, "not to fear death." After fifty, a man lowers his sights.

Then after he returned ignominiously from his last trip to France, that (in retrospect) ridiculous and really stupid attempt to play the role of courtier, Descartes didn't feel so good. It was no particular ailment, he said, he just was worn down and needed to take it easy.

Why hadn't one of his friends in Paris, Picot, for example, written him a frank letter beforehand to tell him that the court was bankrupt, that salaries, let alone pensions, were not being paid, and that it was not exactly the best time for Descartes to make his entrance onto the stage of court life? Ah, his Parisian friends. They wanted to see him. Let him come. They would have some good times together. He would see the lay of the land soon enough. Maybe they could talk him into staying, even if the court pension was not paid. Something could be worked out. The French nobleman Montmort was ready to offer him a country house and a pension.

Descartes returned to Egmond, sat in a chair, looked out the window at the sand-dunes holding back the sea. He had reached the age, it comes to us all, when the future no longer stretches out indefinitely. Of course we all know we are going to die. But for a long time, our minds and bodies do not believe it. We behave as though we will live forever, as though we had all the time in the world. Then one day, there is a subtle change. One day you look back and wonder at those long days and years when you did all those things without a ghost of a thought that you were using up time that would come to an end. You squandered your hours and days as though ... well, you know what I mean. Descartes knew.

Once you reach this stage of awareness in life, you can never recover timelessness — not even in the most idyllic moments. Gone forever is that sense of vast and endless horizons that thoughtlessly framed your life before. The transition takes place at different times for different people. I am sixty-nine (having lived already more than a dozen years longer than Descartes), and it seems to me that sometime between forty-five and fifty, I began to calculate how much time I was spending doing this and that. I started eliminating projects that I had undertaken without thought in the past, before the change. There comes a time when one begins to worry whether there will be time, not just to do all the things one wants to do, but time to finish even one last good one, like writing this book.

We know exactly when the transition took place for Descartes. After he returned from his first trip to Paris in 1644, Descartes wrote to Pollot on 18 May 1645:

> *Since my voyage to France, I have become twenty years older than I was a year ago, so that it is now a greater voyage to go from here [Egmond] to The Hague than it was formerly to go all the way to Rome. It is not that I have any particular indisposition, grace of God. But I feel more feeble and have more need to look after my comforts and my repose.*

It was not so bad for Descartes in 1644, but when he went to Paris the second time, in 1647, when he rubbed up against a genius named Pascal who was hardly out of his teens, he came up short. Roberval harangued and harassed him, and his brother cheated him.

Then on that third voyage in 1648, he really got bombshelled. He made a fool of himself before his friends at the court, and he behaved like a coward on the Day of the Barricades when he ran as fast as he could back home with his tail between his legs. There was no more escaping from himself, no more fantasy. By the time he got back to Egmond, the aging of his mind had finally caught up with his body. He was fifty-two, and to be fifty-two in 1648 was to be an old man. Sure, a few people lived to the same ripe old ages people do now. But the average life span for Descartes's generation was under forty. Descartes had lived already a dozen years past the norm. There were a lot of ways to die then that you could do nothing about. Francine's fever at age five, pneumonia, diarrhea. You could wake up in the morning feeling fine and die a painful death of the plague by noon. A brick could drop from a building and kill you as you walked by, as the doleful Descartes himself remarked to Pollet in a letter in 1648.

The mathematician Pierre de Carcavi, one of the king's librarians, had offered to handle Descartes's correspondence in Paris, but an era had ended for scholars when Mersenne died. Nobody took over his role of keeping everyone informed in all the arts and sciences about what everyone else was doing. Moreover, Carcavi was too close to Gassendi and Roberval. Descartes soon dropped him and turned over his correspondence to Picot.

It was peaceful in Egmond. The post came on Sunday and Descartes could almost forget how old he was as he sat there all day Monday writing letters. Even so, Descartes second-guessed and recriminated. He himself said these were the worst possible things a man could do who wanted to maintain good mental and physical health. But really, Descartes asked himself, *had* he left Paris too soon? The court and Parliament had soon come to an agreement. The barricades were up barely twenty-four hours. Maybe he should have stayed. If he had stayed. Should he have...? What if...?

The old man sat in his study, contemplating his life.

Descartes's rules for life address what he took to be his own deepest flaws. He had loved poetry as a young man. He read novels of chivalry, and he had a tendency toward romanticism. He knew this, so he strove all his life to follow his reason, not his passions. He was not stupid. He knew his weaknesses. He was not at all worried about getting in over his head in mathematics, he would have gone up against God in a poster contest, but just because he knew the depth of those waters, he knew exactly what it was for people to get in over their depth in other matters. So just to make sure he did not get in over his head in the ordinary affairs of life, he ruled that one (he, himself) should figure out what you can influence and what you cannot. If you can't fight it, relax and enjoy it.

We have already seen Descartes dispensing this advice to Princess Elisabeth. It was advice he gave to himself over and over again.

In the *Discourse on Method*, Descartes said that once you have made a decision, act on that decision steadfastly as though it were absolutely certain. Do not waver. Once the decision is made, never consider it again. Never hesitate. Act. And never look back. If you do a thing that your reason tells you is best, then even if you are wrong, you have done the right thing. You are morally clean. You have absolutely no grounds for remorse, none. No recriminations. In *The Passions of the Soul*, Descartes said that regret over what might have been is more than useless, it is devastating. Remorse is the most destructive emotion a human being can have. You can destroy your life by agonizing over what might have been. It is even worse than yearning for what cannot be.

It was right for Descartes to have gone to Paris to collect the pension. Of course in retrospect he had been naive and ignorant. Not stupid, just uninformed. His so-called friends were to be blamed for that. He had their number. "They had wanted to have me in France," as he said later in that letter of 31 March 1649 to Chanut, "like an elephant or a panther because of its rarity, not to be useful for anything." They had deceived him, but there was nothing more he could have done beforehand to find out about the true situation in Paris. So, no regrets about having gone.

That pension...

Stop that!

Stop thinking about it.

Quit going over and over the thing.

Get on with it.

Will you stop thinking about it!

If only he could have followed his own advice. In fact, he vacil-lated, he fussed and fretted, he second-guessed. And he did live in at least eighteen different places during his twenty-one years in the United Provinces. The man could not sit still.

Descartes says that your mind cannot control your passions directly. But in *The Passions of the Soul*, he gives instructions con-cerning how to control them indirectly. Suppose, for example, you are a panic-stricken soldier in battle. It won't work just to tell your-self to be brave. So hold out your trembling hands and say, "Hands be still." Breathe more slowly. Make your heartbeat slow down. You can do these things one at a time. Get your body into a defiant stance. Grip your sword strongly. Put a fierce look on your face. Think how proud you'll be afterward. Shout a battle cry. Louder! Again! Now! The brave man rushes into battle. Soldiers today are trained Des-cartes's way.

Hector-Pierre Chanut, the career diplomat, was attracted to Des-cartes. Chanut was not a philosophically aware admirer like Burman, or a devoted disciple like the duc de Luynes, young male hangers-on. Chanut was only five years younger than Descartes, he had not read Descartes's philosophy, he was not a mathematician.

Descartes was simply the great philosopher admired so much by Chanut's brother-in-law, Clerselier. Clerselier had translated the *Objections and Replies* to the *Meditations* into French. Chanut was pleased to meet the philosopher, to be known as his friend, and in the way of people who make the world go around, Chanut kept in mind — he surely did not even think about it, it was there as an automatic response in an upward oriented diplomat — that he might one day find a place for Descartes in his own plans.

In his unskilled way, Descartes was also on the make. They met in 1644 on Descartes's first return visit to France. Descartes was looking for a position. Maybe he had not yet gathered all the data he thought necessary for making the decision, but Descartes was definitely considering the option of moving back to France. Chanut, like Clerselier, was a man of a kind he knew well. All the men in Descartes's family were in government service. Descartes himself had taken his law degrees. Many years in the past, to be sure, but he knew these people in his blood. Maybe Chanut could help him one day.

Descartes was not subtle about it. He let Chanut know that this philosopher wanted a post, although I cannot decide whether Descartes was being dumb or sarcastic when on 21 February 1648 he wrote to Chanut that he was going to Paris the first of March, but that "I do not want an exacting job that would take from me the leisure to cultivate my mind, even though it would give me a great deal of money and profit." He goes on to say that it seems to him that Chanut's job offers just that leisure. Descartes surely knew how much time a diplomat had to stand around doing nothing, waiting his chance. And how much time he spends thinking of strategy and tactics, what might have been, what might be. All that gossip, intrigue, infighting. Waiting. Yet Descartes could still dream of some nominal administrative post that would give him time to think and write.

There was, for example, the post of librarian, like that of Naudé with Mazarin. That's a traditional sinecure for a thinker. Leibniz thrived as a librarian. Probably not the place for Descartes, though. He might decide to hurry along the replacement of Aristotle with Cartesianism by burning all the old and useless books.

In early October 1645, on his way to be resident in Queen Christina's court in Stockholm, Chanut and his family stopped four days in Amsterdam. Descartes went from Egmond to spend several days with Chanut. There is no record of what they talked about. I wonder where they went out to dinner.

It was on this occasion that Chanut's nephew Porlier, very religious, checked around to see if Descartes was devout. He was reassured by a master of arms who said that Descartes was very pious. But the interesting thing is that this master of arms claimed that he probably knew Descartes better than anybody in Holland, because he had fenced with him many times in many places. For this to be true, Descartes must have frequented the fencing salons.

Descartes's first (known) letter to Chanut is of 6 March 1646, in which he comments that although it is the coldest winter since 1608, he knows that "you have more preservatives against the cold [porcelain stoves] there than in France." Descartes had the same in Holland.

On 1 November 1646, in response to Chanut's plan to give Queen Christina a copy of the French translation of the *Meditations*, and also perhaps with the thought that Chanut might influence the French or even the Swedish court to give him a pension, Descartes says:

> *I have never had enough ambition to desire that people of that rank know my name.... But since ... I am already known by an infinity of Schoolmen who look at my writings the wrong way and look for ways to harm me at all costs, I am greatly inclined to hope also to be known by people of the highest rank, who have the power and the virtue to be able to protect me.*

The immediate reference might seem to be to the good graces of Cardinal Mazarin, who dispensed pensions and protection in the name of Louis XIV and Anne of Austria. But Descartes goes on immediately to repeat the eulogy to Queen Christina given to him by the former French ambassador to Sweden, Thuillerie, who had returned to The Hague. Remember that Descartes was in France from June through September 1647. On 6 June 1647, on his way, he wrote to Elisabeth saying that even though he was changing his place of residence, his devotion for her would not alter. He really was planning to move back to France. But there is nothing of this in his letter to Chanut of the same day. Descartes was covering all three bases. He was seeking a pension from the court in Paris. He had already hinted to Princess Elisabeth that if her brother Charles would support him, he would go to the Palatine to live in the same court with her, or at least nearby. And he was also thinking of possible benefits from Queen Christina. So he says that he would much enjoy private conversations with Chanut on moral philosophy, but (hinting) he doubts he will ever go where Chanut is. In that letter of 1 November 1646 to Chanut, Descartes goes on to say that "From the first hour that I have had the honor of knowing you, I have been entirely yours [the French idiom means your faithful servant, or even your slave] and as I have since then dared to depend on your good will, I beg you to believe that I could not be more for you [the French idiom means in your camp] even if I had lived with you all my life."

Chanut understood immediately. In his letter of 1 December 1646, Chanut says that Thuillerie is right, Christina is a prodigy. She is interested in serious intellectual questions, and she would like to know Descartes's opinion on the question of which can cause more harm if misused, love or hate? In a long discourse of 1 February 1647 (sent to Chanut for the queen), Descartes distinguishes rational from sensual love (both involve wanting to join oneself with the loved object, but in obviously different ways). Descartes concludes that love can be used to cause incomparably more evil than hate, because love by its very nature is much stronger than hate. And to show how much harm love can do, he quotes some lines of a poem ("Stanzas for Mademoiselle M...") by Théophile de Viau.

> *Oh ye gods!*
> *What beautiful prey had Paris, that handsome boy.*
> *So let the young lover have his fame,*
> *Even though he burned down Troy,*
> *To extinguish his own flame!*

A lot has been made of Descartes's quoting these lines by heart after more than twenty years, but I'm not sure why. Maybe he just looked them up.

In early November 1647, Descartes received a letter from Chanut who said that Queen Christina was interested in hearing what the philosopher's position was concerning the nature of the sovereign good. Not only did Descartes immediately send Chanut a letter addressed to the queen containing a treatise on the subject, he included copies of six of the letters he had sent to Elisabeth on the subject of the passions. Everyone thinks this insensitive (dumb) of Descartes, but nobody thinks that Chanut was stupid enough to pass them on to the queen. (In fact, after Descartes's death, Chanut wrote to Elisabeth asking if she wanted those very letters back. Yes.) But Chanut did give Christina the copy of the manuscript of *The Passions of the Soul* that Descartes included. Christina thanked Descartes for it in her own hand on 12 December 1648, nearly a year after she received it. There is no indication that she read it.

Descartes replied to Christina on 26 February 1649 with a letter that could have been copied out of a style book as an example of scrape and bow obeisance at the extreme end of the scale:

> *If a letter had arrived for me from Heaven [he begins], and I had seen it descending from the clouds, I would not have been more surprised, nor would I have received it with more respect and veneration, than I have received the one that it has pleased your majesty to write to me.*

Having thus compared Christina to God, Descartes then simpers about how honored he is that she has taken time from her very important affairs to read his works. She "whose least actions do so much good in general for the whole earth." Anyone who could render her any service can count himself very happy:

> *And since I am one of them, I dare to protest here to Your Majesty that she could command nothing to me so difficult that I would not always be ready to do everything possible to execute it, and that even if I had been born a Swede or a Finn, I could not be more zealous nor more perfectly [for you] than I am, etc.*

Disgusting. All right, you are going to say that I need not be so sarcastic about Descartes's letter. That's the way one wrote to a queen in the seventeenth century. Indeed it is. But even the courtiers of the time made fun of that language in broadsides and the theater. It is not so much what he says and how he says it, but that he says it at all. My point is that Descartes did not have to write to the queen at all, unless he wanted something. What did he want?

If Descartes did not want to go to Sweden, he should not have written that letter. Therefore, he wanted to go to Sweden. Fortune, that fickle bitch, was shining her crooked light on him again, for the very next day after he sent that soppy letter, 27 February 1649, Chanut sent him a letter in which he conveyed Queen Christina's fervent command: Get thee to Stockholm, old boy. The queen wants to learn philosophy at your knee.

Descartes had not been asked to teach Louis XIV. But Princess Elisabeth had studied his works. Now Queen Christina — by all rights of conquest one of the strongest sovereigns in Europe, with armies as powerful as France (but with finances in not much better shape) — the queen was calling him to her court. Not just to be a zoo exhibit, either, but as her private tutor in philosophy. Objectively speaking, this was glory for a philosopher. Vindication for all the attacks on him, that, too. And at a time when he was admitting that his work in medicine was not going at all as well as he would have liked. Descartes ought to have been ecstatic. That is, if that was what he wanted.

So having resolved to a fair degree of satisfaction that Descartes was soliciting patronage from Princess Elisabeth, the court of France, and Queen Christina of Sweden, I now have to figure out why in fact Descartes was not greatly pleased with the invitation from Stockholm. He did, after all, ask for it.

Of course he was fifty-two years old, really fifty-two, not the false-face fifty-two that thinks itself twenty years younger that most of us wear to the masked ball of life. He was tired. And with good cause. Two trips to Paris two years running in pursuit of a pension had come to worse than naught. His prospects there had been flung back in his face. His last act on the Parisian stage had been one of cowardice, and he had been made a fool of.

So he was also a bit tender in the region of self-regard. He told himself to be determined, steadfast, and to go straight for the main chance. Oh yes, oh yes. Were one to know the right course to take. He had already made a play for a new life as a pensioned courtier in Paris, with that fine new apartment in which he anticipated long conversations with the learned, young hangers-on eager to translate his newest writings, perhaps to collect and edit his best letters, that sort of thing. Nothing more than the honor he deserved. All phantoms.

He didn't even know the layout of the playing field, let alone the rules of the game.

Chanut wrote Descartes a second letter of invitation on 6 March 1649. The Swedish Admiral Hermann Flemming was sailing to Holland to get Gerhard Johannes Vossius's library, sold to Queen Christina by his son, Isaac Vossius, who had come as librarian to Christina's court. Descartes could go back to Sweden with the admiral and the books. Both of these letters of invitation are lost, so we do not know what they actually said.

In another lost letter of 27 March 1649, Chanut (Baillet reports) explains that Christina would like Descartes to come in April to be there during the best part of the Swedish year, so he could return to Egmond at the end of summer. That way he would not have to undergo the rigors of the Swedish winter.

On 31 March 1649, his fifty-third birthday (another year gone by!), Descartes wrote two letters to Chanut, one to show to Christina, one not. In the first, he drips with desire to decorate Christina's court.

I have so much veneration for the high and rare qualities of this princess that the least of her wishes are my absolute commands. Thus, I have not even deliberated about this voyage, but have resolved only to obey.

But, he says, he doubts that the summer would be enough time to satisfy the queen, so he proposes that he leave for Sweden in the summer and stay over the winter to return the next summer. In winter you can always sit in a room heated by a porcelain stove.

Ominous kettle drumming in the wings.

Mark well: It was his call.

Christina offered him a season, a couple of months (summer is short up north). Descartes wants a year. He whines to Chanut that twenty-one years of retreat has weakened him (before it was his source of strength), that spring and fall are bad times to travel (too stormy, too muddy), that the weather is calmest for travel in the middle of the summer. Also, Descartes says he has some important affairs to settle before he leaves. This was to get *The Passions of the Soul* published with a dedication to Christina, so he could present it to her.

In a second letter personally to Chanut on the same day, Descartes has a different message; to wit, get me out of this! He starts out by saying, "I have had much more difficulty in resolving to take this voyage than I could ever have imagined." Yes, yes, he would like to be of service to the queen. And he trusts Chanut, all those wonderful things Chanut has reported about Christina's intellect and her desire to learn Descartes's philosophy. If he were only sure that he could be of use. That is, in fact, he does not trust what Chanut and Thuillerie say about Christina as far as you can throw the open sheet of paper it was written on. Despite his faux pas in Paris, Descartes was not born yesterday. But he has already included his letter of acceptance to Christina. It's done! He's not supposed to be waffling. But that is what he does. He vacillates to Chanut:

> *Experience has taught me that even the most intelligent people with a great desire to learn [like Chanut himself] have very little leisure to enter into my thoughts, so I don't have much hope that with an infinity of other occupations a queen will have time for them.*

Moreover, Lady Fortune, she is against him. Those three trips to France were disasters, he says, "particularly the last." If only that last trip had been useful for something! Here is that wonderful passage again:

What disgusts me the most is that none of those who invited me to Paris wanted to know anything more than what I look like, as though they wanted to have me in France only like a panther or an elephant, because of rarity, not to be useful for anything.

This time I will continue with what follows, the last paragraph of Descartes's fifty-third birthday letter to Chanut, the pathetic cry of a desperate man:

I don't suppose it is like that where you are, but the bad success of all the voyages I have made during these last twenty years makes me fear that on this one I'll be robbed by thieves or lose my life in a shipwreck. Nevertheless, this won't stop me if you judge that this incomparable queen continues in her desire to examine my opinions, and that she can take the leisure to do so. Then I will be happy to be able to serve her. But if this is not true, and she has simply had some curiosity that is now gone, without displeasing her, I want to be spared this voyage.

This is a man who was having a great deal of difficulty in relaxing and enjoying it. The tone of hopeless desperation in this letter shows that he knows perfectly well that Chanut is a career diplomat, a procurer, who won't even pause at Descartes's cries for mercy. Chanut was the French resident in Sweden. He was about to be promoted to ambassador. The Swedish queen wanted Descartes. It did not matter whether it was whim or whatever on her part. Chanut had his man. He would deliver.

Meanwhile, Admiral Flemming had come and gone. Descartes purported not to know who Flemming was, and even if he was who he said, Descartes could not believe he had been sent just to pick up little old him. Of course he hadn't. Flemming had been sent to pick up Vossius's library, something like 2,000 volumes. What Christina really lusted after was old books. Adding an old philosopher to that cargo has all the aspects of an afterthought.

Don't worry, Chanut said face-to-face with Descartes during a fast transit through Holland toward the end of May 1649. Chanut was on his way to Paris to be made ambassador to Sweden. If you have any questions, write to Johannes Freinshemsius, the queen's librarian and intellectual advisor (he's read your book).

Chanut was a good friend of Henri Brasset (the perennial secretary to a sequence of French ambassadors to the United Provinces) and exchanged letters with him. Thus Chanut probably knew that after writing that "your slightest whim is my command" letter to Christina and the hysterical letter to Chanut, on that same day, his fifty-third birthday, Descartes wrote two more letters, one to Elisabeth and one to his old friend Henri Brasset. In Descartes's letters to Elisabeth and Brasset, he brags about the invitation from Christina, and says offhandedly that he is going to go.

Descartes told Elisabeth that he was particularly delaying his trip to await any orders she might have to give to him. This has fueled an industry of scholars who argue that Descartes went to Sweden as Elisabeth's agent, to try to further the cause of the house of Brandenburg. But Elisabeth had no orders to give him, and the fate of the house of Brandenburg had already been settled on 17 October 1648 when Elisabeth's brother Charles was given the Lower Palatine. Descartes was simply larding it on again, as he always did when writing to the princess, the queen, and powerful Jesuits. He has already sworn his sword and shield to the service of Queen Christina, and here he is on the same day saying to Princess Elisabeth:

> *I beg very humbly of Your Highness the favor of instructing me in all that she judges I can render her service, to her and hers, and I assure her that she has over me as much power as if I had been all my life her domestic servant.*

Chanut also doubtless knew about the letter Descartes wrote to Brasset on 23 April 1649, with all the fine figures meant to be passed around:

No one finds it strange that Ulysses left the enchanted islands of Calypso and Circe where he could enjoy all imaginable voluptuousness, and that he also scorned the songs of the Sirens to go live in a stony and infertile land because it was his place of birth. But I avow that a man who was born in the gardens of Touraine, and who now inhabits a land where, if there is not as much honey as God promised the Israelites, it is credible that there is more milk, cannot so easily resolve to leave it to go to live in a land of bears, among the rocks and ice.

On the same day, 23 April 1649, Descartes wrote in answer to Chanut's letter of 6 March 1649, which had finally arrived. In it, Descartes lies that had he got it in time to realize that Admiral Flemming was who he was, he would be on his way to Sweden. But he didn't know the man was an admiral. Anyway, he was waiting for an answer to the plea he had written on 31 March 1649 to be excused from the trip.

But when, on Chanut's recommendation, Descartes wrote to Freinshemsius in June 1649, he did not ask questions about the queen's true state of mind. Instead, he said he would rather die on the trip to Stockholm than cause the queen trouble either because of the bad things some of his enemies in her court would say about him, or because someone might say bad things about her for entertaining a Catholic. Descartes seems to throw out these last straws for himself with the realization that they will just be brushed aside, and he goes on immediately to ask whether he should wait to accompany Chanut when he returns to Stockholm or set off at once. He also asks if it is all right to dedicate *The Passions of the Soul* to Christina. Of course.

Mid-August and Descartes is about ready to go. He did not want to go, but he went.

I believe Descartes went to Sweden because he was nearly flat broke.

On 30 August 1649, two or three days before he set sail, Descartes put his affairs in order with Picot in Paris and van Zurk in

Holland. He says he has received two counter deeds or annulments of three contracts for interest he has in Brittany. They are of no value, but van Zurk has taken them to cover Descartes's debts. In another letter to Picot on the same day, Descartes says:

> *Being on the point of parting to go to Stockholm, and consider-*
> *ing that I could die on the voyage, I am writing this letter to*
> *inform you that after having borrowed money at diverse times*
> *from Monsieur Antoine Studler van Zurk, Seigneur de Bergen,*
> *I have computed my accounts with him, and find that I owe*
> *him exactly 9,000 Dutch livres, which comes to more than*
> *10,500 French livres, but that nevertheless, to please me, he is*
> *content to receive in payment both the principal and the inter-*
> *est of two contracts that I have sent to you, the one of which is*
> *for 5,000 livres on Sieur de Trenandan, Malescot & their asso-*
> *ciates, which is about to amortize, if they have not yet amor-*
> *tized it; the other is of 4,000 livres, but it has been around two*
> *years since Monsieur de la Chappelle Boüexic, Counsellor in*
> *the parliament of Brittany, has received, as your procurer, the*
> *4,000 livres plus 800 livres of arrears, and he has retained this*
> *money without your consent nor mine. He tells us that he has*
> *loaned 3,200 livres to one of his friends and 1,600 livres to*
> *another, and that they will pay the interest, which amounts to*
> *600 livres, in two years. With the money that I ought to receive*
> *soon from these two contracts, coming to around 10,400 livres,*
> *I ask in the name of our friendship that you do your best to pay*
> *this money to those to whom I owe it.*

Descartes continues with discussion of other contracts, but there are problems with each, and he finishes by saying that if they are not enough to pay his debts, Picot should apply to his brothers to pay them. The picture of Descartes's financial situation given here is both chaotic and desperate. It fits with his saying about his estate if he dies, "Let whoever get whatever he can," which suggests there isn't much to get. The fact is that van Zurk was subsidizing Descartes.

Descartes had gone through a lot of money. Samuel Sorbière visited Descartes at the Endegeest château in 1642 and reported that Descartes received 2,000 livres a year interest from the Amsterdam bank. At the standard interest rate of 5 percent, this would mean he had 40,000 livres in the bank. But if his bankers gambled on the Dutch East Indies market, earnings could be sky high, so his principal could have been less. In that market you could also lose it all. Descartes sold property for 25,000 livres in 1623, and in 1625 he sold more for perhaps 15,000 livres (which would make the 40,000). And he may have increased (or decreased) his capital by playing cards with his rich friends. Whatever he had was augmented by the 4,000 livres cash and 500 livres annual interest he received after his father died, and then in 1644, there was the additional settlement of (I guess) up to 20,000 livres that was probably not paid in cash, but as annual interest.

On Descartes's death, he had 200 rischedales in cash. This is not much. Half of it was given to his servant Schulter along with Descartes's wardrobe, and the other half went to pay for his funeral.

What a strange little man. Brasset jokes in a letter to Chanut of 7 September 1649 about how Descartes had dressed up in his new green silk suit, white collar, lace-spangled gloves, curly wig, and boots with turned up toes — to get on the ship for the month-long trip to Stockholm. Surely he changed into something more seaworthy when they got underway. The ship's captain is not named, but Baillet tells a charming story of how Descartes awed him with his knowledge of navigation. That is, the captain is supposed to have told the queen when he was asked about his passenger, that Descartes was a semi-god and that he had learned more about navigation from the philosopher in a month than he had learned in all his years as a sea captain. This is amusing, given that Descartes's ideas on navigation were off the wall.

The month of September on the North Sea. Not exactly Descartes's original plan of sailing during the best weather of midsummer. The fall storms have begun by mid-September. Well, we don't have any weather reports. October can be beautiful in Stockholm. But this was, as remarked, in the middle of the Little Ice Age. And here our hero was setting out for the north. This is the man who wrote to Mersenne on 4 September 1646 that "Voyages are incommodious and changes of life are always dangerous for the health."

Descartes arrived in Stockholm the first week of October 1649 at the start of a very cold winter. He was received by Queen Christina on arrival and saw her a second time that first week. Then he was dismissed for six weeks, to get acclimatized, as though he were going to climb Everest. Freinshemsius arranged it so that he need not attend the daily round of court functions. He was not to become a courtier after all. Don't call me, I'll call you.

In a letter to Elisabeth on 9 October 1649, Descartes assures her that after seeing Christina twice, "Nothing has changed or diminished my devotion and my zeal" to serve Elisabeth. He claims that Christina is even more scintillating than described (as Elisabeth had sarcastically predicted he would). Most disturbing, however, was the fact that Christina gave no indication of having studied any philosophy. Instead, she was engaged in learning Greek from the handsome, thirty-two year old Isaac Vossius "and is collecting a lot of ancient books, but," Descartes says grimly, "perhaps this will change." But if her interests do not change, he says, he will tell her what he thinks even if she might not like it.

This was an old line of Descartes's. In 1640, he had told Anna Maria van Schurman — a prodigy in painting, poetry, mathematics, philosophy, and languages — that learning Hebrew to read the Old Testament was a waste of her talents, because even the most ignorant peasant can get to heaven on blind faith alone. That means nobody needs to study theology, or even read the Bible. Descartes says in a letter to Mersenne of August 1638 that even idiots and the feebleminded can get to heaven with faith and grace, but it takes brains to understand science. But Descartes's enemy, Voetius, had mesmerized Schurman. Descartes complained that Voetius had ruined (the French word translates "spoiled," as in rotten meat) Mademoiselle Shurman by getting her involved in theological disputes, which, Descartes said, is an obsessive game that eliminates a person from conversation with honest men. In turn, Schurman thanked God in her private journal for turning her affections away from this most profane man.

Thus I am inclined to accept this story of Sorbière's in his letter to Pierre Petit of 20 February 1659:

> *I have heard say that this princess [Christina] did not have much esteem for the speculations of M. Descartes because to his cost he did not approve the studies of the queen, who at that time was completely bound up with the Greek language taught by young Vossius. Someone assured me that M. Descartes said to the queen that he was astonished that Her Majesty amused herself with such trifles, that he had had his fill of it as a small boy in college, but was happy to have forgotten it all having reached the age of reason. (AT V 460)*

If the queen does not like what I say, Descartes says to Elisabeth, then "at least I will have the satisfaction of having done my duty, and perhaps it will give me the occasion to return to my solitude without which it is difficult to advance in the search for truth, which," he raves on, "constitutes my principal good in this life."

This sort of talk, which got around whether or not he addressed it to the queen, did not endear Descartes to the distinguished philologists who had, at her invitation, been established in Queen Christina's court well before Descartes arrived there.

One who surely did not like Descartes was Christina's Greek teacher Isaac Vossius, whose deceased father's books were, as remarked above, transported to Stockholm in the same ship that later carried Descartes. (Isaac had sold them to Christina.) Isaac's father, Gerhard Vossius, had been professor of eloquence at Amsterdam. Descartes probably knew him.

Another of Christina's Greek teachers must have disliked Descartes even more. This was Nicholas Heinsius, the son of Daniel Heinsius, a professor of history at Leiden. Daniel Heinsius had been in a bitter dispute with Guez de Balzac, and in a letter to Mersenne in December 1640 Descartes said that because he was a friend of Balzac, Heinsius had taken him as an enemy. Heinsius set theses against Descartes at the University of Leiden and was greatly opposed to the New Philosophy. The most amusing thing about Heinsius is that after the Leiden officials had paid the enormous sum of 4,000 livres to get the great philologist Claude de Saumaise to come to the university, Heinsius, who was university librarian and the former reigning philologist, refused to let Saumaise take any books out of the library. Heinsius is also known for his campaign against long hair and wigs.

But besides this background, young Nicholas Heinsius probably disliked Descartes because in a letter (open) to Mersenne of 29 January 1640, Descartes told the following story. When the astronomer Martin Hortensius had been in Italy a few years back, he had his horoscope read and was told that he would die in 1639, which he did. He was also told that the two young men with him would die soon after. Descartes continues: "These two young men had such apprehension of this that one of them has already died, and the other, who is the son of Heinsius, is so languishing and sad that he seems to be doing everything possible in order to prove that the astrologer did not lie. That's a fine science, which makes people die who would not have been sick without it." Nicholas Heinsius had obviously recovered, perhaps to Descartes's amusement and the young man's embarrassment when they met again in Stockholm.

Amusement aside, Descartes was ready to leave almost immediately after arriving. "I don't think," he concluded to Elisabeth on 9 October 1649, "that anything would be capable of keeping me in this land longer than until next summer, but I cannot absolutely speak for the future."

He wrote to Picot the same day (a letter lost), reporting (according to Baillet) that he had seen the queen only to salute her and that comte de Brégy-Flexelles was staying at the Chanut residence, where Descartes had also moved in. De Brégy was French ambassador to Poland and in 1645 had arranged the marriage of King Wladislas IV of Poland to Louise-Marie de Gonzague of France (it was Wladislas's second marriage). Remember that Wladislas had asked for Elisabeth's hand in 1636 and was refused, but later gossip was that the offer to the poor princess was just a ploy in the long process of negotiations with the very rich Gonzagues. Comte de Brégy was well known to Elisabeth's mother, Elisabeth herself, Brasset, and the court in The Hague, as well as to Chanut, and to Picot in France. Descartes could have met him in Holland. So when Descartes asks Picot on 4 December 1649 what he thinks of this de Brégy, he can only be fishing for gossip — what is this slick operator doing hanging around the queen? Christina seemed to be smitten with de Brégy. Was he acting for France, Poland, or for himself?

In the lost letter to Picot, Descartes said that at the second meeting with Christina, she spoke of giving Descartes Swedish citizenship, "but he replied simply with compliments, and strengthened his resolution to live in France after the resolution of the troubles there, or in the Palatine on the Rhine, or to return to his old retreat in North Holland" (B II 388).

Baillet goes on to say that at this meeting, Descartes was given orders to be "in her library every morning at five o'clock" (B II 389). And of course Descartes gallantly did not remark that this would disrupt his habit of lying abed until late in the morning. Whether or not this was his invariable custom (and it may have been), five in the morning would have been severe in any case. But there is little evidence that he met with the queen at that hour more than half a dozen times. Christina probably thought that there was no point in her meeting with Descartes until Chanut was there to be impressed by her doing so.

All we know for sure about Descartes's activities in Stockholm between his second meeting with the queen on 7 October and the arrival of Chanut on 20 December 1649, other than that he wrote a few letters, is that he recorded the reading of Chanut's barometer every morning for transmission to Pascal who was comparing readings from different latitudes.

The Passions of the Soul was published at the end of November by Elzévier in Holland, and Descartes sent instructions to Picot (lost letter, 4 December 1649) to distribute copies to "The Chancellor, the Grand Master, the duc de Luynes, Père d'Estrées, Advocate General Bignon, de Montmort, de Verthamont, etc. He also charged de Martigny to distribute some to the court" (B II 393).

So Descartes was still working on the French connection. Again one wonders why, if he was most rationally and prudently still seeking favor in France, why he did not dedicate the *Passions* to Cardinal Mazarin or Anne of Austria or Louis XIV. For the second time, he dedicated a book to a Protestant woman, a book intended to make a splash among the scholarly and powerful Schoolmen of Catholic France.

What a terribly frustrating time it was for Descartes. It was January, the darkest time of the year. Maybe he had plans to follow up his suggestion to Picot on 9 October 1650 (a week after he had arrived) that he might return overland in January when the ground was frozen. He was isolated from the world.

Back in the world, Descartes's family history was repeating itself. Like his father before him, Pierre Descartes had turned over his counselorship in the Parliament of Brittany to his son, Joachim. Held now into the third generation, the hereditary status of the Descartes family nobility was assured. Again like his father, Pierre had bought another counselorship for himself, which he officially assumed on 10 January 1650. And again like his father, he soon sold it at a profit. That was the counter-life of riches and honor that René Descartes had eschewed. He had no son. In several places he speaks of his books as his children.

On 15 January 1650, Descartes wrote to de Brégy that he had seen the queen only four or five times since 18 December 1649, "always in the morning in her library in the company of Monsieur Freinshemsius." He also remarked that Chanut, now ambassador, had seen her only once since his return on 20 December 1649. There was no news to report.

Descartes's letter to de Brégy also inspired this curious story that Baillet tells about Descartes in Sweden:

M. Descartes was in Stockholm, fatigued by the idleness in which he was retained by the queen, who seemed to have made him come only to divert her. The court was occupied with the celebration of the Peace of Münster, and the queen, who wanted him to play his role, seeing that she could not get him to dance in the ballets, engaged him at least to compose French verse for one of them. [Note in the margin: It was on the Peace, and some fragments of it remain.] He acquitted himself in this task in a sufficiently playful manner to please the court, which already prided itself on imitating French manners. But these verses do not derogate from the wisdom of a philosopher of his rank. They will be found too beautiful to be the fruits of such an advanced age, of an imagination that would seem for forty years to have smothered its poetic genius under the weight of algebra and of even more somber sciences. What remains available [Note in margin: As one judges from fragments collected by Henri Estienne] allows us to judge that M. Descartes would have been just as successful in putting philosophy to verse as were Thales, Xenophon, Empedocles, and Epicurus among the Greeks, and Lucretius, Varron, and Boethius among the Latins. This small success, although regarded by M. Descartes as a childish thing fit more to lower than to raise his status, nevertheless perhaps contributed to the jealousy of the grammarians and pedants who fawned upon the queen, and who would have gained great advantage from a glory that appeared so frivolous and contemptible to M. Descartes.

The title of this ballet is *The Birth of Peace*. It is an allegoric celebration of the Peace of Westphalia signed at Münster on 24 October 1648 to end the Thirty Years' War between the victors Sweden and France, and the losers Germany and the Holy Roman Empire. It was performed on 9 December 1649, the day after Christina's twenty-third birthday. The professional dancers wore masks and acted in pantomime. Christina herself danced the role of Pallas Athena, goddess of peace. The audience read the verses from booklets during the dances — they are not recited by the dancers.

I was charmed by this story, and I also noticed that this, the last work of Descartes's published in his lifetime, had not been translated into English. So some years ago I translated all 344 lines into doggerel verse that is quite as good as the original French. Here are some samples:

THE BIRTH OF PEACE

For Panic Terror Who Dances the Third Dance

> *I, who am much less bark than bite,*
> *I, who am the daughter of the night,*
> *Cold, pale, and with a trembling hand,*
> *When I want to terrorize a man,*
> *Or in a thousand soldiers weakness put,*
> *And trample all their laurels underfoot,*
> *A chimera is all I need,*
> *A dream, a shadow, phantom steed,*
> *So in their brains the monsters leap,*
> *And then they tremble like a herd of sheep.*
> *They flee, turn pale, see elves,*
> *And running, often fling themselves*
> *Into worse states upon the blade*
> *Than those they're trying to evade.*

For the Crippled Soldiers Who Dance the Seventh Dance

> *Who sees how we have been undone,*
> *Yet praises war in beauty's name,*
> *Thinks Peace in worth the lesser one,*
> *Is crippled badly in his brain.*

The psychology of the soldiers in battle has a distinct Cartesian flavor, so I checked again to see what evidence Baillet had for attributing *The Birth of Peace* to Descartes. Here it is. In the postscript to that letter of 8 December 1649 to de Flessel, comte de Brégy, counselor to the king of France and ambassador of France to Poland, Descartes wrote:

In order to enlarge this packet so that it won't be so easy to lose, I have added to it the verses of a ballet that will be danced here tomorrow evening.

That's it. The ballet isn't even named.

If Descartes did write verses in Sweden, he wasn't remembering what he had written to Huygens on 17 February 1645:

The poem you have favored me with by sending it to me is so excellent, and contains a syllogism so ingeniously put in the form and fashion of the School, that seeing you philosophize so well in verse, I almost find myself in a humor to want also to philosophize in verse in an attempt to respond to your courtesies. But remembering that Socrates wrote verse only when he was approaching death, for fear that this would likewise be a bad augury for me, and that one might say in Flemish that I was veygh [at the point of death], I have refrained.

Baillet jumped to the conclusion that the verses with which Descartes weighted down his package were some he wrote himself. But I don't believe it. Here is why.

Rumor said de Brégy, the French ambassador to Poland, was trying to talk Queen Christina into establishing an elite corps of French bodyguards with himself at their head. They could wear fancy hats, brightly colored scarves, shining swords, and make the Swedish court militia furious. This sort of provocative behavior did appeal to Christina. The Swedes were further alarmed by other rumors that de Brégy was trying to become Christina's advisor and first minister as Mazarin was in France. Nothing came of any of this, perhaps because de Brégy's father died in Paris and he had to leave Stockholm before he had planned. But he delayed going until he could see *Diana Vic-*

torious by Hélie Poirier, a ballet performed in November 1649. He nearly got frozen in as ice filled the port.

Comte de Brégy waited to see the ballet because it is the second (and *The Birth of Peace* the third) of five ballets written in French and performed between April 1649 and January 1651, the themes of which closely reflect Christina's political views. Thus these ballets represent pronouncements of royal policy (which was common for court ballets of the time). The five ballets are as follows:

1. *The Passions Victorious and Vanquished* (author not named), performed in April 1649 concerns the subordination of amorous passions so the queen can govern with more honesty and competence.

2. *The Vanquished of Diana* or *Diana Victorious* by Hélie Poirier, a Parisian, was performed twice in November 1649 and is about the decision of the queen not to marry. It is possible to see in this ballet a prefiguring of Christina's abdication of the crown in 1655.

3. *The Birth of Peace* (author of the French version not named, but the German version has Freinshemsius listed as author, and the Swedish version Stiernhielm) was performed on 1 December 1649 (the day after Queen Christina's twenty-third birthday), on the triumph of Pallas, goddess of wisdom, over Mars, god of war, and the imposition of peace by the queen. Authorship attributed to Descartes by Baillet.

4. *The Pomp of Felicity* by Charles de Beys, performed in October 1650 about the submission of Mars, god of war, to Cupid, god of life, and the domination of them both by Felicity, who maintains peace.

5. *Parnassus Triumphant* (French version by Hélie Poirier, Swedish by Stiernhielm) performed in January 1651 on the benefits of the peace, and to celebrate Christina's coronation in 1650.

Given the style, the rhyme schemes, the humor, the nature of the characters, and the development of the themes, either of the two ballets published without the author indicated could have been written by either of the professional writers of French verse, Hélie Poirier or Charles de Beys, who are authors of three of the five.

The chances that Christina turned the composition of these verses over to a politically naive foreign philosopher she had so far met with probably less than half a dozen times, a graybeard whom she had excused from court duties, is close to nil. She did like to tease distinguished old men. But a court ballet was not some trivial bagatelle. The ballets were serious business.

By comparison with *Diana Victorious*, I became convinced that *The Birth of Peace* was also written by Hélie Poirier. I knew Poirier was in Sweden at the right time, because in a letter of 9 December 1649 to Thuillerie, Brasset remarks that Poirier perished in a shipwreck on his return from Stockholm. Brasset goes on to say that Poirier was a man "that I would have expected to drown in wine rather than in the Baltic Sea" (Brasset, f. B587v). But I had to find a smoking gun to support this inference. I would have to go to Stockholm.

"Absolutely not," Pat said. "I will not go with you."

I wanted to take this research trip in the dead of winter, so I could find out what it was like for Descartes as he lay dying.

"At least the queen invited Descartes," Pat said. "And look what happened to him."

"Well, look," I said, "we could take a boat from Amsterdam to Stockholm in September through the North Sea, just like Descartes did." I had checked to see that this was actually possible. "You'd like that."

"I might like it," she said, "but you get seasick. The North Sea in September? Forget it."

Unfortunately, she was right.

"We could fly over," I said, "arrive around the first of October as he did, see the nights get longer, feel how depressed he must have been."

"You're crazy," she said. "Besides, did Descartes take *his* wife?"

A twenty-one-day excursion. Descartes probably would have

jumped at the chance. It took him a week longer than that just to get to Stockholm in a round-bottomed sail boat.

Pat took me to the St. Louis airport. It was balmy, as late January days often are in Missouri. In Newark, I changed to Scandinavian Airlines. The plane was nearly empty. I went to the back to find three seats in the middle empty, lay down and went to sleep, to wake up on the morning of 16 January 1993 as we were landing in Stockholm. It was the same sun shining, same balmy weather as in St. Louis.

Susanna Åkerman met me. She is a Swede who had written her dissertation on the intellectual milieu of Queen Christina at Washington University, where I teach, and published it as a book. I had been on her committee. She had just received an appointment at Stockholm University. Her father drove us to a beautifully situated cottage on the outskirts of Stockholm. I put on my running shoes and ran several miles in the woods, heavy exercise, a partly successful way of tricking your body out of jet lag. When I returned, Susanna's mother gave me a cool drink made by steeping linden tree blossoms in sugared water. They had forgotten to ask the pilot of the plane his impressions of me, but he and I had not spoken anyway.

This was the fourth winter in Stockholm with no snow. There were only about six hours of daylight. But the length of the days increased nearly two hours in the three weeks I was there. Descartes had gotten past the depressing march of darkness to midwinter when on 22 December, the noon sun barely rises above the horizon. But then there is nothing slow about the return of the light. The days race toward the midsummer, midnight sun. Descartes must have felt that he was over the hump, was exhilarated, and could see spring coming. The ice would break up in the harbor, and he could go back home to Holland.

But it was cold, bitter cold in 1650, not balmy. The winter Descartes spent in Sweden was one of the coldest ever recorded in Europe, with temperatures always well below freezing. All was wind and ice and snow. Not just the harbors; the North Sea itself froze over.

The day after I arrived, there began a three-day cold snap with a flurry of snow. But then the temperature rose again, just above freezing every day, just below every night. The sun shown brightly with lovely slanting light. Conditions for ice skating were perfect on the lakes in Stockholm. Bareheaded young parents pushed their babies in perambulators around outdoor markets in the sun to buy fruit and vegetables. You would have thought it was summer. I was at sixty degrees north latitude and might as well have stayed at thirty-eight in St. Louis for all the sense of the dread north that Stockholm offered that winter. True, there was less daylight, but the city was well lighted as I could see out the wide window of my room in the Swedish Writers' Union, electric typewriter provided.

It is a short train ride to Uppsala. Queen Christina went there during the winter of 1649–1650, but there is no evidence that Descartes ever did. Probably not. I went there to work in the Carolina Rediviva, a wonderful research library. They have a beautiful copy of *The Birth of Peace* in mint condition. I busily transcribed into my notebook corrections to the errors published in the revised version of the Adam and Tannery edition of Descartes's works. If they thought Descartes wrote the thing, why had the editors printed an incorrect version from a journal article published in 1920, rather than from an original copy? And no new work was done on the ballet for the new edition.

In my reading I had come across an article by William M. C. Stewart in which he says that in the Carolina Rediviva, *The Birth of Peace* is cataloged as being by Hélie Poirier. And there it was, in the catalog of a collection acquired in 1724. Certainly Poirier is a hot candidate. He had been a priest at Chenevières-sur-Marne in France, and in 1625 he published a book of religious and love poetry, *The Loves of Melissa*. Then in 1640, when he was forty, he went a bit too far with some Melissa, fled to Amsterdam, converted to Protestantism, and in 1649 wrote verses for Axel Oxenstiern, the chancellor of Sweden. Also in 1646, he dedicated a book of verse, *The Salutary Sighs* (all his verses are in French), to Queen Christina. Finally, as remarked, we know that Poirier was in Sweden at the time *The Birth of Peace* was written, because of that letter from Brasset to Thuillerie.

I was used to working in the Bibliothèque Nationale in Paris where you must justify your requests for archival material and are closely supervised while you work with them. In the Carolina Rediviva, the librarians had to be restrained from doing my research for me. They did find copies of the five ballets themselves and the catalog showing Hélie Poirier listed as author of *The Birth of Peace*. One of them pointed out a watermark that identified the paper of the catalog as from Holland. But finally they left me on my own with the eighteen boxes of the papers of Johan Nordström, who had published the article on *The Birth of Peace* in 1920. There was a rumor that in those papers was a note in Nordström's handwriting saying that Poirier was the author of *The Birth of Peace*. I took a couple of days to go carefully through every box. Nordström had copied some of Poirier's letters, but if he thought Poirier wrote *The Birth of Peace*, he made no note of it that I could find.

Back in Stockholm, Susanna knew the ins and outs of the Castle Archive in Stockholm, and she took me there. It is built right into the walls of the old castle and was open for research on Tuesdays from one to four in the afternoon. At eleven o'clock, we ate lunch in the Queen Kristina restaurant, next door to the house in which Descartes died. There was nothing to see inside that old French embassy, for it had been gutted and turned into an office building. Still, one could stand outside looking down toward the water and think of how Descartes went outside every day to record the temperature, humidity, barometric pressure, and wind direction for young Pascal back in Paris. They may have had their differences about the vacuum, but cooperative science had already begun its march.

Promptly at one o'clock the door of the Castle Archive was unlocked, and Susanna and I soon had in our hands the Royal Household Records for December 1649. The pages of the large bound books had charred edges from the burning of the castle on 7 May 1697. We leafed through receipts day by day, and wonder of wonders, there it was. Payment recorded for the ballet performed in December 1649. It was a long receipt. Every musician was listed by name, instrument, and payment.

As for the ballet itself, one large lump sum was paid to the ballet master, Antoine Beaulieu. The name of the author of the ballet was not given. It was quite enough money to pay the dancers and the author, but only the name of the ballet master himself was recorded. What we need are his records and receipts. None are known.

What about the papers of the publisher Jean Janssonius who published *The Birth of Peace*? None are known. He was Dutch with the main office in Amsterdam. Dutch records for the publishing house? None are known. Papers of Poirier in Sweden or Holland? None are known.

I went to sleep on the plane back to the United States and had a dream. I found all the papers used by Baillet in writing his thousand-page biography of Descartes in 1691. They were in an old cottage that had belonged to Legrand's mother, who had put them in a cupboard when her son, to whom Baillet had returned them, died. And in a false wall in Amsterdam, I came across the trunk full of papers Descartes had left with Hogeland, who had not destroyed them after all. On top was a big sheaf of letters to and from Descartes and Helena. Almost incidentally, I found at the Janssonius publishing house that had published the ballet the manuscript of *The Birth of Peace* in Poirier's hand. While still asleep, I interpreted my dream as wishful thinking.

"I think," Descartes said, "that in the winter, men's thoughts here freeze like the water." The queen evidently was cool, too, because Descartes goes on to say that "she shows as much benevolence to me as I could reasonably want. But," he goes on:

I am out of my element here, and I desire only tranquility and repose, which are goods the most powerful kings on earth cannot give to those who cannot obtain them for themselves.

He concludes by directing his thoughts about himself onto de Brégy: "I pray to God that he gives you what you desire."

As the romance writers say, little did he know that seventeen days later he would catch a cold, and that in less than a month he would be dead. Or, as some of his biographers are wont to say, he had premonitions — expressed in his resisting the decision to go, putting his affairs in order before leaving, telling Elisabeth he could not speak for the future, and now this bitter critique of his own fate, with the final wish that de Brégy's desires would be satisfied, because he, Descartes, despaired ever again of satisfying his own.

I am not much for premonitions, despite how one can dredge them up and string them together for dramatic effect after the fact. What is striking here comes from the juxtaposition of this remark to de Brégy with Descartes's maxim: Unfortunate is the man who is well known to everyone else but who dies unknown to himself.

At least since he was twenty-four, snug in that oven-heated room in Germany, Descartes consciously sought tranquility and repose for the purpose of advancing mechanics, medicine, and morals for the benefit of mankind.

Descartes did attain such peace occasionally in his life, even for months at a time. But he never settled down. It had been twenty-one years since he had arrived in the United Provinces, but during those years he lived in at least those eighteen different places we know of, and he had traveled to France three times and to Denmark once. He apparently carried his papers with him wherever he went. And he wrote a deep *Meditations*. But in his fifty-third year in that letter to de Brégy, he looked within himself and saw a failure and in some way a fraud. He was wrong — he was as far from being a failure and a fraud as any human being could ever be — but that is the judgment of history, and he didn't know.

Descartes certainly did not doubt the value of his work. I am not talking about his work. I am talking about his life, the man, his maxims, his ideals, his inner self. Let's assume he truly did want tranquility and repose. People often do want what they say, despite actions and appearances to the contrary. Some part of Descartes wanted that peace, wanted to believe that he truly could study and work for himself alone, never publish a book, be unknown to everyone — and be happy. But even the outer man could not pretend to himself and to others that he lived by that inner creed. All those fights with the Dutch preachers he could have avoided. All that pay-ing court in France and Sweden. Alas, he said, I was not a clever monkey. I did not shut up. I wrote books and am known to every-one. Will I die unknown to myself?

Descartes did not die unknown to himself. That last letter to de Brégy was his confession, the only one of his we have. Why am I in this frozen hell? he interrogates himself. Because I am a man who wants to be known by everyone. And knowing this, our hero knew himself.

The end came abruptly, as it often does. Chanut caught cold on 18 January 1650. It developed into pneumonia, but Chanut was well cared for and he was up and around by 29 January. Descartes — they say — helped take care of him. This is likely. Descartes played physician and gave medical advice whenever he could.

On 1 February 1649, presumably at five o'clock in the morning, Descartes delivered the statutes of a Swedish Royal Academy to the queen. She had asked him to write them up. Provision number two, Descartes's contribution, not something the queen specified, reads firmly: Only natural-born Swedish citizens can be members.

On 2 February 1649, Descartes participated in Candlemas cere-monies in Chanut's residence, where he took communion from Père Viogné. (The only recorded occasion.) Then he went to bed with a chill. He had told Burman that by the time a man is thirty, he ought to know enough to be his own physician. Descartes prescribed for himself a few spoonfuls of eau-de-vie, a powerful dose for someone who ordinarily drank only a little wine. Then he slept for two days. Apparently he got brain fever. It is hard to say, because the evidence always given to prove he was out of his mind is that he refused to be bled. Descartes had long thought that bleeding to reduce fever was harmful. He was right. But he also apparently refused to eat or drink anything, and he knew this was wrong. Descartes believed it was good to have something in your stomach at all times, to keep the machine working. So if he wasn't eating, he wasn't thinking.

The queen's personal physician, François du Ryer, was a French-man, a defrocked Jacobin monk turned Protestant. Descartes might

have followed his prescriptions, but du Ryer was in Germany examining some property, spoils of war — a nunnery in fact — whose
income the queen had transferred to du Ryer (to the detriment of the
nuns), the sort of thing Descartes knew she might also do for him.
The other court physician was a Dutchman named Wullen, whom
Descartes counted as an enemy and would have nothing to do with.
The queen sent Wullen over every day anyway. Chanut or his wife or
Descartes's servant Henry Schulter would describe Descartes's condition, and Wullen would prescribe, but Descartes resisted all med-
ication. Chanut wrote after Descartes's death that for several days
Descartes had denied he had a fever, saying he just had a cold.

Wullen kept wanting to bleed him. Wullen himself, in a letter
written on the day of Descartes's death, reports Descartes's pathetic
plea, "Spare this French blood" (AT V 477). In commenting on this,
Wullen cites Horace: "To save someone in spite of himself is to kill
him." As for Descartes's aversion to him, Wullen said philosophically, "If he must die, he'll die more contentedly if he doesn't see me"
(AT V 478). But it would not have been any different if du Ryer had
been there. He, too, would have prescribed bleeding, because bleeding was his cure-all.

Chanut had just recovered from pneumonia. If Descartes had
done what they told him, he might have survived even the bleeding.
After a week, he (as they say) came to his senses and allowed himself to be bled. François Belin, who was there, said Descartes's blood
was like oil.

Too late! Too late!

Wullen reports that Descartes was so filled with phlegm he could
barely cough. Still treating himself, Descartes asked for an old wives'
remedy, some wine into which some tobacco had been dipped, to
make him vomit up the phlegm. Wullen thought that would kill
him, but the man was going to die anyway, so why not?

On the fifth day — the world continued to turn. On 5 February
1650, while Descartes was dying, his old opponent Pierre Gassendi
was climbing Mount Faron in Toulon to repeat the experiment Pascal's brother-in-law had done the year before at Puy-de-Dôme to

demonstrate the weight of the air. "Oh flesh," as Descartes called him in his replies to Gassendi's objections to the *Meditations*, lived another five years. (Gassendi had called Descartes ironically, but flatteringly, "Oh spirit!" Descartes's return jibe was not friendly.) Gassendi had taken up Montmort's offer of a pension and house in the country, so Montmort finally did get his philosopher in residence. Another old opponent, Descartes's archenemy Roberval collected another professorship and lived to 1675.

The ninth day, according to Belin, Descartes asked his manservant Schulter to prepare him some parsnip soup, because he was worried now that his bowels would retract, and he wanted something for his stomach to work on. He was sitting in an armchair when he suddenly collapsed, and gasped, "Ah, my dear Schulter, after that blow I must part" (B II 422). Schulter put him back in bed, but Descartes spoke no more. He could not be given last rites, but — so Baillet says in classic form — when the priest spoke to him, he tilted his head and raised his eyes to heaven. Absolution! The entire Chanut household was on their knees around the bed. That is Baillet's rendition of the classic way a pious Catholic dies.

It is clear from René Descartes's letters that he disliked both his father and his brother Pierre (and there is evidence that they disliked him in turn). He did like his niece Catherine, Pierre's daughter, who was only nine years old when he sent her a copy of the French translation of his *Meditations* in 1646. Catherine is the only member of the Descartes clan who ever wrote anything about the philosopher. Unfortunately, she made most of it up.

For example, Catherine wrote forty years after the event that a few hours before his death, Descartes dictated to Chanut a letter to his brother and half brother in which he asks them to continue a small pension he was paying to his old nurse. The problem with this is that his manservant Henry Schulter reports that Descartes died without saying a word. And Pierre Chanut says in his letter to Princess Elisabeth that Descartes could not speak on the night of his death (he died at 4 o'clock in the morning, about the time he might have been getting up for a 5 o'clock rendezvous with the queen, had he been in health). Chanut is at great pains to tell how pious Descartes was the day before he died and how he had recently made the duties of a true Catholic, which means that he went to confession and took holy communion.

If Descartes had done such a noble thing as asking his brothers to continue a pension to his old nurse (this would have been his wet nurse), Chanut would certainly have reported it to Elisabeth, which he does not. Neither does Chanut in any of his letters report any last words of Descartes, such as given by Baillet, "Ah, my dear Schulter, it is the final blow and I must depart," or by Clerselier, "Ah, my soul, it has been a long time that you have been captive; now is the hour that you can escape your prison and leave the embrace of your body; it is necessary to suffer this disunion with joy and courage." Clerselier, you remember, is the one to whom the publication of Descartes's letters was entrusted and who cleaned them up a bit.

Catherine Descartes's story of the deathbed behest by Descartes to his nurse certainly has all the elements of a made-up family story, particularly given that she goes on to say that Descartes then spent five or six hours before his death with his confessor in continual acts of piety and religion. Nevertheless, in a 20 February 1657 letter to Pierre Petit, Samuel Sorbière has heard the story, for he says of Descartes that "the care he made for the provision of his nurse is a convincing proof of his goodness," and Sorbière goes on to say that he has heard several stories about Descartes's goodness when he was in The Hague. Of course Sorbière also says that he thinks the jealous grammarians in the Stockholm court poisoned Descartes, which is about on the order of the rumor that Lyndon Johnson and Richard Nixon conspired to assassinate both President Kennedy and his brother Robert.

I wonder about that nurse. You know, Helena nursed Francine. After Francine died, Helena went on her way. A servant in service somewhere. So much is made of this improbable story of Descartes on his deathbed asking his brothers to continue a pension for his

DESCARTES BY JAN LIEVENS, SOMETIME AFTER 1647

Groningen Museum, Groningen

old nurse that I wonder, what about Helena? Could that story about Descartes's nurse have as its source his having left some sort of legacy for Helena? One would like to think so.

Descartes's manservant Schulter wrote a letter about Descartes's death to Schooten, who sent a copy to Dirck Rembrantz, the shoemaker to whom Descartes taught mathematics, who became a famous astronomer. That report goes as follows:

Yesterday [11 February 1650] between three and four o'clock in the morning, Monsieur Descartes died.

On February 3rd at four o'clock in the morning, on his way to meet the Queen in her library as he did even when it was extremely cold (the Swedes say it has not been so cold in a long time, which possibly caused his death), he was stricken with a severe fever. He said it came from phlegm that was so heavy in his stomach that he believed his natural fires were almost extinguished. He was extremely cold, had a bad headache, and ate nothing but three or four spoonfuls of brandy. Then he slept for two days. On Friday, he had a wine sop. He complained of severe heat and pain in his side that increased every day, and he could hardly breathe. He had pneumonia, but refused to believe it. On Monday, the Queen sent her physician who prescribed bleeding and other remedies, but M. Descartes said he had too little blood, that he wanted remedies only from the kitchen, and he refused to see the physician again. On Tuesday, he finally allowed himself to be bled three times, but it did no good because his blood was corrupted and yellow. He will be buried at four o'clock this afternoon. (AT V 576-577)

But give the last word to Baillet, who puts it most precisely:

He died the eleventh day of February at four o'clock in the morning, aged fifty-three years, ten months, and eleven days. (B II 423)

CONCLUSION

The ghost in the machine fights
the last battle for the human soul.

ENÉ DESCARTES'S *Discourse on Method* was published in 1637 and his *Meditations on First Philosophy* in 1641. Both books have been in print ever since. Descartes's mathematical method and mind-body metaphysics have directed the course of Western philosophy and science now for three and a half centuries. I remarked in the introduction that our whole Western culture — both humanistic and technological — is Cartesian to the core. So it is not surprising that Descartes's ideas also set the agenda for the twenty-first century, for a great battle. The results of that battle will lead to the the greatest revolution that humankind will ever undergo. That battle is the last battle for the human soul.

The most recent revolution on this level took place during Descartes's own lifetime when Kepler and Galileo displaced man from the center of the cosmos. Earth was shown not be the center of the universe at all but rather a minor planet circling a minor star far out on the edge of a galaxy. Moreover, this sparse edge is virtually in the dark compared to the brightness of that tightly gathered collection of stars at the galaxy's center.

God, if He exists, surely inhabits that hot central core of stars so much greater than our own. If God cares about the human inhabitants of our insignificant planet, his eye is certainly on the sparrow. But that decentering was only the beginning of man's degradation. Man's place in the universe only got worse as astronomical knowledge increased, and we found that even our own galaxy of billions of stars is itself trivial and insignificant in size and place compared to billions of other galaxies that make up our universe. There is now even talk of other universes.

So what about me, one tiny human being, the tiniest of sparrows, what about me in that vast cosmos? What is my place and purpose in the universe? Well, although my tiny light of consciousness seems to dwindle to a point of nothingness in this vast cosmos, God *could*, after all, care about *me*. If we have diminished the place of human-kind in the universe, we have not necessarily detracted from the message of the good book, that the peoples who revere the book — Jews, Christians, and Muslims — are special in God's eye.

All we have really done, it might be said, is discover the true im-mensity and magnificence of God's creation. Even should we detect other creatures as intelligent as we are on some far distant planet, or even should they visit us here on earth, they still could be shel-tered under the mantle of God's grace and be welcomed as our brothers. Descartes in fact thought it very likely that God has popu-lated other planets, and he hoped to build a telescope so powerful that we could see whether or not there are creatures like us on the moon. If there were, and if it turned out that we could converse with them as we do with each other — and as we cannot do with mere animals — then we would be assured that they are conscious and have souls as do you and I.

But no, the last battle for the human soul is *not* going to be over whether the extraterrestrials convert us to their gods or we convert them to ours. It is rather over whether or not we have souls at all. Descartes set the stage for this battle with his dualism of two sub-stances that are diametrically different from one another. According to Descartes, each human being consists of a mental, thinking, active, unextended soul-mind united with a material, unthinking, passive, extended body. Most people in the Western world believe that this is true, that we have bodies and we have souls.

A prime motive behind Descartes's dualism is summed up in a saying of his times: If immaterial, then immortal. Because the soul is unextended and has no parts, it cannot break up. When one's body dies and disintegrates, one's soul is simply released. The soul cannot rot as does the body. If immaterial, then immortal. This is the principle behind the Cartesian notion — the Western world's notion — that the soul is entirely separate from the body and that when the body dies, the soul is unharmed and unchanged.

This is a powerful doctrine. It is the primary promise and main attraction of Christianity. Descartes's dualism of soul separate from body supports the Christian belief in the survival after death and the immortality of the human soul. Of the human person, of you and me. Following the death of our bodies, our souls receive their last judgments and henceforth exist eternally in the ecstasy of heaven or the agony of hell.

This Christian dualism commits Descartes to another view, one that sets up the twenty-first century's battle for the human soul, a battle, by the way, that has already begun.

Descartes was a vivisectionist. Let's look at some results of his research on the living bodies of animals, which, he says, do *not* have souls and so are not self-conscious and do not feel pain. All animals are insentient machines.

Descartes was the first physiologist to work out in detail the reflex arc theory of stimulus and response. This is an essential step toward understanding cybernetic steady-state mechanisms and evolution. Here is how it goes.

Living machines respond when the sense organs are stimulated. These organs are activated by direct contact with large bodies in touch, with small particles in smell and taste, and with light and sound waves in sight and hearing. According to Descartes, each impact on a sense organ tugs cords in the hollow nerves in a unique way. For example, the cords in the nerves of the eye are jerked differently for each different pulse of light that hits the eye.

The cords in the nerves extend, Descartes says, to a cavity in the brain. At that endpoint, they terminate at valves called ventricles. When a nerve cord attached to a ventricle is pulled, the end of the nerve is aimed in a certain direction, the ventricle is opened a certain amount, and a certain quantity of a fine, fluid matter flows out.

Now in this cavity in the brain sits the teardrop-shaped pineal gland. The exact direction the ventricle points, the size of its opening, and thus the amount of fluid matter that flows out is specific and unique to each type and degree of stimulus that hits each sense organ, jerks the cords to aim and open the ventricles, and releases a blast of fluid matter aimed at the pineal gland. This is the stimulus.

The next step for the animal machine is the response. According to Descartes, the pineal gland is quite loosely attached. What happens is that the inflowing fluid matter points the pineal gland at certain other ventricles. The pineal gland can manufacture this fluid matter itself. So pushed and pointed by the inflow from one set of ventricles, the pineal gland aims and fires off an outflow at another set of ventricles. This blast is powerful enough to crack the nerve cord whips and activate the muscles to which they are attached. Then the body runs or jumps or whatever. This is the response.

Thus, if bright light hits your eyes, almost instantly you blink your eyelids shut, because your eye cords jerk open brain ventricles to release fluid matter aimed at the pineal gland that fires off a return shot that jerks the cords of your eyelid muscles. It's all automatic.

Now we know that the nerves are not hollow, they have no cords in them, and no ventricles at their ends in the brain. The pineal gland does not hang loose in a cavity in the brain, and it does not shoot out fluid matter to activate the muscles.

But the theory! The mechanistic model! The working out of how the body is stimulated and responds as a machine! This is genius of the highest order. Descartes is absolutely right about what happens. He is the first to describe the principle of the reflex arc. And he anticipates Pavlov concerning conditioned reflexes. Remember the dog beaten to the sound of a violin playing. So Descartes gets the neurophysiology a bit wrong, who cares? Certainly no philosopher does: It's the principle that counts. In general terms, Descartes is right about the way the animal machine works. Biology has been Cartesian ever since.

Descartes's theory of stimulus and response is the same as that taught in medical schools and biology and psychology departments today. The details are different, but the principles are the same. For each distinctive sensory stimulus on the sense organs, energy is transported through the nerves to the brain where it is recorded as a brain state or neural net configuration unique to that stimulus. This brain event evokes nerve reactions that cause a muscular response. An important point about this theory is this: Consider, say, the causal chain from a vibrating gong to its internal impact in the brain. If you were to look only at this brain registration — a specific orientation of the pineal gland, neural net, or whatever — theoretically you could tell from its distinctiveness that a gong had rung, what note, how loud, where, and so on.

This mechanistic model of the body and brain is an explanation of how the animal machine works according to physical laws. It can thus be used to predict and control the movements of animal bodies. Descartes's method is an immense advance over the previous scholastic Aristotelian notion that everything behaves the way it does because it is each thing's nature to behave as it does. The classic putdown of these animistic or "tree-spirit" explanations that appeal to a thing's desires or nature was made by Molière. In his play, *The Hypochondriac*, he has the physician explain that opium puts us to sleep because it has a dormative power. That is, the reason opium puts you to sleep is because opium has the power to put you to sleep. End of explanation. But by using Descartes's method of mechanistic models, one can show how opium turns off switches in the brain to put the body into that inactive state we call sleep. On the Aristotelian view, all we can do is say that it is the nature of opium to put us to sleep, but we don't know how. With Descartes's mechanistic explanation, we can manufacture other compounds that put us to sleep, and also design defenses against sleep-producing substances. By understanding the body as a machine, we can control the body. And we have not appealed at all to the notion of a spirit or a soul or a nature. The mechanistic explanation applies only to how the parts of things interact. In this sense, it is sheerly behavioristic.

So much for the mechanistic model of the material body and

brain. It is time to talk about the main bone of contention in the battle for the human soul, the ghost in the machine.

Lights! Camera! Action! For the classic model of human sensory perception is that of the theater, with a little man inside the head reading off a screen what is happening outside. That little man is the human soul, the ghost in the machine. It is connected with the pineal gland (or, in today's terms, with the whole brain). Now note carefully: The screen is *not* in the brain. The screen is in the soul or the mind. It is in the little man himself. And that little man has the power — free will — to override the natural responses of the body to make it do whatever the little man wants it to do. It works this way.

The movements of the pineal gland or the firings of the neural network in the brain cause the display on the screen in the mind. The display is a representation or picture of what is going on in the outside world. This representation is in all sensory modes — passional, kinesthetic, visual, tactile, auditory, olfactory, and gustatory. And *only* the human soul in the human animal has this display of passions, pleasures, and pains, bodily orientation, colored images, tactile feelings, sounds, smells, and tastes. Only the human soul is conscious. There it sits, alert in the brain, like the captain in a ship or the pilot in the cockpit, watching the screen with ghostly hands on the body's controls to make it do its bidding. As a matter of fact, Descartes explicitly says that the soul is *not* in the body like a captain in a ship but rather is in union with the body. But his description of what this union means sounds very much like the way a driver can feel the movements of the automobile he is driving. So Descartes gets stuck with the ghost in the machine after all. And then what rears its ugly head is the mind-body problem that philosophers have wrestled with ever since Descartes set it up. The mind-body problem stems from the fact that mind and matter are completely unlike one another, and the problem has two parts: causation and consciousness.

First, causation. You remember that Princess Elisabeth nailed Descartes on that one. If the soul is unextended as the good Christian philosopher Descartes says it is, then how can it act on an extended body? Here is how to see the problem. Remember that old medieval question: How many angels can dance on the head of a pin? You must know that your first answer to any philosophical question should be: It depends. Angels are unextended souls. They are not made of matter, they are immaterial ghosts. So the answer to the question of how many angels can dance on the head of a pin is either an infinite number because they don't take up any space, or else none because they have no feet. Either answer makes it clear that an unextended soul cannot kick a material body, and since material bodies can be moved only by bodily impact, immaterial souls cannot budge bodies because souls cannot bump bodies. Neither bodies souls. Just as the soul cannot act on the body by bumping the body because the soul is not the sort of thing that can bump, neither can the body act on the soul by bumping the soul because the soul is also not the sort of thing that can be bumped. So neither can souls move bodies, nor can bodies make souls feel anything. Causal interaction between minds and bodies is impossible. But let's suppose causal interaction does take place. That is, Descartes argues that obviously we have souls and bodies, and obviously they interact, and obviously God is powerful enough to make this happen, so what's the problem?

This reminds me of an explanation once given by Ring Lardner: Shut up, he explained. When Princess Elisabeth asked Descartes to explain how mind and body could possibly interact, he replied: Don't worry about it.

So to set up the second part of the mind-body problem (consciousness), let's assume that mind (or soul) and body can interact because they do and God makes it happen. Now we have to refine the model of the ghost in the machine. What naturally happens is this. Not only do motions of the pineal gland (or firings in the neural net) act to cause reflex muscular action, they also act on the mind-soul to cause it to have sensory experiences of sight, touch, sound, taste, and smell. Because of this sensory display in the theater in the mind, we automatically think we are seeing things in the external world. But this is naive. We are just seeing *representations* of things in the material world. Remember that the visual image of the sun that you see now is not of the sun as it is now, but is rather of the sun as it was eight minutes ago. All that we experience in the theater in the mind is a display of representations of how things were out there in the world a split second ago if we are touching them, and as they were millions of years ago if we are looking at the stars. Fortunately, most of our representations are close enough in time to the things out there that we don't even notice the difference.

This theory of perception has led mad scientists to speculate about how to program this inner theater so you can have whatever glorious sensations you want. In his novel, *Brave New World* (1932), Aldous Huxley predicted that it could be done with drugs. Opium and LSD cause you to have some fabulous experiences, but drugs are hard to control. In his science fiction novel *The Big Ball of Wax* (1954), Shepard Mead suggested a better way, the electronic feelies. Today we have computer freaks perfecting virtual reality. Before long we will be able to strap in to get electronic jolts on every sense organ all over our bodies so that we — me Tarzan, you Marilyn Monroe — can experience in the theater in our minds ... well, I shudder to think.

Here is the picture. God makes it so that your mind has sensory experiences correlated with your body's causal interaction with other bodies in the outside world. All sensory experience occurs in the theater in your mind where your soul — the ghost in the machine — learns to interpret what you see on the screen. And with this information you command your body — in general — to seek out interactions with other bodies that cause you pleasure and to avoid bodily interactions that cause you pain.

This is a causal theory of representational perception, the view that we do not have direct experience of bodies but only of sensations that are caused by bodies. This representationalism gives rise to the very difficult second part of the mind-body problem: Is the world really like the sensory pictures we have of it in the theater in the mind?

Descartes himself says absolutely not. For example, visual extension is not like real extension because visual extension is not really extended. It cannot be, you see, because it is in the mind and the mind is unextended. That's a hard one, and we had best just take Descartes's word for it. But it can make sense to a mathematician who thinks that sensory representations, although not themselves spatial, are related to one another in a way isomorphic to the way points are related in space.

John Locke and Immanuel Kant, however, say that we cannot ever know whether or not the real world of bodies is like the sensory pictures shown in the theater in the mind. The reason is that to know whether or not these pictures show the external world as it really is, we would have to be able to compare the inner pictures with the outer things, but in fact we can know about the outer things only *indirectly* by way of the inner pictures. And after all, if we *could* perceive the outer world directly, we would not need a system by which we perceive that outer world indirectly by way of pictures of it.

But enough of the details. Let's get on with the fight. The last battle for the human soul is being waged by religious mentalists on the one side who argue that the human soul exists independently of bodies, opposed to atheist materialist scientists — neurophysiologists, psychologists working on artificial intelligence, and computer scientists working on network theory — materialists who argue on the other side that the mind or soul just is the brain. It is a battle of religious dualists fighting for the independent existence of a spiritual human soul against atheistic monists who say the human soul is just the material brain. And the amazing thing is that the materialists are winning.

That the materialists are winning is paradoxical because Descartes's proof for the existence of an independent soul-mind seems to be very strong. In his *Discourse* and *Meditations*, he argues that you are certain that you exist because you experience yourself directly, but you cannot be certain that your body exists because you know about it only by way of representations in your mind. And then Descartes presents his demonic proof of the mind's independence of the body. Even if there were no bodies in the world, God or a demon could cause you to have sensory experiences in the theater in your mind just as if there were.

All your experience is inner, subjective, private, and you can never know whether or not the external world is like your inner experience, or even if there is an external world at all. But one thing you can be absolutely certain about is that you exist — or, rather, *I* can be absolutely certain that I exist as a thinking thing. About *your* existence, you will have to decide for yourself — like Professor Cohen's student who wondered if he existed.

The materialists respond to the mentalists' argument for the soul-mind as follows. We agree that no one can be absolutely certain that anyone else is thinking except himself. But it would be pretty stupid (downright crazy, in fact) to act as though there were no other minds.

As for the external world, we can show you that we *probably* know that it exists and what it is like to such a high degree of probability that it would be insane to doubt it. We learn what the external world is like — as Descartes taught us — by forming mechanistic theories and hypotheses about its smallest parts, atoms, and subatomic particles. Then we predict what the results will be if we conduct certain experiments on the basis of these theories and hypotheses. If our predictions are borne out, then this helps confirm our belief that there is a material world out there and that we know what it is like. Our test is this: Does it work? It does. Look what we can do — make bridges, atom bombs, false teeth. We are, as Descartes predicted man could be, masters and possessors of nature. We can control the material world.

The soul people do have a comeback. Nonsense, they say, your theories and hypotheses are merely instrumental. They are *useful* for doing things, but that is all. They do not describe the world the way it really is.

Oh, sure, the materialists reply. That is the trick Galileo used to avoid condemnation by the church. He agreed to the ruse that his heliocentric theory is only a calculational device. He agreed that really the earth is at the center of the universe, it is just easier instrumentally to calculate the position of the planets by pretending that the sun is at the center. And what do we think about that now?

As for the mind or the soul, neuroscientists today are discovering how the material brain works. Eventually, materialists say, maybe in the next hundred years, everything that goes on in the neural network will be mapped so that all you need to do is flash it on a screen and you can read off what that *brain*, not the soul, mind you, but what the *brain* is thinking. Already at the Washington University Medical School, Professor Raichel can tell you which parts of your brain will light up under a PET scan when this or that word is said to you. It is crude, but it represents immense progress. I have no doubt that eventually neuroscientists will be able to show which brain events correlate with all our thoughts. And, of course, like good Cartesian scientists, they will have incidentally discovered how to control all our thoughts. All brain research of this sort originates in Descartes's mechanistic model of the body — and thus of the brain — as a machine. Materialists conclude that the soul is just the brain and sensations are nothing but brain events.

Descartes's own model of the brain in fact raises a very serious problem for mentalists like himself. He shows that the soul-mind (the ghost in the machine) knows what is happening outside the mind only by observing the sensory show in the theater in the mind. These inner reports are caused by brain events that also leave traces in the brain. So when the soul-mind wants to remember something, it checks the brain traces left by past events. Descartes's disciple Louis de La Forge pointed out the disturbing implication that when the body dies and the brain disintegrates, the surviving soul-mind no longer has access to the memory traces recorded in the brain. The soul after death thus cannot remember its former life on earth. A disembodied soul cannot remember the person it was when united with a body.

This result provides one motivation for the Christian doctrine of the rapture and the resurrection of the body after the last judgment. The important thing is not so much that dem *bones* gonna rise again, but that your *brain* must be reconstituted and your soul-mind reunited with it. For if *you* are going to enjoy heaven (or suffer in hell), your soul-mind must be able to remember that you *are* you.

Materialists comment on this that if you can believe that disintegrated bodies are going to be resurrected and transported into heaven, you really are, as Kierkegaard says, Knights of Infinite Faith. And if you do accept this absurd doctrine, they say, you are just showing that you accept the view that the brain is the soul-mind. The materialist neuroscientists have not yet, however, fully shown that the mind is the brain. One thing that might stop their progress toward doing so would be a religious revival and revolution against science. Probably not the Jews, but maybe the orthodox Christians or Muslims might sweep the earth and wipe out brain research. Religious mentalists might win the battle for the human soul by enforcing a time-honored rule: Convert, or we'll slit your throat.

Think of it. What if the twenty-first century is a century of religious wars, just like Descartes's seventeenth century. Maybe they have already started in Bosnia, Herzegovina, and Kosovo, or in Israel and Palestine, or in India and Pakistan, or in Chechnya. Or New York City and Afghanistan. Another battle for the human soul. Christians vs. Muslims, Muslims vs. Jews, Hindus vs. Sikhs, East vs. West. But wait a minute. Religious wars never have slowed the advancement of science in the past. There is nothing like war to spur invention. King Gustavus Adolphus of Sweden invented the modern army and won the Thirty Years' War for the Protestants against the Catholics in Descartes's time. Ayatollahs today approve of machine-guns.

Back to arguments. No material activity in the brain, mentalists say, is *like* the subjective sensory experience we have in the theater in the mind. A *feeling* of pain obviously is not a brain event. That Technicolor sunset we see is obviously different from a pattern of neurons firing in a neural net. Yes, there are correlations between brain events and sensory experience, but they do not prove that sensory experiences are identical with brain events. A colored shape *as seen*, a tickle or an itch *as felt*, a sound *as heard*, an odor *as smelled*, and a taste *as tasted*, all sensory experience is totally unlike the material events that take place in the brain, no matter how closely and in what detail sensory experience is correlated with brain events. This qualitative difference shows that the mind is totally different from the brain.

Most telling of all, mentalists say, the mind is conscious of its own sensory experience. You know that *you* are having your subjective experience. No mere animal machine is conscious. No animal machine knows itself. Only human soul-minds are conscious. There can never be a mechanistic explanation or a material equivalent of consciousness. If there ever is a conscious computer, it won't be because the machine is conscious but because a mind has occupied it. Hal in the movie *2001* is in heaven; the computer he occupied blew up.

Sensory experience *as sensed* certainly does not seem to be identical with brain events, or consciousness with, say, modulated brain waves in the 40-Hertz range. But even though both materialists and mentalists agree that brain event correlates for all sensory experiences will probably be found, mentalists still argue that this will not prove that the brain is the mind. So materialists revert to the problem of mental causation. All brain events are caused by the causal interactions of material bodies. It is not just crude bumping, of course, it is all the subatomic and electrico-chemical interactions that follow physical laws. *All* brain events can be traced to material causes. There is no way for an immaterial mind to cause bodily motions. The mentalists' mind is merely an angel uselessly dancing on the head of a pin. Finally, even if the mind could cause the body to move, if it did, it would disrupt and counteract the chain of material causes. And this would be a miracle. We do not see many miracles these days. None, in scientific fact.

Remember now, mentalists give no explanation of how unextended mental souls or minds can act causally on material bodies. They just claim that obviously minds do act on bodies. But this, materialists say, is just to assume that there are minds separate from brains, which is the very issue in question.

Here is the crucial problem: If a mind *did* act on a body to make the body do what the mind wants it to do, the action of that mind would have to overcome the material causes acting on the body. For example, my arm might be hanging down naturally in accord with the law of gravity, but if my mind makes my arm rise in salute, then my mind has to overcome the material forces of physical attraction that naturally cause my arm to hang down. How can the mind *do* that?

Materialists have elaborate mechanistic models showing how the brain operates according to physical laws. Mentalists have no models that show how the mind can act on the body. Materialists have elaborate theories of how the brain evolved over geologic time in contact with the material world, so it operates in a stimulus-response manner. Mentalists say that God made the mind and gave it the power to act on the body, but they do not know how the mind *does* it. Mentalists have no explanatory, diagrammatic models, of *how* the mind acts on the body. All they can say is that it is the nature of the mind to have the power to act on the body.

And that, materialists say, is magic. The independent mind has no other way of acting except by magic. Every time the mind acts on the body (if it does), it miraculously overcomes the laws of physics. Every time the body moves according to the mind's orders, a miracle takes place. The religious Cartesian Père Malebranche, of dog-kicking fame, even agreed that this was true. Minds and bodies do not really interact, he said. It only looks as though they do. In fact, on the occasion, for example, of your willing to raise your arm, God makes it rise, miraculously. Most modern mentalists do not countenance this occasionalist solution to the causation problem. But they still call on God to explain interaction.

Materialists point out that by appealing to God to carry out the mind's will, mentalists admit that the notion of an independent mind acting on a body is baloney. And if the mind can't do anything, who needs it?

To be sure, sensory experience, thinking, and willing take place. But all mental activity is caused by brain events. It is just an illusion that brain or bodily events are caused by mental events. For example, some admittedly controversial PET-scan brain research shows that the brain lights up in areas whose actions cause certain bodily motions *before* a person (the mind) consciously "decides" to do those things. An example would be someone's brain firing up to make his body get up from a chair, just prior to that person's consciously deciding to get up from that chair. So by stimulating certain parts of the brain, you could theoretically cause a person both to do something and to "decide" to do it.

If so, then your self-conscious thoughts are not the causes of your actions but are rather nearly instantaneous — but still after the fact — reports of your body's responses to environmental stimuli. There is no conscious mental self separate from the body that makes decisions and causes the body to act; rather, the body's responses and actions cause self-conscious thoughts to arise.

But what about when you agonize over a decision and cannot decide what to do? Then your body is stuttering. It is stymied in its response, it is rapidly starting and stopping an action, and until your body firmly responds one way or another to an environmental stimulus, you will experience that self-conscious state we know as indecision. But as soon as the body acts one way or another, the report of that act will flash into your self-consciousness in the form of a decision to do it. Actually, we know how to overcome nervous indecision. Just pop a pill.

Thus materialists say that the body is fully in command and that we are conscious only of reports of how the body is responding to the environment. So is all our self-conscious experience of making decisions an illusion?

No, in fact, it is not an illusion. Your body is doing what *you* want to do because your body *is* you.

Even if your self-conscious feelings of being in command are only reports of bodily action, it is still *you* who are acting. Your experience, your existential way of being in the world, does not change, cannot change, simply because you learn that causation takes place only in your body and that you have no mind-soul that issues commands to make the body act.

Here is the grand, overall situation.

The last battle for the human soul was set up by two central doctrines in Descartes's philosophy. First, that our real selves, our persons, are mind-souls that have an existence independent of our bodies, and that these mind-souls command and control our bodies like ghosts in a machine.

Descartes's second crucial doctrine is that all animals — including human animals — are machines that behave the way they do in response to external stimuli from the material environment in strict accord with the laws of physics and neurophysiology.

These two Cartesian doctrines contradict one another. If our bodies are determined according to these natural laws, then no independent mind-soul can act on our bodies to cause them to behave in ways counter to natural laws. If my body is a machine, then, it would seem, I am *not* free either to continue writing or to stop writing. I do what my body must do. But if I am my body, I am doing what I want to do.

It sounds like a trick. Spinoza is one of Descartes's successors who is famous for arguing that all our actions are absolutely and totally determined and *that* is what makes us free. The more you will yourself to do what you must do anyway, the freer you are. Of course, you are also determined to will yourself to do (or not do) what you must do anyway. And so on ad infinitum. It is not a doctrine of free will of the sort most people think they have, neither does it make any sense. But it is, materialists say, all we've got.

In the twenty-first century, this is how the last battle for the human soul will go. Materialists will discover more and more about how the brain works. Mentalists will never be able to show how an independent mind works. One day, one hundred, two hundred years down the line, everyone will finally realize that the materialists have won and that the mentalists have lost this last battle for the human soul. When humankind finally faces the fact that the mind is the brain, that there is no independently existing mental soul to survive the death of the body, that none of us chirpy sparrows is immortal, when Descartes's ghost in the machine finally fades away and his animal machine is triumphant, then there will be a revolution in human thought the like of which none has gone before.

ACKNOWLEDGMENTS

I thank Patty Jo Watson for her assistance and enthusiasm in pursuing Descartes. My research was facilitated greatly by Richard H. Popkin, Jean-Henri Roy, Susanna Åkerman, Theo Verbeek, and Jean-Robert Armogathe.

Anna Watson, Steven Nadler, Thomas Lennon, Justin Leiber, Charles Newman, Eric Simonoff, Eric Chinski, and Carl W. Scarbrough read one or another version of the entire manuscript and made many perceptive comments for which I am most grateful. Alan Gabbey did a wonderful final check.

Outstanding among many others who helped are: Roger Ariew, Jean-Marie Beyssade, Erik-Jan Bos, Harry Bracken, Hiram Caton, Claude Chabert, Daniel Garber, William H. Gass, Lars Gustafsson (of Örebro), Kurt Hawlitschek, Patrick Henry, Zbigniew Janowski, Geir Kirkebøen, Pauline Kleingeld, Elisabeth Labrousse, José-Raimundo Maia Neto, Kenneth Manders, Jean-Luc Marion, Att McDowell, Philippe Mensier, Fenella Middleton, Georges Moyal, Dugald Murdoch, Matthijs van Ortegem, Geneviève Rodis-Lewis, Susan Rosa, Maya Rybalka, Michel Rybalka, Jerome Schiller, Alexandre Schimmelpenninck, Ivo Schneider, Paul Schuurman, Gregor Sebba, Susan H. Sims, Emma Lewis Thomas, Erik Trinkaus, Steven Voss, and Gerhardus Wiersma.

I thank librarians at the Carolina Rediviva in Uppsala, the Kungl. Biblioteket and the Slottsarkivet in Stockholm, University Libraries of Amsterdam and Leiden, the Herzog August Bibliothek in Wolfenbüttel, the Bibliothèque Nationale in Paris, and the Washington University Library in St. Louis. I also appreciate the hospitality of the Swedish Writers' Union.

The leisure Descartes said a thinker needs was provided by research grants from the National Science Foundation, the University of Michigan, and Washington University, and by fellowships from the American Council of Learned Societies, the Center for Advanced Study in the Behavioral Sciences, the Camarago Foundation, and the Bogliasco Foundation.

At the Center for Advanced Study in the Behavioral Sciences, I thank three successive directors: Ralph W. Tyler, Gardner Lindzey, and Philip E. Converse, and two successive associate directors: Preston S. Cutler and Robert A. Scott. They and their fine staff provided an intellectual ambiance that fulfilled those romantic dreams I had about the life of a scholar when I was young. Then I thank Michael Pretina, director, and his assistant Anne-Marie Franco of the Camarago Foundation, where I wrote the first draft of this book. I also thank James Harrison, president; Anna Maria Quaiat, director; and Alan Rowlan, associate director of the Bogliasco Foundation, where I completely rewrote it.

At Washington University, I thank the staff and my colleagues in the Department of Philosophy, Departmental Chairs Roger Gibson and William Bechtel, Deans of Arts and Sciences Martin Israel and Edward Macias, and Chancellors William Danforth and Marc Wrighton.

"On the Zeedijk" appeared in different form in *The Georgia Review* and was included in *The 1990/1991 Pushcart Prize: Best of the Small Presses*. I thank editors Stanley W. Lindberg, Stephen Cory, and Bill Henderson for permission to use this material again. "The Ghost in the Machine Fights the Last Battle for the Human Soul" appeared in different form in *Kriterion*. I thank editor José R. Maia-Neto for permission to use this material again.

Finally, I thank that most independent of publishers, David R. Godine.

BIBLIOGRAPHY

Citations in parentheses in the text: A = Adam 1910, B = Baillet 1691, C = Cohen 1920, AT = Adam and Tannery *Oeuvres de Descartes*, D&D = Verbeek *Descartes and the Dutch*, Q = Verbeek *Descartes et Martin Schoock, la querelle d'Utrecht*. Letters quoted by date in the text are in AT. Translations are my own unless otherwise indicated.

Adam, Antoine. *Théophile de Viau et la libre pensée française en 1620*. Paris: E. Druz, 1935.

Adam, Charles. *Descartes: ses amitiés féminines*. Paris: Boivin, 1937.

———. "Descartes: ses correspondants anglais," *Revue de littérature comparée*, Vol. 17, 1937, pp. 437-460.

———. "Quelques questions à propos de Descartes," *Revue bimensuelle des cours et conférences*. Series II, Vol. 38, 15 Juillet 1937, pp. 577-589; Vol. 39, 15 December 1937, pp. 3-8.

Adam, Charles and Paul Tannery, eds. "Descartes: sa vie et ses oeuvres, étude historique," in *Oeuvres de Descartes*. Vol. 12. Paris: Léopold Cerf, 1910.

Adam, Charles and Paul Tannery, trans. *See* Descartes.

Åkerman, Susanna. *Queen Christina of Sweden and Her Circle*. Leiden: Brill, 1991.

———. *Rose Cross Over the Baltic: The Spread of Rosicrucianism in Northern Europe*. Leiden: Brill, 1998.

Alexander, Tangren. *Kristina, So Far*. N.p., 1991.

Anderson, Daniel E. "Descartes and Atheism," *Tulane Studies in Philosophy*. Vol. 29, 1980, pp. 11-24.

Ariès, Philippe. *L'Enfant et la vie familiale sous l'ancien régime*. Paris: Plon, 1960. *Centuries of Childhood: A Social History of Family Life*. New York: Alfred A. Knopf, 1962.

Ariew, Roger. *Descartes and the Last Scholastics*. Ithaca: Cornell University Press, 1999.

Ariew, Roger, and Marjorie Grene, eds. *Descartes and His Contemporaries: Meditations, Objections, and Replies*. Chicago: University of Chicago Press, 1995.

Armogathe, Jean-Robert. "Descartes, philosophe des lumières, ou l'effet Baillet," *Enlightenment Essays In Memory of Robert Shackleton*. Oxford: Voltaire Foundation at the Taylor Institution, 1988, pp. 1-28.

———. "L'Approbation des *Meditationes* par la Faculté de Théologie de Paris (1641)." *Bulletin cartésien*, 21: 1-3, in *Archives de philosophie*. Vol. 57, 1994, pp. 1-3.

Armogathe, Jean-Robert, Vincent Carraud, and Robert Feenstra. "La Licence en droit de Descartes, un placard inédit de 1616," *Nouvelles de la république des lettres*. Vol. 2, 1988, pp. 125-145.

Arnold, Paul. "Descartes et les Rose-Croix." *Mercure de France*. No. 1166, October 1960, pp. 266-284.

———. *Histoire des Rose-Croix et les origines de la Franc-Maçonnerie*. Paris: Mercure de France, 1955.

———. "Le 'Songe' de Descartes," *Cahiers du sud*. No. 312, 1952, pp. 274-291.

Bacon, Francis. *The Twoo Bookes of Francis Bacon. Of the Proficience and Advancement of Learning, Divine and Humane*. London: Henrie Tomes, 1605.

Baillet, Adrien. *La Vie de monsieur Des-Cartes*. 2 vols. Paris: Daniel Horthemels, 1691; New York: Garland, 1987.

———. *La Vie de Mr. Des-Cartes réduite en abrégé*. Paris: Daniel Horthemels, 1692.

Balzac, Jean-Louis Guez de. *Oeuvres de Balzac*. Vol. 2, *Dissertations chrestiennes et morales* (1627-1629), three letters dedicated to Descartes, V. Le Sophiste chicaneur, VI. Le Chicaneur convaincu de faux, VII. La Dernière objection du chicaneur réfutée. Paris: T. Jolly, 1665.

Barbier, Alfred. "Sur le lieu ou est né Descartes," *Mémoires de la société des antiquaires de l'ouest*. Series II, Vol. 20, 1897 (1898), pp. 775-803.

———. "Trois médecins Poitevins au XVIe siècle ou les origins Châtelleraudaises de la famille Descartes," *Mémoires de la société des antiquaires de l'ouest*. Series II, Vol. 19, 1897 (1898), pp. 51-250.

Barr, Mirjam de, Machteld Löwensteyn, Marit Monteiro, and A. Agnes Sneller, eds. *Choosing the Better Part: Anna Maria van Schurman (1607–1678)*. Dordrecht: Kluwer, 1996.

Baret, Eugéne. *De L'Amadis de Gaule, et son influence sur les moeurs et la littérature au XVIe et au XVIIe siècle*. Paris: Firmin-Didot, 1873.

Barnouw, A. J. *The Making of Modern Holland*. New York: W. W. Norton, 1944.

Bates, E. S. *Touring in 1600: A Study in the Development of Travel as a Means of Education*. London: Constable & Houghton Mifflin, 1911.

Batiffol, Louis. *La Duchesse de Chevreuse: une vie d'aventures et d'intrigues sous Louis XIII*. Paris: Hachette, 1913.

Beaussire, M. E. "Deux étudiants de l'université de Poitiers, François Bacon et René Descartes," *Mémoires de la société des antiquairies de l'ouest*. Vol. 32, 1807, pp. 65-87.

Beeckman, Isaac. *Journal tenu par Isaac Beeckman de 1604 à 1634*. Ed. Cornélis de Waard. 4 vols. La Haye: Nijhoff, 1939-1953.

Behn, Irene. *Der Philosoph und die Königin: Renatus Descartes und Christina Wasa, Briefwechsel und Begegnung*. Freiburg/München: Karl Alber, 1957.

Beijer, Agne. "La Naissance de la paix: ballet de cour de René Descartes." In *Le Lieu théâtral à la Renaissance*. Ed. Jean Jacquot. Paris: Centre National de la Recherche Scientifique, 1964, pp. 409-422.

Bertrand, Joseph. "Une Amie de Descartes, Élisabeth, princesse de Bohême," *Revue des deux mondes*. Vol. 102, 1890, pp. 93-121.

Betts, C. J. *Early Deism in France*. The Hague: Martinus Nijhoff, 1984.

Beyer, Charles Jacques. "Comment Descartes combattit Gassendi," *PMLA*. Vol. 59, 1944, pp. 446-455.

Beys, Charles de. *La Pompe de la félicité*. Stockholm: Jean Janssonius, 1650.

Beyssade, Jean-Marie. "Descartes et Corneille ou les démesures de l'ego," *Laval théologique et philosophique*, Vol. 47, 1991, pp. 63-82.

————. "La Mort de Descartes selon Baillet. Du récit édifiant à ses composantes philosophiques," *Review des sciences philosophiques et théologiques*, 1992, pp. 14-28.

Biegel, Heidi. *La Naissance de la Paix: A Ballet by René Descartes*. MS. Department of Dance, University of California, Los Angeles. 21 pp.

Billacois, François. *Le Duel dans la société française des XVIᵉ–XVIIᵉ siècles: Essai de psychosociologie historique*. Paris: École des Hautes Études en Sciences Sociales, 1986.

Bitton, Davis. *The French Nobility in Crisis, 1560–1640*. Stanford: Stanford University Press, 1969.

Blom, John J. *Descartes: His Moral Philosophy and Psychology*. New York: New York University Press, 1975.

Blondel, Maurice. "Le Christianisme de Descartes," *Revue de Métaphysique et de Morale*. Vol. 4, 1896, 551-567.

Bordonove, Georges. *Louis XII le juste*. Paris: Pygmilion/Gérard Watelet, 1981.

Borel, Pierre. *Vitae Renati Cartesii, Summi Philosophi, Compendium*. Paris: Joannem Billaine et al., 1656.

Bos, Erik-Jan. "Descartes's *Lettre Apologétique aux Magistrats d'Utrecht*: New Facts and Materials," *Journal of the History of Philosophy*. Vol. 37, 1999, pp. 415-433.

Bosseboeuf, Louis. "Les Ancêtres de René Descartes," *Bulletin de la société de Touraine*, Vol. 12, 1900. pp. 50-68, 248-264.

————. "L'Iconographie de Descartes," *Bulletin Trimestriel de la société archéologique de Touraine (Tours)*. Vol. 9, 1897, pp. 68-82.

Bougerel, Joseph. *Vie de Pierre Gassendi*. Paris: Jacques Vincent, 1738.

Bourke, Vernon J. "An Illustration of the Attitude of the Early French Jesuits Towards Cartesianism," *Cartesio nel Terzo Centenario nel "Discorso del Metodo*. Milan: Vita e Pensiero, 1937, pp. 129-137.

Brassett, Henri. *Registre des lettres et des despaches que j'ay escrittes en l'année 1649 durant ma Residence en Holland*. Brasset à de la Thuillerie de 9 December 1649, BN.fr.17901, f 857v.

Braudel, Fernand. *Les Structures du quotidien: le possible et l'impossible*. Paris, Armand Colin, 1979. *The Structure of Everyday Life: The Limits of the Possible*. New York: Harper & Row, 1981.

Brugmans, Henri L. "Descartes et les pasteurs de Hollande," *Revue de littérature comparée*. Vol. 17, 1937, pp. 499-521.

Brunschvicg, Léon. *René Descartes*. Paris: Rieder, 1937.

Buzon, Frédéric de. "Un Exemplaire de la *Sagesse* de Pierre Charron offert à Descartes en 1619," *Bulletin Cartésien XX, Archives de philosophie*, Vol. 55, Cahier 1, 1992, pp. 1-3.

Campbell, Dorothy de Brissac. *The Intriguing Duchess, Marie de Rohan, Duchesse de Chevreuse*. New York: Covici, Friede, 1930.

Cantecor, G. "L'Oisive adolescence de Descartes," *Revue d'histoire de la philosophie*. Vol. 4, 1930, pp. 1-38, 354-396.

————. "La Vocation de Descartes." *Revue philosophique de la France et de l'étranger*. Vol. 95, 1923, pp. 372-400.

Carmona, Michel. *La France de Richelieu*. Paris: Fayard, 1984.

————. *Les Diables de Loudun, sorcellerie et politique sous Richelieu*. Paris: Fayard, 1988.

————. *Marie de Médicis*. Paris: Fayard, 1981.

————. *Richelieu*. Paris: Fayard, 1983.

Carraud, Vincent. "Descartes et l'écriture sainte," in *L'Écriture sainte au temps de Spinoza et dans le system spinoziste*. Paris: Presses universitaires de Paris, 1992, pp. 41-70.

Cassirer, Ernst. *Descartes, Corneille, Christine de Suède*. Paris: J. Vrin, 1942.

Caton, Hiram. "Descartes' Anonymous Writings: A Recapitulation," *Southern Journal of Philosophy*. Vol. 20, 1982, pp. 299-310.

————. *The Origin of Subjectivity, an Essay on Descartes*. New Haven: Yale University Press, 1973.

————. "The Problem of Descartes' Sincerity," *The Philosophical Forum*. Vol. 2, 1971, pp. 355-370.

Champigny, Robert. "Corneille et le Traité des passions," *The French Review*. Vol. 26, 1952, pp. 112-120.

Chappell, Vere, and Willis Doney, eds. *Twenty-Five Years of Descartes Scholarship, 1960– 1984: A Bibliography*. New York: Garland, 1987.

Chartier, Roger, Marie-Madeleine Compère, and Dominique Julia. *L'Éducation en France du XVIe au XVIIIe siècle*. Paris: Société d'Édition d'Enseignement Supérieur, 1976.

Chevalier, Jacques. "La Spiritualité de Descartes," *XVIIe siècle*. No. 19, 1953, pp. 155-172.

Chusman, Robert E. "Barth's Attack Upon Cartesianism and the Future in Theology," *The Journal of Religion*. Vol. 36, 1956, pp. 207-223.

Clarke, Jack Alden. *Huguenot Warrior: The Life and Times of Henri de Rohan, 1579–1638*. The Hague: Martinus Nijhoff, 1966.

Cochos, Paul. *Bérulle et l'école française*. Paris: Seuil, 1963.

Cohen, Gustave. "Descartes et le ballet de cour," *Revue international de musique*. Vol. 9, 1950, pp. 233-237.

————. *Écrivains français en Hollande dans le première moité de XVIIe siècle*. Paris: Édouard Champion, 1920. (Livre III is entitled *La Philosophie indépendante, Descartes et Hollande*.)

Cohen, Gustave, and G. Lucas de Pesloüan. *Le Dernier projet littéraire de Maurice Barrès: Descartes et la Princesse Élisabeth*. Abbeville: F. Paillart, 1929.

Cole, John R. *The Olympian Dreams and Youthful Rebellion of René Descartes*. Urbana: University of Illinois Press, 1992.

Comar, Philippe. *Mémoires de mon crâne René Des–Cartes*. Paris: Gallimard, 1997.

Cottingham, John. *Descartes*. Oxford: Basil Blackwell, 1986.

Cottingham, John, Robert Stoothoff, Dugald Murdoch, and Anthony Kenny, trans. *See* Descartes.

Couderc, Camille. "Nouveau documents sur la situation de fortune de la famille de René Descartes," *Bibliothèque de l'École des Chartes revue d'érudition*. Vol. 78, 1917 (1918), pp. 269-293

Cousin, Victor. "La Conspiration de Henri de Talleyrand, Comte de Chalais," *Journal des savants*, April, 1862, pp. 197-221.

————. *Madame de Chevreuse et Madame de Hautefort*. Paris: Didier, 1856.

————."Vanini ou la philosophie avant Descartes," In *Fragments philosophiques pour servir à l'histoire de la philosophie*. Vol. 3, Paris: Didier, 1886; Geneva: Slatkine Reprints, 1970, pp. 1-92.

Crété, Liliane. *La Vie quotidienne à La Rochelle au temps du grand siège 1627–1628*. Paris: Hachette, 1987.

Dainville, F. de. *Les Jésuites et l'éducation de la société française, la naissance de l'humanisme moderne*. Paris: Beauchesne, 1940

Davidenko, Dimitri. *Descartes le scandaleux*. Paris: Robert Laffont, 1988. (Presented as a historical study, this work would be better classified as a novel.)

Davies, Penny. *Growing Up in Medieval Times*. London: B. T. Batsford, 1977.

Dear, Peter. *Mersenne and the Learning of the Schools*. Ithaca: Cornell University Press, 1988.

d'Haucourt, Xavier. "Une Dynastie de 'non-originaires' au parlement de Bretagne, la famille Des-Cartes (1585-1736)," *Annales de Bretagne (Rennes)*. Vol. 44, 1937, pp. 408-432; Vol. 45, 1938, pp. 3-24.

Delblanc, Sven. "Baletten som glorifierade Kristina." *Svenska Dagbladet*. 6 June 1985, p. 14 (10).

De Sacy, Samuel S. *Descartes par lui-même*. Paris: Seuil, 1956, 1996.

Descartes, René. *Discours de la méthode pour bien conduit sa raison, et chercher la verité dans les sciences. Plus la dioptrique, les météores, et la géométrie, qui sont des essais de cette methode*. Leyde: Jan Maire, 1637.

———. *Epistola RENATI DES-CARTES, Ad celeberrimum virum D. Gisbertum Voétium. In quâ examinantur duo libri, nuper pro Voetio Utrajecti simul editi, unus de Confraternitate Marianâ, alter de philosophiâ Cartesianâ*. Amstelodami: Ludovicum Elzevirium, 1643.

———. *Magni Cartesi Manes ab ipsomet defensi, sive N. V. RENATI DES-CARTES Querela Apolgetica ad Amplissimum Magistratum Ultrajectinum, Quâ technae, calumniae, mendacia, falsorum testimoniorum fabricae, aliaque crimina Voetiorum & Demantii, plenè reteguntur. Opusculum antea ineditum, nunc veró opponendum quotidianis Voetii & Voetianorum criminationibus, iis nominatim quas sub Theolgiae Naturalis Reformatae titulo haud ita pridem emiserunt*. Vristadii: Lancellotum Misopodem, 1656.

———. *Les Méditations métaphysiques de René Descartes touchant la première philosophie, dans lesquelles l'existence de Dieu, & la distinction réelle entre l'âme & dans le corps de l'homme sont démonstrées*. Traduites du latin de l'Auteur par M. de D.D.L.N.S. *Et les Objections faites contre ces Méditations par diverses personnes très-doctes, avec les réponses de l'Auteur*. Traduites par M. C.L.R. Paris: Jean Camusat et Pierre le Petit, 1647.

———. *Meditationes de prima philosophia, in qui dei existentia et animae immortalitas demonstrantur*. Paris: Michaelem Soly, 1631.

———. *Les Passions de l'âme*. Paris: Henry Le Gras, 1649.

———. *Principia philosophiae*. Amstelodami: Ludovicum Elzevirium, 1644.

———. *RENATI DES-CARTES Notae in Programma quoddam, sub finem anni 1647 in Belgio editum, cum hoc Titulo: Explicatio Mentis humanae, sive Animae rationalis, ubi explicatur quid fit, & quid esse possit*. Amstelodami: Ludovici Elzevirii, 1648.

———. *Oeuvres de Descartes*. Eds. Charles Adam, Paul Tannery, and others. 11 vols. Paris: J. Vrin, 1996.

———. *The Philosophical Works of Descartes*. Trans. Elizabeth S. Haldane and G.R.T. Ross. 2 vols. Corrected edition. Cambridge University Press, 1934.

————. *The Philosophical Writings of Descartes*. Trans. John Cottingham, Robert Stoothoff, Dugald Murdoch, and Anthony Kenny. 3 vols. Cambridge: Cambridge University Press, 1984-1991.

Descartes, René [?]. *La Naissance de la paix*. Stockholm: Jean Janssonius, 1649; German trans. by Johannes Freinshemsius, *Des Friedens Geburts-tag*. Stockholm: Heinrich Keysern, 1649; Swedish trans. by Georg Stiernhielm, *Freds-Afl*. Stockholm: Heinrich Keysern, 1649. In *Samlade Skrifter av Georg Stiernhielm*. Ed. Johan Nordstrom and Berndt Olsson. Vol. 8. Lund: Carl Bloms, 1976, pp. 303-316; German trans. by Johannes Freinshemsius, *Des Friedens Geburts-tag*. Ibid., pp. 316-329; Swedish trans. by Georg Stiernhielm, *Freds-Afl*, *Samlade Skrifter av Georg Stiernhielm*. Ed. Johan Nordström, Bernt Olsson, and Per Wieselgren. Vol. 8. Lund: Carl Bloms, 1973, pp. 81-99.

Descartes, René [?] and Louis Aragon. *La Naissance de la paix*. Paris: Bibliothèque Française, 1946; German trans. by Hans Paeschke, *Die Geburt des Friedens*. Neuwied am Rhein: Lancelot Verlag, 1949.

Deviosse, Jen, and Jean-Henri Roy. *Châtellerault*. Tours: NR Éditions, 1986.

Dickerman, Edmund H. "The Conversion of Henry IV: 'Paris is well worth a Mass' in Psychological Perspective," *The Catholic Historical Review*. Vol. 63, 1977, pp. 1-13.

Dimier, Louis. *La Vie raisonnable de Descartes*. Paris: Librairie Plon, 1926.

Dulmet, Florica. "Voyage autour de Descartes," *Écrits de Paris*. Vol. 240, 1995, pp. 88-102.

Dulong, Claude. *Anne d'Autriche*. Paris: Hachette, 1980.

Du Perron, Jacques Davy. *Les Ambassades et négotiations*. Paris: A. Estienne, 1623.

Du Port, François. *La Décade de médecine ou le médecin des riches et de pauvres*. Paris: Laurent d'Houry, 1694. *The Decade of Medicine or The Physician of the Rich and the Poor in which all the Signs, Causes, and Remedies of Disease Are Clearly Expounded*. Ed. H. Diehl. Berlin: Springer-Verlag, 1988.

Eddy, John A. "The Maunder Minimum," *Science*. Vol. 193, 1976, pp. 1189-1192.

Espinas, Alfred. *Descartes et la morale*. Vol. 1. Paris: Bossard, 1925.

Fagan, Brian. *The Little Ice Age: How Climate Made History, 1300–1850*. New York: Basic Books, 2000.

Féret, Abbé. *Le Cardinal Du Perron*. Paris: Didier, 1877.

Ferrand, Jean I. *De eo habentur: de nephrisis et lithiasis, seu de renum, et vesicae calculi definitione, causis, signis, praedictione, praecautione & curatione. Ex Hippocrate, Discoride, Galeno, Avicenna, Aetio, & Paulo Aeginenta, aliisque celeberrimis medicis, collectis*. Parisiis: Michaelem Sonnium, 1570.

Ferrand, Jean II. *De febris libellus ex variis auctoribus collectis*. Parisiis: Michaelem Sonnium, 1602.

Ferrier, Françis. *La Pensée philosophique du Père Guillaume Gibieuf: 1583–1650*. Lille: Atelier Reproduction de Thèses, 1976.

Ferrier, Françis. *Un Oratorien ami de Descartes: Guillaume Gibieuf, et sa philosophie de la liberté*. Paris: J. Vrin, 1980.

Ferrier, Jacques. *Un Gentilhomme nommé Descartes, soldat, philosophe et mathématicien, 1596–1650*. Bruxelles: Cahiers de la Fondation Nicolas-Claude Fabri de Peiresc, 1996.

Fitzgerald, Desmond J. "Descartes: Defender of the Faith." *Thought, Fordham University Quarterly*. Vol. 34, 1959, pp. 383-404.

Foucher de Careil, A. *Descartes et la Princesse Palatine*. Paris: August Durand, 1862.

Frédérix, Pierre. *Monsieur René Descartes en son temps.* Paris: Gallimard, 1959.

Friedrich, Carl J. *The Age of the Baroque, 1610–1660.* New York: Harper & Row, 1952.

Gabbey, Alan. "Gilles Personne de Roberval (1602–1675). Un savant révélé par ses arch-ives: Catalogue des manuscrits et des documents. Documents inédits." Unpublished MS. Archives de l'Académie des Sciences, Paris.

———. "Henry More lecteur de Descartes, philosophie naturelle et apologétique." *Arch-ives de philosophie,* Vol. 58, 1995, pp. 355-369.

———. "Mersenne et Roberval," In *1588–1988, Quatrième centennaire de la naissance de Marin Mersenne.* Eds. Marie Constant and Anne Fillon. Le Mans: Université du Maine, 1994.

Gabbey, Alan, and Robert E. Hall. "The Melon and the Dictionary: Reflections on Des-cartes's Dreams." *Journal of the History of Ideas.* Vol. 59, 1998, pp. 651-668.

Gäbe, Lüder. *Descartes' Selbstkritik, Untersuchungen zur Philosophie des jungen Descartes.* Hamburg: Felix Meiner Verlag, 1972.

Galard, Jean. "Descartes en Nederland," Eds. Paul Blom, et al. In *La France aux Pays-Bas.* Vianen: Kwadraat, 1985, pp. 51-88. "Descartes et les Pays-Bas." N.p, n.d. 31 pp.

Gambier, Paul. "Un Autre ennemi de Descartes, le Pasteur André Rivet," *Revue du Bas-Poitou et des provinces de l'ouest.* Vol. 75, 1964, pp. 184-194.

Garrison, Janine. *L'Édit de Nantes.* Paris: Fayard, 1998.

Gaukroger, Stephen. *Descartes: An Intellectual Biography.* Oxford: Oxford University Press, 1995.

Gaultier, Jules de. "Le Problème de Descartes," *La Revue des idées.* Vol. 2, 1905, pp. 89-107.

Georges-Berthier, A. "Descartes et les Rose-Croix," *Revue de Synthèse.* Vol. 18, 1939, pp. 9-30.

Germe, Jean-Marie. "Origines paternelles de René Descartes," *Les Amitiés généalogiques canadiennes-françaises.* 1996, pp. 3-40.

Gilson, Étienne. "Descartes en Hollande," *Revue de métaphysique et de morale.* Vol. 28, 1921, pp. 545-556.

———. *La Liberté chez Descartes et la théologie.* Paris: Librairie Félix Alcan, 1913.

Gouhier, Henri. *L'Anti-humanisme au XVIIᵉ siècle.* Paris: Libraire Philosophique J. Vrin, 1987.

———. *Descartes essais.* Paris: J. Vrin, 1949.

———. "Descartes et la religion," *Cartesio, nel terzo centenario nel "Discorso de metodo."* Milano: Vita e Pensiero, 1937, pp. 417-424.

———. *La Pensée religieuse de Descartes.* Paris: J. Vrin, 1924.

———. *Les Premières pensées de Descartes, contribution à l'histoire de l'anti-renaissance.* Paris: Libraire Philosophique J. Vrin, 1958.

Goupille, André Haya. *La Haye en Touraine, La Haye Descartes, Descartes, des origines à nos jours,* 2nd ed. Tours: Chavanne, 1980.

Grandmaison, Louis de. "Actes relatifs à la famille Descartes," *Bulletin de la société archéol-ogique de Tourraine.* Vol. 13, 1901, pp. 45-49.

———. *Nouvelles recherches sur l'origine et le lieu de naissance de Descartes,* Paris, 1899. Nogent-le-Rotron: Daupeley-Gouveneuve, 1899.

Greengrass, Mark. *France in the Age of Henri IV: The Struggle for Stability.* London: Long-man, 1984.

Grove, Jean M. *The Little Ice Age*. London: Routledge, 1988.

Guenancia, Pierre. *Descartes bien conduire sa raison*. Paris: Gallimard, 1996.

——. *Lire Descartes*. Paris. Gallimard, 2000.

Guerrieri, Lorenzo. "Cartesio, Maestro di Christina di Svezia," *Firenze: Atti de XXII Congresso Nazionale di Storia della Medicina (Roma)*, 1966, pp. 260-280.

Gustafsson, Lars. "Amor et Mars vaincus: allégorie politique des ballets de cour de l'époque de la Reine Christine." In *Queen Christina of Sweden: Documents and Studies*. Ed. Magnus von Platen, Nationalmusei skriftserie nr. 12, Analecta Reginesia 1, Stockholm: P. A. Norstedt & Soner, 1966, pp. 87-99.

Haldane, Elizabeth S. *Descartes: His Life and Times*. London: John Murray, 1905.

Haldane, Elizabeth S. and G. R. T. Ross (translators). See Descartes.

Harth, Erica. *Cartesian Women: Versions and Subversions of Rational Discourse in the Old Regime*. Ithaca: Cornell University Press, 1992.

Hawlitschek, Kurt. "Die Deutschlandreise des René Descartes," *Ulm and Obserschwaben: Zeitschrift für Geschichte und Kunst*. Forthcoming.

——. *Johan Faulhaber, 1580-1635, Eine Blütezeit der Mathematischen Wissenschaften in Ulm*. Ulm: Stadtbibliothek Ulm, 1995.

——. "Niederländische Mathematik und Technik. Ihr Einfluss auf Ulm im 17. Jahrhundert.' *Ulm and Obserschwaben: Zeitschrift für Geschichte und Kunst*. Vol. 51, 2000, pp. 23-41.

Herman, Arthur. "The Huguenot Republic and Antirepublicanism in Seventeenth-Century France." *Journal of the History of Ideas*. Vol. 53, 1992, pp. 249-269.

Héroard, Jean. *Journal de Jean Héroard sur l'enfance et la jeunesse de Louis XIII, (1601-1628)*. 2 vols. Paris: Firmin-Didot, 1668.

Hervey, Helen. "Hobbes and Descartes," *Osiris*. Vol. 10, 1952, pp. 67-90.

Houssaye, M. *Le Cardinal de Bérulle et le Cardinal de Richelieu, 1625-1629*. Paris: E. Plon, 1875.

Huet, Pierre-Daniel. *Nouveaux mémoires pour servir à l'histoire du cartésianisme*. Lyons: Mercure Gallant, 1692.

Hunt, David. *Parents and Children in History: The Psychology of Family Life in Early Modern France*. New York: Basic Books, 1970.

Huppert, George. *Les Bourgeois Gentilshommes. An Essay on the Definition of Elites in Renaissance France*. Chicago: University of Chicago Press, 1977.

Huppert, George. *Public Schools in Renaissance France*. Urbana: University of Illinois Press, 1984.

Huxley, Aldous. *The Devils of Loudun*. New York: Harper & Brothers, 1953.

Jacquot, Jean. "Un Amateur de science, ami de Hobbes et de Descartes, Sir Charles Cavendish, 1591-1654," *Thalès*. Vol. 6, 1949-1950, pp. 81-88.

Jama, Sophie. *La Nuit de songes de René Descartes*. Paris: Aubier, 1998.

James, Susan. *Passion and Action, the Emotions in Seventeenth-Century Philosophy*. Oxford: Oxford University Press, 1997.

Janet, Paul. "Descartes: son caractère et son génie," *Revue des deux mondes*. Vol. 73, 1865, pp. 345-369.

Jolibert, Bernard. *L'Enfance au XVIIe siècle*. Paris: J. Vrin, 1981.

Judovitz, Dalia. "Autobiographical Discourse and Critical Praxis in Descartes," *Philosophy and Literature*. Vol. 5, 1981, pp. 91-107.

Lachèvre, Frédéric. "Hélie Poirier," *Glanes bibliographiques et littéraires*. Vol. 2. Paris: L. Giraud-Badin, 1929, pp. 124-137.

———. *Le Libertinage au XVIIe siècle, disciples et successeurs de Théophile de Viau, la vie et les poésies libertines inédites de des Barreaux (1599–1673) — Saint-Pavin (1595–1670)*. Paris: Librairie Ancienne Honoré Champion, 1911.

———. *Le Prince Des libertiens au XVIIe siècle, Jacques Vallée des Barreaux (1599–1673)*. Paris: Librairie Ancienne Honoré Champion, 1907.

Lalanne, Abbé. "Notice sur l'origine de la famille Descartes," *Bulletins de la société des antiquaires de l'ouest et de musées de Poitiers*. 1857, pp. 233-251.

Lalot, J.-A. *Essai historique sur la conférence tenue à Fontainebleau entre Duplessis-Mornay et Duperron le 4 mai 1600*. Paris: Fishbacher & Grasart, 1889.

Lanson, Gustave. "Le Héros cornélien et le 'généreux' selon Descartes." *Revue d'Histoire littéraire de la France*. Vol. 1, 1894, pp. 397-411.

Larousse, Pierre. *Grand dictionnaire universel du XIXe siécle*. 17 vols. Paris: Administration du Grand dictionnaire universal, 1866-[90].

Lécuyer, Raymond. "René Descartes, gentilhomme et propriètaire Châtelleraudais," In *Demeures inspiréees et sites romanesques*. By Raymod Lécuyer and Paul-Émile Cadilhac. Paris: Éditions S.N.E.P., pp. 65-76.

Lefebvre, M. H. "De la morale provisoire a la générosité," in *Descartes, Cahiers de Royaumont*, Philosophie No. 11. Paris: Les Éditions de Minuit, 1957, pp. 237-272.

Lefèvre, Roger. *La Vocation de Descartes*. Paris: Presses Universitaires de France, 1956.

———. *L'Humanisme de Descartes*. Paris: Presses Universitaires de France, 1957.

———. "Quand Descartes dîne à Douai," *Revue des sciences humaines*. Fasc. 107, nouvelle série, 1962, pp. 314-326.

Lenoble, Robert. "La Vocation et l'humanisme de Descartes." *Revue de métaphysique et de morale*. Vol. 63, 1958, pp. 349-357.

Lenoble, Robert. *Mersenne ou la naissance du mécanisme*. Paris: J. Vrin, 1943.

Leroy, Maxime. *Descartes le philosophe au masque*. 2 vols. Paris: Rieder, 1929.

———. "Descartes, précurseur du social moderne." *Revue de synthèse*. Vol. 63, 1948, pp. 59-67.

Leroy, Pierre, and Hans Bots. *Claude Saumaise (1588–1653) & André Rivet (1587–1651), correspondence échangée entre 1632 et 1648*. Amsterdam: Holland University Press, 1987.

Lewis, Hine William. *The Interrelationship of Science and Religion in the Circle of Marin Mersenne*. Ph.D. diss., University of Oklahoma, 1967.

Ligou, Daniel. *Le Protestantisme en France de 1598 à 1715*. Paris: Société d'Édition d'Enseignement Supérieur, 1968.

Lindborg, Rolf. "Filosofen Descartes och Kristina vasa." *Svenska Dagbladet*. 29 May 1985, p. 14 (10).

Lindeboom, G. A. *Descartes and Medicine*. Amsterdam: Rodopi, 1978.

———. "Dog and Frog: Physiological Experiments at Leiden in the Seventeenth Century." In *Leiden University in the Seventeenth Century: An Exchange of Learning*. Eds. Th. H. Unsingh Scheurleer and G. H. M. P. Meyjes. Leiden: Leiden University, 1975, pp. 279-293.

Lipstorp, Daniel. *Specimina Philosophiae Cartesianae*. Lugduni: Johannem & Danielem Elsevier, 1653.

Livet, Georges. *La Guerre de trente ans*. 4th ed. Paris: Presses Universitaires de France, 1983.

Lot, Germaine. *René Descartes: esprit-soleil*. Paris: Seghers, 1966.

Louise, Gilbert. "Une Oeuvre poétique de Descartes, les vers du ballet 'La Naissance de Paix,'" *Mémoires de l'Académie Nationale des Sciences, Arts et Belles-lettres de Caen*. Vol. 20, 1982, pp. 175-203.

Maar, Vilhelm. *Lidt om Descartes og Danmark*. Kopenhagen: H. H. Thieles, 1931.

MacDonald, Paul S. "The Lost Episodes," *Journal of the History of Philosophy*. Forthcoming.

Mahmood, Cynthia Keppley. *Frisian and Free: Study of an Ethnic Minority in the Netherlands*. Prospect Heights: Waveland Press, 1989.

Mandrou, Robert. *Des Humanistes aux hommes de science, XVIe et XVIIe siècles*. Paris: Éditions du Seuil, 1973.

Maritain, Jacques. *Three Reformers: Luther — Descartes — Rousseau*. New York: Thomas Y. Crowell, 1929.

Marvick, Elizabeth Wirth. "Nature Versus Nurture: Patterns and Trends in Seventeenth-Century French Child-Rearing." In *The History of Childhood*. Ed. Lloyd de Mause. New York: Psychohistory Press, 1974, pp. 259-301.

———. *The Young Richelieu: A Psychoanalytic Approach to Leadership*. Chicago: University of Chicago Press, 1983.

Mause, Lloyd de. "The Evolution of Childhood." In *The History of Childhood*. Ed. Lloyd de Mause. New York: Psychohistory Press, 1974, pp. 1-73.

Méchoulan, Henry. *Amsterdam au temps de Spinoza: argent et liberté*. Paris: Presses Universitaires de France, 1990.

Mersenne, Marin. *Correspondance du P. Marin Mersenne, relegieux minime*. Ed. Cornélis de Waard. Paris: Presses Universitaires de France, CNRS, 1932.

Mesnard, Pierre. *Essai sur la morale de Descartes*. Paris: Boivin, 1936.

Méthivier, Hubert. *La Fronde*. Paris: Presses Universitaires de France, 1984.

———. *Le Siècle de Louis XII.*, 6th ed. Paris: Presses Universitaires de France, 1987.

Meyer, Jean. *La Naissance de Louis XIV*. Paris: Complexe, 1989.

Michel, Erich. "Descartes und Prinzessin Elisabeth von Böhmen," *Sudentland*. Vol. 22, 1980, pp. 250-254.

Milhaud, Gérard. "Chronologie de Descartes," *Europe revue littéraire mensuelle*. Vol. 56, 1978, pp. 147-155.

Milhaud, Gaston. "La Question de la sincérité de Descartes," *Revue de métaphysique et de morale*. Vol. 26, 1919, pp. 297-311.

———. "Une Crise mystique chez Descartes en 1619," *Revue de métaphysique et de morale*. Vol. 23, 1916, pp. 607-621.

Moore, A. Lloyd. *Louis XII The Just*. Berkeley: University of California Press, 1989.

Morgan, Vance G. *Foundations of Cartesian Ethics*. Atlantic Highlands: Humanities Press International, 1994.

Morhof, Georgi. *Polyhistor.* Vol. 2, Lubeciae: Petri Beeckmanni, 1747.

Morris, John M. "Letter commenting on Richard A. Watson's note and translation 'Descartes's Ballet?'" *American Philosophical Association Proceedings.* Vol. 63, No. 5, p. 61.

Mousnier, Roland. *La Famille, l'enfant et l'éducation en France et en Grande-Bretagne du XVIᵉ et XVIIIᵉ siècle.* 2 vols. Paris: Center de Documentation Universitaire, 1975.

————. *The Assassination of Henry IV: The Tyrannicide Problem and the Consolidation of the French Absolute Monarchy in the Early Seventeenth Century.* London: Faber and Faber, 1973.

Neel, Marguerite. *Descartes et la Princesse Élisabeth.* Paris: Elzévir, 1946.

Nelson, Robert J. "Descartes and Pascal: A Study of Likenesses." *PMLA.* Vol. 69, 1954, pp. 542-565.

Nerlich, Michael. *Kritik der Abenteuer-Ideologie: Beitrag zur Erforschung der bürgerlichen Bewusstseinsbildung, 1110-1750.* Berlin: Akademic-Verlag, 1977; *Ideology of Adventure: Studies in Modern Consciousness, 1100-1750,* Minneapolis: University of Minnesota Press, 1987.

Nordström, Johan. "Till Cartesius' Ikonografi," *Lychonos.* Vol. 17, 1957-1958, pp. 194-250.

Nye, Andrea. *The Princess and the Philosopher: Letters of Elisabeth of the Palatine to René Descartes.* Lanham: Rowman & Littlefield, 1999.

Orcibal, Jean. *Le Cardinal de Bérulle: Évolution d'une spiritualité.* Paris: Cerf, 1965.

Otegem, Matthijs van. *A Bibliography of the Works of Descartes (1637-1704).* 2 vols. Utrecht: Zeno, 2002.

Ouvré, Henri. "Essai sur l'histoire de la Ligue à Poitiers," *Mémoires de la Société des Antiquaires de l'ouest* (Poitiers). 1ère série, tome 21, 1854, pp. 85-245.

————. "Essai sur l'histoire de la ville de Poitiers, depuis la fin de la Ligue jusqu'au Ministère de Richelieu," *Mémoires de la Société des Antiquaires de l'ouest (Poitiers).* tome 22, 1855, pp. 567-728.

Pagès, Frédéric. *Descartes et le cannabis.* Paris: Éditions Mille et Une Nuits, 1996.

Parker, Geoffrey, and Lesley M. Smith, editors. *The General Crisis of the Seventeenth Century.* London: Routledge & Kegan Paul, 1978.

Payot, Roger. *René Descartes (1596-1650) et le primat de la raison.* Lyon: LUGD, 1996.

Pelseneer, Jean. "Gilbert, Bacon, Galilée, Kepler, Harvey et Descartes: leur relations," *Isis.* Vol. 17, 1932, pp. 171-208.

Perrot, Maryvonne. "Descartes, Saumaise et Christine de Suède," *Les études philosophiques.* No. 1, 1984, pp. 1-9.

Petit, Léon. "Descartes en Italie sur les pas de Montaigne," *Bulletin de la société des amis de Montaigne.* Series III, No. 13, 1960, pp. 22-33.

————. *Descartes et la Princesse Elisabeth: roman d'amour vécu.* Paris: A.-G. Nizet, 1969. (Despite the title, this is a historical study, not a novel.)

————. "Descartes et trois poètes au siège de La Rochelle," *Cahiers de l'ouest (Paris).* No. 21, January–February, 1958, pp. 39-49.

Pickman, Edward Motley. "Libertine Ideas in the Time of Richelieu and Mazarin," *Proceedings of the Massachusetts Historical Society.* Vol. 68, 1994-1996, pp. 3-41.

Pintard, René. *Le Libertinage érudit dans le première moitié du XVIIe siècle.* Paris: Boiven et Cie., 1943.

Pirro, André. *Descartes et la musique*. Paris: Feschbacher, 1907.

Poirier, Hélie. *La Diane victorieuse*. Stockholm: Jan Janssonius, 1649 (*Le Vaincu de Diane*. Stockholm: Jan Janssonius, 1649.)

———. "Letters to Saumaise," in the Johan Nordström collection in the Carolina Rediviva. Box No. 10, 3N ms. fr. 3970. 128 & 130.

———. *La Naissance de la paix*. Stockholm: Jan Janssonius, 1649.

———. *Parnasse triomphant*. Stockholm: Jan Janssonius, 1651.

———. *Les Passions victorieuses et vaincues*. Stockholm: Jan Janssonius, 1649.

Popkin, Richard H. *The History of Skepticism from Erasmus to Spinoza*. Berkeley: University of California Press, 1964.

———. *The Third Force in Seventeenth-Century Thought*. Leiden: E. J. Brill, 1992.

Porschnew, B. F. "Descartes und die Fronde," In *Beiträge zur Französischen Aufklärung und zur Spanischen Literatur, Festgabe für Werner Krauss zum 70. Geburtstag*. Ed. Werner Bahner. Berlin: Akademie-Verlag, 1971, pp. 281-287.

Prawdin, Michael. *Marie de Rohan, Duchesse de Chevreuse, 1600–1679*. London: Allen & Unwin, 1971.

Ranum, Orest. *Parisians in the Seventeenth Century*. New York: John Wiley, 1968.

Rébelliau, Alfred. "Un Épisode de l'histoire religieuse du XVIIe siècle: La Compagnie du Saint-Sacrement." *Revue des deux mondes*. Vol. 16, 1903, pp. 49-82.

Rée, Jonathan. *Descartes*. London: Allen Lane, 1974.

Reinhard, Marcel. *Henri IV ou la France sauvée*. Paris: Hachette, 1943.·

Reith, Herman R. *René Descartes, the Story of a Soul*. Lanman: University Press of America, 1986.

Richeome, Louis. *Le Pèlerin de Lorette*. Bordeaux: Millanges, 1604.

Ripault, Louis. "La Naissance de René Descartes," *Le Glaneur Châtelleraultdais*. No. 14, 1937, pp. 5-9.

Rochemonteix, Camille de. *Un Collège de Jésuites aux XVIIe et XVIIIe siècles: Le Collège Henri IV et de La Flèche*. 4 vols. Le Mans: Leguicleux, 1899.

Rochot, Bernard. "A propos des Rose-Croix, de Descartes et des rêves de 1619," *Revue de synthèse*. Vol. 77, 1956, pp. 351-361.

Rodis-Lewis, Geneviève. "Descartes' Life and the Development of His Philosophy," In *The Cambridge Companion to Descartes*. Ed. John Cottingham. Cambridge: Cambridge University Press, 1992, pp. 21-57.

——— . *Descartes: Biographie*. Paris: Calmann-Lévy, 1995; *Descartes: His Life and Thought*. Ithaca: Cornell University Press, 1998.

———. *Descartes: Textes et débats*. Paris: Libraire Génénerale Française, 1984.

———. "Quelques questions disputées sur la jeunesse de Descartes," *Archives de philosophie*. Vol. 46, 1983, pp. 613-619.

Roger, Jacques. "L'Univers médical de Guy Patin," *Travaux de linguistique et littérature Strasbourg*. Vol. 12, 1975, pp. 91-101.

Rondeau, J. "Le Lieu de naissance de Descartes," *L'Illustration*. No. 4929, 21 August 1937, pp. 531-532.

Ropartz, Sigismond. *La Famille Descartes en Bretagne, 1586–1762*. Rennes: Verdier, 1877.

Rosa, Susan. "Pierre Chanut and the Conversion of Queen Christina of Sweden." MS. 15 pp.

Roth, Leon, editor. *Correspondence of Descartes and Constantyn Huygens, 1635–1647.* Oxford: Oxford University Press, 1926.

Roy, Jean-Henri. *Descartes et Châtellerault.* Folder. N.p., n.d, 22 pages.

———. "Sur la date et le lieu de la naissance de René Descartes." MS. 18 pp.

Saumaise, Claude. *Correspondence.* MS. Bibliothèque Nationale, Paris. 13n fonds lat. 8596.

Scarre, Geoffrey. "Demons, Demonologists, and Descartes," *Heyforth Journal.* Vol. 31, 1990, pp. 3–22.

———. *Witchcraft and Magic in Sixteenth- and Seventeenth-Century Europe.* Atlantic Highlands: Humanities Press International, 1987.

Schama, Simon. *The Embarrassment of Riches: An Interpretation of Dutch Culture in the Golden Age.* New York: Alfred A. Knopf, 1987.

Scheurleer, Th. H. Lunsingh, and G. H. M. P. Meyjes, eds. *Leiden University in the Seventeenth Century: An Exchange of Learning.* Leiden: Leiden University, 1975.

Schilte, Pierre. *La Flèche intra-muros.* Cholet: Farré et Fils, 1980.

Schneider, Ivo. *Johannes Faulhaber 1580–1635, Rechenmeister in einer Welt des Umbruchs.* Basel: Birkhäuser Verlag, 1993.

Sebba, Gregor. *Bibliographia Cartesiana: A Critical Guide to the Descartes Literature: 1800–1960.* The Hague: Martinus Nijhoff, 1964.

———. *The Dream of Descartes.* Carbondale: Southern Illinois University Press, 1987.

Serrurier, Cornelia. *Descartes: Leer en Leven.* s'Gravenhage: Nijhoff, 1930.

———. "Descartes l'homme et le croyant." In *Descartes et le cartésianisme hollandais*, Ed. E. J. Dijksterhuis. Paris: Presses Universitaires de France, 1950, pp. 45–70.

———. *Descartes: l'homme et le penseur.* Paris: Presses Universitaires de France, 1951.

———. "Saint-François de Sales — Descartes — Corneille." *Neophilologus.* Vol. 3, 1918, pp. 89–99.

Shapin, Steven. "Descartes the Doctor: Rationalism and Its Therapies," *British Journal for the History of Science.* Vol. 33, 2001, pp. 133–154.

Shea, William R. "Descartes and the Rosicrucian Enlightenment." In *Metaphysics and Philosophy of Science in the Seventeenth and Eighteenth Centuries.* Ed. R. S. Woolhouse. Leiden: Kluwer, 1988, pp. 73–99.

———. *The Magic of Numbers and Motion: The Scientific Career of René Descartes.* Canton: Science History Publications, 1991.

Sirven, J. *Les Années d'apprentissage de Descartes (1596–1628).* Albi: Imprimerie Coopérative du Sud-Ouest, 1928; Paris: J. Vrin, 1930; New York: Garland, 1987.

Six, Karl. "Descartes im Jesuitenkolleg von La Flèche," *Zeitschrift für Katolische Theologie.* Vol. 38, 1914, pp. 404–508.

Snelders, H.A.M. "Descartes et les Pays-Bas," *Septentrion, revue de culture néerlandaise.* Vol. 11, 1982, pp. 19–25.

Snyders, Georges. *La Pédagogie en France aux XVIIe et XVIIIe siècles.* Paris: Presses Universitaires de France, 1965.

Sortais, Gaston. "Descartes et la Compagnie de Jésus, menaces et advances (1640-1646)," *Estudios, Revista Mensual redactada por la Acadamia Literaria del Plata.* Vol. 57, 1937, pp. 441–468.

———. *Le Cartésianisme chez les Jésuites Français au XVIIe et au XVIIIe siècle.* Paris: Gabriel Beauchesne, 1924.

Stewart, William McC. "Descartes and Poetry." *The Romanic Review*. Vol. 29, 1938, pp. 212–242.

Stiernhielm, Georg. *Samlade Skrifter*. Eds. Johan Nordstrom, Bernt Olsson and Poetiska Skrifter. Vol. 8. Lund: Carl Bloms, 1976.

Stolpe, Sven. *Christina of Sweden*. London: Burns & Oates, 1966.

Suchodolski, Bogdan. "La Solitude de Descartes," *Mélanges de littérature comparée et de philologie offerts à Mieczyskaw Brahmer*. Warsaw: PWN-Éditions Scientifiques de Plogne, 1967, pp. 511–520.

Swarte, Victor de. *Descartes, directeur spirituel, correspondence avec la Princess Palatine et la Reine Christine de Suède*. Paris: Félix Alcan, 1904.

Tabaraud, M. *Histoire de Pierre de Bérulle*. 2 vols. Paris: Adrien Égron, 1817

Tallon, Alain. *La Compagnie du Saint-Sacrement*. Paris: Cerf, 1990.

Tanaka, Hitohiko. "Où se situe le 'poêle' de Descartes?" *Études de language et littérature françaises (Tokyo)*. Vol. 34, 1979, pp. 11–18.

Temple, William. *Nature, Man, and God*. London: Macmillan, 1934.

Thibaudet, Albert, and Johan Nordstrom. "Un Ballet de Descartes: La Naissance de la paix." *La Revue de Genève*. Vol. 1, 1920, pp. 163–185.

Thouverez, Émile. "La Famille Descartes d'après les documents publiés par les sociétés savantes de Poitou, de Touraine et de la Bretagne," *Archiv für Geschichte der Philosophie*. Vol. 12, 1899, pp.505–528; Vol. 13, 1900, pp. 550–577.

————. "La Vie de Descartes d'après Baillet," *Annales de philosophie chrétienne*, Vol. 117, 1899–1900, pp. 646–667; Vol. 118, 1899, pp. 58–78, 160–176, 440–452, 523–542, 618–630.

Tillinac, Denis. *L'Ange du désordre: Marie de Rohan, Duchesse de Chevreuse*. Paris: Robert Laffont, 1985.

Tricht, H. W. "Hélie Poirier, Translator of Erasmus," *Quaerendo*. Vol. 10, 1980, pp. 153–155.

Van der Wal, Th. Oenema. *De Mens Descartes*. Brussels: A. Manteau, 1960.

Van Veen, Joh. *Dredge, Drain, Reclaim! The Art of a Nation*. The Hague: Martinus Nijhoff, 1955.

Vauciennes, Lingage de, editor. *Mémoires de ce qui s'est passé en Suède et aux provinces voisines, depuis l'année 1645 jusques en l'année 1655: ensemble le demêlé de la Suède avec la Pologne, tirez des depesches de Monsieur Chanut Ambassadeur pour le Roy en Suède*. 3 Vols. Paris: Pierre du Marteau, 1677.

Verbeek, Theo. *Descartes and the Dutch: Early Reactions to Cartesian Philosophy 1637–1650*. Carbondale: Southern Illinois University Press, 1992.

————. "Regius et Descartes, histoire d'une rupture." MS. 18 pp.

————. "Regius's *Fundamenta Physices*." *Journal of the History of Ideas*. Vol. 55, 1994, pp. 533–551.

————. *Une Université pas encore corrompue, Descartes et les premières années de l'Université d'Utrecht*. Utrecht: Universiteit Utrecht, 1993.

Verbeek, Theo, editor. *Descartes et Regius, autour de l'explication de l'esprit humain*. Amsterdam: Rodopi, 1993.

————. *René Descartes et Martin Schoock, la querelle d'Utrecht*. Paris: Les Impressions Nouvelles, 1988.

Vértes, Augusta O. "Descartes chez les Lapons," *Revue de littérature comparée*. Vol. 17, 1937, pp. 488–498.

Villard, F. "Le Séjour à Châtellerault des enfants Descartes," *Bulletin de la société des antiquaires de l'ouest et des musées de Poitiers*. Vol. 7, 1964, pp. 465–466.

Vrooman, Jack R. *René Descartes: A Biography*. New York: G. P. Putnam's, 1970.

Wang, Leonard J. "A Controversial Biography: Baillet's *La vie de monsieur Des-Cartes*," *Romanische Forschungen*. Vol. 75, 1963, pp. 316–331.

Watson, Richard A. *The Breakdown of Cartesian Metaphysics*. Rev. ed. Indianapolis: Hackett, 1998.

———. "Descartes and Cartesianism," *Encyclopaedia Britannica*. Vol. 15. 15th ed. Chicago: Encyclopaedia Britannica, 1989, pp. 588–595.

———. "Descartes's Ballet?" *American Philosophical Association Proceedings*. Vol. 63, No. 1, 1989, pp. 10–12.

———. *Descartes's Ballet: His Doctrine of the Will and His Political Philosophy*. South Bend, St. Augustine's Press, 2002.

———. "The Ghost in the Machine Fights the Last Battle for the Human Soul," *Kriterion*. No. 94, 1996, pp. 55-63.

———. *The Downfall of Cartesianism*. The Hague: Martinus Nijhoff, 1966.

———. "On the Zeedijk." *The Georgia Review*. Vol. 43, 1989, pp. 19–32.

———. *The Philosopher's Demise: Learning French*. Columbia: University of Missouri Press, 1995; Boston: David R. Godine, forthcoming.

———. *The Philosopher's Diet: How to Lose Weight and Change the World*. Boston: Atlantic Monthly Press, 1985; Boston: David R. Godine, 1998.

———. "René Descartes n'est pas l'auteur de 'La naissance de la paix,'" *Archives de philosophie*. Vol. 53, 1990, pp. 389–401.

———. *Representational Ideas from Plato to Patricia Churchland*. Dordrecht: Kluwer Academic Publishers, 1995.

Weibull, Curt. *Christina of Sweden*. Stockholm: Svenska Bokförlaget Bonniers, 1966.

Williams, H. Noel. *A Fair Conspirator*. London: Methuen, 1913.

Wootton, David. "Lucien Febvre and the Problem of Unbelief in the Early Modern Period." *Journal of Modern History*. Vol. 60, 1988, pp. 695–730.

Yates, Frances A. *The Rosicrucian Enlightenment*. London: Routledge and Kegan Paul, 1972.

Zack, Naomi. *Bachelors of Science: Seventeenth-Century Identity, Then and Now*. Philadelphia: Temple University Press, 1996.

Zumthor, Paul. *La Vie quotidienne en Hollande au temps de Rembrandt*. Paris: Hachette, 1959.

INDEX OF NAMES

GENERAL INDEX

COLOPHON

Cogito, Ergo Sum has been set in Kepler, a multiple-master typeface designed by Robert Slimbach for Adobe in 1996. Rooted in the so-called modern types of the late eighteenth century, Kepler was designed to be free of the coldness and formality of its forebears while capitalizing on their refined appearance. Its multiple-master features endow it with the flexibility needed to serve a wide variety of typographic purposes and styles.

Design and composition by Carl W. Scarbrough